Industry and Higher Education

Leigh Wood · Lay Peng Tan · Yvonne A. Breyer ·
Sally Hawse
Editors

Industry and Higher Education

Case Studies for Sustainable Futures

 Springer

Editors
Leigh Wood
Macquarie Business School
Macquarie University
Sydney, NSW, Australia

Lay Peng Tan
Macquarie Business School
Macquarie University
Sydney, NSW, Australia

Yvonne A. Breyer
Macquarie Business School
Macquarie University
Sydney, NSW, Australia

Sally Hawse
UTS Business School
University of Technology Sydney
Sydney, NSW, Australia

ISBN 978-981-15-0876-9   ISBN 978-981-15-0874-5   (eBook)
https://doi.org/10.1007/978-981-15-0874-5

This Springer imprint is published by the registered company Springer Nature Singapore Pte Ltd.
The registered company address is: 152 Beach Road, #21-01/04 Gateway East, Singapore 189721,
Singapore

Acknowledgements

We wish to acknowledge the support and contributions of all authors, reviewers and the Macquarie Business School research incentive fund for supporting the research. The idea for this book grew out of the nationally funded research project 'Aligning business education with industry expectations on sustainability and employability' (Lead: Yvonne A. Breyer; Team: LayPeng Tan, Hasnain Zaheer, Leanne Denby, Sara Rickards). The final report can be accessed here: https://ltr.edu.au/resources/SD15-5133_Breyer_FinalReport_2019.pdf.

We are grateful to the Department of Education, Australia, who funded the original project and to all involved especially our industry partners and our student researchers who contributed greatly to the project. Last but not least, we would like to acknowledge the enormous help and support that Jemima Moore provided as our copy editor.

Contents

About the Editors

Prof. Leigh Wood is a pioneering leader in student success. Her research spans the transition to university and the transition to professional work as well as curriculum design to facilitate these transitions. Her research contribution includes 5 books, 150 articles and multimedia learning resources. She has had over $A2 million in learning and teaching grants. She is proud of her student experience teams, her students and her Ph.D. graduates and their contributions to our communities.

Dr. Lay Peng Tan is an experienced and stimulating researcher with awards for outstanding teaching. Her research interests lie within the broad areas of consumer behaviour, digital marketing, retailing and green marketing with a focus on the attitude-behaviour gap and the roles of marketing in the face of the green challenge. Her publications have appeared in the *Journal of Business Ethics, Marketing Intelligence and Planning*, *Journal of Marketing Management*, *Australasian Marketing Journal*, *The International Review of Retail, Distribution and Consumer Research* and *Asia Pacific Journal of Marketing and Logistics*.

Assoc. Prof. Yvonne A. Breyer is an award-winning academic with expertise in student success, online learning and digital transformation in the higher education sector. She has led several highly successful strategic initiatives with national and international reach. Most recently, she led the 'Excel Skills for Business' specialisation, which received the Coursera Outstanding Educator Award for Student Transformation on the back of exceptional learner feedback, global reach and impact. She holds a Ph.D. (Macquarie University), a Master of Arts (University of Essen, Germany) and a Postgraduate Certificate in Higher Education, Leadership and Management (Macquarie University).

Dr. Sally Hawse is an organisational knowledge and learning specialist with expertise in knowledge management strategy and project delivery. She is currently a Learning and Development Consultant, where she is involved in the design, implementation and evaluation of people development and capability initiatives to support knowledge transfer and workplace learning as part of a NSW Australia local government workforce sustainability and transformation agenda.

Chapter 1
Towards Sustainable Futures

Leigh N. Wood, Lay Peng Tan, Yvonne A. Breyer and Sally Hawse

Abstract Case studies are an important way for learners to develop professional skills. In this book, we present ten case studies in the area of business sustainability that address the United Nations' Sustainable Development Goals. Each case study is accompanied by teaching notes and assessment questions as well as marking guides.

Keywords Business · Industry · Higher education · Case study · Sustainability · Global

1.1 Introduction and Background

Business is leading the way toward sustainable futures—futures for their own company, their shareholders, their employees, and for the planet. Sustainable practices make good sense for the continuing viability of an enterprise. They build reputation and value, and signal that an enterprise is here for the long-term.

Naturally, business is now looking to tertiary education to help equip graduates with the knowledge, skills, and attitudes needed to be productive and harmonious members of their enterprises. We need creative and applied thinkers to tackle the difficult challenges we face every day, in every board room, by every enterprise, around the globe.

1.2 What Do We Mean by Sustainable Futures?

In 1987, the United Nations defined sustainable development as:

> … meeting the needs of the present without compromising the ability of future generations to meet their own needs. (Report of the World Commission on Environment and Development, 10 Jan 2008)

L. N. Wood (✉) · L. P. Tan · Y. A. Breyer · S. Hawse
Macquarie University, Sydney, Australia
e-mail: leigh.wood@mq.edu.au

© Springer Nature Singapore Pte Ltd. 2020
L. Wood et al. (eds.), *Industry and Higher Education*,
https://doi.org/10.1007/978-981-15-0874-5_1

1

In this book, we are informed by the United Nations' 17 Sustainable Development Goals (UN SDGs) for the 2030 Sustainability Development Agenda. Our case studies contribute to these goals as we give examples of how we can educate our university students to incorporate sustainability into their learning.

By using "sustainable futures", we recognise that we can choose the type of future that we want and that different people will choose different futures. Some will want to move off-grid or grow their own food; many will choose to live in cities. How can we—educators, business and industry leaders—support these different choices and create viable, inclusive futures?

Our case studies address sustainability in the way the UN SDGs do. We examine sustainability from many perspectives, including education, work, health, communities, consumption and production and the environment.

1.3   Why Case Studies?

We want to showcase the excellent education that is happening within universities and industry. Active learning through case studies opens opportunities to change attitudes and to find creative solutions. Just as case studies work in the classroom, case studies also work for faculty and industry to change attitudes and look to what is possible. Ultimately, we need to live together and find solutions to the UN SDGs. To do this we need to work together.

This book is targeted toward capstone students, postgraduate business students, and students in environmental studies. Therefore, the case studies offered sit at the microeconomic level. These learners are, or soon will be, in a position to make a difference to their chosen industry and may well need a model for how to do it.

The dilemma of creating value while preserving and enhancing the planet is a difficult one that is part of boardroom discussions globally. It is easy to find "causes" that are important—the importance of music, of astronomy, of science, of knowledge—but how to pay for all this? And how to create space for other life on this planet? It is not enough to say that a content area (for example, Mathematics) is the most important knowledge and, therefore, everyone needs to know it, without some idea of the contribution of that knowledge to employment, life, and happiness. Is food and fuel for a family more important than the habitat of a tiger? What of swimmers and sharks? Households and mosquitoes? Farmers and vegans?

The UN SDGs try to balance the needs of people versus other life. Some have criticised the goals for being more about the needs of people than other life forms; only two of the 17 goals target other life. Nevertheless, the goals will lead to better conditions for all life forms when implemented.

Case studies are presented as dilemmas with no clear outcome. Even in situations where we know the outcome, there is still the dilemma about whether this outcome was the correct one given the context. Take the tourism development on the Freycinet peninsula as an example. Was this outcome the best? If not, why not? How could the participants have found a better solution? Case studies put the learners in the shoes of the decision makers. What would you do in this situation?

Case studies elicit emotions as participants work individually or in teams to develop solutions, business plans, and recommendations. The lens of sustainability—broadly defined—encourages participants to set aside their own views and to examine the situation from different perspectives. We also encourage learners to critique the established theories and examine ways to improve methods to cater for global applications. We take what has been achieved and examine whether it is still relevant and viable for the particular context.

The case studies we present in this volume are able to be adapted to short or long teaching timeframes. All have a key sustainability issue at their heart. The case studies can be used as a trigger for a semester-long course or can be adapted for a one-week study.

1.4 Teaching with Case Studies

Much has been written about the use of case studies in learning. It is a key area of expertise in business schools. The following suggestions can be used in face-to-face teaching or online.

There are several fundamental ways of teaching with case studies:

- **Stakeholder analysis**: Participants take on the role of different stakeholders.
- **Decision analysis**: Participants use decision tools to evaluate outcomes and make recommendations.
- **Communication theory**: Participants use communication and negotiation skills to push through a recommended decision.
- **Learning theory**: Participants use human resource management practices and learning theory to prepare a workforce for a change.
- **Marketing and brand**: Participants use marketing theory and practice to sell their ideas and products.
- **Analysis**: Participants use qualitative and quantitative analysis to make and support decisions.
- **Ethical practice**: Participants are able to use critical thinking and ethical theories to construct arguments about their ethical viewpoints.
- **Cultural awareness**: Participants are aware and act with respect to different cultures. Participants are able to adapt to different cultural contexts to achieve mutually desirable outcomes.

Harvard Business School and The Case Centre, among others, run courses on how to teach with case studies. If you are new to the case method, observe a class that uses the method, read up about it, or take one of the courses. Forward planning and clear goals are important for the success of the method. The right cases are critical—which is where this book will help!

1.5   Assessing Case Studies

Assessment depends on the learning outcomes of the course. The same case study can be used in many situations—as a study of stakeholder theory or as an ethical dilemma, for example. Case studies can be used for learning activities and assessment tasks.

1.5.1   Short Case Studies

These are good for short, individual, or small group activities. The students are put under pressure to understand the situation, gather information, and respond relatively quickly. These rely on prior knowledge and skills, including the processing of information and making decisions. Short case studies can be used in formal written or oral examinations.

1.5.2   Detailed Case Studies

Longer, more detailed case studies require in-depth thinking, analysis, and research and need time for students to prepare solutions at the required level. Students are able to prepare responses to the questions ahead of the assessment or class activity. The case studies in this volume all present teaching questions and options that can be adapted for class use.

The instructor has several options:

- Ask all students to prepare individual responses to the questions.
- Ask all students to submit their solutions at a set time.
- Randomly call on a selection of students to submit their solutions.
- Call on a particular student to present their solution with the rest of the class critiquing the solution (grades allocated for the solution and for the critiques). The student may or may not be given warning that you will call on them.
- Ask a small number of students to prepare a solution and encourage other students to challenge that solution.
- Break the class into teams—either self-selected teams or instructor selected. There is evidence to suggest that diverse teams will present better outcomes. Therefore, teams assembled by the instructor are recommended.

    - Teams submit a response.
    - Selected teams present a response. Other teams critique and challenge the response.

- Students or teams should critique one or two responses by others. The critique is graded.

- Roleplay examples:
  - Students are allocated roles. For example—the junior (preparing the response), the manager (making changes and presenting to the board), the Board (who question, negotiate and make recommendations to the CEO) and the CEO who signs off on the recommendations.
  - Stakeholder analysis. Students are allocated to one of several stakeholder groups and prepare responses to the case based on their allocated stakeholder group. A board of other students then negotiate an outcome.

1.5.3 Using Case Studies in Formal Written or Oral Examinations

Case studies can be used in examinations. These can be seen or unseen case studies. If a formal oral or written examination is required, we recommend a seen case study so students have time to prepare answers. Consider that, under the time pressure of an examination, students may not read carefully, which can give an unfair advantage to native speakers of the language. Case studies can be distributed one day before the examination or longer if it is a detailed study. The questions may or may not be distributed before the examination.

1.6 Marking of Case Studies

1.6.1 Radar Charts

Radar charts are useful for assessing changes in learning and can easily be created in Excel (e.g., Fig. 1.1). Radar charts allow a student to assess themselves against capability criteria and then repeat the assessment at the end of the activity or course. The two sets of results provide a clear demonstration of how far they have progressed during their study. You can also use radar charts for peer and instructor marking. It works best with between four and ten criteria. Scales on each axis should be a maximum of 10. In Tables 1.1 and 1.2 we have used a scale of 5.

1.7 Preparing to Learn Using Case Studies—Students

Harvard Business School, the EFMD Global and others have good resources to assist learners to make the most from case study learning.

Fig. 1.1 Radar chart for assessment of graduate skills

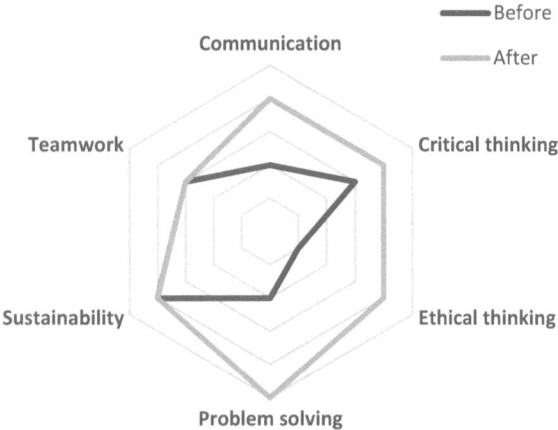

In summary:

- There is no one correct answer. Also, there may be better answers.
- There is never enough information. We are always dealing with imperfect data. What information you don't have may be more important than the data you have.
- There is never enough time. You have to work smarter.
- Use your team. Be open to new methods and solutions. Diversity is an asset.
- You cannot be a perfectionist. You have to make a call with the resources available.
- Hindsight is a lovely thing. You may only know later whether your solution was the best.
- Always reflect on your solution and the process to come to that solution. You will be building skills for your future.

1.8   How to Use This Book

The ten case studies presented here can be used in flexible ways. This book can be used as a textbook with one case per week (although that would be a huge workload for students) or one case per semester for an in-depth case upon which to hang the rest of the course. They are ideal for a capstone to bring together learning from a program of study.

We have enjoyed working with our talented authors for this book and hope you enjoy working with the cases.

Leigh, Lay Peng, Yvonne, and Sally
May 2019

Table 1.1 Generic marking guide for case studies—assessment of achievement by conceptual, procedural, and professional categories

Grade	Conceptual: what	Procedural: how	Professional: why	Mark
High distinction A, A+	Theories and concepts are linked and integrated, resulting in a new understanding. The depth and breadth of the concept is understood in such a way that the individual is inspired to re-organise other concepts, and motivated to make creative and innovative applications	Demonstrates the capacity to create or develop new valid procedures and applications. Rules are applied in novel ways, or new rules are derived from deep understanding	Demonstrates a strategic view to enable innovative outcomes in complex situations Applies the concepts and procedures of sustainability in a business context with clear communication of the outcomes	80–100
Distinction B, B+	The understanding of the concept is broadened, appreciated from different angles, and this elaboration reflects in the ability to consider the concept in other contexts and from different perspectives	Demonstrates the ability to select appropriate procedures and apply them in a given context	Demonstrates the ability to adapt to new environments. Works with a team to develop clear outcomes	70–80
Credit C, C+	The concept has become a part of their knowledge. Nevertheless, it remains narrow and shallow and relatively disconnected from other concepts	Demonstrates the ability to apply given rules and procedures in a variety of contexts and to novel problems	Can evaluate a professional situation and identify key issues	60–70

(continued)

Table 1.1 (continued)

Grade	Conceptual: what	Procedural: how	Professional: why	Mark
Pass D, D+	Demonstrates the ability to describe and define the basic concepts of the skill, subject matter, and/or knowledge domain, but has not demonstrated an ability to be able to elaborate or reflect on the meaning of the concept(s)	Demonstrates knowledge of the rules and can practice the rules of a given procedure and/or skill	Demonstrates a basic understanding of processes and functions and a basic understanding of the significance of these in professional practice	50–60
Fail F	Is unable to describe and define the basic concepts of the skill, subject matter, and/or knowledge domain	Demonstrates little knowledge of the rules and is not able to practice the rules of a given procedure and/or skill	Demonstrates little understanding of processes and functions or the significance of these in professional practice	0-50
F	No attempt or substantially copied			0

Source Adapted from Wood et al. (2012)

Table 1.2 Assessment of case studies—overall criteria

Grade	Criteria	Mark
High distinction	Innovative, creative, and critical responses to the case study assignment	80–100
Distinction	Selects and adapts known knowledge, skills, and attitudes to the case study questions and produces well-argued critical responses	70–80
Credit	Uses known knowledge, skills, and attitudes to address the case study questions. The argument and responses may not be complete	60–70
Pass	Uses known knowledge, skills, and attitudes to address the case study questions. The responses are satisfactory with some errors	50–60
Fail	Uses known knowledge, skills, and attitudes incorrectly or inappropriately	0–50
Fail	No attempt or substantially copied	0

References

EFMD Global. Retrieved from https://www.efmd.org/business-schools/case-competition

Harvard Business School. The Case Method. Retrieved from https://www.hbs.edu/mba/academic-experience/Pages/the-hbs-case-method.aspx

Report of the World Commission on Environment and Development (2008) Retrieved from https://sustainabledevelopment.un.org/milestones/wced

United Nations Sustainable Development Goals. Retrieved from https://sustainabledevelopment.un.org/

Wood LN, Reid A, Petocz P (2012) Becoming a mathematician. Springer, Dordrecht

Prof. Leigh N. Wood is a pioneering leader in student success. Her research spans the transition to university and the transition to professional work as well as curriculum design to facilitate these transitions. Her research contribution includes 5 books, 150 articles and multimedia learning resources. She has had over $A2 million in learning and teaching grants. She is proud of her student experience teams, her students and her Ph.D. graduates and their contributions to our communities.

Dr. Lay Peng Tan is an experienced and stimulating researcher with awards for outstanding teaching. Her research interests lie within the broad areas of consumer behaviour, digital marketing, retailing and green marketing with a focus on the attitude-behaviour gap and the roles of marketing in the face of the green challenge. Her publications have appeared in the *Journal of Business Ethics, Marketing Intelligence and Planning, Journal of Marketing Management, Australasian Marketing Journal, The International Review of Retail, Distribution and Consumer Research* and *Asia Pacific Journal of Marketing and Logistics.*

Assoc. Prof. Yvonne A. Breyer is an award-winning academic with expertise in student success, online learning and digital transformation in the higher education sector. She has led several highly successful strategic initiatives with national and international reach. Most recently, she led the 'Excel Skills for Business' specialisation, which received the Coursera Outstanding Educator Award for Student Transformation on the back of exceptional learner feedback, global reach and impact. She holds a Ph.D. (Macquarie University), a Master of Arts (University of Essen, Germany) and a Postgraduate Certificate in Higher Education, Leadership and Management (Macquarie University).

Dr. Sally Hawse is an organisational knowledge and learning specialist with expertise in knowledge management strategy and project delivery. She is currently a Learning and Development Consultant, where she is involved in the design, implementation and evaluation of people development and capability initiatives to support knowledge transfer and workplace learning as part of a NSW Australia local government workforce sustainability and transformation agenda.

Part I
Industry Case Studies

Chapter 2
Health System Sustainability: The Pharmaceutical Benefits Scheme in Australia

Joanne Epp, Bonny Parkinson and Sally Hawse

Abstract The Australian Federal Government's National Medicines Policy aims to create positive health outcomes for all Australians by providing appropriate access to medicines. Underpinning the policy is the Pharmaceutical Benefits Scheme (PBS), which subsidises the cost of medicines. However, like many healthcare systems around the world, governments are struggling with the challenge of how to manage escalating healthcare expenditure. The landscape is dotted with competing agendas: increased demand for healthcare due to population growth and ageing; patient preferences over treatment options; improved technologies and medicines; the need for pharmaceutical companies to recoup research and manufacturing costs—all have been seen as culprits behind a rising national healthcare bill. Further, spending a dollar on one form of healthcare means not spending a dollar on another. In other words, providing healthcare has an opportunity cost. Increasingly, decision-makers are using economic evaluations as a tool to balance these agenda trade-offs. Only through balance can we ensure that healthcare continues to provide value for money and the system remains sustainable. This chapter explains how the PBS works—its decision-making bodies and processes, how economic evaluation is key to recommending which new medicines are listed on the PBS, and the industry's perspective on the PBS. The case study focuses on the human papillomavirus (HPV) vaccine to highlight the competing resource demands, business interests, and societal needs that influenced its listing on the PBS. The case study also considers how making the vaccine available through the National Immunisation Programme has contributed to making Australia's healthcare system more sustainable.

Keywords Vaccine · Human papillomavirus (HPV) · Pharmaceutical Benefits Scheme (PBS) · Health technology assessment (HTA) · Economic evaluation · Health system sustainability

J. Epp (✉) · B. Parkinson · S. Hawse
Macquarie University Centre for the Health Economy, Sydney, Australia
e-mail: joanne.epp@mq.edu.au

© Springer Nature Singapore Pte Ltd. 2020
L. Wood et al. (eds.), *Industry and Higher Education*,
https://doi.org/10.1007/978-981-15-0874-5_2

13

2.1   The case at a glance

Key concepts	• Healthcare system sustainability • Opportunity cost • Australia's Pharmaceutical Benefits Scheme (PBS) • Economic evaluation
Level of study	• MBA students
Subject areas	• Economics, social policy, health policy

Graduate capabilities

Graduate outcomes	%
Critical thinking	30
Problem solving	10
Teamwork	5
Communication	5
Ethical thinking	10
Sustainability	40
Total	**100%**

Time required	• Preliminary reading activities:	45 mins
	• During reading activities:	20 mins
	• Post-reading assignments:	60 mins

Activity type

Individual:
• Pre-reading
• Assignment questions
• Supplementary multimedia activities – YouTube videos
• Supplementary further reading

Team-based:
• Group discussion questions

Additional Materials

• http://www.pbs.gov.au/pbs/home
  A website containing information on the PBS, including details of the medicines subsidised by the Australian government as well as information for consumers, carers, health professionals, and the pharmaceutical industry. The PBS is part of Australia's broader National Medicines Policy.

- https://pbac.pbs.gov.au/
  Guidelines for preparing submissions to the Pharmaceutical Benefits Advisory Committee (PBAC) Information on the evidence considered by PBAC when considering which medicines to recommend for PBS subsidy.

2.2   Introduction

Australia is recognised globally as providing affordable access to medicines while concurrently encouraging the development of new medicines. This chapter explains how Australia's National Medicines Policy achieves these two competing goals and, in doing so, contributes to maintaining a sustainable healthcare system. This chapter explains how the Pharmaceutical Benefits Scheme (PBS) works, its decision-making bodies and processes, how economic evaluation is key to recommending which new medicines are listed on the PBS, and the industry's perspective on the PBS through a case study on the HPV vaccine.

2.3   Background

> Australian spending on health has grown by 50% between 2006 – 2007 and 2015 – 2016, from $113 billion to $170 billion. In 2015 – 2016, spending on health amounted to nearly $7,100 per person … Governments fund the majority of spending (67% or $115 billion), and non-government sources fund the remaining $56 billion (33%). Individuals contributed more than half ($29 billion) of the non-government funding. (Australian Institute of Health and Welfare 2018, p. 38)

A person's health generally depends on two things: the factors that influence health, such as lifestyle, environment, and genetics; and the interventions and actions taken to improve health. Health interventions differ in terms of overall survival rates and gains to quality of life; however, they all typically require: resources, such as doctors, hospitals, and medical equipment; access to quality medicines; health literacy; and research to develop new health practices and new or improved medicines.

Healthcare systems throughout the world are struggling with the challenge of how to manage escalating healthcare expenditure. The competing agendas of increased public demand due to population growth, ageing and patient preferences on treatment options, improved technologies and medicines, and the need for pharmaceutical companies to recoup research and manufacturing costs are often seen as the culprits behind rising healthcare costs (Jonsson and Banta 1999; Productivity Commission 2005; Parkinson 2013).

Access to care, the quality of that care, and the cost of providing it are often used to measure and assess the performance of a healthcare system. However, greater healthcare expenditure does not necessarily mean that a healthcare system performs better or that it delivers a net gain in population health. A dollar spent on one form of healthcare means a dollar that is not available for another. Thus, providing healthcare involves an opportunity cost.

2.4   Health System Sustainability

Pressures on healthcare budgets have led to a focus on system sustainability. According to international health expert, Crisp (2017), the sustainability of a healthcare system depends on seven factors:

Internal factors:

- the efficiency and effectiveness of healthcare provision;
- the availability of well-trained healthcare workers; and
- its cost and economic benefits.

External factors:

- the overall health and resilience of the population;
- the availability of carers and informal networks of care; and
- the integration of policy and practice with other health-building groups.

Overall:

- public and political acceptance and support.

Crisp (2017) explains that what is needed is a focus on providing the most effective care at the best price in the most appropriate setting—i.e., the right care, at the right time, in the right place. This could mean, for example, that some patients receive healthcare services in the home as an alternative to using expensive hospital resources. Crisp also stresses the importance of undertaking research on the cost and benefits of healthcare, including preventative healthcare, medicines, and alternative models of care.

This chapter shows how Australia's National Medicines Policy supports healthcare system sustainability.

2.5   Medicines Policy in Australia

2.5.1   The National Medicines Policy

The Australian Federal Government's National Medicines Policy aims to improve positive health outcomes for all Australians through access to and wise use of medicines (Department of Health and Ageing 2000). The principles that underpin the policy are (p. 1):

- timely access to the medicines that Australians need, at a cost individuals and the community can afford;
- medicines meeting appropriate standards of quality, safety and efficacy;
- quality use of medicines; and
- maintaining a responsible and viable medicines industry.

Essentially, the policy forms a partnership between the Australian federal and state governments, health educators and practitioners, healthcare providers and suppliers, the pharmaceutical industry, and healthcare consumers.

2.5.2 The Pharmaceutical Benefits Scheme

The PBS was established in Australia in 1953 under the *National Health Act* 1953 to subsidise the cost of medicines as one of three complementary cornerstones of Australia's government-funded medical system. These cornerstones are the PBS, the Medicare Benefits Schedule, and free treatment in public hospitals.

The aim of the PBS is to provide Australians with affordable, timely, and equitable access to necessary medicines at an economically viable cost to the government (Parkinson 2013). This is achieved by subsidising medicines prescribed by clinicians outside a hospital setting and dispensed at community pharmacies, along with some of the more expensive medicines dispensed at public hospitals or specialist treatment centres.

Under the PBS, pharmacies purchase medicines from wholesalers or manufacturers. When a patient goes to a pharmacy to fill a prescription, they pay a small co-payment and the Australian government reimburses the difference in cost to the pharmacy—costs that may amount to thousands of dollars. However, access to subsidised medicines is restricted to patients with certain conditions or those who meet certain clinical criteria. If a medicine is not listed on the PBS or the patient does not meet the clinical criteria, they have to pay full price as a private prescription. Additionally, under the National Immunisation Programme, the government covers the cost of vaccines with no applicable co-payment.

The PBS accounts for the majority of medical prescriptions and payments. Today, the PBS lists around 793 medicines in 2,066 forms and dosages, sold as more than 5,300 differently branded items (Department of Health 2015). In 2016/17, more than 195 million prescriptions were dispensed under the PBS at a cost of $8.7 billion. This represents an 9.6% increase on the previous year's expenditure of $7.9 billion (Department o f Health 2019).

The cost of the PBS to the federal government is "uncapped" (Parliament of Australia 2016), such that it has no fixed budget. The cost of the scheme can therefore increase to accommodate need as new medicines are added and the demand for PBS-listed medicines grows. Figure 2.1 illustrates how the cost of the PBS has increased exponentially over time. Understandably, these increases have raised concerns over the sustainability of the PBS.

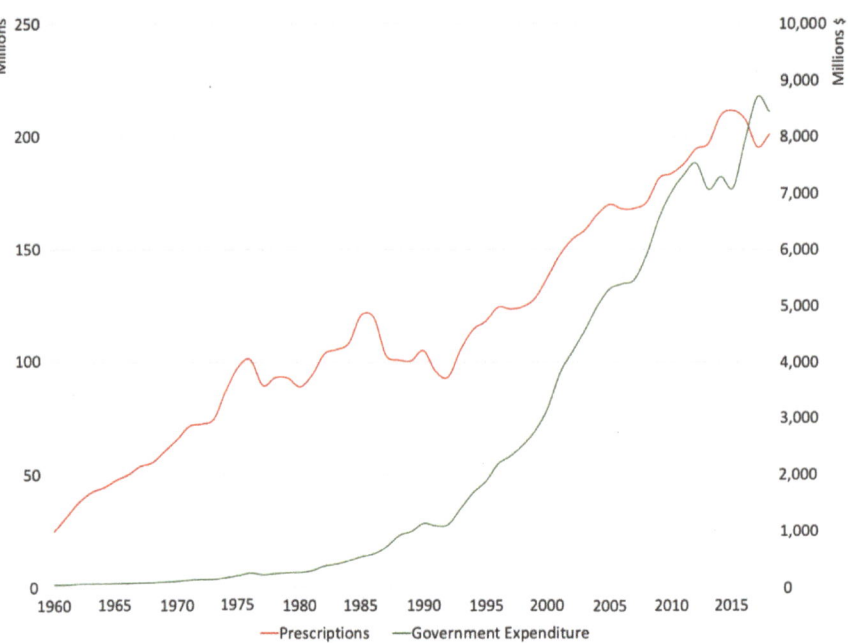

Fig. 2.1 PBS prescriptions and expenditure, 1960–2016. *Source* Department of Health (2019)

2.6   Managing Cost Versus Demand for PBS Medicines

One approach the federal government has used to address the issue of sustainability is to balance the cost of medicines listed on the PBS versus demand through patient co-payments, price discounts, and price disclosure polices.

2.6.1   Co-payments

Co-payments for medicines on the PBS were first introduced on 1 March 1960. This was one of the first attempts by the Australian government to control expenditure. By acting as a price signal to patients, this initiative helped to deter over-use, making the PBS more sustainable (Sloan 1995).

There are two co-payment arrangements: concession and general population. As of 1 January 2018, concession card holders pay a maximum of $6.40 for most prescriptions, while the general population pays $39.50. When a patient reaches a total co-payment threshold for the year, the amount paid per prescription falls to nil for concession patients and to the concession rate for the general population. This is referred to as the pharmaceutical safety net threshold (Department of Health 2018c).

While evidence suggests that co-payments have helped to reduce the use of medicines, the initiative has also had unintended consequences—for example, discouraging patients from filling some necessary prescriptions (Hynd et al. 2008). In turn, reduced treatment rates may have longer-term impacts on health expenditure if the medicine prevents the onset of health problems (e.g., cardiovascular medicines) or slows the progression of a disease (e.g., osteoporosis medicines).

2.6.2 Price Discounts and Reference Pricing

In Australia, a 20-year patent on new medicines protects R&D investments made by pharmaceutical companies. During this time, other companies are not allowed to manufacture or market the medicine. This patent protection incentives pharmaceutical companies to invest money in further research toward new medicines and allows the company to recoup its research, development, and marketing costs (Lavelle 2006). After 20 years, other companies are able to manufacture and market the medicine under other brand names. These medicines are referred to as 'generics'.

Theoretically, generics should introduce price competition, thus lowering the price of both the branded and the generic medicine. However, this does not always occur in practice, as doctors and patients are generally shielded from the full cost of PBS-listed medicines.

Historically, the federal government has used generic medicines entering the market as an opportunity to reduce its own costs by either imposing mandatory price discounts for every new generic listed on the PBS or using reference pricing to other similar medicines (Parkinson 2013).

Unfortunately, mandatory price discounts and reference pricing had limited success in reducing medicine prices, and the price of medicines with a generic option remained higher than in other countries (Bulfone 2009; Clarke and Fitzgerald 2010).

2.6.3 Price Disclosure Policies

Surprisingly, a more successful solution was inspired by the pharmaceutical industry. As a way to compete for market share, generic medicine companies began to offer pharmacists discounts on the PBS list price (e.g., ten for the price of nine), who then encouraged patients to substitute a generic over the original brand (Lofgren 2007).

In response, the federal government introduced price disclosure in 2007, where companies submit their total sales and revenue information, including any discounts and non-price benefits given to pharmacists. Based on this information, the price the government pays for a medicine is adjusted to more closely reflect the price the pharmacists pay (Department of Health 2018b). These reforms have been highly effective in reducing the price of medicines with a generic alternative (Sweeny 2013).

2.6.4 Impact on Health System Sustainability

As mentioned, co-payments had limited success at improving the sustainability of the healthcare system and may have even been detrimental. However, price discounts, reference pricing and, more recently, price disclosure have made an impact. The resulting reductions in expenditure have provided the federal government with some headroom to pay for new, innovative, and more expensive medicines.

2.7 The Process for Listing New Medicines on the PBS

> The paradigm of HTA emerged as a response to decision-makers' questions about the uncontrolled diffusion of costly medical equipment. HTA began in the early 1970s, when the rapid demand for computer-assisted tomography (CT scans) became a public policy issue due to the very high cost per unit, often in excess of US \$300,000. (WHO 2011, p. 11)

The Pharmaceutical Benefits Advisory Committee (PBAC) recommends which new medicines should be listed on the PBS and which vaccines should be listed on the National Immunisation Programme. Under the National Health Act 1953 Section 101 and the 1987 Amendment to the National Health Act (1953), PBAC is required to consider:

> … the [clinical] effectiveness and cost of therapy involving the use of the drug, preparation or class, including by comparing the effectiveness and cost of that therapy with that of alternative therapies, whether or not involving the use of other drugs or preparations.

PBAC consists of clinicians, pharmacists, epidemiologists, health economists, health consumer advocates, and a pharmaceutical industry representative. Subcommittees provide advice and guidance on specialist knowledge areas, such as analysing clinical and economic data, budget impacts, and, vaccines.

The diagram in Fig. 2.2 summarises the key decision-making processes and bodies for listing medicines on the PBS and the National Immunisation Programme. These steps involve:

1. A submission to the Therapeutic Goods Administration (the Australian equivalent of the US Food and Drug Administration) is lodged for approval to market a new medicine in Australia. The submission contains evidence regarding the medicine's efficacy, safety, and quality of manufacture. If approval is given, the medicine is listed on the Australian Register of Therapeutic Goods.
2. A submission to PBAC for a PBS listing is then lodged. The submission contains information regarding the requested listing and a health technology assessment (HTA).
3. PBAC has 17 weeks to consider the submission, which involves an evaluation by an academic research centre and a review by several subcommittees. Companies and patients are not allowed to attend the subcommittee meetings; however,

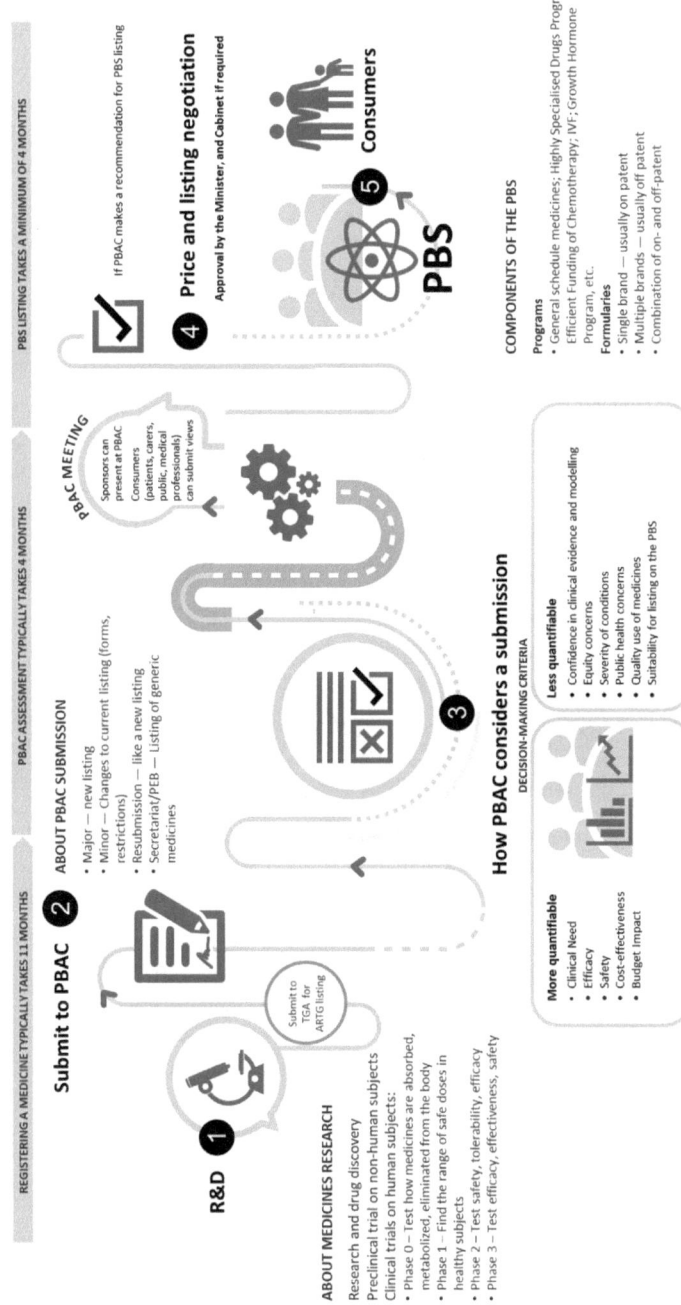

Fig. 2.2 Process of listing on the PBS. *Source* Adapted from GSK Australia and ViiV Healthcare (2018)

companies are given an opportunity to respond to any concerns raised during the process. PBAC may also hold a short hearing to seek patient and company views.

4. When PBAC recommends a medicine should be listed, the price and details of the listing can be further negotiated and, once those negotiations are complete, the Minister for Health, and subsequently Cabinet, formally approves or rejects PBAC's recommendation. If approved, the medicine is listed on the PBS.

5. If PBAC rejects a medicine, it cannot be listed. However, companies may choose to revise their application and re-submit.

2.8   Health Technology Assessment and Economic Evaluation

There is enormous variation in the price of PBS-listed medicines, with some costing less than a dollar and others costing more than $800 per day (Viney et al. 2017). These price variations raise questions—for example: What will the government pay for? and How is the price of new medicines decided?

2.8.1   What Is HTA?

In January 1993, PBAC's submission guidelines became mandatory for the sponsors of major applications (PBAC 2008). This effectively ensured that a process called health technology assessment (HTA) was conducted on all new medicines seeking a PBS listing. According to the World Health Organisation (WHO 2011, p. 8):

> HTA is the systematic evaluation of properties, effects, and/or impacts of health technology. Its main purpose is to inform technology-related policy-making in healthcare, and thus improve the uptake of cost-effective new technologies and prevent the uptake of technologies that are of doubtful value for the health system.

Figure 2.3 summarises the current PBAC guidelines for preparing a major submission to list a new medicine on the PBS (PBAC 2016). These guidelines outline the structure of an HTA and, hence, the information required by PBAC and its economic subcommittee to support a proposed new medicine. This information includes:

- scientific evidence regarding the clinical effectiveness and safety of a medicine;
- an economic evaluation to assess the cost-effectiveness of the medicine; and
- an estimate of the total budget impact.

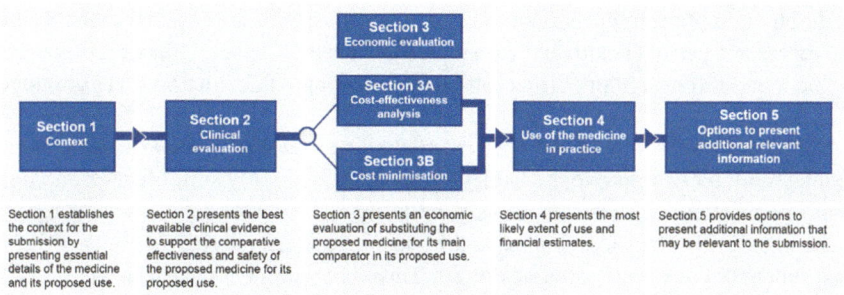

Fig. 2.3 Summary of PBAC's guidelines. *Source* PBAC (2016)

2.8.2   What Is Economic Evaluation?

As a tool to balance the trade-offs between cost and demand, decision-makers are increasingly using economic evaluations to ensure that healthcare provides value for money and the healthcare system is sustainable. In healthcare, economic evaluation involves evaluating the gain in health and the additional cost of a new medicine compared to using those funds on an alternative, often current clinical practice.

A great deal of evidence is required to conduct an economic evaluation, such as health outcomes without treatment, the efficacy of the medicine, the impact on quality of life, healthcare resource use and, of course, its cost. Sometimes all the evidence required for an economic evaluation is captured within a clinical trial. These cases are referred to as 'within-trial analysis'. However, it is more likely that evidence from a clinical trial will be combined with other evidence from a variety of sources, such as observational studies, surveys, and expert opinions. This evidence is then synthesised using an economic model to predict health outcomes and costs over time.

Some medicines may improve symptoms immediately; others may prevent the onset of a disease; others still may stop, slow, or reverse a disease's progression. Consequently, economic evaluations do not simply consider the immediate costs of a medicine, they also consider longer-term impacts on resource use, medicine use, and reduced requirements for doctor visits, hospitalisations, and diagnostic tests.

2.8.3   What Are Quality-Adjusted Life Years (QALYs)?

According to the PBAC guidelines, health outcomes should be reported in terms of quality-adjusted life years (QALYs) (PBAC 2016). QALYs are a general measure of 'disease burden' that combines survival and quality of life into a single measure (Drummond et al. 2015). They are calculated by weighting a patient's expected survival time by the quality of life experienced during that period. The weights applied are referred to as utility weights or utility values. Utilities are estimated based on the strength of preferences across different health states on a cardinal scale, where one represents perfect health and zero represents death. The strengths of preferences can be measured using "time trade-off" or "standard gamble" methods (Drummond et al. 2015).

Figure 2.4 shows how QALYs are calculated in an economic evaluation and how an intervention can improve the QALYs gained. In the highly simplified example in Fig. 2.4a, a patient experiences full health (utility = 1) until they have a car accident at the age of 40. They live with their injuries for another 40 years (utility = 0.5), then suddenly die of a heart attack at 80. Thus, the patient experiences 60 QALYs ($1 \times 40 + 0.5 \times 40$). In Fig. 2.4b, the patient receives an intervention that improves their quality of life after the accident (thus, the utility weight increases to 0.75), but this does not prevent their heart attack. However, they now experience 70 QALYs— a gain of 10 QALYs. In Fig. 2.4c, the patient has a car accident, but the selected intervention delays the heart attack until the age of 100. Again, they experience 70 QALYs, i.e., the same 10 year gain.

This example illustrates why policy decision-makers prefer health outcomes to be reported in terms of QALYs when making funding decisions—QALYs allow an explicit comparison of the trade-offs between different treatments and different diseases.

2.8.4 How Does PBAC Use HTAs and Economic Evaluations to Make Decisions?

In maintaining the financial viability of the PBS, PBAC's decisions are influenced by five measurable quantitative factors and a range of less quantifiable factors. Together, these factors help to determine whether a medicine should be listed on the PBS. Table 2.1 lists these factors.

The results of the economic evaluation are essential to this decision-making process. PBAC is likely to recommend a medicine for the PBS if:

- the medicine is cheaper and more effective;
- the medicine is equally effective (or 'non-inferior') to the comparator and is the same price or cheaper—referred to as a cost-minimisation analysis; or
- the medicine is more effective but also more expensive, and the incremental cost-effectiveness ratio (ICER) is below the threshold line—referred to as a cost-effectiveness or cost-utility analysis.

ICER is an often-used statistic in economic evaluation, and is calculated as follows:

$$ICER = \frac{Cost_A - Cost_B}{Effectiveness_A - Effectiveness_B}$$

(a) Quality of life of an individual over time

QALYs = Utilities x time in each health state
= 1 x 40 years + 0.5 x 40 years = 60 QALYs

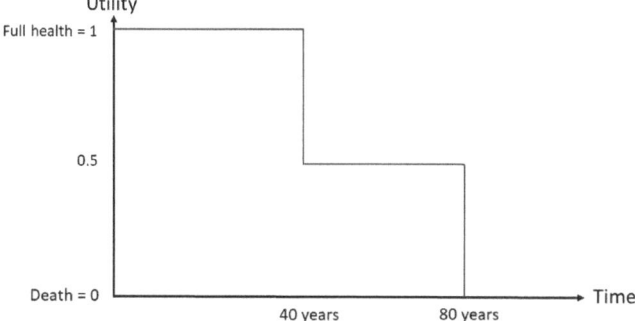

(b) The intervention improves quality of life (i.e., utility):

QALYs = Utilities x time in each health state
= 1 x 40 years + 0.75 x 40 years = 70 QALYs

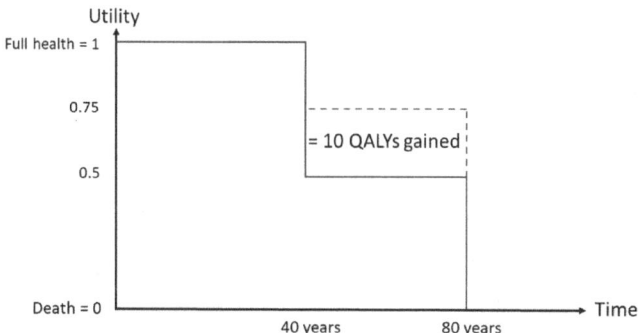

(c) The intervention increases life expectancy

QALYs = Utilities x time in each health state
= 1 x 40 years + 0.5 x 60 years = 70 QALYs

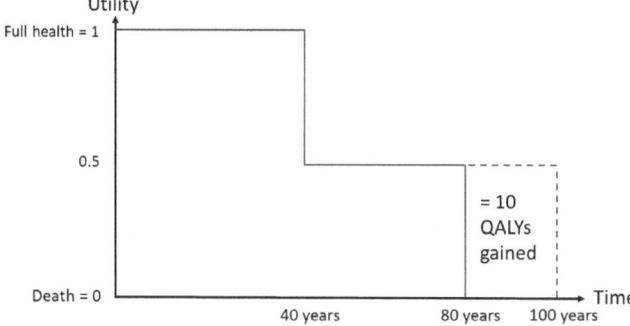

Fig. 2.4 Quality-adjusted life years (QALYs)

Table 2.1 Factors in determining a PBS listing

Quantifiable	Less quantifiable
• Health benefits: does the medicine offer significantly better outcomes compared to existing medicines? • Cost-effectiveness: considering health gain and healthcare costs, is the medicine reasonably priced compared to similar medicines? • Affordability: is a PBS subsidy required to meet the NMP aims of access and equity? • Uptake and impact on PBS budget: would the medicine have a significant impact on PBS costs? • Impact on health budget: even if the medicine has a high cost to the PBS, does it offer an overall cost reduction to the health system/net benefit?	• Confidence—confidence in the clinical evidence and assumptions relied upon in the economic analysis • Equity—the background and geographical status etc. of those most likely to require treatment • Effective alternative treatments—treatments that may influence the clinical need for a proposed medicine • Severity of the medical condition treated—treating more serious conditions receives a higher weighting • Ability to target—targets people most likely to benefit most from it, increasing the cost-effectiveness and societal benefits • Public health issues—the development of population resistance • Other relevant factors—factors that may affect the suitability of the medicine for listing on the PBS

Source Adapted from GSK Australia and ViiV Healthcare (2018) and PBAC (2016)

where A represents the medicine and B represents the comparator. Effectiveness is typically measured in QALYs.

Figure 2.5 illustrates how ICERs provide a way to assess whether a medicine represents value for money. Intervention A is less effective and more costly, and thus would not be recommended for funding. Intervention B is more effective and less costly, and thus would be recommended for funding. Intervention C is more effective and more costly. In this case, if the ICER falls below the threshold, the intervention would be considered value for money, i.e., cost-effective, and recommended for funding. In a cost-utility analysis, ICERs are reported in terms of incremental cost per QALY gained. Intervention D is less effective and less costly, which means the ICER would also be compared to the threshold. Note, however, that PBAC very rarely considers such cases.

Harris et al. (2008) analysed PBAC's recommendations on major submissions lodged between February 1994 and December 2004. In this study, effectiveness was measured using either life years gained (LYG) (n = 138) or QALYs gained (n = 116) with ICERs greater than zero. They found that PBAC does not have a single threshold but, rather, that increasing the ICER by \$10,000/QALY reduces the probability of a recommendation by 6% (95% CI: 4–10%). PBAC also considers other factors. For example, the study shows that, when the condition is not life-threatening, confidence in the clinical significance of the medicine increases the probability of a recommendation by 23% (95% CI: 14–44%) and by 36% (95% CI: 3–68%) when the condition is life-threatening. This is not surprising as PBAC generally makes recommendations, first based on an assessment of the clinical evidence and the need

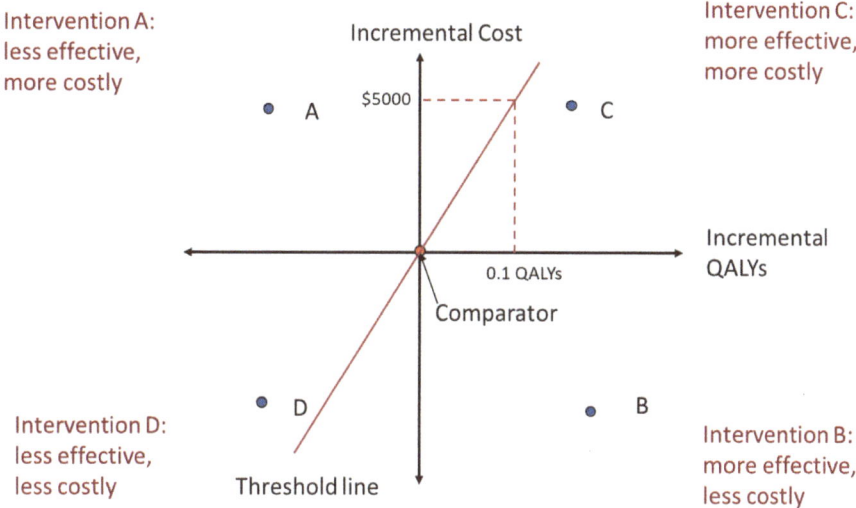

Fig. 2.5 Incremental cost-effectiveness ratio. *Source* Parkinson (2013)

for a medicine, and then on value for money. If there is significant clinical uncertainty, the ICER is also likely to be highly uncertain.

2.8.5 HTA and Economic Evaluation Around the World

Many countries use HTA and economic evaluation as criteria for funding health interventions to help ensure the sustainability of their health systems, including New Zealand, England, Japan, the Netherlands, and Portugal, among others (International Society for Pharmacoeconomics and Outcomes Research 2018). Table 2.2 compares the key criteria for funding medicines in the UK, Australia, and New Zealand. This comparison highlights that, while all three nations consider clinical effectiveness and cost-effectiveness, Australia also includes the price of alternative medicines and the impact of listing a medicine on the health budget in its decision-making process.

2.8.6 Impact on Health System Sustainability

HTA has been highly successful in contributing to the sustainability of the PBS and, thus, the Australian healthcare system. Subsidising vaccines and preventative medicines reduces the onset and progression of diseases, which, in turn, improves the overall health and resilience of the population. PBAC's evidentiary standards ensure the safest, most effective medicines are available, while its restrictions ensure

Table 2.2 Criteria used for funding new medicines

England (NICE)	Australia (PBAC)	New Zealand (PHARMAC)
• Clinical effectiveness and cost-effectiveness (cost/QALY) • Uncertainty • Nature of the health condition • Technological innovation • Wider costs and benefits • Precedents	• Clinical effectiveness and cost-effectiveness (largely cost/QALY) • The price of alternative brands or medicines in the same therapeutic class • Budget impact • 'Rule of rescue' (where appropriate)	• Clinical effectiveness and cost-effectiveness (cost/QALY) • Health needs, including those of Māori and Pacific Islander peoples • Budget impact • Cost-effectiveness of medicines versus other interventions • Clinical benefits and risk • Direct costs to users • Availability of alternative treatments

NICE National Institute for Health and Clinical Excellence; *PBAC* Pharmaceutical Benefits Advisory Committee; *PHARMAC* Pharmaceutical Management Agency; *QALY* quality-adjusted life year
Source Raftery (2008)

that only the patients who are most likely to gain a benefit are treated. These two factors improve the efficiency and effectiveness of healthcare provision. Economic evaluation ensures that both short-term treatment costs and the longer-term impact on health are taken into account, which implies that resource use is also considered. ICERs reflect the opportunity cost of listing one medicine but not another. Therefore, decision-makers consider both the costs and economic benefits of healthcare. Finally, HTAs have general public and political support (GSK Australia and ViiV Healthcare 2018). However, more can be done to increase HTA's acceptance in society. This is discussed next.

2.9   Industry Perspective

The cost of new medicines may amount to thousands of dollars per month per patient. As Viney et al. (2017) state:

> For any new medicine, there will be years of research and development in terms of drug discovery, and many more years in terms of clinical testing and trials to demonstrate their safety and effectiveness. Pharmaceutical companies tell us for each new drug they bring to market, there will be many that fail along the way—and the cost of the research on these medicines needs to be recouped.

Without the PBS, some medicines would be otherwise unaffordable for some patients. Hence, listing a medicine on the PBS significantly expands market access for pharmaceutical companies.

Pharmaceutical companies recognise that the sustainability of the PBS is important, and that price reductions increase the federal government's capacity to reinvest in new, innovative, and life-changing medicines (Medicines Australia 2017). The net result is a system that helps to build partnerships between the government and Australian researchers, and one that encourages innovative companies to invest in local clinical trials and manufacturing.

However, pharmaceutical companies have struggled with the PBS process over the years, particularly with regard to the moderate, and sometimes significant, regulatory burden the submission process imposes (PWC 2015). There have been some improvements in recent years, including the introduction of the 'parallel process' where a medicine can be considered by the Therapeutic Goods Administration and PBAC simultaneously, and/or granting conditional approvals subject to further data. Both reforms reduce the time to market and, hence, increase revenue for companies.

However, other concerns remain. According to PWC (2015), these include:

- a lack of resources to prepare submissions and manage the process;
- high expectations regarding clinical evidence;
- conditional approvals that require costly data collection and re-submissions; and
- comparator price erosion resulting in knock-on effects for the price of new medicines, or the need to show very large gains in health outcomes.

There are several points along the PBAC decision-making process where companies and patients are able to submit their views to PBAC, but both groups have indicated they would like more two-way communication flows. Companies would like more transparent and consistent access to PBAC officials during the submission process to clarify assumptions, calculations, methodologies, and comparator selections (PWC 2015). Patient groups would like to be informed when a submission is made by a company, and more information and notification about when patient inputs are accepted during the listing process (GSK Australia and ViiV Healthcare 2018).

2.10 Case Study: Gardasil

2.10.1 About the Human Papillomavirus (HPV)

A virus is a small infectious biological agent that reproduces inside other living organisms. Every animal and plant on this planet is infected with a virus of some form. As early as 1908, it was discovered that some viruses could cause cancer, and it is now estimated that viruses contribute to 20% of all human cancers (Dimmock et al. 2007).

Human papillomavirus, or HPV, is a very common virus in both men and women. There are over 100 types of human papillomavirus (HPV) (Dimmock et al. 2007).

This virus causes anal, vaginal, and cervical cancers, penis cancers, and oropharyngeal cancers (Cancer Council Australia 2017). There is no way to predict who will get cancer or other health problems from HPV, and there is currently no cure. The scale and reach of HPV statistics give pause for thought. It is estimated that up to 79% of the population will be infected with at least one type of genital HPV at some time in their lives (Department of Health 2017). One of the best defences for viruses is protection through immunisation. Therefore, it is much easier to prevent HPV cancers than to treat them.

2.10.2   Development of an HPV Vaccine

Ellerman and Bang reported the cell-free transmission of chicken leukaemia in 1908, and in 1911 Rous discovered that solid tumours of chickens could be transmitted. These were the first indications that some viruses can cause cancer. (Dimmock et al. 2007, p. 5)

The HPV vaccine and our current understanding of how viruses are implicated in cancer owe much to Harald Zur Hausen, Jian Zhou, and Ian Frazer. Zur Hausen (1976) was the first to theorise that HPV caused cervical cancer. In response, medical research was galvanised to find a cancer vaccine. In 1991, Zhou, Frazer, and their team at the University of Queensland found a way to form non-infectious virus-like particles co-expressing the L1 protein, which strongly activates the immune system against HPV Type 16 (Zhou et al. 1991). This research was further built on by researchers at the Georgetown University Medical Center, the University of Rochester, and the US National Cancer Institute. Early work on the vaccine by the University of Queensland was supported by an Australian company, CSL, resulting in the development of Gardasil. CSL then licensed Gardasil to Merck to commercialise the technology, conduct appropriate clinical trials, gain regulatory approval, and market the vaccine in the US. The European rollout of Gardasil was licensed to Sanofi-Pasteur (McNeil 2006; Krelle 2005).

Gardasil protects against four types of HPV—Types 16 and 18 are responsible for 70% of the HPV infections that cause cervical cancer, while Types 6 and 11 cause genital warts. A decade on, Frazer recounts that, "We realise now that about 20% of cancers are caused by virus infections … It's much easier to prevent an infection [than cancer]." (Moss 2017).

The vaccine is made from tiny proteins that look like the outside of the HPV cells. In response, the body creates antibodies to the protein and, if a person is subsequently exposed to the real virus, those antibodies prevent the virus from creating an infection (Cancer Council Australia 2017).

The HPV vaccine is on the *WHO Model List of Essential Medicines*. The WHO notes that each country determines its own vaccination regime "after consideration of international recommendations, epidemiology and national priorities", but recommends that the HPV vaccine be "polyvalent", meaning that it is active against several HPV types (WHO 2018, p. 43).

2.10.3 National Immunisation Programme Listing of Gardasil

When PBAC makes a decision to recommend a medicine on the PBS, it makes public summary documents (PSDs) about the recommendation available to the public. These documents provide information on the evidence and reasons behind PBAC's recommendations. ICER statistics are generally not made available; however, a range is provided. Table 2.3 summarises the PSDs for Gardasil.

Initially, PBAC rejected Gardasil for the National Immunisation Programme on the basis that it was not cost-effective. The public summary document indicates the cost of vaccinating females within the National Immunisation Programme at over $100 million, with an ICER of between $16,000 and $70,000 per QALY gained.

However, the Australian government supported the vaccine and convened discussions with the company to lower its price. A special meeting of PBAC was held in late November 2006 (only a few weeks after the initial meeting) where they reversed their decision to reject Gardasil. Among the revised conditions contributing to this reversal were a price reduction, a more comprehensive risk-share arrangement around the possibility of a booster, and an immunisation register to recall patients if a booster was required in future. PBAC's ultimate decision to include the HPV vaccine in the Programme was attributed to strong government and public support (Haas et al. 2009) For example, Ian Frazer was made Australian of the Year in 2006, and there was significant media attention to his key role in the development of the HPV vaccine. In 2007, Australia became one of the first countries to introduce a federal government-funded national HPV vaccine program to prevent HPV-related infections (Tabrizi et al. 2012).

Subsequently, in 2011, PBAC recommended subsidies for male Gardasil vaccinations. HPV infection in males is usually asymptomatic but can result in a number of anogenital diseases, including genital warts, anal and penile cancer, and potentially oral cavity and oropharyngeal cancers. Further, HPV vaccinations in males may result in additional benefit to unvaccinated females through interruption of transmission. The public summary document indicates that the cost of vaccinating males to be as low as $5–$30 million, which in part reflects the lower negotiated price, with an ICER of between $15,000 and $45,000 per QALY gained.

In 2018, Gardasil was replaced by Gardasil 9, which protects against nine HPV types. While Gardasil covers the HPV types associated with around 71.8% of cervical cancer cases (i.e., HPV Types 16 and 18), Gardasil 9 protects against an additional 14.7% (HPV Types 31, 33, 45, 52, and 58). The submission also proposes switching from three doses to two doses. The public summary document indicates that a 2-dose Gardasil 9 vaccination schedule would result in more QALYs and lower costs than a 3-dose Gardasil schedule, with cost savings to the National Immunisation Programme of around $10 million.

Currently, two doses of Gardasil 9 are administered at schools free of charge via the National Immunisation Programme to both females and males between 12 and 13 years old. Adolescents under the age of 19 who missed out on a vaccination at

Table 2.3 PBAC's evaluation for Gardasil and Gardasil 9

2007 Gardasil for females	
Target population	Females aged 12 to 26 years
Comparator	Screening for cervical cancer as part of standard medical management, including the National Cervical Screening Program (NCSP)
Clinical evidence and claim	The submission included data from six randomised control trials comparing Gardasil to placebo in females. The submission claimed that Gardasil is superior compared to no vaccine
Economic analysis	Nine economic evaluations were modelled: one for the 12-year-old cohort, along with eight additional models for the catch-up cohorts. The models assumed that the effectiveness of Gardasil does not taper over time and, therefore, provides lifetime protection for vaccinated females The estimated ICERs for all women aged 12 to 26 years included: – $16,000–$44,000/QALY gained (overall base case) – $15,00 –$38,000/QALY gained (overall base case) for the first catch-up cohort in a school-based program – $18,000–$70,000/QALY gained (overall base case) for the second catch-up cohort
Cost	The total cost of the program in its first four years was estimated to be >$100 million
2011 Gardasil for males	
Target population	Males aged 12–13 years and a catch-up program over two years for year 9 males
Comparator	No vaccination (placebo) in males as the main comparator and the current female-only vaccination program as a secondary comparator
Clinical evidence and claim	The submission presented three randomised control trials comparing Gardasil to placebo in healthy males
Economic analysis	A Markov model was used to examine the cost-effectiveness of the primary comparator (males vs. placebo). A hybrid model, comprising a dynamic infectious diseases model and a Markov model, was used to examine the cost-effectiveness of the secondary comparator (male + female vaccination vs. females only). Again, the models assumed that Gardasil's effectiveness does not taper over time and offers lifetime protection to those vaccinated The results of the economic evaluation produced a base case ICER for all diseases of less than $15,000/QALY gained in males + females versus females only based on herd immunity. However, PBAC subsequently considered that a base case of $15,000 to $45,000/QALY gained was more likely
Cost	The cost was estimated at $5-$30 million per year

(continued)

Table 2.3 (continued)

2017 Gardasil 9 for females and males	
Target population	Females and males aged 12–13
Comparator	Gardasil
Clinical evidence and claim	One randomised control trial comparing a 3-dose schedule of Gardasil 9 to a 3-dose schedule of Gardasil in females only, plus three immuno bridging studies (No data on a randomised control trial comparing a 2-dose schedule of Gardasil 9 to a 3-dose schedule of Gardasil in adolescents was included.)
Economic analysis	A modelled cost-utility analysis comparing: a 2-dose Gardasil 9 program to a 3-dose Gardasil program; and a 3-dose Gardasil 9 program to a 3-dose Gardasil program The economic model captured the incremental clinical benefits of Gardasil 9 compared to Gardasil in preventing HPV disease attributable to the additional HPV types. It also captured the cost savings of implementing a 2-dose, rather than a 3-dose, vaccination schedule on the assumption that implementing a 2-dose versus a 3-dose Gardasil 9 schedule would have no clinical impact. Further, a 2-dose schedule would result in more QALYs and lower costs than the 3-dose schedule The ICER of the 3-dose Gardasil 9 schedule, versus the 3-dose Gardasil schedule, was estimated at $15,000/QALY–$45,000 QALY gained
Cost	At year six, the cost savings to the National Immunisation Programme was estimated at less than $10 million per year

Adapted from PBAC (2007, 2011) Public summary documents for Quadrivalent Human Papillomavirus (Types 6, 11, 16, 18) recombinant vaccine, injection, 0.5 mL, Gardasil and 2017 Public summary document for Human papillomavirus 9-valent vaccine: Injection 0.5 mL, pre-filled Syringe Gardasil® 9

school can access the vaccine through a catch-up program (Cancer Council Australia 2017). The National Immunisation Programme listing of Gardasil and a subsequent health promotion program have greatly contributed to the success of the vaccine's take-up. In 2017, 79% of girls and nearly 73% of boys aged 15 were fully immunised against HPV (Australian Institute of Health and Welfare 2018).

Figure 2.6 provides a summary of Gardasil's development timeline and its listing on the National Immunisation Programme.

2.10.4   Impact on Health System Sustainability

In the early 1980s a research group headed by Harald Zur Hausen at the German Cancer Research institute discovered that cervical cancer was associated with infection with Human Papillomavirus (HPV). This discovery was later recognised by being awarded the Nobel Prize in Physiology or Medicine in 2008. (Frazer 2016)

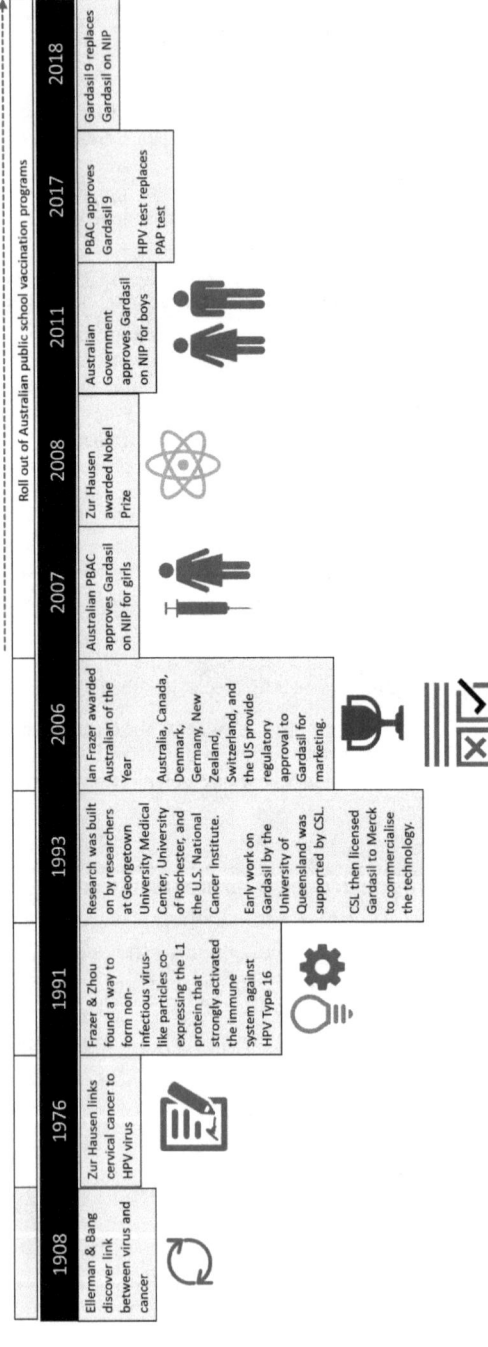

Fig. 2.6 A timeline of Gardasil's development and listing in the National Immunisation Programme

From the public summary documents, it is clear that PBAC comprehensively considered the effectiveness of the vaccine. However, PBAC also considered the costs and economic benefits through economic evaluations. It is also clear that these economic evaluations accounted for future healthcare savings in terms of both costs and resource use. The US National Cancer Institute (2018) summarises these savings:

> Widespread vaccination has the potential to reduce cervical cancer deaths around the world by as much as two-thirds if all women were to take the vaccine and if protection turns out to be long-term. In addition, the vaccines can reduce the need for medical care, biopsies, and invasive procedures associated with the follow-up from abnormal Pap tests, thus helping to reduce healthcare costs and anxieties related to abnormal Pap tests and follow-up procedures.

The public summary documents for Gardasil highlight that the vaccine's role in reducing cervical and related cancers will not be evident for some time given that cervical cancer usually develops over 10 years or more. However, statistics from the Cancer Council Australia (2017) indicate early signs of the vaccine's success, including:

- a 77% reduction in the HPV types responsible for almost 75% of cervical cancer;
- almost a 50% reduction in the incidence of high-grade cervical abnormalities in females under the age of 18; and
- a 90% reduction in genital warts in men and women under 21 years old.

Thus, funding Gardasil through the National Immunisation Programme has helped to strengthen the health and resilience of the population. Further, this is likely to have downstream impacts on workforce productivity as the number of people experiencing these diseases dwindles.

While HPV vaccination does not remove the requirement for cervical screening tests, the National Cervical Screening Program has been changed from testing every two years to every five years (Department of Health 2018a). Moreover, the healthcare savings relating to HPV cancer diagnosis and treatment could fund health programs or interventions aimed at treating other patients, further bolstering the sustainability of the healthcare system.

The public summary documents for females (2007) and males (2011) also reveal that PBAC initially rejected Gardasil's listing on the basis that it was not cost-effective. In both cases, the pharmaceutical company, CSL, responded with a second submission at reduced prices to meet PBAC's cost-effectiveness thresholds. This reveals two key points: (1) how motivated CSL was to gain market access; and (2) the influential position the federal government holds as a monopoly buyer. Both parties recognised the significant potential benefits of listing Gardasil on the National Immunisation Programme. The lower price also provided the federal government with some leeway to fund other treatments to further improve the system's sustainability.

In addition to price reductions, the federal government was able to negotiate support from CSL for an HPV vaccine register. Established in 2008, the register plays an important role in monitoring and evaluating the vaccine program. The register also feeds into new research on the effectiveness of the HPV vaccine, which contributes to further disease prevention, further improvements to the health and resilience of the population, and, hopefully, future medical discoveries. In this way, the National Immunisation Programme directly supports job creation in Australian medical research and manufacturing, and indirectly through royalties to CSL and the University of Queensland.

Despite Gardasil's initial rejection by PBAC, there was strong public support for its listing. It is likely that the final outcome of PBAC's positive recommendation will be increased public and political support for the PBAC process and improved sustainability in the healthcare system.

2.10.5 Summary

Publicly-funded healthcare costs matter because health budgets and resources are limited. Cost outlays for one intervention often compete for claims to invest in others. Balancing these competing claims means that "decisions based on economic evaluation are really about identifying the alternative which offers the greatest net health benefits overall" (Drummond et al. 2015, p. 82).

Australia's National Medicines Policy illustrates how economic evaluation helps decision markers allocate resources for new medicines. The case of Gardasil shows the strength of PBAC's cost-effectiveness thresholds in supporting the government's negotiation position to reduce the cost of medicines, and how it helped Australia lead the way in providing important protection against HPV-related cancers. Haas et al. (2009) argue that Australia's approval of Gardasil and its support for a school immunisation program may have influenced other countries to follow Australia's lead. This is due to Australia's reputation for a healthcare policy that supports both access and affordability.

Crisp (2017) notes a country's health expenditure generally rises as its economy grows. This has been the experience in Australia in recent years. Therefore, it is important to continue to support economic evaluation for new medicines and to consider extending this analysis in other areas of health expenditure to ensure that our health system is achieving value for money and future sustainability.

2.11 Teaching Notes

2.11.1 Synopsis of the Case

The Australian Federal Government's National Medicines Policy aims to create positive health outcomes for all Australians by providing appropriate access to medicines, underpinned by the Pharmaceutical Benefits Scheme (PBS), which subsidises the cost of medicines. However, like many healthcare systems around the world, governments are struggling with the challenge of how to manage escalating healthcare expenditure. Competing agendas are all seen as culprits: increased demand for healthcare due to population growth and ageing; patient preferences over treatment options; improved technologies and medicines; the need for pharmaceutical companies to recoup research and manufacturing costs. Further, spending a dollar on one form of healthcare means not spending a dollar on another, in other words, healthcare has an opportunity cost.

Economic evaluations are a useful tool for balancing these agenda trade-offs to that healthcare continues to provide value for money and the system remains sustainable. This chapter explains how the PBS works—its decision-making bodies and processes, the industry's perspective, and how economic evaluation is key to recommending which new medicines are listed on the PBS. The case study focuses on the human papillomavirus (HPV) vaccine to highlight how sustainability can be found among the competing resource demands, business interests, and societal needs.

2.11.2 Target Learning Group

- Level of study—MBA students
- Subject areas—economics; social policy; health policy; finance

2.11.3 Learning Objectives

2.11.3.1 Key Issues

- Build awareness of the complexity in the concept of sustainability in healthcare.
- Create understanding that health system sustainability is about balancing a range of competing factors and forces—that there is an opportunity cost in providing healthcare interventions, but these interventions may result in downstream impacts on other areas of the system.

- Introduce the Australian National Medicines Policy and its function as one of the key pillars of the Australian healthcare system, i.e., the PBS, the Medicare Benefits Schedule, and free treatment in public hospitals.
- Build awareness of how HTAs and economic evaluations are used in policy decision making and how those tools contribute to the sustainability of a healthcare system.

2.11.3.2   Specific Objectives

- Examine how decision-makers use economic evaluation to make funding decisions.
- Explore health sustainability through the lens of the PBS and Australia's provision of the HPV vaccine as a protective measure against a range of cancers.

2.11.4   Reading Activities

2.11.4.1   Pre-reading

To help you get the most out of the case study, complete the following activities before you read the case study in detail.

Skim the case study:

- Set a 5-minute timer and skim the whole chapter. Get as good an idea as you can of what the chapter and the case study is about within the time limit.
- Summarise the chapter in 3–5 dot points.

2.11.4.2   In-Depth Reading

Summarise each of these key sections in 1–2 sentences.

- Introduction
- Medicines policy in Australia
- Managing cost versus demand for PBS medicines
- Listing new medicines on the PBS
- Industry perspective
- Case study: Gardasil.

2.11.5 Discussion Activities

2.11.5.1 Video and Discussion

View the Department of Health's PBS Animation http://www.pbs.gov.au/info/about-the-pbs

- What statement indicates the scale of the PBS?
- What types of medicines does the video say the PBS provides access to?
- What reason does the narrator give for these types of medicines?
- What is the economic implication?

2.11.5.2 Group Discussion Questions

- Why do you think Gardasil manufacturers were willing to negotiate a price reduction to gain a PBAC recommendation for listing their medicines in the National Immunisation Programme?
- Do you think the Australian government's role as a single purchaser of medicines supports the system's sustainability?
- Do you think there is too much regulation governing market access for medicine manufacturers in Australia? What could the possible consequences of less regulation be?
- What are the main benefits of medicine regulation in Australia?
- How does economic evaluation support sustainability in a healthcare system?

2.11.6 Assignment Questions

Public summary documents are available for every medicine considered by PBAC. Select a handful of interesting public summary documents for students to summarise. Students could answer all or a selection of the following questions.

- What is the medicine?
- When was the application for PBS approval submitted and who was the sponsor?
- Which patients does the medicine treat and for what condition?
- What was the comparator? Why was this comparator chosen?
- What type of clinical evidence was presented to PBAC? What health outcomes were reported? What did PBAC consider to be the key sources of uncertainty surrounding the clinical data?
- What type of economic evaluation was conducted? Did the submission estimate QALYs?

- Did PBAC consider the medicine to be cost-effective? What did PBAC consider to be the key sources of uncertainty surrounding the economic evidence?
- What was the total cost to the PBS/National Immunisation Programme? What else could have been funded with this money?
- What other factors did PBAC consider when making their decision?
- Did PBAC recommend or reject the application?

2.11.7   Multimedia Activities

2.11.7.1   PBS Overview

These animated videos summarise what the PBS is and the process of listing medicines on the PBS. It also outlines the role of PBAC.

- DoH. 2018. *About the PBS* http://www.pbs.gov.au/info/about-the-pbs.
- GSK AUSTRALIA. 2018. *Pulling back the PBS curtain* https://www.youtube. com/watch?v=cTJNoOWjZ_k.

2.11.7.2   How the HPV Vaccine Works

- WHO. 2017. How the HPV vaccine works https://www.youtube.com/watch?v= qF7pBzU4D20.
  A video from the WHO regional office for Europe that shows how HPV can progress into cervical cancer, how the HPV vaccine works, and how it was tested for safety and efficacy before it was approved.
- DoH. 2014. *How the HPV vaccine works* https://www.youtube.com/watch?v= FaHrhKvPZ2w.
  A video from the Department of Health that demonstrates how the HPV vaccine works to protect against HPV-related cancers and disease.

2.11.7.3   Competing Interests and Needs: Social and Political Dimensions of the HPV Vaccine

Describe the focus and audience of the following HPV informational web sites:

- Cancer Council Australia. 2017. What is HPV? https://www.cancer.org.au/about-cancer/types-of-cancer/hpv.html.
- Seqirus Australia. 2013. What is HPV? https://www.hpv.com.au/what-is-hpv.

Further Reading

- **GSK Australia and ViiV Healthcare** (2018). The Pharmaceutical Benefits Scheme in Australia: An explainer on system components. GSK Australia.
  This reading is targeted at medicine consumers. Its purpose is to present the complexities of legislation and the policies and decision-making processes of the PBS in a comprehensive format. The aim of this paper… is to provide an engaging, constructive, and informative resource to aid understanding of a complex and often emotive policy issue. We hope it enables an ongoing informed discussion on the Australian health system and how the PBS will evolve to continue to provide universal access to innovative medicines and vaccines when people need them.
- **Harris, A. H., Hill, S. R., Chin, G., Li, J. J. & Walkom, E.** (2008). The role of value for money in public insurance coverage decisions for drugs in Australia: a retrospective analysis 1994-2004. *Medical Decision Making,* 28, 713–22.
  This article provides a statistical analysis of the factors that influence PBAC.
- **Cancer Council Australia** (2017). What is HPV?. Retrieved from https://www.cancer.org.au/about-cancer/types-of-cancer/hpv.html.
  A website that provides more information about the HPV vaccine program in Australia.

References

Amendment to the National Health Act 1953 Subsection 3(a). Commonwealth Government of Australia

Australian Institute of Health and Welfare (2018) Australia's health 2018. Australian Institute of Health and Welfare, Canberra, ACT

Bulfone L (2009) High prices for generics in Australia—more competition might help. Austr Health Rev 33:200–214

Cancer Council Australia (2017) HPV vaccine. Cancer Council Australia, Victoria, Australia. Retrieved from http://www.hpvvaccine.org.au/parents/parents-what-is-hpv.aspx

Clarke PM, Fitzgerald EM (2010) Expiry of patent protection on statins: effects on pharmaceutical expenditure in Australia. Med J Aust 192:633–636

Crisp N (2017) What would a sustainable health and care system look like? BMJ 358:1–3

Department of Health (2015) Annual Report 2014–2015. Commonwealth of Australia, Canberra, ACT

Department of Health (2017) The Australian immunisation handbook, 10th edn. Commonwealth of Australia, Canberra, ACT

Department of Health (2018a) National cervical screening program. Department of Health, Canberra, ACT. Retrieved from http://www.cancerscreening.gov.au/internet/screening/publishing.nsf/Content/about-the-new-test

Department of Health (2018b) Price disclosure. Retrieved from http://www.pbs.gov.au/info/industry/pricing/price-disclosure-spd

Department of Health (2018c) Fees, patient contributions and safety net thresholds. Retrieved from http://www.pbs.gov.au/info/healthpro/explanatory-notes/front/fee

Department of Health (2019) Historical pharmaceutical benefits scheme expenditure (1948–49 to 2017–18). Retrieved from http://www.pbs.gov.au/info/statistics/expenditure-prescriptions/expenditure-prescriptions-twelve-months-to-30-june-2018

Department of Health and Ageing (2000) National medicines policy. Department of Health and Ageing, Canberra

Dimmock NJ, Easton AJ, Leppard KN (2007) Introduction to modern virology. UK, Blackwell Publishing, Oxford

Drummond MF, Sculpher MJ, Claxton K, Stoddart GL, Torrance GW (2015) Methods for the economic evaluation of health care programmes. Oxford University Press, Oxford

Frazer I (2016) 2016: 10th anniversary of world's first HPV vaccine. Australian Cancer Research Foundation (ACRF). Retrieved from https://home.cancerresearch/10th-anniversary-of-worlds-first-hpv-vaccine/

GSK Australia and ViiV Healthcare (2018) The pharmaceutical benefits scheme in Australia: an explainer on system components. GSK Australia

Haas M, Ashton T, Kerstin B, Christiansen T, Conis E, Crivelli L, Kin LM, Lisac M, Macadam M, Schlette S (2009) Drugs, sex, money and power: an HPV vaccine case study. Health Policy 92:288–295

Harris AH, Hill SR, Chin G, Li JJ, Walkom E (2008) The role of value for money in public insurance coverage decisions for drugs in Australia: a retrospective analysis 1994–2004. Med Decis Making 28:713–722

Hynd A, Roughead E, Preen D, Glover J, Bulsara M, Semmens J (2008) The impact of co-payment increases on dispensings of government-subsidised medicines in Australia. Pharmacoepidemiol Drug Saf 17:1091–1099

International Society for Pharmacoeconomics and Outcomes Research (2018) Pharmacoeconomic guidelines around the world. Retrieved from https://www.ispor.org/PEguidelines/

Jonsson E, Banta D (1999) Management of health technologies: an international view. BMJ British Med J 319:1293

Krelle R (2005) CSL, Merck strengthen bid to be first to market with HPV vaccine. Retrieved from https://www.labonline.com.au/content/life-scientist/news/csl-merck-strengthen-bid-to-be-first-to-market-with-hpv-vaccine-1142801499

Lavelle P (2006) Saving money on medicines. ABC. Retrieved from http://www.abc.net.au/health/consumerguides/stories/2006/04/17/1837734.htm

Lofgren H (2007) Reshaping Australian drug policy: the dilemmas of generic medicines policy. Australian and New Zealand Health Policy 4:11

McNeil C (2006) Who invented the VLP cervical cancer vaccines? J Natl Cancer Inst 98:433

Medicines Australia (2017) Strengthening the PBS: agreement with medicines Australia on behalf of the innovative medicines sector. Canberra, MA. Retrieved from https://medicinesaustralia.com.au/wp-content/uploads/sites/52/2017/05/09-May-2017-Summary-Document-Strenghtening-the-PBS.pdf

Moss E (2017) Ten years on, Professor Ian Frazer recalls 'lucky' discovery of cervical cancer vaccine. ABC. Retrieved from http://www.abc.net.au/news/2017-03-25/ian-frazer-recalls-lucky-discovery-of-cervical-cancer-vaccine/8385872

National Health Act (1953) Commonwealth Government of Australia. Retrieved from https://www.legislation.gov.au/Details/C2018C00308

National Cancer Institute (2018) Human papillomavirus vaccines (HPV). NCI. Retrieved from https://www.cancer.gov/about-cancer/causes-prevention/risk/infectious-agents/hpv-vaccine-fact-sheet

Parkinson B (2013) Pharmaceutical policy in Australia. CHERE Working Paper 2013/01. UTS, Sydney, Australia, CHERE, University of Technology, Sydney

Parliament of Australia (2016) The pharmaceutical benefits scheme: a quick guide. Commonwealth of Australia, Canberra, ACT, 7 Apr 2016

Pharmaceutical Benefits Advisory Committee (2007) Public summary document for quadrivalent human papillomavirus (Types 6, 11, 16, 18) recombinant vaccine, injection, 0.5 mL, Gardasil. Commonwealth of Australia, Canberra, ACT

Pharmaceutical Benefits Advisory Committee (2011) Public summary document for quadrivalent human papillomavirus (Types 6, 11, 16, 18) recombinant vaccine, injection, 0.5 mL, Gardasil. Commonwealth of Australia, Canberra, ACT

Pharmaceutical Benefits Advisory Committee (2016) Guidelines for preparing submissions to the Pharmaceutical Benefits Advisory Committee (PBAC). Retrieved from https://pbac.pbs.gov.au/

Pharmaceutical Benefits Advisory Committee (2017) Public summary document: Human papillomavirus 9-valent vaccine: injection 0.5 mL, pre-filled Syringe Gardasil® 9. Commonwealth of Australia, Canberra, ACT

Pharmaceutical Benefits Advisory Committee December (2008) Guidelines for preparing submissions to the Pharmaceutical Benefits Advisory Committee (Version 4.3). Department of Health and Ageing, Canberra, ACT

PWC (2015) Challenges and change: a report on the Australian pharmaceutical industry. PWC, Sydney

Productivity Commission (2005) Impacts of advances in medical technology in Australia, research report. Melbourne, PC

Raftery JP (2008) Paying for costly pharmaceuticals: regulation of new drugs in Australia, England and New Zealand. Med J Aust 188:26

Sloan C (1995) A history of the Pharmaceutical Benefits Scheme 1947–1992. Commonwealth Department of Human Services and Health, Canberra

Sweeny K (2013) The impact of further PBS reforms: report to medicines Australia. Victoria University

Tabrizi SN, Brotherton JM, Kaldor JM, Skinner SR, Cummins E, Liu B, Bateson D, Mcnamee K, Garefalakis M, Garland SM (2012) Fall in human papillomavirus prevalence following a national vaccination program. J Infect Dis 206:1645–1651

Viney R, Haywood P, De Abreu Lourenco R (2017) Explainer: how is the price of medicine decided in Australia? The conversation. Retrieved from https://theconversation.com/explainer-how-is-the-price-of-medicine-decided-in-australia-83633

WHO (2011) Health technology assessment of medical devices. World Health Organisation. Retrieved from http://apps.who.int/medicinedocs/en/d/Js21560en/

WHO (2018) WHO essential medicines list (EML). World Health Organisation. Retrieved from http://www.who.int/medicines/publications/essentialmedicines/en/

Zhou J, Sun XY, Stenzel DJ, Frazer IH (1991) Expression of vaccinia recombinant HPV 16 L1 and L2 ORF proteins in epithelial cells is sufficient for assembly of HPV virion-like particles. Virology 185:251–257

Zur Hausen H (1976) Condylomata acuminata and human genital cancer. Can Res 36:794

Dr. Joanne Epp is a health economist with extensive international experience in economics, research and policy analysis including work at the World Bank (USA), UNFPA (USA), the Ontario Treasury (Canada), AMP Capital Investors, the Centre for Health Economics Research and Evaluation, NSW Treasury, KPMG, and Primary Health Care Limited. Dr. Epp is currently a Senior Research Fellow at the Macquarie University Centre for the Health Economy (2017–), where she is involved in evaluating outcomes-based funding models, integrated care programs, and health policy impacts.

Dr. Bonny Parkinson is a health economist with expertise in pharmaceutical policy in Australia and in conducting and reviewing economic evaluations of healthcare interventions and technologies. Dr Parkinson is currently a Senior Research Fellow at the Macquarie University Centre for the Health Economy (2015–), where she leads a team of researchers conducting evaluations of submissions to the Pharmaceutical Benefits Advisory Committee (PBAC). She also teaches health economics to students undertaking a Masters of Public Health at Macquarie University and regularly teaches short courses on economic evaluation.

Dr. Sally Hawse is an organisational knowledge and learning specialist with expertise in knowledge management strategy and project delivery. Dr. Hawse is currently a Learning and Development Consultant, where she is involved in the design, implementation, and evaluation of people development and capability initiatives to support knowledge transfer and workplace learning as part of a NSW Australia local government workforce sustainability and transformation agenda.

Chapter 3
Ensuring Healthy Lives: Saving Lives at Birth in Indonesia

Salut Muhidin, Rachmalina Prasodjo, Maria Silalahi and Jerico Pardosi

Abstract Programs for saving lives at birth have been implemented in many countries, especially in the less developed countries, such as Indonesia, where maternal and child deaths are still too high. Internationally, ensuring healthy lives and promoting well-being for all is one of the 17 United Nations Sustainable Development Goals (UN SDGs) launched in 2015. The UN SDGs is a global plan of action for prosperity, people, and the planet that presents an opportunity to mobilise both government and society to ensure no one is left behind and equality for all. This chapter represents an attempt to understand the varying results achieved at a sub-regional level by a saving lives at birth program in the eastern part of Indonesia. Through this case study, we focus on identifying the barriers to program participation and the enablers that successfully prompt women to give birth at a health facility. We also explore two theoretical frameworks used in business and economics—social marketing for health promotion and shared leadership—to ascertain whether they might improve the region's saving lives program.

Keywords Saving lives a t birth · Indonesia · Social marketing · Shared leadership · Maternal health · Mortality

S. Muhidin (✉)
Macquarie University, Sydney, Australia
e-mail: salut.muhidin@mq.edu.au

R. Prasodjo
Ministry of Health, South Jakarta, Indonesia

M. Silalahi
NTT Provincial Women Empowerment and Child Protection, Kupang, Indonesia

J. Pardosi
Queensland University of Technology, Brisbane, Australia

© Springer Nature Singapore Pte Ltd. 2020
L. Wood et al. (eds.), *Industry and Higher Education*,
https://doi.org/10.1007/978-981-15-0874-5_3

45

3.1   The Case at a Glance

Key concepts	• Public health: sustainable health development
	• Management: shared leadership
	• Marketing: social marketing of health promotion

Level of study	• Undergraduate, postgraduate

Subject areas	• Economics, management, marketing, public health

Graduate capabilities	Graduate outcomes	%
	Critical thinking	20
	Problem solving	
	Teamwork	20
	Communication	
	Ethical thinking	20
	Sustainability	40
	Total	**100%**

Time required	• Out-of-class preparation:	60 min
	• In-class discussion:	60 min
	• Out-of-class assignments:	180 min

Additional Materials

• **United Nations' Sustainability Development Goals**
http://www.undp.org/content/undp/en/home/sustainable-development-goals.html
This website summarises the 17 interconnected UN SDGs. These goals are a universal call to action to end poverty protect the planet and ensure that all people enjoy peace and prosperity.

• **Social ecological model**
https://www.unicef.org/cbsc/index_43099.html
UNICEF was one of the first UN organisations to advocate for and address behavioural and social change as a way of reducing maternal, newborn, and child morbidity and mortality. Through a paradigm called Communication for Development (C4D), UNICEF integrates behavioural and social change into its programs throughout the developing world. C4D is based on a theoretical framework called the Social-Ecological Model, which helps to interpret the personal and environmental factors that determine behaviour and its complex effects. With this knowledge, one can identify leverage points for behavioural and social change.

- **Social marketing in health care**
  https://doi.org/10.1177/0272989X08318464
  These three case studies illustrate how social marketing can be used as a strategy for impacting health care providers and broad consumer behaviour across a population. The techniques outlined can be applied at the individual clinical settings or as a complement to reinforce wider community-level messages.

- **Shared leadership in health care**
  https://www.ted.com/talks/eric_dishman_health_care_should_be_a_team_sport
  Eric Dishman uses his experience as a medical specialist to put the patient at the centre of a treatment team as a way to reinvent health care. He says that it is time to update our thinking that healthcare revolves around a hospital "because these places are often the wrong tool, and the most expensive tool, for the job". Dishman argues that while three pillars of personal health—care anywhere, care networking, and care customisation—are currently coming into focus, efforts are piecemeal. To have patient-centric healthcare succeed, caregivers and patients need to take on new roles.

3.2 Introduction

High rates of maternal and child mortality have been one of the big challenges in many less developed countries, including in Indonesia. It is not surprising, therefore, that the United Nations (UN) through its SDGs has provided recommendations and guidance to all countries to achieve substantial reductions in their maternal and child mortality rates (WHO 2017). It is this global agenda for sustainable development that presents an opportunity to mobilise both government and society to ensure that future generations are not deprived of the resources and conditions necessary to live dignified, healthy, and meaningful lives—and that the environments that support their well-being remain intact (WHO 2017).

In the context of the Asia Pacific region, Indonesian mortality rates are still considered high. In 2010, Indonesia's under-five mortality rate was 151 per 1000 live births compared to Malaysia and Thailand's 3 and 11 in 1000, respectively (UN 2010). The 2012 Demographic Health Survey shows Indonesia's maternal mortality rate (MMR) was similarly high, with 239 deaths per 100,000 live births. Moreover, the report shows significant variations at the provincial level. For example, Yogyakarta's MMR was 104 per 100,000 live births, but the MMR in *Nusa Tenggara Timur* (NTT) was 307 per 100,000 live births.

Given these statistics, the government of Indonesia has made several attempts to combat this unresolved health challenge. One of these initiatives is the "*Revolusi KIA*" Saving Lives at Birth Program, which is specifically targeted at NTT where the mortality rates are among the highest in the country. The idea behind *Revolusi KIA* is to save the lives of both mothers and their children by encouraging child delivery at a health facility. In tandem, in-centre deliveries can help to equalise the distribution and quality of health care throughout the population.

This case study focuses on the implementation and impact of *Revolusi KIA* in NTT. We outline the health issues associated with maternal and child mortality and its context in the global SDGs. We examine some of the challenges and enablers to participation in *Revolusi KIA* and explore some theoretical frameworks that could be used to analyse the program's implementation. We also consider how some of the concepts central to social marketing and shared leadership could be used to improve the saving lives program in the region.

3.3   Health and the UN SDGs

In September 2015, the UN adopted a global agenda for sustainable development called the SDGs. The SDGs are a follow-on action of the Millennium Development Goals (MDGs) that were established in 2000 and ended in 2015. While some progress was made toward certain goals in the MDGs and toward global partnerships for development, by 2015, the global promise the MDGs embodied had not been realised. As a result, the UN introduced the SDGs as an improved version, and particularly to tackle the issue of inequality. The main objectives of the SDGs are to eradicate poverty, to protect the planet, and to ensure equality and prosperity for all by focussing on three main pillars of sustainability: economic, social, and environmental. The SDGs consist of 17 primary goals that are further detailed in 169 specific development targets for 2030. Through these targets, governments, civil society, and the private sector can guide and measure their contributions toward achieving global sustainable development (WHO 2016).

Health issues are addressed in the third goal of the SDGs, which focusses on the development of inclusive and sustainable health and well-being by ensuring healthy lives and promoting well-being for all—including mothers and children. In this context, development is considered to be 'sustainable' when resources are managed by and for all individuals in ways that support the health and well-being of present and future generations. Within the larger framework of the SDGs, the development targets for health actually contribute either directly or indirectly to all 17 SDGs, as shown in Fig. 3.1. Here, health and well-being is a central and basic requirement for social inclusion, poverty reduction, and environmental protection (WHO 2016).

In terms of saving lives at birth, Goal 3 emphasizes programs relating to reproductive, maternal, and child health. It gives attention to the performance of whole health systems, including health facilities and services. It also emphasizes the need for universal health coverage and financial risk protection delivered via an equitable and resilient health system. This includes full access to, and coverage of, health facilities for childbirth.

Fig. 3.1 Health within the UN's SDGs. *Source* WHO (2016)

3.4 Saving Lives at Birth and *Revolusi KIA*

Specific health programs on saving lives at birth have traditionally been adopted at the global and regional levels because many women, particularly in less developed countries, still die every year as a result of complications during pregnancy and childbirth. In 1987, for example, a global program called the Safe Motherhood Initiative was introduced at the International Conference on Safe Motherhood held in Nairobi, Kenya (Sai 1987; Sai and Measham 1992). Since then, this global advocacy program has been adopted in more than 100 countries, including Indonesia, with the support of five international agencies (the Population Council, the UN Development Program, the UN Population Fund, WHO, and the World Bank). In its initial stages, the main agenda of the program centred on the relationships between maternal health and child survival, socio-economic development, and family planning. The target was to reduce the worldwide MMR by 50% by the year 2000 (Sai and Measham 1992).

Indonesia adopted the Safe Motherhood Initiative in 1988 with the target of reducing Indonesia's MMR from 450 to 340 per 100,000 live births by 1993. The initiative has indeed reduced national mortality rates, but results at the sub-national level have been variable. Accordingly, the government of Indonesia has made a strong commitment to addressing this challenging issue and is paying more attention to the regions where mortality rates are still high, such as NTT. In this province, the MMR is 307 maternal deaths per 100,000 live births with 45 infant deaths per 1000 live births. These figures are relatively higher than the national level of 239 per 100,000 and

Fig. 3.2 Map of the NTT Province, Indonesia

32 per 1000 live births, respectively (Statistics Indonesia and Macro International 2013). The lack of proper health care at the front line, or village level, in NTT has been claimed as the main reason. In general, access to health services among disadvantaged and remote communities has remained a substantial challenge for the NTT government given the vastness of the region, which has 22 main districts with 3270 villages and more than 566 islands. Based on a 2017 Statistical Report, NTT has a population of 5.3 million, the vast majority of whom are young and rural. The median age is 22 years old, and 80% live in rural areas that are spread across the three main islands (Sumba, Flores, and Timor). These regions are characterised by diverse races, ethnicities, and languages. Figure 3.2 shows the geographical location of NTT within Indonesia.

In terms of health development, NTT has experienced high rates of maternal and child mortality for several decades. Hence, the local government has launched a series of three major national campaigns under the umbrella brand "*SIAGA*", which literally means '*ALERT*'. The *Suami SIAGA* or 'Alert Husband' campaign launched in 1999 aimed to improve paternal knowledge about pregnancy and delivery by focussing on maternal mortality prevention. Evaluation studies showed that the majority of husbands lack the interpersonal skills to communicate with local nurses or midwives and instead relied on their wives' understanding of reproductive health issues (Cholil et al. 1998; Shefner-Rogers and Sood 2004). The *Bidan SIAGA* or "Alert Midwives" campaign followed. This was an improvement program on the earlier action in the 1980s when traditional birth attendances (TBA) at the village level were involved in helping mothers to give births at home. At the time, TBA services were considered inadequate, especially for dealing with antenatal care, which then led to recommendations for additional midwives and trained healthcare workers at the village level. Consequently, the government attempted to ensure that each village had at least one midwife responsible for providing antenatal care. Village midwives, however, still had difficulties engaging with the local communities and building partnerships with local organisations, which limited their ability to support obstetrics and emergency services (D'Ambruoso et al. 2009). Hence, in 2006, the *Desa SIAGA* or 'Alert Village' campaign was launched to mobilise community involvement. The program included a pregnancy register, financial support, transport availability, blood donations, and family planning information (GIZ 2011). Overall, the *Desa SIAGA* program was successful in terms of community mobilisation. For example, men's involvement during prenatal care and delivery increased from 16 to 32% (Fachry and Sofiarini

2010). However, low levels of knowledge and awareness of the danger signs during pregnancy and delivery continued (Sood et al. 2004).

Thus, despite SIAGA, many regions, including NTT, experienced difficulties with implementing the SIAGA programs (Titaley et al. 2010) and maternal and child mortality in NTT remained high. Many mothers still preferred to give birth at home (i.e., 78% in 2007 and 57% in 2012) or be assisted by a TBA as indicated in Figs. 3.3 and 3.4. In women with a higher risk of haemorrhage or other complications during delivery, home births have a much greater risk of both maternal and neonatal death, as confirmed by a recent study on this topic in NTT (Pardosi et al. 2017).

Facing the serious challenges described above, in 2009, the NTT government made a strong commitment to improving maternal and child health by launching a health program called *Revolusi Kesehatan Ibu dan Anak* (*Revolusi KIA*) or 'Maternal and Child Health (MCH) Revolution' (Dinas Kesehatan Provinsi 2012). To reinforce the NTT government's commitment to this program, *Revolusi KIA* was officially adopted into Provincial Act. No. 42/2009 and eventually adopted in all 22 districts. Table 3.1

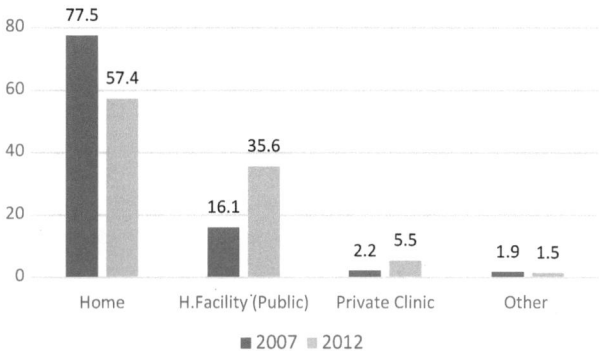

Fig. 3.3 Birthplace in NTT (% of pregnancies). *Source* Statistics Indonesia-BPS et al. (2008, 2013)

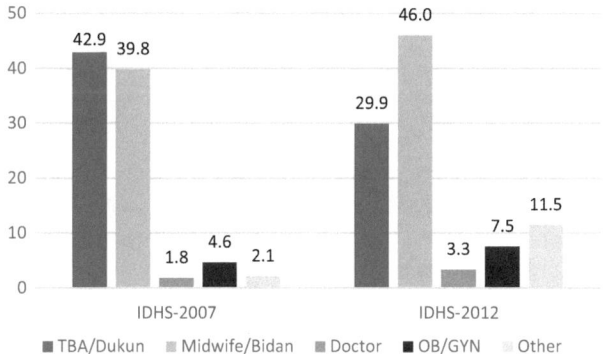

Fig. 3.4 Birth attendance in NTT (% of pregnancies). *Source* Statistics Indonesia-BPS et al. (2008, 2013)

Table 3.1 Supporting regulations of *Revolusi KIA* in NTT and its districts

No.	District/city	Supporting regulation	No./year
1.	NTT Province	Provincial Act	No. 42/2009
2.	Kupang City	Peraturan daerah	No. 7/2013
3.	Kupang District	Peraturan Bupati	No. 16/2011
4.	TTS—Timor Tengah Selatan	Instruksi Bupati	No. 25/2010
5.	TTU—Timor Tengah Utara	Peraturan daerah	No. 4/2012
6.	Belu	Bupati Instruction	No. 44/2011
7.	Alor	Peraturan Bupati	No. 12/2011
8.	Lembata	Peraturan Bupati	2012
9.	Flores Timur	Peraturan daerah	No. 9/2011
10.	Sikka	Peraturan Bupati	No. 8/2011
11.	Ende	Peraturan Bupati	No. 22/2011
12.	Ngada	Perda KIBBLA	No. 11/2012
13.	Nagekeo	Peraturan Bupati	No. 1/2011
14.	Manggarai	Peraturan Bupati	No. 7/2011
15.	Manggarai Timur	Peraturan Bupati	No. 1/2011
16.	Manggarai Barat	Peraturan daerah	No. 12/2010
17.	Sumba Timur	Peraturan daerah	No. 3/2011
18.	Sumba Barat	Perda KIBBA	No. 4/2012
19.	Sumba Tengah	Peraturan Bupati	No. 3/2012
20.	Sumba Barat Daya	Peraturan Bupati	No. 17/2011
21.	Rote Ndao	Peraturan Bupati	No. 5/2011
22.	Sabu Raijua	Peraturan Bupati	2012
23.	Malaka	Peraturan Bupati	2014

shows that many district governments only began to fully support the program in 2011—two years after the program was launched. The Malaka district was the last region to adopt *Revolusi KIA*; however, Malaka was part of the Belu district prior to 2012.

In its operationalisation, *Revolusi KIA* is defined as a strong effort to ensure all mothers give birth at an adequate health care facility (NTT PHO 2012). The program provides for a *Puskesmas* (a community health centre) at the sub-district level and a hospital at the district level. However, not all *Puskesmas* in NTT can be considered as adequate. Adequacy means complying with three basic requirements. First, it should have five midwives who have been trained in neonatal obstetric management, which means both normal and emergency deliveries. Second, it should have five nurses who have also been fully-trained in neonatal obstetric services, as well as basic cardiac support and asphyxia. Third, there should be at least one other health professional with specialised training; dentists and lab technicians are considered specialties (NTT PHO 2012).

Safety issues are emphasized as the main reason to promote childbirth at an adequate health facility as opposed to homebirths or other facilities where emergency support is usually unavailable. Many healthy women experience problematic births, and these can arise without any warning. In the absence of medical equipment, even well-trained health workers cannot provide adequate medical care when faced with an emergency like postpartum haemorrhage.

Hence, *Revolusi KIA* has two main objectives. First, to safeguard both mothers and their children during delivery in an equipped health facility; and, second, to improve the quality of health care services by improving and strengthening existing health facilities with support through the six elements outlined in Fig. 3.5. 'Health staff', at number 1, means both quantity and quality. In the short term, a system of staff outsourcing and sister hospitals has been implemented where advanced hospitals in Bali, Yogyakarta, and Makassar partner with the local hospitals in NTT. Knowledge is shared through staff exchanges between facilities to improve expertise and the quality of care over the long term (NTT PHO 2012). 'Equipment', 'Health supplies/medicine', 'Buildings', and 'Systems', are usually considered as a package and have been delivered as a prototype adequate health centre for other centres to model. Budgets and financial management are also a part of the program.

Like the SIAGA program, *Revolusi KIA* acknowledges the importance of multiple levels of influence at the interpersonal, organisational, community, and policy levels. In this way, it can be thought of as a form of social-ecological model (see Fig. 3.6) that builds a supportive environment (Hoek and Jones 2011). The program's interventions take place at: (1) the policy level with a government-operated health insurance scheme; (2) the organisational level with the introduction of new healthcare facilities; (3) the interpersonal level to influence social and cultural norms; and (4) the individual level to increase knowledge and change attitudes toward birth practices. The primary audiences are women of reproductive age, their husbands, families, and influential community members, such as the village head and local religious leaders.

The social-ecological model in *Revolusi KIA's* referral system is a 2H2 system. Pregnant women are intensively monitored two days before and two days after the

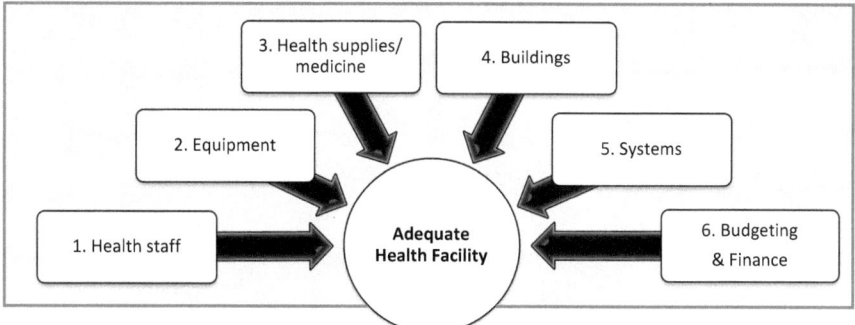

Fig. 3.5 Support elements in *Revolusi KIA*

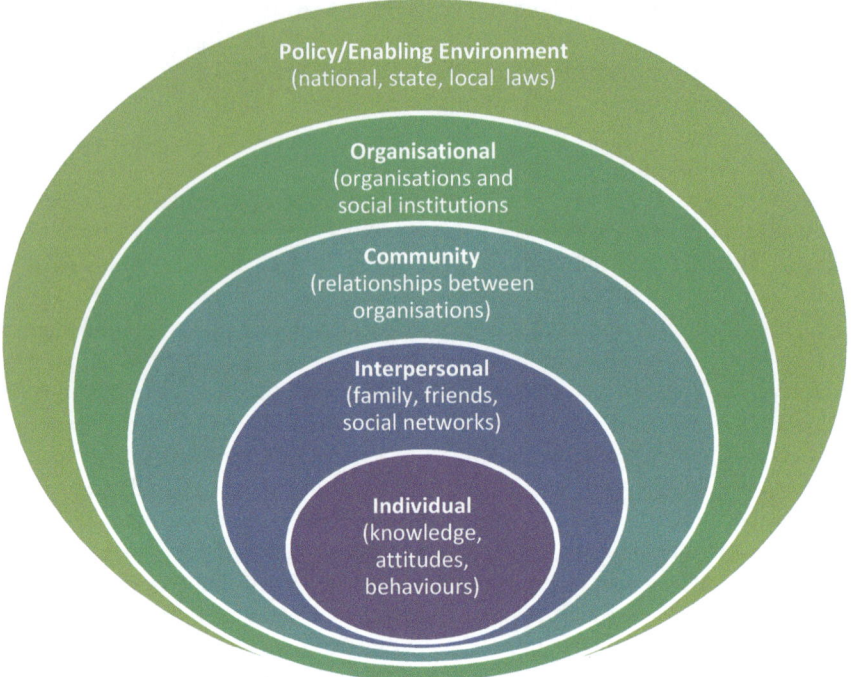

Fig. 3.6 The Social-Ecological Model. *Source* UNICEF (2016)

due date. (The 'H' comes from two *Hari sebelum* and two *Hari sesudah* in Bahasa Indonesian.) This 4-day period is considered a critical period, as 90% of maternity deaths in NTT occur during or soon after delivery (MoH 2001). 2H2 aims to mobilise community elements at different levels to ensure that women arrive at an adequate health facility in time. Figure 3.7 shows the three levels of community involved in the 2H2 system: pregnant women and their family; community members, e.g., neighbours, village health cadres/volunteers, the village midwife, traditional birth attenders, local community leaders, etc.; and government leaders and health facilitators, such as the 2H2 coordinator and hospital.

3.5   Achievements and Challenges of *Revolusi KIA*

Since *Revolusi KIA* was introduced in late 2009, there has been some improvement in health indicators. Between 2009 and 2016, health facility births in NTT increased significantly from 44.9% to 93.5% (NTT PHO 2017). The proportion of health facility births also increased, yet at a lower percentage than previously reported. In 2007, health facility births were still at 16.1%, increasing to 35.6% in 2012 and 65.8% in

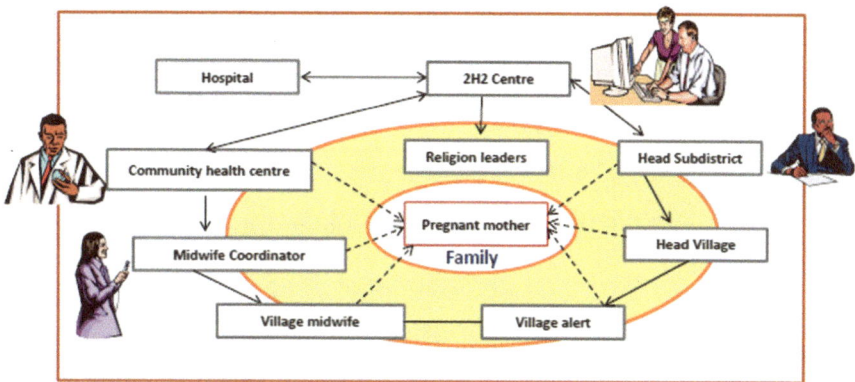

Fig. 3.7 *Revolusi KIA's* implementation of the Social-Ecological Model

2017 (Statistics Indonesia and Macro International 2008, 2013; Statistics Indonesia 2018). However, at the sub-provincial and district level, progress has varied, as shown in Fig. 3.8 and Table 3.2. For example, in Flores Timur, 69% of women gave birth in a health facility in 2009 but, by 2016, this number had increased to 98%, whereas in Alor these numbers have risen and fallen and risen again. Yet despite these variations, the overall trends are moving in a positive direction.

The program has also significantly impacted MMRs at both provincial and sub-regional levels, as presented in Table 3.2. Clearly, these statistics indicate that some women were avoiding birth at a health facility, either voluntarily or forcefully due to certain circumstances. Studies suggest some mothers prefer home deliveries due to a misalignment between the antenatal care provided and the social-cultural context (Finlayson and Downe 2013; Pardosi et al. 2017). Distance and poor road conditions can also be a factor (Pardosi et al. 2017; Thaddeus and Maine 1994; Titaley et al. 2010).

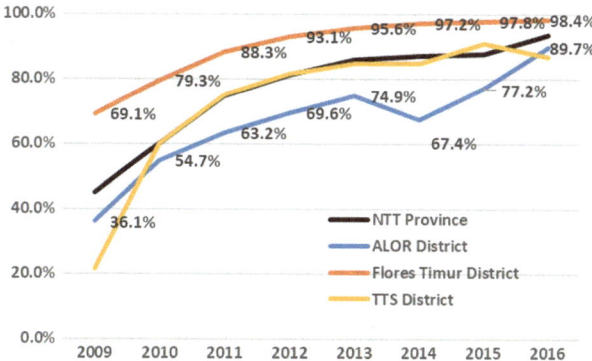

Fig. 3.8 Health Facility Birth in NTT, 2009–2016

Table 3.2 Percentage of health facility birth and maternal deaths in NTT: 2009 and 2016

No.	District/city	Urban pop. 2015 (%)	Health facility births (%)			Maternal deaths (per 100,000 live births)		
			2009	2016	Diff.	2009	2016	Diff.
Timor Island								
1.	Kupang City	96.0	78.51	99.28	20.77	208	59	149
2.	Kupang District	6.7	15.43	90.47	75.04	287	258	28
3.	Timor Tengah Selatan	9.1	21.47	86.68	65.21	531	326	205
4.	Timor Tengah Utara	13.8	53.62	96.14	42.53	402	135	267
5.	Belu	22.1	62.70	91.64	28.94	262	113	149
6.	Malaka	21.1		97.65	97.65		116	−116
Flores Island								
7.	Alor	22.7	36.09	89.68	53.59	356	468	−112
8.	Lembata	18.1	83.53	98.37	14.84	174	187	−12
9.	Flores Timur	20.9	69.12	98.38	29.27	307	152	156
10.	Sikka	19.8	84.09	94.14	10.06	183	249	−65
11.	Ende	32.2	80.52	94.14	13.62	249	317	−68
12.	Nagekeo	0.0	89.30	98.21	8.91	288	149	139
13.	Ngada	14.1	73.32	96.76	23.45	242	216	26
14.	Manggarai Timur	0.0	13.37	84.25	70.87	463	250	212
15.	Manggarai	25.7	20.29	91.20	70.91	254	113	142
16.	Manggarai Barat	9.7	20.06	90.04	69.98	255	224	31

(continued)

Table 3.2 (continued)

No.	District/city	Urban pop. 2015 (%)	Health facility births (%)			Maternal deaths (per 100,000 live births)		
			2009	2016	Diff.	2009	2016	Diff.
Sumba Island								
17.	Sumba Barat Daya	8.1	13.76	95.19	81.43	288	195	93
18.	Sumba Barat	19.7	48.35	96.77	48.42	105	184	−79
19.	Sumba Tengah	0.0	21.08	95.13	74.06	269	160	109
20.	Sumba Timur	21.0	43.06	97.66	54.60	249	268	−19
21.	Rote Ndao	6.9	7.77	92.78	85.01	420	328	92
22.	Sabu Raijua	0.0		93.06	93.06		704	−704
NTT Province (Total)		20.5	44.92	93.45	48.53	304	209	95

Source NTT Provincial Health Office Report (2010–2017)

Based on the percentage of health facility births in 2009 (as a starting point of *Revolusi KIA*), it was as low as 8% in Rote Ndao, 13% in Manggarai Timur, and 15% in the Kupang district to as high as 89% in Nagekeo. The districts with the lowest proportion of health facility births are predominately rural districts. By 2016, seven years after *Revolusi KIA* was launched, most districts in NTT had improved their figures in terms of health facility births. The lowest was 84% in Managgarai Timur, and the highest was 99% in Kupang City (i.e., 96% urban population). In a recent study on a meta-synthesis of underutilisation of health services in low-to-middle income countries (LMICs) (Finlayson and Downe 2013).

However, when MMRs are considered, a different figure emerges. Table 3.2 indirectly indicates that a higher proportion of health facility births does not necessarily mean a decrease in the MMR. For example, on Flores Island, three districts with 98% of births at a health facility each show a different statistic for MMR. Figure 3.9 lists the place of birth statistics at the district level according to three categories: adequate health facilities, inadequate health facilities, and non-health facility or at home. As is clear from the table, the numbers vary wildly from district to district.

In our discussions of the key challenges to participation in *Revolusi KIA*, we have drawn heavily on the findings from a recent study conducted by Muhidin et al. (2016). That study evaluated the implementation of the *Revolusi KIA* program with the aim of determining the barriers and enablers that impacted equitable access to health facility deliveries in NTT. The authors conclude that there are four key challenges to participation in *Revolusi KIA*.

The first challenge is about awareness and knowledge of the program benefits. At the community level, most people have heard of *Revolusi KIA*, but do not necessarily support the idea of giving birth in a health facility. The program has often been perceived as a health-related program rather than an inter-sectoral program that involves different stakeholders in the community. These perceptions may be related to the low

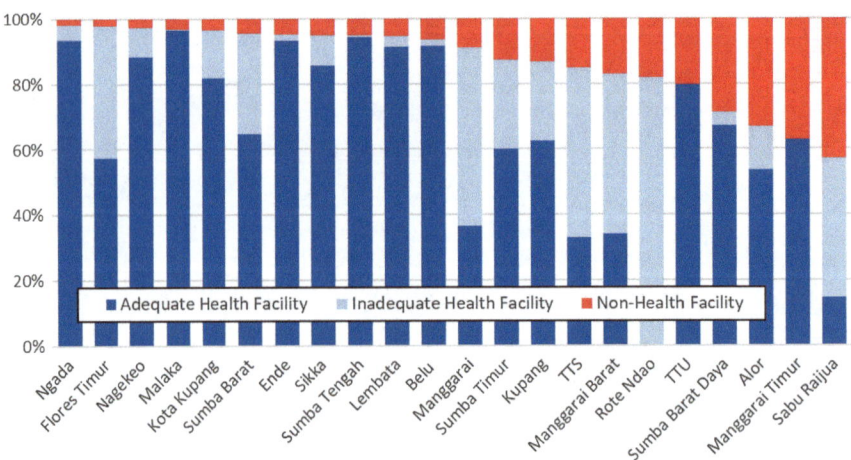

Fig. 3.9 Births by place of delivery in NTT (%). *Source* NTT PHO (2014)

level of education and minimum health information received in NTT province Additionally, some districts still have low levels of awareness of the program's benefits, which leads to low participation rates.

The second challenge is traditional health beliefs and practices that are still strongly exercised in NTT. As a matter of fact, such practices are still common in various cultures around the world, including Indonesia (i.e., Agus et al. 2012; Swasono 1998; Wulandari and Whelan 2011). Of the 1331 ethnic groups currently living in Indonesia, around 370 ethnicities practice local traditions. Pregnancy and delivery are considered to be a normal phenomenon and, thus, giving birth at home with help from a TBA is more conventional. TBAs play an important role in home deliveries as they not only help to deliver babies, they also provide emotional support and practical assistance during pregnancy and after delivery. TBAs are valued and influential members of the community. Therefore, they would be valuable assets to the cause to encourage better maternal health. However, in NTT, most villages have instituted regulations that penalise TBA-assistance. An interview with a village leader suggests these regulations are often ignored as some women feel it is unnecessary to go to a health facility unless complications arise.

The third challenge is individual perception and motivation related to giving births at home or at a health facility. A home birth is perceived by some families as less disruptive and less costly. With home births, there is no need to travel and extended family can easily visit and provide assistance. Hospital births are perceived as special occasions, and visits by extended family members to be involved in the celebration would require a special invitation. Also, accommodation for the family members would need to be arranged at a significant cost. Moreover, due dates are unpredictable, with historical figures from MoH (2001) showing that about 40% of women give birth earlier and about 27% women after. This unpredictability discourages some from travelling to the health facility at the appropriate time, particularly those families who live far away. Women who are in their last gestational stage are advised to be brought to a waiting house located close to the health facility between 2 and 7 days before their estimated due date as 90% of maternal deaths in NTT occur during this critical time. While beneficial to mortality rates, this mobilisation strategy is seen as inconvenient, costly, and time-consuming.

The last challenge is the cost of giving birth at the health facilities, especially at a hospital, which is one of the reasons why the government of Indonesia implemented health insurance for the poor. Called *Jamkesmas*, the insurance provides free primary health care services, including maternity care at a community health centre. Since 2011, the Ministry of Health has also put in place universal maternity benefits, *Jampersal,* for all pregnant women not covered by any maternity scheme. However, it seems knowledge of these schemes has not reached all families. A critical issue is the lack of the father's involvement. In NTT, as in many parts of Indonesia, a patriarchal family structure is very common. Men are typically the breadwinners and hold the decision-making power. Many mothers expressed they did not have the power to decide on a health facility birth unless the father agreed, and many fathers only have superficial knowledge and engagement with pregnancy.

In summary, *Revolusi KIA* has achieved varying results in different areas of NTT; however, despite the conjectures above, the reasons why remain unclear. Further studies using different approaches are needed to gain a better understanding of the program's achievements and challenges. It is also worthwhile exploring whether applying some of the frameworks from the business and economic fields, such as social marketing and shared leadership, might improve *Revolusi KIA's* participation rates.

3.6 Business and Economics Frameworks

3.6.1 Social Marketing

Studies have shown that a social marketing approach can be used to influence health behaviour (Hoek and Jones 2011). For example, a wide range of health communication strategies can be applied to promote, disseminate, and leverage community-level outreach. The same approach could be used to improve the success of *Revolusi KIA* in Indonesia by improving the health status of mothers and their new-born babies. The strategies need to be constructed by taking the barriers and enablers to the program into account.

Some strategies that following social marketing principles, such as audience segmentation and branding, could be used as an effective way to change health behaviour in this region. In the context of NTT, one of the biggest challenges is the difficulty in accessing health information given its low-income, poorly-educated population. Accordingly, creating effective health messages in a social marketing campaign and rapidly identifying and adapting them to appropriate audiences may be essential to the main objective of the program. Social marketing might also be applied to correct misconceptions or to increase awareness of the program and its benefits.

3.6.2 Shared Leadership

Given its structure and operationalisation, *Revolusi KIA* in NTT can be defined as a community-based health intervention that involves active partnerships with multiple stakeholders within and across a community—better known as community engagement. In the context of health programs, Farnsworth et al. (2014) highly recommend a level of shared leadership as an effective measure to produce better outcomes in community engagement programs, such as *Revolusi KIA*. These authors find that higher levels of community engagement occur when close collaboration and shared leadership is present within the community. Thus, MCH might be improved significantly by actively mobilising mothers and their families to use a health facility for childbirth through partnerships between the local governments and community organisations.

Farnsworth et al. (2014) also consider the importance of shared leadership, which usually happens in the latest stage of the community engagement process. Earlier stages of engagement are characterised as outreach, consult, involve, and collaborate. Community engagement is seen as a continuum of community collaborations, which ideally lead to active engagement. Over time, a specific collaboration is likely to move along this continuum toward greater community involvement. It also frequently evolves into long-term partnerships that shift from the traditional focus on a single health issue to address a range of social, economic, political, and environmental factors that affect community health.

In this case, leadership could be used as a primary enabling factor in transforming actions toward attaining the health program's goals. Once a goal has been set, leaders must champion it to ensure that it will be achieved. In this context, leaders from all levels of a community must work together towards the same broad, long-term vision for better health. In other words, shared leadership facilitates the community engagement process in a number of ways, including building trust and mutually beneficial relationships, enlisting and utilising new resources and allies, creating effective communication channels, and improving overall health outcomes as projects evolve into lasting collaborations (Shore 2007). Nevertheless, there are some challenges in implementing the concept of shared leadership in the context of LMICs.

3.7 Teaching Notes

3.7.1 Synopsis of the Case

Programs for saving lives at birth have been implemented in many countries, especially in the less developed countries, such as Indonesia, where maternal and child deaths are still too high. Internationally, ensuring healthy lives and promoting well-being for all is one of the 17 United Nations Sustainable Development Goals (UN SDGs) launched in 2015. The UN SDGs are a global plan of action for prosperity, people, and the planet that presents an opportunity to mobilise both government and society to ensure no one is left behind and equality for all.

This chapter represents an attempt to understand the varying results achieved at a sub-regional level by a saving lives at birth program in the eastern part of Indonesia. Through this case study, we focus on identifying the barriers to program participation and the enablers that successfully prompt women to give birth at a health facility. We also explore two theoretical frameworks used in business and economics—social marketing for health promotion and shared leadership—to ascertain whether they might improve the region's saving lives program.

3.7.2 Target Learning Group

- Level of study—BA and MA students
- Subject areas—public health and health sustainability; social marketing; shared leadership; maternal health.

3.7.3 Learning Objectives

- Infant mortality and maternal health in Indonesia
- Sustainability health development
- Shared leadership in health management
- Social marketing on health promotion.

3.7.4 Teaching Strategy

This case study examines the barriers and opportunities for innovation in reducing infant and maternal mortality in rural Indonesia.

The case highlights the need to address infant mortality and maternal health in these regions. It contextualises *Revolusi KIA* or the 'MCH Revolution' program within the UN SDGs and discusses the challenges presented by geography and location, economic factors, community and tradition, and individual knowledge to the program's success. The case also examines how a social-ecological model has been implemented within *Revolusi KIA,* and how social marketing and shared leadership can positively influence the success of MCH programs.

The discussion questions and assignments should promote awareness of how social-ecological models support *Revolusi KIA* and how social marketing and shared leadership may help to overcome barriers to program participation.

3.7.5 Reading Questions

3.7.5.1 Pre-reading

- What does the title, "Program of Saving Lives at Birth in Indonesia" suggest about the content of this case study?
- Does the chapter abstract answer your predictions about the content of the case study?

3.7.5.2 Skim Reading

Skim the chapter to find the meaning of these acronyms and key terms. Depending on class size and time, instructors may wish to use a 'read, pair, share' activity, where participants work in pairs with each responsible for half of the acronym/term list. Partners should skim the chapter for their respective acronyms/terms and share their findings.

Acronym/term	Definition
SDG	Sustainable development goals: a UN global action plan for prosperity, people, and the planet
LMICs	Low-middle income countries: a country categorisation based on the population's income level
MMR	Maternal mortality rate: the WHO defines the MMR as the number of women who die while pregnant or within 42 days of giving birth/termination from birth-related issues
NNT	Nusa Tenggara Timur (East Nusa Tenggara), a province in Indonesia
Revolusi KIA	Also known as *Revolusi Kesehatan Ibu dan Anak* or 'MCH Revolution': an NNT government initiative to improve child and mother mortality rates
MDGs	Millennium development goals: eight international development goals that all UN members committed to helping achieve by the year 2015. Of these, two related to mother and child health—to reduce child mortality and to improve maternal health
Safe motherhood initiative	A global program introduced in 1987 focussing on the relationships between maternal health and child survival, development, and family planning with the target of reducing MMR by 50% by the year 2000. In Indonesia, the Safe Motherhood Program was first adopted in 1988 with the target of reducing the MMR from 450 to 340 per 100,000 live births by 1993
TBA	Traditional birth attendances: valued and influential members of the community who help to deliver babies and also provide emotional support and practical assistance during pregnancy and after delivery
Puskesmas	*Pusat Kesehatan Masyarakat* or a community health centre
2H2	2 *Hari sebelum* (2 days before) and 2 *Hari sesudha* (2 days after): an intensive health monitoring program targeted at pregnant women for the two days before and two days after delivery
Jamkesmas	Free basic health insurance for the poor provided by the Indonesian government, including maternity care at community health centres
Jampersal	A free maternity benefit for pregnant women who are not covered by any other maternity scheme

3.7.5.3   Charts and Tables

Examine the figures and tables in the case study. What is their relation to the Saving Lives a t Brth program?

3.7.5.4   In-Depth Reading

Note that, while the questions above are aligned with the structure of the case study, participants may occasionally need to read further in the text for the answers.

3.7.6   Discussion Questions

3.7.6.1   Introduction

- What are the key principles of the SDGs?
- What statistics indicate that Indonesia has a high proportion of birth mortality?
- How do the figures for NTT compare?
- What are the aims of *Revolusi KIA*?

3.7.6.2   Health and the UN SDGs

- What target did international agencies set for the MDGs to reduce the MMR? Was this target achieved?
- How do mortality rates in NTT compare with the rest of Indonesia?

3.7.6.3   Saving Lives a t Brth and the *Revolusi KIA* Program

- Why was the Safe Motherhood Initiative introduced?
- What are some of the reasons given for this mortality rate?
- Why were the SIAGA programs launched?
- Despite the SIAGA program, NTT continues to face a high birth mortality rate. What reasons are given for this?
- When was *Revolusi KIA* adopted as a Provincial Act? Why?
- How has the first objective of *Revolusi KIA* been implemented?

3.7.6.4 Achievements and Challenges of *Revolusi KIA*

- What important barriers to participation does *Revolusi KIA* still need to overcome?
- Involving men in the process of giving birth remains critical to the success of the Saving Lives a t Birth program. Why?

3.7.6.5 Other Discussion Areas

The discussion questions aim to establish connections between program interventions and the SDGs. They also serve as a lead-into the suggested assignment task. The discussion questions help highlight that, while *Revolusi KIA* has been impactful in reducing maternal and child deaths, it has not been as influential in the rural areas of NTT.

- What four key challenges have been identified as barriers to maximising participation in *Revolusi KIA*?
- What suggestions are offered to address traditional health beliefs and practices?
- What were the SIAGA awareness campaigns, and what was the motivation for each? How effective were these campaigns?
- How does the SIAGA program relate to the Social-Ecological Model that underpins *Revolusi KIA*?

3.7.6.6 Suggested Approach

Depending on class size, instructors may wish to divide participants into three groups and assign each group to one of *Siami SIAGA*; *Bidan SIAGA*; *Desa SIAGA*. After 5–10 min, each group should summarise their assigned campaign. The instructor may wish to lead a class discussion on the relationship between the SDGs and the SIAGA campaigns.

3.7.7 Suggested Assignments

3.7.7.1 Social Marketing

The authors note that, "a social marketing approach can be used to influence health behaviour (Hoek and Jones, 2011). For example, a wide range of health communication strategies can be applied to promote, disseminate, and leverage community-level outreach. The same approach could be used to improve the success of *Revolusi KIA* in Indonesia by improving the health status of mothers and their newborn babies."

Taking the barriers and enablers of *Revolusi KIA* into account, develop a social marketing campaign to improve one aspect of how the program might reach its target audiences.

3.7.7.2   Shared Leadership

Shared leadership generally occurs in the later stages of the community engagement process. Over time, collaboration is likely to evolve toward greater community involvement and long-term partnerships to address a range of factors that affect community health. Community leaders can serve as key enablers to transformative action in reaching health program goals.

Taking the barriers and enablers of *Revolusi KIA* into account, develop a shared leadership intervention to improve one aspect of how the program might reach its target audiences.

3.7.7.3   Suggested Assignment Approach

UNICEF's Communication for Development (C4D) initiative uses the Social-Ecological Model to understand the complex and interrelated impacts of personal and environmental factors that determine behaviours and to identify behavioural and organisational levers for change. The authors summarise the achievements and challenges of *Revolusi KIA* in NTT. They also identify that social marketing and shared leadership can be employed in C4D efforts.

- Participants should select either the social marketing or shared leadership assignment. Resources in the ancillary materials can be used for assignment pre-work, or to help guide the topic choice:

  - Social marketing in health care: https://doi.org/10.1177/0272989X08318464
  - Shared leadership in health care: https://www.ted.com/talks/eric_dishman_health_care_should_be_a_team_sport.

- Participants could work individually or in small groups to research and collaborate on ideas with high potential for impact on MHC outcomes.
- The proposed solutions should be feasible, cost-effective, and relatively easy to deploy.
- The proposed solutions should relate to Social-Ecological Model and *Revolusi KIA's* implementation of Social-Ecological Model provided in Figs. 3.6 and 3.7 of the case study. For assistance, participants can refer to Modules 1 and 2 of the *MNCHN C4D Guide: Communication Strategy Guide for Maternal, Newborn, Child Health and Nutrition* (https://www.unicef.org/cbsc/index_43099.html)

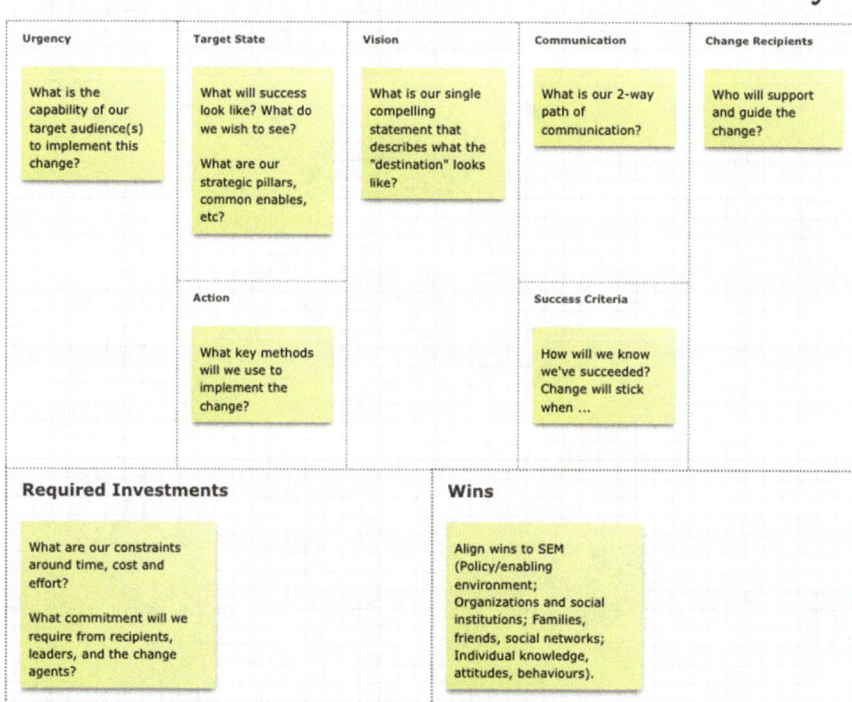

Fig. 3.10 Example of a social marketing change canvas. *Source* Adapted from Canvanizer (2018)

- Module 1: Understanding the Social-Ecological Model and Communication for Development
- Module 2: Steps for Developing a Strategic C4D Program Plan.

• Participants should present a social marketing/shared leadership proof-of-concept aimed to create positive MCH outcomes in the short or medium term. The examples of a Change Canvas (Fig. 3.10) and a Partnership Canvas (Fig. 3.11) can be used as planning and presentation tools. The Change Canvas is tailored to social marketing activity; the Partnership Canvas is tailored to the shared leadership activity. Groups can create their own Change Canvas at: https://canvanizer.com/new/lean-change-canvas. For the Partnership Canvas, participants will need to create two plans—one to capture the viewpoint of community leaders and one to capture the view of healthcare advocates. Participants should then compare what each party needs, offers, and how they can co-create a mutually beneficial outcome. See: Instructions for the Partnership Canvas in the *Additional resources* section below.

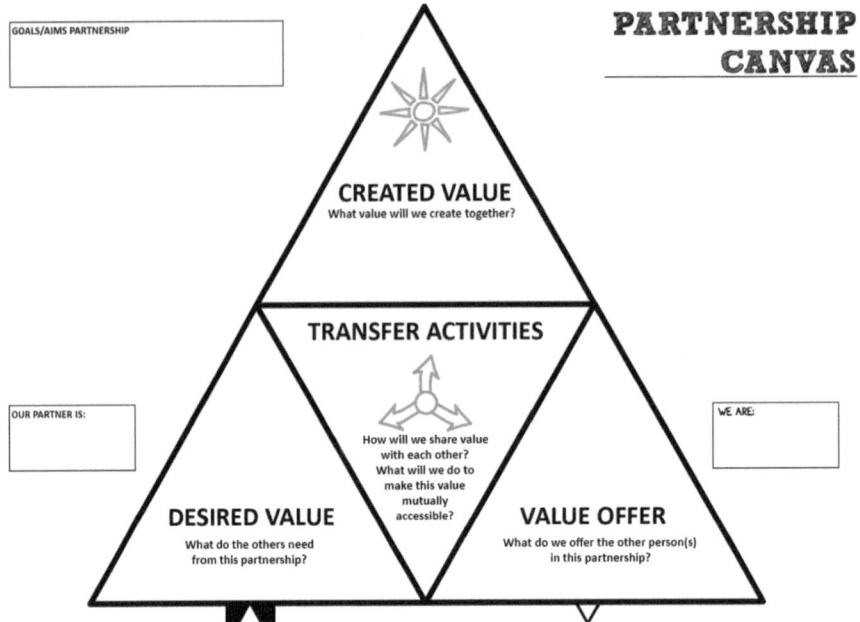

Fig. 3.11 Example of shared leadership/partnership canvas. *Source* Adapted from Doorneweert (2014)

3.7.8 Additional Resources

- **Communication for Development (C4D). Behaviour and social change** https://www.unicef.org/cbsc/index_65736.html
- **Communication for Development (C4D). Community engagement** https://www.unicef.org/cbsc/index_65175.html
- **The Compass: Your Guide to Social Impact Measurement** https://www.csi.edu.au/research/project/compass-your-guide-social-impact-measurement
- **The Navigator: Your Guide to Leadership for Social Purpose** https://www.csi.edu.au/research/project/navigator-your-guide-leadership-social-purpose
- **Canvanizer** https://canvanizer.com/new/lean-change-canvas
- **Lean Change Part 1—Combining Kotter and Running Lean** http://agileconsulting.blogspot.com/2012/08/lean-change-part-1-combining-kotter-and.html
- **Instructions for the Partnership Canvas** https://valuechaingeneration.com/2014/10/17/the-partnership-canvas.

References

Agus Y, Horiuchi S, Porter SE (2012) Rural Indonesia women's traditional beliefs about antenatal care. BMC Research Notes 5:589

Canvanizer [Change Canvas] (2018) Available at https://canvanizer.com/new/lean-change-canvas

Cholil A, Iskandar MB, Sciortino R (1998) The Mother Friendly Movement in Indonesia. The state ministry for the role of woman and the Ford Foundation, PT Panji Graha Semarang

D'Ambruoso L, Achadi E, Adisasmita A, Izati Y, Makowiecka K, Hussein J (2009) Assessing quality of care provided by Indonesian village midwives with a confidential enquiry. Midwifery 25:528–539

Dinas Kesehatan Provinsi (Provincial Health Office) Nusa Tenggara Timur (2012) Pedoman Revolusi KIA di Provinsi NTT [Guidance of MCH Revolution in NTT Province]. Revised edn

Doorneweert B (2014) The partnership canvas. Retrieved from https://valuechaingeneration.com/2014/10/17/the-partnership-canvas

Fachry A, Sofiarini R (2010) Evaluasi Desa Siap Antar Jaga di Provinsi NTB. Ministry of Health, GTZ, DFID

Farnsworth SK, Böse K, Fajobi O, Souza PP, Peniston A, Davidson LL, Griffiths M, Hodgins S (2014) Community engagement to enhance child survival and early development in low-and middle-income countries: an evidence review. J Health Commun 19:67–88

Finlayson K, Downe S (2013) Why do women not use antenatal services in low-and middle-income countries? A meta-synthesis of qualitative studies. PLoS Med 10. https://dx.plos.org/10.1371/journal.pmed.1001373

GIZ (2011) Persalinan sebagai Urusan Desa: sebuah publikasi dalam. German Health Practice Collection. Deutsche Gesellschaft für Internationale Zusammenarbeit (GIZ), Bonn, Germany

Hoek J, Jones SC (2011) Regulation, public health and social marketing: a behaviour change trinity. J Soc Market 1:32–44

Ministry of Health (2001) Indonesia Health Survey (Survei Kesehatan Nasional-Surkesnas) 2001. Ministry of Health, Indonesia. http://ghdx.healthdata.org/record/indonesia-health-profile-2011

Muhidin S, Prasodjo R, Pardosi JF, Silalahi M (2016) How does community engagement improve maternal and newborn health? Paper presented at the 4th global symposium on health system research (HSR 2016), Vancouver BC, Canada, 14–16 Nov 2016

NTT PHO (2012) Pedoman Revolusi KIA di Provinsi NTT [Guidance of MCH Revolution in Nusa Tenggara Timur Province], Revised edn. NTT Provincial Health Office, Kupang, Indonesia

NTT PHO (2014) Profil Kesehatan Nusa Tenggara Timur [Health profile of Nusa Tenggara Timur]. NTT Provincial Health Office, Kupang, Indonesia

NTT PHO (2017) Profil Kesehatan Nusa Tenggara Timur [Health profile of Nusa Tenggara Timur]. NTT Provincial Health Office, Kupang, Indonesia

Pardosi JF, Parr N, Muhidin S (2017) Local government and community leaders' perspectives on child health and mortality and inequity issues in rural eastern Indonesia. J Biosoc Sci 49:123–146

Sai FT (1987) The safe motherhood initiative: a call for action. IPPF Med Bull 21:1–2

Sai FT, Measham DM (1992) Safe motherhood initiative: getting our priorities straight. Lancet 339:478

Shefner-Rogers CL, Sood S (2004) Involving husbands in safe motherhood: effects of the SUAMI SIAGA campaign in Indonesia. J Health Commun 9:233–258

Shore N (2007) Community-based participatory research and the ethics review process. J Empirical Res Human Res Ethics 2(1):31–41

Sood S, Chandra U, Palmer A, Molyneux I (2004) Measuring the effects of the SIAGA behavior change campaign in Indonesia with population-based survey results. USAID, John Hopkins Bloomberg & Maternal and Neonatal Health, Baltimore, MA

Statistics Indonesia and Macro International (2008) Indonesia Demographic and Health Survey 2007. Statistics Indonesia-BPS, National Population and Family Planning Board-BKKBN, Ministry of Health-Kemenkes/Indonesia, and ICF International, Jakarta, Indonesia

Statistics Indonesia and Macro International (2013) Indonesia Demographic and Health Survey 2012. Statistics Indonesia (BPS), National Population and Family Planning Board (BKKBN), Ministry of Health, and ICF International, Jakarta, Indonesia

Statistics Indonesia (2018) Indonesia Demographic and Health Survey 2017. Statistics Indonesia (BPS), National Population and Family Planning Board (BKKBN), Ministry of Health, and ICF, Jakarta, Indonesia

Swasono MF (1998) Kehamilan dan kelahiran dalam konteks budaya dan implikasinya terhadap kesehatan bayi dan ibu [Pregnancy and delivery in cultural context and its implication to child's and mother's health]. In: Swasono MF (ed) Kehamilan, kelahiran, perawatan ibu dan bayi dalam konteks budaya [Pregnancy, delivery, maternal and neonatal cares in the context of cultural]. UI Press, Jakarta, Indonesia

Thaddeus S, Maine D (1994) Too far to walk: maternal mortality in context. Soc Sci Med 38:1091–1110

Titaley CR, Hunter CL, Dibley MJ, Heywood P (2010) Why do some women still prefer traditional birth attendants and home delivery? A qualitative study on delivery care services in West Java Province, Indonesia. BMC Pregnancy Childbirth 10:43

UNICEF (2016) Module 1. Understanding the Social Ecological Model and Communication for Development. Retrieved from https://www.unicef.org/cbsc/index_43099.html

United Nations (2010) The Millennium development goals report 2010. UN Publishing, New York

WHO (2016) Health in the UN-Sustainable Development Goals

WHO (2017) World health statistics 2017: monitoring health for the sustainable development goals. World Health Organization, Geneva, Switzerland

Wulandari LPL, Whelan AK (2011) Beliefs, attitudes and behaviours of pregnant women in Bali. Midwifery 27:867–871

Dr. Salut Muhidin is a Senior Lecturer at the Department of Management, Macquarie University in Sydney, Australia. He has been involved in both teaching and research roles, especially on the study of international business as well as population issues and its consequences in different settings such as Asia, West Africa and Australia. Dr. Muhidin's most recent study focuses on the community engagement in reducing maternal and child mortality through 2H2 system in NTT Province, Indonesia and the evaluation of "Revolusi KIA" health program on health facility birth in the same region.

Mrs. Rachmalina Prasodjo is a Senior Researcher at the National Institute of Health Research and Development (NIHRD), the Ministry of Health-Indonesia. She is an anthropologist and social behavioral researcher. She has strong skills in qualitative analysis and has been involved in many research projects focused on socio-behavioral, ethnographic, and cultural determinants of health in Indonesia. Dr. Prasodjo was appointed as a survey coordinator in Indonesian School Health Survey and as a qualitative research consultant in several research projects related to health promotion and health policy.

Ms. Maria Silalahi, MPHM is the Head of Gender Equality, Institutional and Partnership at NTT Provincial Women Empowerment and Child Protection, Indonesia. Previously, she was the Head of Community Health Division at NTT Provincial Health Office, and the Head of Health Promotion Section and the Head of Maternal Neonatal Health Section, Community Services Division at the same organization. She has been actively involved in the NTT region's health policy. As the Head of Community Health Division, she has responsible to monitor and supervise the districts in NTT Province on health programs in order to improve community health in general and to reduce maternal and neonatal mortality rates in particular.

Dr. Jerico Pardosi is a Lecturer at the School of Public Health and Social Work, Queensland University of Technology (QUT) in Brisbane, Australia. He is also a researcher at the National Institute of Health Research and Development (NIHRD) of the Ministry of Health-Indonesia. Previously, Dr. Pardosi was involved in research projects focused on developing adolescent health integrated health intervention, reconstructing women's reproductive health rights, needs and services in rural Alor region and postnatal danger signs in Indonesia.

Chapter 4
Sustainability for Organisational Success: How Is Optus Joining the Dots?

Zak Baillie, Lay Peng Tan, Yvonne A. Breyer and Andrew Buay

Abstract Singtel Optus Pty Ltd ("Optus") is an Australian telecommunications company in a highly competitive industry. While expanding its network, value proposition, and achieving superior customer experience is a key driver of market growth, Optus has embedded sustainability across its business as a market differentiator. In Optus, sustainability informs decision-making, the culture of its business, its operations, and its products and services. Optus believes that making sustainability a part of its DNA will establish the foundations for long-term success. This case study outlines four sustainability initiatives Optus is pursuing and how these initiatives are integrated into its daily business. Yet some key challenges face Optus on the way ahead and, as this case study shows, long-term sustainability requires a collaborative, innovative, and holistic approach. This case study was developed based on primary and secondary research about Optus' sustainability initiatives up till June 2016.

Keywords Systems thinking · Integrative thinking · Strategy · Strategic framework

Z. Baillie · L. P. Tan (✉) · Y. A. Breyer
Macquarie University, Sydney, Australia
e-mail: laypeng.tan@mq.edu.au

A. Buay
Vice President, Group Sustainability, Singtel, Sydney, Australia

Vice President, Group Sustainability, Singtel, Singapore, Singapore

Talent Coach, Optus, Sydney, Australia

4.1   The Case at a Glance

Key concepts	• Systems thinking • Strategic framework • Stakeholder theory • Sustainability as a driver for long-term success
Level of study	• Undergraduate capstone units, postgraduate, executives, MBA
Subject areas	• Strategic management, marketing management, systems thinking, corporate social responsibility

Graduate capabilities

Graduate outcomes	%
Critical thinking	20
Problem solving	10
Teamwork	20
Communication	10
Ethical thinking	10
Sustainability	30
Total	**100%**

Time required	• Out-of-class preparation:	180 min
	• In-class discussion:	120 min
	• Out-of-class assignments:	180 min

Activity type	Individual: • Pre-reading, skim reading, in-depth reading • Reading discussion Team-based: • Group discussion
Ancillary materials	• **Optus sustainability web page** Our sustainability vision and focus areas https://www.optus.com.au/about/sustainability The Optus sustainability vision is to deeply embed sustainability in its culture, values, decision-making, operations, and products and services to create a sustainable business.

4.2   Introduction

Sustainability has emerged as a critical element of a successful business. Recent evidence highlights that businesses that embed sustainability into their policies and practices enjoy 4.8% higher returns than those who that do not (Eccles et al. 2014).

While this data comes from a study conducted in the US, similar trends are occurring in Australia where companies are considering sustainability as more than just an obligation under corporate social responsibility (CSR) but as a critical means to long-term success. One such company is Optus. As Andrew Buay, the Vice President, Group Sustainability at Singtel & Talent Coach at Optus, points out, "Sustainability creates shared value for the business, and it's not just about philanthropy."

Optus is an Australian company in the highly competitive telecommunications industry. It is the second-largest company in an oligopolistic market, i.e., where only a few firms dominate the market. Its main competitor, Telstra, is the most dominant in terms of infrastructure and market share. For example, as of 2015, Telstra held 45% of the market share in mobile handset services and 64% in wireless broadband services (ACCC 2016).

However, consumer demand in the telecommunications industry is increasing rapidly. Between June 2014 and June 2015, the total volume of data downloads increased substantially—40% for fixed-line broadband services and 85% for mobile devices (ACCC 2016). Further, these numbers are expected to increase as on-demand television services, such as Netflix and Stan, gain in popularity (ACCC 2016). The increase in demand for services is likely to stoke more competition as firms seek to capture additional customers. Optus, for example, invested AUD $1.5 billion into its mobile network in the 2015–2016 financial year. However, Telstra, as the largest telecommunications operator in Australia, and Vodafone Hutchison Australia, as the third-largest, have also made similar investments. These statistics show that Australia's telecommunications industry is both intensely competitive and projected to grow significantly.

While expanding its network is a means of both expanding its operations and a way of capturing additional market share, the way Optus has embedded sustainability into each layer of its business is a crucial differentiator in the market. In 2015, Optus grew its market share in the postpaid mobile market by 2% and increased its profit over the three financial years from 2013 to 2015 (see Table 4.1). Optus is growing, and sustainability is a critical component of this success.

Optus has a broad definition of sustainability, and it has sought to embed these values throughout its business. For Optus, sustainability informs its decision-making, the culture of the business, its operations, and its products and services (see Fig. 4.1).

Table 4.1 Three years of financial details for Optus

Variables	2015–2016 ($m)	2014–2015 ($m)	2013–2014 ($m)
Economic value generated	9115	8790	8466
Operating costs	5143	5002	4851
Staff costs	1299	1246	1171
Dividends to shareholders	600	560	560
Tax expense	379	360	361
Economic value retained	1685	1613	1513

Fig. 4.1 Sustainability governance structure

Optus believes that by embedding sustainability into the DNA of their business, it is priming itself for long-term success.

This case study is organised into four sections. The next section provides a background to Optus, followed by an outline of its four sustainability initiatives. The major themes that act as common threads between the four sustainability initiatives are then discussed, along with some of the challenges facing Optus in the sustainability sphere ahead.

4.3 Background

Optus employs the equivalent of 9000 full-time staff and operates 342 shop fronts. In total, they serve 10 million customers each day. Since 2001, they have been a wholly-owned subsidiary of Singtel. The Singtel Group is based in Singapore but has operations in 25 countries serving over 600 million mobile customers. Optus is Australia's second-largest telecommunications operator. Its 4G network covers 94% of Australia's population through 4850 base stations, while its 3G network covers 98.5% of the population. Table 4.1 details the key financial information for the years 2013–2016.

4.4 Sustainability as a Driver of Long-Term Success

4.4.1 Four Pillars

Optus has embedded sustainability into four key areas of their business. These four 'pillars' are how Optus defines sustainability: (1) marketplace and customers; (2) community; (3) our people; and (4) the environment. Within each pillar are a number of focus areas. These are deemed material to Optus and their stakeholders and are where they believe they can make a positive impact (see Tables 4.2, 4.3, 4.4 and 4.5). These initiatives are a good means of understanding how Optus approaches sustainability, the fundamental components of their sustainability agenda, and how sustainability is integral to its long-term success. Figure 4.2 presents the Optus approach to sustainability.

4.4.2 Pillar 1: Marketplace and Customers

To achieve status as Australia's top service provider, Optus must offer high-quality customer service. This customer service element is delivered via information and communications technology. It is with this technology that Optus aims to improve

Table 4.2 Marketplace and customer pillar

Initiative	Description	Achievements to date	Goals
Supply chain management (2015-present)	Optus seeks to deal with partners who share similar values. Part of this process has been to conduct an LCA on its value and supply chain to identify the areas with the greatest environmental, social, and economic impacts	Completed a global-scale LCA	To be an industry leader in sustainable supply chain management by 2020
Supplier performance assessment (2015-present)	In conjunction with its parent company, Optus has devised a supplier code of conduct that is written into any new contract worth AUD $5000 or more. This ensures that all suppliers share common values with Optus. Optus also reviews prospective suppliers with regard to human rights, worker health, safety, and environmental practices	A new supplier code of conduct that aligns with UN stipulations and has been integrated into all supplier contracts worth more than $5000 Contracts over $200,000 undergo an environmental conduct and worker welfare inspection	To ensure no major material environmental, social, or corporate governance issues arise in the supply chain
Advanced Security Operations Centre (2016-present)	ASOC is a new cybersecurity initiative to help protect businesses from cybercrime. A detect and response feature ensures that data are monitored and Optus is notified if a threat is detected		Not publicly available
Big Data (2016-present)	Optus' Big Data application can be used by customers to monitor and manage their data usage		Not publicly available

Table 4.3 Community pillar

Initiative	Description	Achievements to date	Goals
DTP (2013–present)	The DTP program is an educational program for secondary school students designed to inform participants about how to use technology safely and properly	3000 sessions have been conducted, reaching over 88,000 students	To reach 37,000 students in 2017 with 1350 sessions. Expand to interstate and regional areas
Kids Helpline @ School (2013–present)	This program connects primary school students with a counsellor via video link. The sessions cover topics such as family arguments, how to cope with change, and information about using technology correctly	18,000 children participated in sessions in 2015	Not publicly available
Future Makers (2016–present)	Future Makers provides funding and professional guidance to not-for-profits and social entrepreneurs to develop technologies that address the social challenges young people face. AUD $350,000 and up to 4 months of capacity building is available for successful participants		Not publicly available

(continued)

Table 4.3 (continued)

Initiative	Description	Achievements to date	Goals
student2student (2010–present)	The student2student program pairs school students who read at a level below the national average with a 'buddy'. The student and their buddy read together over the phone weekly. Working with the Smith Family, this program has recently been expanded into rural areas where Optus provides a mobile phone for those who do not have a landline	In 2015, 600 pairs of students took part in the program. 95% of those who finished the course said their reading was improved	770 reading pairs by the end of 2017
Australian Business and Community Network (ABCN) mentoring (2005–present)	This mentoring program pairs Optus staff with students to discuss their career prospects and education opportunities. In 2015, the ABCN issued a scholarship, which is awarded to vulnerable youth who have prevailed over hardship to succeed in their schooling. Worth $7000 per annum, the scholarship supports students from Year 11 to the end of their first year of tertiary studies	500 Optus staff mentored 900 students in 2015	Not publicly available
yes4good (2005–present)	yes4good allows Optus employees to donate their time to their favoured charities or provide mentoring	In 2015, $8.7 million was donated by Optus staff (this includes cash donations as well as hours volunteered)	15,000 volunteer hours in the 2016/2017 financial year

Table 4.4 Our people pillar

Initiative	Description	Achievements to date	Goals
Think Big (2015-present)	Think Big incentivises employees to think innovatively and to develop ideas into concepts. A small number of concepts are then chosen and developed into products		Have 1000 Big Ideas submitted by 2017. Host 8-10 Think Big challenges
Healthy Body at Work (2014-present)	This eight-week program is designed to encourage employees to become more active, get more sleep, and reduce their stress levels	The program was presented at the 2016 Corporate Health and Wellbeing summit	Not publicly available
Happy, Healthy Minds (2014-present)	Happy, Healthy Minds aims to improve worker mental health. To do so, managers have taken courses so they can better identify and assist mental health issues in their team. Optus has also started the My Life Hub, which gives support to people and their families. Additionally, onsite counselling is available at the Sydney and Melbourne offices	In 2015, 500 managers undertook training in mental health awareness	Not publicly available

how people live and work. Table 4.2 summarises all the initiatives within this pillar. A key initiative is sustainable supply chain management.

4.4.2.1   Initiative 1—Sustainable Supply Chain Management

Optus is attempting to create a supply chain that practices responsible business activity. That is, Optus seeks to engage suppliers who reflect its own ethical, social, and environmental values. To do this, Optus conducted a lifecycle assessment (LCA) to

Table 4.5 Environment pillar

Initiative	Description	Achievements to date	Goals
Energy efficiency	Increasing the energy efficiency of Optus' network in a range of ways, such as installing smart metres at base stations, replacing older inefficient equipment with new more efficient equipment, and making its vehicle fleet more fuel-efficient	In 2015, smart meters were installed at 640 base stations; 3000 air conditioners were replaced with thermostat-controlled fans; and printers were upgraded to reduce their energy use by 80%	Reduce emissions intensity by 30% by 2020 and 50% by 2050
Future-proofing our infrastructure (2014-present)	Using regional climate predictions, Optus aims to build a network that is more resilient to a changing climate		To operate a network that meets or exceeds regulatory standards
Mobile Muster (1998-present)	This program recycles disused mobile phones	In 2015, 3.6 tonnes of mobile phones were acquired	To contribute a volume of mobile phones commensurate with Optus' market share

identify where in its broader supply and value chains it has high exposure to environmental pressures, governance issues, or social and human rights risks (see Breakout: 'What gets measured what gets managed'). An LCA identifies issues of material importance, and its findings can be integrated into a sustainable supply chain management strategy.

The scope of the initial LCA was global, encompassing Optus' entire operation, to provide the best opportunity for identifying all the risks present in the whole value and supply chain. The LCA allowed Optus to identify 'hotspots' for future focus, i.e., areas of greater exposure. Optus included both its large and small suppliers in the LCA. It was important for Optus to assess the risks in both its large and small suppliers, especially since some of its largest suppliers, for example, Apple and Samsung, are industry-best sustainability practitioners.

The LCA was initiated in 2015 and concluded in 2016 and identified several significant issues in Optus' supply and value chain. For example, worker health, safety, and well-being were the key labour issues in its outsourced contact centres in India and the Philippines. Also, staff engagement and retention were issues for these contact centres as the market is very competitive and labour is highly mobile. Consequently, any factors affecting staff motivation could cause workers to seek employment elsewhere. Further, low staff motivation could impact the service they

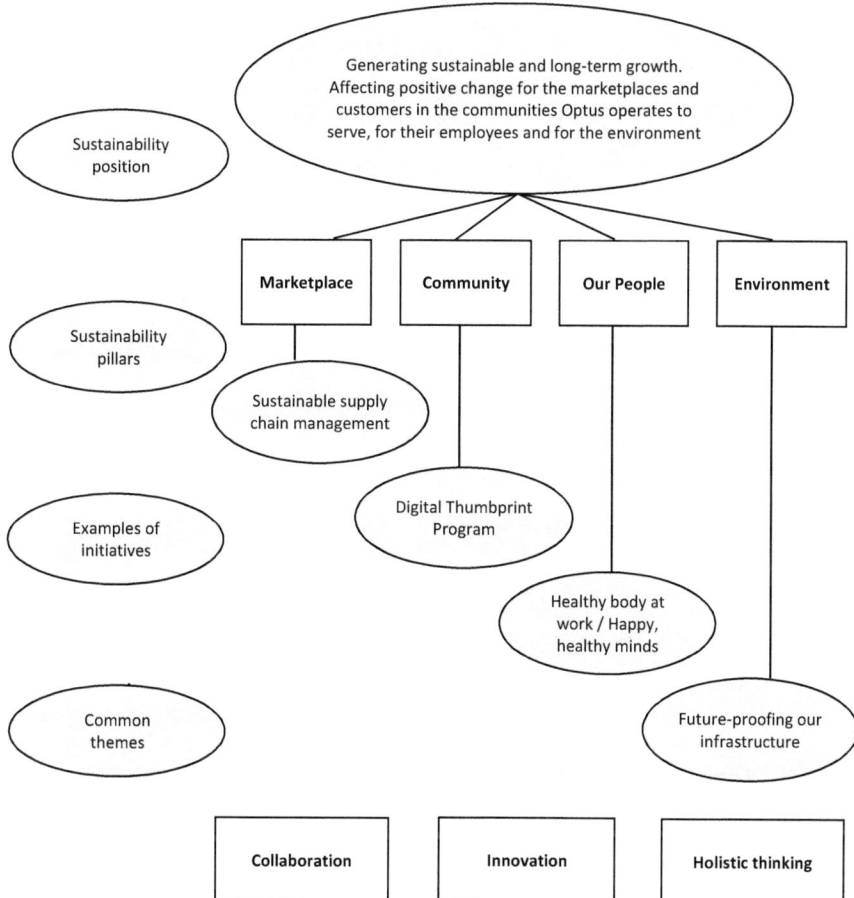

Fig. 4.2 A schematic illustrating Optus' definition of sustainability and how that informs the development of its initiatives

deliver to Optus customers and the training they provide to their own staff. These are critical issues for Optus. To address these labour-related issues, senior management regularly met with the supplier and its staff to share Optus' vision and strategy. The intention was for the supplier's staff—Optus' indirect staff—to gain a sense of shared ownership in what Optus is trying to achieve, so they felt and behaved as if they worked for Optus. A sense of shared ownership can change the way staff deal with customers. It also creates shared value, which, in this case, would benefit all three parties—Optus, the supplier, and the staff. Optus' Net Promoter Score (NPS) is among the top three telecommunication companies in Australia. The Net Promoter Score is indicative of overall customer satisfaction with a company's products and its services. An important component of the NPS is frontline customer service, and this high rating is partly attributed to addressing the issues highlighted above.

Optus has also developed local community programs in the Philippines that make CSR volunteering opportunities available to staff and contact centre partners. The positive feedback and success of these programs led to an expansion in the program's scope and scale the following year, and it is now also run in India where the other contact centres are located.

Breakout: Life Cycle Assessment

A lifecycle assessment (LCA) is an assessment of the environmental impact of a product (Klöpffer 2014). An LCA employs a 'cradle-to-grave' approach, and this is what differentiates it from other environmental assessments (Klöpffer 2014). Not to be confused with a product's lifecycle, an LCA is the sum of all the environmental impacts of a product in all stages of the product's life. That is, from the gathering of initial raw materials to how it is disposed of when the product is discarded.

Take, for example, a bottle of tomato sauce. An LCA would look at how the tomatoes are grown – even at the origin of the soil in which the tomatoes were planted – how they are harvested and transported to the factory, and how the sauce is produced. Further, an LCA would also look at the packaging and labelling, how the bottles are transported to the store, the retail outlet where the sauce is sold and whether, once purchased, it is kept in the fridge or in the cupboard. Finally, once the sauce has been consumed, whether the packaging is recycled or whether it ends up in landfill.

Depending on the scope and resolution of the LCA, the process can be incredibly time-consuming and expensive; however, the 'systems thinking' of the approach is critical. An LCA does not view a product in isolation; it considers all the processes that have taken place to create the product. This is vital because there are a number of environmental impacts across the creation of a product and the net of these must be considered to properly understand the environmental impact of a product. The popularity of LCAs has resulted in international guidelines and standards to homogenise the LCA process (see ISO 2006).

However, to make informed and sustainable decisions, information on environmental impact is not enough. Information on social impact is also important and, thus, a social lifecycle assessment (S-LCA) has also been devised (UNEP 2009). Bearing great similarity to the LCA, the S-LCA assesses social impacts over the lifecycle of a product. For example, returning to our example of tomato sauce, an S-LCA may look at the rights of the workers who grow the tomatoes or the wages of those who transport them (UNEP 2009). Optus also reviewed the social impacts of their supply and value chain, and this is discussed in the next section.

Having completed the initial LCA, Optus now aims to focus on the areas of interest identified in the study along with detailed reviews of their top 50 vendors. Through a review process, Optus will design a strategy to deal with the areas of higher risk and exposure. This was the primary purpose of the LCA—to shape Optus' materiality focus. Hence, its results are used to inform many of Optus' sustainability initiatives.

4.4.3 Pillar 2: Community

The community pillar focuses on using Optus' infrastructure and capabilities to help connect disconnected communities. More specifically, there is a focus on reconnecting vulnerable or marginalised young people who can become removed from the broader community as a result of their socio-demographics, cultural background, educational shortcomings, or family circumstances.

There are four key initiatives under this pillar:

- education and employment—technology as a means of educating and helping young people find work;
- digital citizenship—informing young people on how to be safe and responsible online users;
- inclusion and well-being—increasing employment prospects for disadvantaged youth; and
- engaging our people—allowing Optus staff members to contribute to causes they believe in.

Teaching young people to be safe and capable digital users is a key component and, therefore, is the focus of the Digital Thumbprint Program (DTP).

4.4.3.1 Initiative 2—The DTP

The rapid increase in our use of technology has had many unintended negative consequences. Examples include social media addiction, bullying via social media, and data privacy issues. Pitched at Generation Z—the generation after Millennials—the DTP acknowledges the academic, networking and professional opportunities the internet can provide but also the social issues that can result from its use.

The DTP consists of three workshops for secondary school students—the age at which young people gain more autonomy and greater access to technology. As of June 2016, 3478 sessions had been conducted reaching a total of 108,776 students with the program gaining accreditation from the Australian government in the process. In 2015, the program won the Security and Online Safety Award at the annual Australian and New Zealand Internet Awards. Survey data collected after the program shows that 97% of teachers believe the course has helped students improve their online competencies.

The program was devised in collaboration with experts from backgrounds in education, technology, data privacy, internet security, and youth mental health. Students are encouraged to take home what they have learned and teach their parents. This tenet recognises that participant's parents may not have the required knowledge to inform their children about how to use the internet properly.

While Optus is not directly responsible for the unintended negative consequences of technology, they do provide access via products and services. As a result, Optus is, in part, responsible for disseminating information to users about proper conduct with regard to its use. This initiative has similarities to the example given above about addressing worker conditions: Optus acknowledges that it is in their value chain. As Andrew Buay explains: "If people start to abuse or misuse technology … the government could come in and clamp down on how people can use the internet … and that can undermine customer freedom and privacy." If a customer's privacy is undermined, it could also lead to customers having less trust in their service provider as they expand into new digital businesses like mobile advertising. Again, because it is in their value chain, Optus has a responsibility to ensure their customer's data is safe and that their privacy is protected. Optus believes that if customers lose trust in them as a service provider, it could undermine their current and future business.

4.4.4   Pillar 3: Our people

'Our People' is about being an employer that people want to work for. Part of this is creating a workforce that is diverse, collaborative, and inclusive, as well as ensuring that employees are able to reach their highest potential. This has obvious implications for Optus. As the market evolves, it becomes more competitive; as customer expectations change, Optus' workforce must be equally adept and constantly evolving. As depicted in Table 4.4, initiatives within this pillar are directed at developing employee ideas, offering learning and development programs for their workforce, and improving the well-being of employees.

4.4.4.1   Initiative 3—Healthy Body at Work/Happy, Healthy Minds

An effective worker is one who is not only physically safe when they go to work, but also one who is mentally happy, has aspirations, is motivated, and who has a sense of purpose. This initiative is about ensuring workers are healthy and physically fit and that they are in good mental health. The Healthy Body program is an eight-week program aimed at improving workers' sleeping habits, activities, and stress levels. The Healthy Minds program aims to create an environment where staff feel they can talk openly about any mental health issues. Staff can disclose these issues to the company, or they can keep them confidential. All team leaders have undertaken a Healthy Minds Psychological Capability Training program to better enable them to identify and address possible mental health issues in their respective teams. Further, Optus launched My Life Hub, which is an onsite counselling service for people and their families at their Sydney and Melbourne offices.

Both programs have had positive impacts. After the Healthy Body at Work program, staff productivity and satisfaction increased. Further, staff were more aware of stress, better at improving sleep habits, were sitting less, and were active more. Additionally, the demand for the onsite counselling service has increased by 30% over the past year.

Mental health is now regarded as the most important issue when it comes to worker well-being. This is partly because mental health issues can lead to physical health issues over time. Optus has identified two primary links between worker well-being and worker productivity. First, having a workforce that is driven, ambitious, and enjoys their job is more productive. Second, when someone is struggling with mental health issues, they may lack focus. This could materialise, for instance, in an avoidable incident like a car accident. There are no regulations in place when it comes to worker mental health. However, the issue is perceived as material and, therefore, Optus addresses it.

4.4.5   Pillar 4: Environment

This pillar describes Optus' attempts to minimise the environmental impact of its network. The Optus network consumes a lot of energy, which in turn produces a lot of greenhouse gas emissions, given the bulk of energy supply in Australia is still from coal-based generation. Thus, tackling climate change has taken both mitigation and adaptation. Optus is upgrading its network to become more energy-efficient and is lowering its emissions intensity. It is also designing infrastructure to cope with new and varied climatic pressures. 'Futureproofing Our Infrastructure' is an initiative with the aims of creating a network that is more resilient to these new climatic pressures. Refer to Table 4.5 for a summary of all initiatives within this pillar.

4.4.5.1   Initiative 4—Futureproofing Our Infrastructure

When planning new infrastructure, Optus is now taking the threats from climate change into account. That is, Optus now aims to build infrastructure according to both present standards and future climates to increase infrastructure resilience. However, new designs require an understanding of how the climate is likely to change on a regional scale. As such, Optus commissioned a study to understand the impact of climate change on their operations. The findings of this study are now being used to inform a plan on how to best lessen the impacts of a changing climate on their infrastructure.

Working with the Australian scientific body, the Commonwealth Scientific and Industrial Research Organisation (CSIRO), Optus sought to understand the specific vulnerabilities its network will face according to climate projections. Climate scientists from the CSIRO modelled likely climate changes on a regional scale, and Optus used these findings to understand what conditions its network would be exposed to in the future. One particular example is the changing pattern of storms. It is forecast that cyclones are now going to be moving further south and into NSW with greater frequency and intensity. The network in Queensland is designed to withstand cyclones, but not all parts of the NSW network were designed for strong cyclonic events. Based on the results of this study, Optus plans to upgrade its northern NSW network to the same standards as Queensland. Adaptation, in this case, is considered to be the most cost-effective approach. These findings are supported by the Australian Business Roundtable for Disaster Resilience and Safer Communities (hereafter referred to as ABR), of which Optus is a founding member.

While climate projections have supported Optus' approach to building a resilient network, natural disasters have also emphasized the importance of a network that can withstand inclement weather. In 2011, Cyclone Yasi, an incredibly destructive tropical cyclone, struck the northern Queensland coast. During this storm, and in the aftermath, Optus realised the importance of their network to emergency services in coordinating assistance and so that family and friends could contact one another. Optus found that, even when the electricity grid fails, it is important for their network to remain operational. During the storm, emergency personnel took six days to reach the most heavily affected areas. Therefore, their network needed to operate on generators for six days. Previously, most Optus power generators could only last up to three days without electricity from the grid. Optus is now progressively upgrading some parts of its network to extend the self-sufficiency of power generators during outages.

To better prepare for such extreme weather, Optus founded the ABR along with other top private sector companies and the Red Cross. The guiding principle of the ABR is that, today, money is better spent improving the resilience of communities to help them deal with the extreme weather events of tomorrow and that such development will mitigate the costs of an extreme weather event. They provide research and recommendations to the government for developing long-term policies to inform future infrastructure standards. A recent report by the ABR finds that investing in the short term and designing and building infrastructure for the long term leads to net positive gains (Deloitte 2013). These findings underpin the construction of a resilient network.

4.5   Joining the Dots

While the above four initiatives appear to have little in common, they do share common themes (see Fig. 4.3). Each initiative is a product of Optus' vision for sustainability and, in turn, all initiatives embody many core components of systems thinking. These components—collaboration, innovation, and holistic thinking—are critical to the success of these sustainability initiatives and, thus, critical to Optus' long-term success.

4.6   The Role of Core Initiative Components on Systems Thinking

4.6.1   Collaboration

Optus believes that sustainability issues must be addressed from a collaborative standpoint. In the past, companies have sought brand equity through uniqueness and differentiation. However, if common goals are set (e.g., the UN SDGs), meaningful progress is possible through collaboration. For example, the DTP was devised with experts from fields ranging from mental health and educators to data privacy

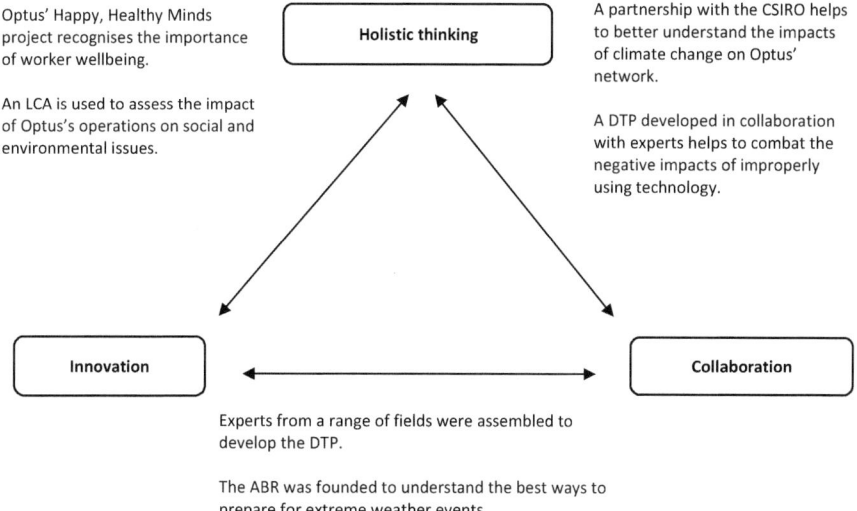

Optus' Happy, Healthy Minds project recognises the importance of worker wellbeing.

An LCA is used to assess the impact of Optus's operations on social and environmental issues.

Holistic thinking

A partnership with the CSIRO helps to better understand the impacts of climate change on Optus' network.

A DTP developed in collaboration with experts helps to combat the negative impacts of improperly using technology.

Innovation

Collaboration

Experts from a range of fields were assembled to develop the DTP.

The ABR was founded to understand the best ways to prepare for extreme weather events.

Fig. 4.3 A schematic of the interactions between the three fundamental components of Optus' sustainability strategy

and internet security. The program has reached thousands of students and has been accredited and endorsed by the e-safety Commission of the Australian government, adding legitimacy to the program and its content. In another example, the ABR examined ways of creating communities that are more resilient to natural disasters. This is another example of where Optus has worked with other large corporates and non-government organisations to achieve a common goal. A report commissioned by the ABR (see Deloitte 2013) showed that if $250 million was invested annually in pre-disaster resilience, it would lead to savings of $12.2 billion by 2050.

Collaboration as a means for success is also found in another of Optus' initiatives—the Healthy Body at Work/Happy, Healthy Minds program. This physical exercise program was developed with fitness experts, while the various mental health initiatives were devised with aid from mental health professionals. The program won the 2016 Mental Health Matters Award for best Mental Health Promoting Workplace NSW, demonstrating the importance of collaboration in designing sustainability initiatives.

4.6.2 Innovation

Innovation is necessary to realise opportunities. The Happy, Healthy Mind program recognises the importance of addressing both the physical and mental well-being of workers. It demonstrates innovative benefits of applying a common approach to a new need. Instead of addressing only physical well-being, Optus recognised there was a need to also address mental health.

The work the ABR has conducted to prepare for extreme weather events further demonstrates innovation. The ABR's innovative approach acknowledges the significant cost facing governments after an extreme weather event. In recognising this issue, the ABR set about finding a potential solution—that investment in infrastructure which can survive extreme weather events can prove to be a cost-effective solution. A similar translation of an idea put into practice can be seen with the DTP program. Here, Optus identified that if technology continued to be improperly used, it might have negative consequences for their brand. Thus, Optus implemented an educational program to improve the online conduct of young users.

Another example is the (now superseded) Optus' $2 SIM. The $2 SIM offered people who could not afford a pre- or post-paid plan unlimited calls and SMS messages but only on the day of purchase. The initiative was particularly popular with homeless people, but the downside was that people were once again uncontactable after the SIM expired—an especially problematic situation for those seeking help from social services and charities. Thus, Optus modified the SIM so that certain charity organisations and social services could be contacted for free regardless of expiry. This example is a good illustration of innovation in practice. That is, using a common product, a SIM card, and slightly modifying it to provide communications access to an entirely new group of people. Optus has since stopped the $2/day SIM and replaced it with even better innovation in practice. It now runs a program called Donate Your Data (Gifted), which enables customers to donate their unused data, matched by Optus, to customers from low-income families and students who cannot afford mobile services. This is a way to engage Optus's customers into helping the vulnerable in the community. The project was piloted with the Smith Family.

4.6.3   Holistic Approach

Optus has employed a holistic approach to understanding how one issue may affect another part of the business. This approach is used in all four of the initiatives highlighted above and is crucial to Optus' success and their definition of sustainability. The first initiative, which addresses the sustainability of their supply chain, is a good example of a holistic approach in practice. Optus recognises that poor working conditions in their supply chain can impact the service workers provide to their customers. Further, the competitive nature of the industry also means that any declines in worker satisfaction may lead to those employees seeking work elsewhere. These two factors led Optus to address workers' rights. This example is also good because the workers in question are not direct employees of Optus but rather are employed by a firm that Optus outsources to. Optus recognises that they are indirect employees of the company and should be treated as such.

The other three highlighted initiatives also employ a holistic approach. The DTP recognises that, as a service provider, Optus has a responsibility to teach young people how to use the internet and technology properly. Failure to do so may have negative implications for technological autonomy, and this can undermine public trust in services providers. The Happy Body/Happy, Healthy Minds program acknowledges the links between worker productivity, satisfaction, and well-being. Through Futureproofing Our Infrastructure, Optus acknowledges the gains from investing in infrastructure today to withstand the climate of tomorrow.

All these programs employ collaboration, innovation, and a holistic approach—three elements that are critical to their success. It is these components that directly link each program together and to sustainability (see Fig. 4.3).

4.7 Key Challenges

Sustainability is a disputed concept to define, let alone to measure. However, tracking the performance of sustainability initiatives is critical to understanding their contribution to the long-term success of a business and to demonstrate short-term gains. There are several reporting frameworks companies can use to track and communicate the progress of their sustainability initiatives and compare their progress with others (see Breakout box 2). One such framework is the GRI employed in Optus' Sustainability Report. Another is the CDP which Singtel uses to reports its carbon emissions, energy usage, and climate change strategy. Optus also gets its data and performance assured by an external auditor.

4.7.1 Difficulty in Measuring Performance

Measuring the performance of sustainability initiatives is important for establishing links to long-term growth and for setting and meeting goals. Optus has set goals for some of their sustainability initiatives which reflect how they envisage them progressing (see Tables 4.2, 4.3, 4.4, 4.5 for a comprehensive summary of the goals of Optus' sustainability initiatives). For example, Optus aims to reach an additional 37,000 students with its DTP program in 2017. However, while some programs have easily measurable components, tracking others is more complex. For example, survey data collected after sessions of the DTP program (see Table 4.3) indicate those who took part in the program found it beneficial. However, one of the primary motivations of the DTP initiative is to create responsible technology users. The challenge then becomes: How does Optus show it is creating responsible technology users to validate its DTP initiative?

4.7.2   Balancing Short-Term Gains with Long-Term Goals

Sustainability is regarded as essential for Optus' long-term success. However, quantifying initiative performance is also important to prove the existence of short-term benefits stemming from these initiatives. For a successful business, a mixture of both short-term and long-term goals is necessary to show shareholders that a business is thinking about the future without disregarding the present. That is, if only short-term results are considered, sacrifices must be made in the long-term. Conversely, if decisions are made only for the long-term, a business can struggle to demonstrate short-term progress. Programs such as the DTP are inherently long-term programs, but survey results show it is having immediate impacts, too. So, initiatives must balance short and long-term goals. However, this distinction is not so clear for initiatives such as an LCA, where the benefits are only realised long after the LCA had been conducted.

Breakout: 'What Gets Measured Gets Managed': GRI, CDP, and UN SDGs

The Global Reporting Initiative (GRI) is a reporting framework that companies use to communicate the economic, social, and environmental impacts of their operations. This kind of reporting, also referred to as sustainability reporting, recognises that a sustainable business is a business that is both profitable and one that is environmentally and socially responsible (GRI 2016).

The GRI takes a fundamentally quantitative approach to sustainability reporting. When preparing a GRI report, companies can choose to follow the 'core' or 'comprehensive' guidelines. Obviously, following the comprehensive guidelines is more onerous in terms of report content. The reporting framework is then split into two components: standard disclosures, which include elements such as governance, strategy and analysis, organisational profile; and specific disclosures, which include information on economic, environmental, and social performance. The level of information a company must disclose is dictated by which report option they choose. The quantitative approach is designed to let companies set goals and benchmark their performance toward achieving them.

The CDP, formerly known as the Carbon Disclosure Project, takes a different approach. It surveys companies, states, and cities about their environmental conduct. It then collates this data to track progress on environmental issues – carbon dioxide emissions, for example.

The distinct benefit of using a standard reporting framework is that it makes information more comparable. In quantify information, companies translate absolute numbers into relative figures (e.g., total greenhouse gas emissions). This allows companies to track both how they are progressing toward their own goals and how they compare to other companies globally. According to the GRI (2016), 74% of the world's largest companies prepare sustainability reports using GRI guidelines. Further, following a predetermined methodology adds consistency to measurements, which means data are readily comparable.

Additionally, the use of reporting frameworks creates inadvertent collaborations. The content of these frameworks is considered to be important in the sustainability sphere. Therefore, companies shaping their initiatives to the framework's requirements generates a concentrated approach toward addressing global issues, and a collective effort is more likely to drive change than individual companies pursuing the issues they deem to be important. The United Nations Sustainable Development Goals (SDGs) is another example of setting common goals for a greater net outcome. These goals cover 17 specific sustainability issues deemed to be universally important and serve to foster widespread cooperation in solving these issues. Like the GRI, the fundamental benefit of the SDGs is that they create a common language.

In its sustainability initiatives, Optus is addressing the SDGs, in part, because it adds legitimacy to Optus' initiatives and, in part, to ensure those initiatives target issues of global concern. In the past, Optus has used the SDGs to determine whether the issues they are addressing are material issues. The next step for Optus is to work more closely with specific SDG outcomes and tailor initiatives to make specific contributions toward achieving them.

4.8 Conclusion

This case study demonstrates how Optus has embedded sustainability into its business. This has only been possible due to Optus' broad definition of sustainability. As a result, the way it engages with sustainability is dynamic and covers a broad spectrum of activities. To illustrate this, four sustainability initiatives are described in detail. These initiatives are very different in subject matter, but each shares three common themes: collaboration, innovation, and a holistic approach. Ultimately, Optus has adopted this approach for long-term success. As Andrew Buay explains: "Sustainability is ... not only about how we grow and sustain long-term growth in our business but also about doing it in a way that positively shapes and impacts our many stakeholders."

A dedicated sustainability group is responsible for managing sustainability throughout the Singtel Group, headed by a Vice President who reports to the Group Chief Human Resources Officer. The group works in collaboration with group strategy, group risk management, procurement, and other business units to oversee and report on the development and execution of the Group's sustainability strategy. The Singtel Management Committee, comprising the eight most senior executives of the Singtel Group and chaired by the Group CEO and including the Optus CEO, provides strategic direction to the sustainability group and approves the Group's sustainability strategy.

Sustainability is on the Board's agenda, and the Group's sustainability strategy is presented to the Board annually. The Group CEO provides the Board with regular updates on Optus' various sustainability programs, upcoming activities, and the global and local trends that may impact their sustainability strategy. At the execution level, Singtel and Optus have formulated working groups for Singapore, Australia, and regional associates comprising representatives from business and support units. These working groups are actively involved in developing and implementing sustainability strategies and programs in their respective countries. Various working groups are brought together to drive and collaborate on sustainability programs in key markets, as well as sharing best practices across the Singtel Group of companies.

4.9   Teaching Notes

4.9.1   Synopsis of the Case

Optus is an Australian telecommunications company in a highly competitive industry. While expanding its network is a key driver of market growth, Optus has embedded sustainability across its business as a market differentiator. In Optus, sustainability informs decision-making, the culture of its business, its operations, and its products and services. Optus believes that making sustainability a part of its DNA will establish the foundations for long-term success. This case study outlines four sustainability initiatives Optus is pursuing and how these initiatives are integrated into its daily business. Yet some key challenges face Optus on the way ahead and, as this case study shows, long-term sustainability requires a collaborative, innovative, and holistic approach.

This case study demonstrates how an organisation like Optus embeds the value of sustainability throughout all aspects of its business. It particularly highlights how Optus is 'joining the dots' of various initiatives through holistic thinking, collaboration, and innovation.

This case study was developed based on primary and secondary research about Optus' sustainability initiatives up till June 2016.

4.9.2   Target Learning Group

This case study is ideal for executive education, undergraduate capstone units, or postgraduate classes with a particular emphasis on integrative thinking.

4.9.3   Learning Objectives

- Demonstrate the role of sustainability in creating a competitive edge for business and driving long-term success.
- Emphasise the importance of adopting systems thinking as fundamental to embedding sustainability throughout a business.
- Appreciate the challenges of integrating sustainability in all aspects of business.

4.9.4   Teaching Strategy

This is a comprehensive case. It is ideal for undergraduate capstone units or PG classes with a particular emphasis on integrative thinking. Alternatively, the instructor could adopt a modular approach allocating 60 min for each session.

4.9.5   Reading Activities

4.9.5.1   Pre-reading

Sustainability's links to business and employment and the video and questions handout listed in the Multimedia section can be provided as a pre-reading and discussion activity or used in-class as a guided listening activity.

4.9.5.2   Skim reading

- From the chapter abstract, how does sustainability inform Optus business practices?
- Numerous acronyms are used throughout the chapter. What do these acronyms mean? Skim the chapter to find out. Alternatively, students could work in pairs, with each student responsible for half the acronym list. Partners share the acronyms on their list. The instructor checks any acronyms that are challenging or ambiguous with the group.

4.9.5.3   In-depth reading

- How is the expression 'joining the dots' explained?
- The authors use the expression, 'oligopolistic market':

  - What does this mean in relation to the telecommunications industry?
  - How might this market structure be relevant to sustainability?

- What does the abstract suggest are the main reasons for Optus' focus on sustainability?
- What are the 'four sustainability' pillars that support a culture of sustainability at Optus?
- What key challenges has Optus faced integrating sustainability as an organisational framework?
- Examine the explanation of Optus' LCA approach in Breakout Box 1: Life cycle assessment. How do the authors define "systems thinking" in relation to Optus' sustainability agenda?

4.9.6   Discussion Activities

- Comment on the definition of sustainability Optus has provided. What is the meaning and scope of sustainability in the eyes of Andrew Buay?
- Optus has chosen four 'pillars' to implement their sustainability mission. Comment on why (or why not) these four are the most appropriate ones for the business?
- Why is it important for organisations like Optus to appear sustainable? How would you test whether their claims are substantiated and that the initiatives are actually leading to a substantial impact?
- Suppose you have just started as a new human resources manager at Optus. Write a plan to implement the Healthy Body at Work/Happy, Healthy Minds program. How would you know if your program was successful?
- Why has Optus undertaken the Digital Thumbprint Program?
- What role do collaboration, innovation, and systems thinking play in the company's initiatives?

4.9.6.1   Discussion Notes

Discussions may lead to how the meaning and scope of 'sustainability' has evolved from externally mandated CSR, where corporations have a regulatory responsibility for the economic, social, and environmental consequences of their activities into becoming integral to a company's DNA—its values and business model. An alert student may take the initiative of checking the LinkedIn profile of the group head of sustainability at Singtel Optus and note that he has a business strategy background.

How Optus leverages its four pillars to implement its sustainability agenda may lead to a discussion on how a sustainability strategy needs to be uniquely tailored for each company to ensure appropriateness or 'fit for purpose' initiatives. Discussions might reinforce the evolution of sustainability from a function centred on communications and marketing to its integration into core business models and associated elements, such as revenue, profits, how we make money, how we operate, etc. Discussions could involve the measurability and specificity of targets.

4.9.6.2   In-depth Discussions

- Discuss whether and how collaboration, innovation, and a holistic approach are reflected in the initiatives described in this case study. Print "The role of core initiative components on systems thinking" and the Conclusion separately from the case study. Discuss these two sections, then provide the authors' analysis of the topic.
- Debate the topic: "Corporate Social Responsibility (CSR) or sustainability activities are undertaken with revenue-generation as the main objective".

- This is a devil's advocate/ polemical discussion topic that is counter to contemporary systems-oriented thinking on sustainability measures, such as CSR and the Triple Bottom Line. This activity could be conducted as a debate, with half the class taking a pro-sustainability stance and the other half taking a pro-revenue stance.
- Participants should work in groups to draw up a list of 3–5 points in favour of their position.
- Groups should then re-form into smaller groups or pairs to debate their position.
- Ask the groups to summarise the key points for both the pro-sustainability and pro-revenue positions.
- What is the general position of the class? Why?

4.9.7 Suggested Assignment

Research the sustainability strategy and initiatives of one of Optus' market competitors. What are the key similarities or differences in their approaches to sustainability? Example organisations:

- Telstra: https://exchange.telstra.com.au/sustainability/
- Vodafone: https://www.vodafone.com.au/about/sustainability
- iiNet: https://www.iinet.net.au/about/
- nbn.co: https://www.nbnco.com.au/corporate-information/about-nbn-co/corporate-responsibility.html
- Macquarie Telecom Group: https://macquarietelecomgroup.com/ or see reports under https://macquarietelecomgroup.com/investors.

4.9.7.1 Assignment Questions

- How do other Australian telecommunication provider sustainability strategies and/or initiatives differ from Optus?
- Are there common themes?
- How does your chosen provider rate in CSR? (for example, see: https://www.csrhub.com/csrhub (Note: this is a paywall site, but some information is freely available).
- The Optus NPS (Net Promoter Score) is among the top three telecommunication companies in Australia. The NPS is an indicator of overall customer satisfaction with a company's products and services. For example, "How likely are you to recommend our company to a friend or colleague?" An important component of the NPS is frontline customer service, and Optus' strong NPS score is partly attributed to its focus on staff engagement and motivation. What is the NPS for your chosen provider? Are any indicators provided for this score?

4.9.7.2 Data Analysis

- The authors state, "… Australia's telecommunications industry is both intensely competitive and projected to grow significantly". Find statistics to support this statement.
- The authors present several statistics relevant to Optus' sustainability focus. Skim the chapter to find the relevant statistics. What is their significance?

4.10 Multimedia Activities

Sustainability's links to business and employment: https://www.youtube.com/watch?v=I2zlzGCBYwU.

Guided listening to consolidate the chapter reading. Alternatively, use as a pre-reading and discussion activity.

- Set the context for listening: Andrew Buay, Optus Vice President, Group CSR and Talent Coach, discusses the necessity for sustainability skills and knowledge at Optus.
- Provide the video questions as a separate handout.
- Participants should review the questions and predict the answers based on the chapter reading.
- Play the video, stopping at video section placeholders to discuss the questions for the section.

Video Questions:

Section 1:

- Why is sustainability important to Optus?
- How does Andrew Buay summarise Optus' approach to sustainability?
- He talks about 'shared-value thinking'. What does he mean by this?
- How does Optus' "core value of integrity" impact on the business?
- How does Buay express his belief that sustainability creates value for the business?

Section 2:

- Why is a sustainability skillset and mindset important for business?
- Why is it important to embed a sustainability mindset through leadership? What example does Buay give?

Section 3:

- Does an understanding of sustainability help students stand out in terms of employability?
- Does sustainability awareness help gain employment?

Section 4:

- How has having employees with an understanding of sustainability positively impacted Optus as a business and competitor?
- How does employee understanding of sustainability impact Optus? What two points does the speaker make?

Section 5:

- Is sustainability literacy something your clients and customers are seeking from Optus employees?

References

ACCC (2016) Competition in the Australian telecommunications sector: Report to the Minister of Communications. Australian Competition and Consumer Commission, Canberra, ACT. Retrieved from https://www.accc.gov.au/system/files/ACCC%20Telecommunications%20reports%202014%E2%80%9315_Div%2011%20and%2012_web_FA.pdf

Deloitte (2013) Building Australia's resilience to natural disasters. Deloitte Access Economics. Retrieved from https://www2.deloitte.com/au/en/pages/economics/articles/building-australias-natural-disaster-resilience.html

Eccles RG, Ioannou I, Serafeim G (2014) The impact of corporate sustainability on organizational processes and performance. Manage Sci 60:2835–2857

GRI (2016) GRI Standards Download Centre. Global Reporting Initiative. Retrieved from https://www.globalreporting.org/standards/gri-standards-download-center/

ISO (2006) Environmental management—Life cycle assessment—principles and framework, ISO 14040:2006. International Organization for Standardization. Retrieved from https://www.iso.org/obp/ui/#iso:std:iso:14040:ed-2:v1:en

Klöpffer W (2014) Introducing life cycle assessment and its presentation in 'LCA Compendium'. In: Klöpffer W (ed) Background and future prospects in life cycle assessment. Springer, Dordrecht, Netherlands. https://doi.org/10.1007/978-94-017-8697-3_1

UNEP (2009) Guidelines for social life cycle assessment of products. United Nations Environment Programme. Retrieved from http://www.unep.fr/shared/publications/pdf/dtix1164xpa-guidelines_slca.pdf

Mr. Zak Baillie has University degrees in economics and science (environment, climate) and is interested in the interface of the two. He has worked in academia and public policy in Australia. He is currently completing a research degree looking at how hot it might get in Sydney in 2030–40 and whether our energy system is appropriately preparing for that kind of heat.

Dr. Lay Peng Tan is an experienced and stimulating researcher with awards for outstanding teaching. Her research interests lie within the broad areas of consumer behaviour, digital marketing, retailing, and green marketing with a focus on the attitude-behaviour gap, and the roles of marketing in the face of the green challenge. Her publications have appeared in the Journal of Business Ethics, Marketing Intelligence & Planning, Journal of Marketing Management, Australasian Marketing Journal, The International Review of Retail, Distribution and Consumer Research, and Asia Pacific Journal of Marketing and Logistics.

Associate Professor Yvonne A. Breyer is an award-winning academic with expertise in student success, online learning and digital transformation in the higher education sector. Yvonne has led several highly successful strategic initiatives with national and international reach. Most recently, she led the 'Excel Skills for Business' specialisation, which received the Coursera Outstanding Educator Award for Student Transformation on the back of exceptional learner feedback, global reach and impact. She holds a Ph.D. (Macquarie University), a Master of Arts (University of Essen, Germany) and a Postgraduate Certificate in Higher Education, Leadership and Management (Macquarie University).

Mr. Andrew Buay is the Vice President, Group Sustainability at Singtel, Talent Coach at Optus. An unassuming, but highly agile, versatile and experienced senior telecom and ICT executive with over 26 years of experience with Asia's leading telecom company. Andrew's career has spanned all aspects of the telco business from Corporate Sustainability, Talent Development, IT, networks investments, product development, marketing, account management, corporate strategy, business development, technology investments and development, and end to end operations. His business and cultural adaptability spans across several countries in Asia including Singapore, Philippines and Australia, having also done business and partnership development in US, Israel and Asia.

Chapter 5
Climate Change and Extreme Events: Risk Assessment of Adaptation in Sydney

Stefan Trück, Chi Truong, Tim Keighley, Feng Liu and Supriya Mathew

Abstract Measuring the potential costs of catastrophic climatic events is a challenging but important exercise, as the occurrence of such events is usually associated with substantial damage and high uncertainty. Risk assessments and measures to evaluate adaptation should focus on an appropriate time horizon that is consistent with the frequency of events, since a short-term view may disproportionally deflate the risk involved. This chapter illustrates key concepts that need to be considered when quantitatively evaluating adaptation to extreme climate events. Important issues include: measuring uncertainty using a probability distribution; the time value of money; the choice of discount rate values; the costs and benefits of adaptation; and sustainable decision making.

Keywords Climate change · Extreme events · Probability distributions · Adaptation · Time value of money · Discount rates · Cost-benefit analysis · Sustainable decision making

S. Trück (✉) · C. Truong · T. Keighley · F. Liu
Macquarie University, Sydney, Australia
e-mail: stefan.trueck@mq.edu.au

S. Mathew
Menzies School of Health Research, Alice Springs, Australia

L. Wood et al. (eds.), *Industry and Higher Education*,
https://doi.org/10.1007/978-981-15-0874-5_5

5.1   The Case at a Glance

| Key concepts | <ul><li>Climate change</li><li>Extreme events</li><li>Uncertainty</li><li>Discount rates</li><li>Cost-benefit analysis</li></ul> |

Key concepts
- Climate change
- Extreme events
- Uncertainty
- Discount rates
- Cost-benefit analysis

Level of study
- BA and MA students

Subject areas
- Management, economics, finance, statistics

Graduate capabilities

Graduate outcomes	%
Critical thinking	15
Problem solving	15
Teamwork	5
Communication	5
Ethical thinking	30
Sustainability	30
Total	**100%**

Time required
- Out-of-class preparation: 45   min
- In-class discussion: 30   min
- Out-of-class assignments: 120   min

Activity type

Individual
- Pre-reading
- Assignment questions
- Additional practice question
- Supplementary multimedia activities—YouTube videos
- Supplementary further reading

Team-based
- Group discussion questions

Additional materials

Online Resources:

- **Adapting to a changing climate**
  https://www.youtube.com/watch?v=lGMx2xP3dcM
  A new video documentary by the UNFCCC Adaptation Committee aims to raise awareness of climate change adaptation. The 20-min documentary "Adapting to

changing climate" introduces viewers to the topic of climate change adaptation, weaving in inspiring stories of adaptation action and interviews with experts.

- **A Climate Adaptation decision support Tool for Local Governments: CAT-LoG**
  https://www.nccarf.edu.au/publications/climate-adaptation-decision-support-tool-local-governments
  A decision support tool for investment into climate adaptation developed during a research project for the National Climate Change Adaptation Research Facility. The tool uses a combination of quantitative (cost-benefit analysis) and qualitative (multi-criteria analysis) methods. It allows users to conduct sensitivity tests, examine the impact of uncertain parameters ranging from climate impacts to discount rates. The final product is a user-friendly decision tool in the form of an Excel add-in together with a user manual booklet that demonstrates sample worked out projects. The tool is made flexible so that stakeholders can adopt or refine or upgrade it for their context-specific applications.
- **Climate change adaption: It's time for decisions now**
  https://www.youtube.com/watch?v=FO46sPwm4xk
  Animation film by the International Climate Initiative (ICI) of the Federal Ministry for the Environment, Nature Conservation and Nuclear Safety (BMU), produced by the Deutsche Gesellschaft für Internationale Zusammenarbeit (GIZ) GmbH in cooperation with the Potsdam Institute for Climate Impact Research (PIK).
- **Climate change is happening. Here's how we adapt**
  https://www.youtube.com/watch?v=fw01_q0cxM8
  TED Talk: Imagine the hottest day you've ever experienced. Now imagine it's 6°, 10°, or 12° hotter. According to climate researcher Alice Bows-Larkin, that's the type of future in store for us if we don't significantly cut our greenhouse gas emissions now. She suggests that it's time we do things differently—a whole system change, in fact—and seriously consider trading economic growth for climate stability.
- **The Intergovernmental Panel on Climate Change (IPCC)**
  https://www.ipcc.ch/
  IPCC is the United Nations body for assessing the science related to climate change. It publishes assessment reports on climate change, its causes, potential impacts, and response options. It also oversees the Data Distribution Centre, which provides data sets, scenarios of climate change, and other environmental and socio-economic conditions, as well as other materials.

Journal Papers:

- **Keighley, T., Longden, T., Mathew, S., & Trück, S. (2018).** Quantifying catastrophic and climate impacted hazards based on local expert opinions. *Journal of Environmental Management*, 205, 262–273.
  The *Journal of Environmental Management* is a journal for the publication of peer-reviewed, original research for all aspects of management and the managed use of the environment, both natural and man-made. As governments and the

general public become more keenly aware of the critical issues arising from how humans use their environment, this journal provides a forum for the discussion of environmental problems around the world and for the presentation of management results. It is aimed not only at the environmental manager, but at anyone concerned with the sustainable use of environmental resources.

Additional Journal Articles and Publications:

- **Mathew, S., Trück, S., & Henderson-Sellers, A. (2012)**. Kochi, India case study of climate adaptation to floods: ranking local government investment options. *Global Environmental Change*, 22(1), 308–319.
- **Aerts, J.C. & Botzen, W.W. (2011)**. Flood-resilient waterfront development in New York City: Bridging flood insurance, building codes, and flood zoning. *Annals of the New York Academy of Sciences*, 1227(1), 1–82.
- **Intergovernmental Panel on Climate Change (2012)**. *Managing the risks of extreme events and disasters to advance climate change adaptation: Special report of the intergovernmental panel on climate change*. Cambridge University Press. Chaps. 5 and 8.

5.2   Introduction and Background

The Intergovernmental Panel on Climate Change (IPCC) states that "existing environmental stresses will interact with, and [can] in many cases be exacerbated by, shifts in mean climatic conditions and associated change in the frequency or intensity of extreme events, especially fire, drought and floods" (IPCC 2014, p. 16). In other words, climate change is likely to impact how often extreme events occur and the severity of their damage. Alleviating the increased risk exposure caused by these events at the national and local level requires preparatory measures designed to mitigate the ill-effects of these events—or at least to help people adapt to them. Risk assessments, sustainable decision-making, and evaluating adaptation measures are complex problems. This chapter illustrates key concepts that need to be considered when quantitatively evaluating adaptation to extreme climate hazards. Important issues include measuring uncertainty with a probability distribution, the time value of money, the choice of a discount rate, the costs and benefits of adaptation, and sustainable decision making.

5.2.1   Adaptation and Mitigation

Climate change is expected to increase both the frequency and severity of natural disasters across the world, such as tropical storms, droughts, bushfires, and flooding. Irrespective of the level of mitigation one tries to achieve, the typical atmospheric lifetime of greenhouse gases means that any mitigation effort will take a long time to have an impact. Therefore, in the interim we must also formulate plans for adapting to the damage arising from climate change. The effects of climate change on extreme events will vary across locations, signifying the importance of local decision-making. Yet analysing extreme events in isolation is challenging because: (i) these events rarely occur; (ii) even fewer observations are likely to be available at a local level; and (iii) past observations may not have been recorded properly or completely (see, e.g., Mathew et al. 2012). Despite these challenges, the extent of the damage associated with extreme events makes adaptation responses crucial for vulnerable locations. For instance, in 2015, there were 346 reported disasters with more than 22,000 lives lost. Further, almost 100 million people were affected in some way, and extreme events are estimated to have caused US$66.5 billion in economic damages (UNISDR 2016).

5.2.2 Losses from Extreme Weather Events

Various regions in Australia may be prone to increased flooding, storm, and bushfire activities in the future, as suggested by several studies (see, e.g., Garnaut 2011; Hasson et al. 2009; Murphy and Timbal 2008). Australia is unusual in the sense that each of these disasters can cause a probable maximum loss event that may result in significant damage to the community.

The total insured economic losses from disaster events based on data provided by the Insurance Council of Australia (ICA) indicate that losses from extreme events have risen over time. Figure 5.1 plots the cumulative annual insured losses arising from bushfires, cyclones, flooding, hail storms, storm flooding, and tornados. While the graph suggests an increasing trend, it is important to note that cumulative annual losses are often driven by a single or small number of extreme events. For example, in 2011, over 60% of insured losses were attributable to the Brisbane floods and

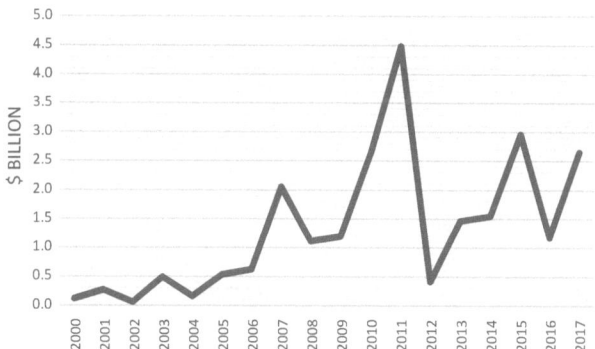

Fig. 5.1 Annual total insured economic losses in Australia (2000–2017) from bushfires, cyclones, flooding, hail storms, storm flooding, and tornados. *Source* Historical Catastrophe Database of the Insurance Council of Australia (ICA)

Cyclone Yasi while, in 2017, Cyclone Debbie was responsible for approximately 65% of the losses. The average annual loss over the 2000–2017 period was $1.33 billion and, over the last five years, this figure has increased to $1.96 billion. Bushfires are also a relatively common and regular phenomenon, with the annual probability of a non-zero property loss for Australia during the 20th century falling somewhere between 48 and 57% (McAneney et al. 2009).

5.3 Modelling Impacts from Extreme Events

In the following, we outline an approach for quantifying potential losses from catastrophic events, like storms, droughts, or bushfires, that may further increase due to climate change. Unfortunately, there are several problems when it comes to finding an appropriate quantitative model for this task. First, the number of observations is rather limited, particularly at the local scale, where adaptation investments need to be applied. Hence, only a small number of observations are usually available to calibrate a probability distribution and the loss model. This means that parameter estimates of the distributions might be quite sensitive to the addition of new events. Further, in using historical observations, databases may contain reporting bias. For example, extreme events may be well recorded, but smaller fires or storms may have been neglected. In addition, considering that some of the records on bushfires or storms go back almost 100 years, it might be necessary to consider how our society has changed in the intervening years when assessing the potential for damage, i.e., increases in the population density, the amount of at-risk property, infrastructure, and so on.

5.3.1 The Loss Distribution Approach

The loss distribution approach (LDA) is a statistical technique for generating an aggregate loss distribution based on separate distributions for the frequency and severity of an event. It is particularly popular in the finance and insurance industry (see, e.g., Bank for International Settlement 2001; Klugman et al. 2012; Shevchenko and Wüthrich 2006) and is often used to model risk from storm surges (West et al. 2001), bushfires (Truong and Trück 2016; Truong et al. 2018), and other natural disasters.

One of the underlying assumptions of LDA is that the frequency distribution and the severity distribution of an extreme climate event are independent and can be modelled separately. Hence, to calculate the probability distribution of the aggregate loss over a time horizon (e.g., one year), all that is required is to estimate the probability distribution function for the magnitude of a single event loss as well as the frequency distribution, in other words, the distribution of the number of events in one year.

5.4   Modelling the Frequency of Events

The frequency of an event is usually modelled as a discrete distribution, such as a Bernoulli, binomial, Poisson, or geometric distribution. Discrete distributions apply to a random variable where the set of possible values is finite or countable. Hence, the frequency of an event can be modelled with a discrete distribution as a countable discrete random variable.

One of the most popular approaches to modelling frequency is through a Poisson distribution because it is particularly good at representing the chances that a relatively rare event will occur within a given period of time (see, e.g., Keighley et al. 2018; Klugman et al. 2012; Mathew et al. 2012; Trück et al. 2010). To illustrate how a Poisson distribution describes these probabilities, assume we are interested in the annual frequency of catastrophic events. The probability mass function of the Poisson distribution is given by

$$P(N = k) = \frac{\lambda^k}{k!}e^{-\lambda}$$

where k denotes the number of events. λ is the sole parameter of the Poisson distribution, which represents the average number of events over a specified time horizon—for example, one year. Now assume that the expected number of events per year is given by $E[N] = \lambda$.

Figure 5.2 provides a plot of the probability mass function of the Poisson distribution with the values for λ at 0.2 (*left*) and 4 (*right*). When $\lambda = 0.2$, which corresponds to an average of 0.2 events per year, the distribution is skewed to the right. Here, zero

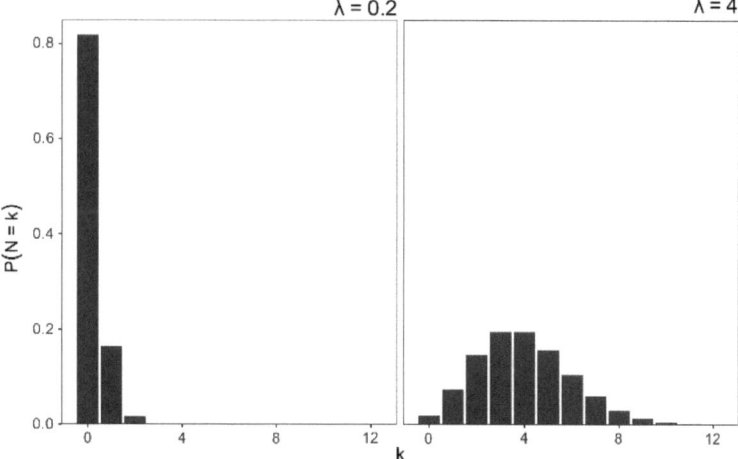

Fig. 5.2   Probability mass function for a Poisson distribution with parameter $\lambda = 0.2$ (left panel) and $\lambda = 4$ (right panel)

has the highest probability, i.e., no event is likely to occur during this period with a probability of P(N = 0) = 0.8187 (i.e., 82%), while the probability of one event occurring is approximately 16%. The remaining 2% is the probability that more than one event will occur. However, when λ is adjusted to 4, i.e., an average of 4 events per year, the distribution is more symmetric. The highest probabilities are now given to three or four events: P(N = 3) = P(N = 4) = 0.1954 (i.e., 20%).

5.5   Modelling the Severity of Events

Extreme events are rare. Accordingly, it can be difficult to acquire sufficient historical data to fit a distribution. However, as decision-makers are faced with the possibility of extreme losses, calculating a distribution that estimates the magnitude of future events is important. Usually, a continuous distribution is used to model the severity of disasters associated with climate or weather. The literature on catastrophic losses typically suggests using right-skewed and/or heavy-tailed distributions, such as the Weibull, lognormal, Burr, or Pareto distribution because these distributions have been designed to quantify rare but extreme outcomes. A lognormal distribution is probably the most common approach.

Figure 5.3 presents a probability density function for a lognormal distribution with the parameter settings μ = 3.40 and σ = 1.15. The black area between 0 and 30 to the left of the specified median illustrates that there is a 50% probability for the loss to be less than or equal to 30. Whereas, the black area to the right of 200 is

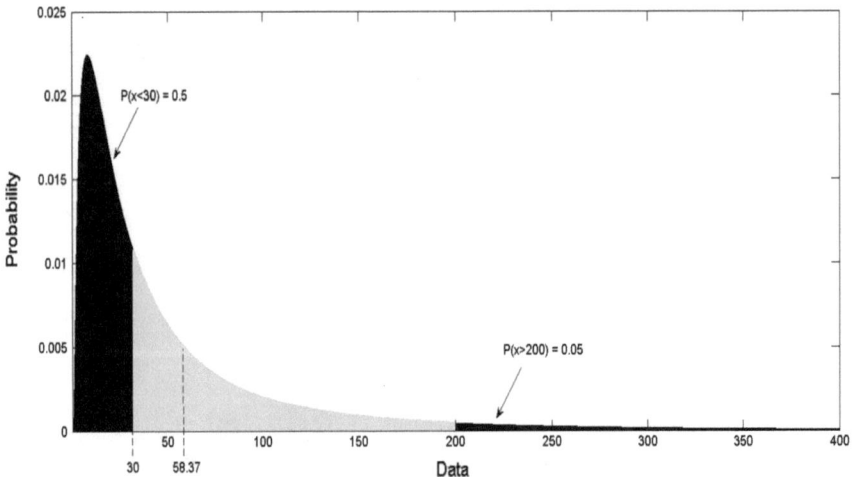

Fig. 5.3 A probability density function for a lognormal distribution. $\mu = 3.40$ and $\sigma = 1.15$. The specified distribution has a mean of $E(X) = 58.37$ and a median of 30

equal to 0.05, indicating only a 5% probability of losses greater than 200. This figure illustrates that for a heavy-tailed distribution such as the lognormal distribution, the median (med = 30) can be significantly smaller than the mean, E(X) = 58.37.

5.5.1 Cumulative Losses Over Time

As mentioned earlier, a key assumption of LDA is that the frequency and severity distributions for the losses are assumed to be independent. For example, consider a cumulative loss over one year, expressed as

$$G = \sum_{i=1}^{N} X_i$$

where N is the number of events that occur in that year. N is modelled as a random variable from a discrete distribution, while $X_i, i = 1, \ldots, N$ are the severities of each event modelled as independent random variables from a continuous distribution. Usually, a Monte Carlo simulation is used to compound the severity and frequency distributions and calculate the aggregate losses from all the events of that type (see, e.g., Fishman 1996; Klugman et al. 2012). A simulation algorithm then generates an annual loss distribution through the following process:

1. Take a random draw from the frequency distribution: suppose this simulates N events per year.
2. Take N random draws from the severity distribution: denote these simulated losses as $X_1, X_2, \ldots, X_N$.
3. Sum the N simulated losses to obtain an annual loss $G = X_1 + X_2 + \cdots + X_N$.
4. Return to step 1, and repeat k times (usually the number of simulation runs is relatively large, e.g., $k = 10,000$, $k = 100,000$, or even higher). The process returns $G_1, G_2, \ldots, G_k$, where k is a large enough number to produce an adequate distribution for the aggregate losses.

Thus, LDA not only provides a method for computing the expected loss, but also the loss at a confidence level α. The expected loss EL and the loss at a confidence level α, $L(\alpha)$, are thus defined as

$$EL = \int_0^{\infty} x \, dG(x) \text{ and}$$

$$L(\alpha) = \inf\{x | G(x) \geq \alpha\}.$$

The expected loss is the expected value of the aggregate loss distribution function G, whereas the loss at confidence α is the quantile for the level α. With a Monte Carlo simulation, the aggregate loss distribution of the event can be generated with quantiles at, say, the 90%, 95%, or 99% confidence levels.

5.6   Discounting and the Time Value of Money

Discounting involves expressing future and present values of particular variables in a common unit so that decisions regarding possible courses of action in the present can be made rationally. There is considerable ambiguity, and indeed controversy, in the literature concerning which discount rate should be used to evaluate the losses arising from climate change, or the costs and benefits of actions taken to mitigate or adapt to its effects. The choice depends on two key issues: (i) the differences between discounting in a financial sense and discounting in an economic sense; and (ii) the magnitude of the discount rate required (in the economic sense).

5.6.1   *Financial Versus Economic Discounting*

The key difference between the two discounting 'senses' are the past and future variables being compared—financial sense means a monetary variable; economic sense means a welfare variable.

Financial discounting involves comparing *explicit monetary flows*. Hence, discounting is necessary to convert future dollars into present dollars so that a valid cost comparison can be made in terms of today's money. For example, the maximum price one should pay for an asset can only be answered by appropriately discounting future net earnings. In a financial context, the ideal discount rate is one that reflects the actual cost of capital or the cost of acquiring funds in the likelihood that an adaptation project will be funded with borrowed money. A significantly lower discount rate than the cost of the project capital will most likely lead to an underestimation of the project's actual costs. Hence, if an organisation is subject to a binding budget constraint, such as a local or state government, using an artificially low discount rate in the financial sense will usually mean expenditure has to be reallocated away from other uses to cover the shortfall.

Discounting in the economic sense involves comparisons between future and present *welfare* and so raises a different set of questions. Of course, welfare cannot be measured directly, so it is standard practice in economics to use a proxy representative of monetary value, such as 'willingness-to-pay'. A paradigmatic case relevant to climate adaptation is one of making the best choice from a number of public investment projects, each of which uses present resources to create welfare in the future. The optimal investment is the one that maximises welfare, but this requires converting the forecast welfare into a present-day equivalent, i.e., discounting.

Unlike the financial sense, there is no obvious 'common sense' discount rate to use in economics. The choice comes down to the weight given to the interests of particular agents in the present and near future, and the interests of the same or other agents once the project is complete. High discount rates favour projects with immediate benefits and/or deferred costs. The implication here is that the cost of foregoing the future welfare is low. Conversely, low discount rates carry high costs justifiable in the present on the basis that the future welfare gains will be worth it. Clearly, the choice of discount rate in economic terms has a significant, if not decisive, ethical component. This has been a source of much debate in the literature and, obviously, in response to the famous reviews on the economics of climate change by Stern (2006) and Garnaut (2011). In both reports, a discount rate below 2% had been proposed, what was lower than discount rates recommended in most previous economic studies on climate change.

5.6.2 Economic and Social Discount Rates and Intergenerational Equity

In economic theory, welfare means the satisfaction of preferences. By definition, an increase in welfare for an agent involves moving to a more preferred outcome. Preferences are defined over consumption, so an increase in welfare is defined as a move to a more preferred combination of goods consumed. Economists represent preferences for technical purposes through the use of a *utility function:*

$$U = u(c)$$

where U is the utility, which is an index that indicates the place of a given consumption combination (c) relative to others. Higher utility numbers indicate more preferred combinations. A typical investment project will carry a consumption trajectory over a given time horizon (possibly infinite) giving rise to a total welfare effect of

$$U_0 = \int_0^\infty u(c_t)dt$$

where U_0 is the total utility of the stream of c's over time, evaluated in period 0, i.e., the time during which the project will be implemented.

As noted (and decried on ethical grounds) by Ramsay (1928), there is a *technical* need for discounting if a choice is to be made among possible consumption paths (i.e., projects). The zero discount rate case involves summing finite quantities over an infinite horizon, in which case project choice would require an illegitimate comparison of infinities. However, discounting utilities converts the stream into a declining geometric series, which therefore has a finite sum:

$$U_0 = \int_0^\infty u(c_t)e^{-\theta t}dt$$

Given the differing consumption paths, choosing an appropriate adaptation project would be determined by the value taken by the discount rate θ as applied to the utilities.

It is at this point that the ethical/governance aspects of the discount rate chosen begin to become a subject of discussion. The first issue concerns the role of 'pure time preference' or 'intrinsic discounting'. This concept involves assigning different weights to consumption baskets purely on the basis that they will occur at different points in time. In other words, a positive rate of pure time preference means that a given quantity of consumption over n future periods is deemed inferior to the same quantity experienced now, *ceteris paribus*. Economists generally agree that pure time preference is unjustifiable in terms of the collective good. That is, when considering which investment project is best, a government should not treat the welfare of future generations as less important than the current generation simply because of the displacement in time.

This position is reflected in the Garnaut Report (2011). Here, a baseline value of zero is chosen for pure time preference, with only a slight adjustment to allow for the possible occurrence of an extinction event. A discount rate of zero means that the welfare of the current generation has equal weight to that of a million years in the future. The 0.05% rate set by Garnaut means that the welfare of people around 1400 years in the future is worth half of that of people alive today. For more relevant timeframes, such as 100 years, the 0.05% rate only carries a marginal decrease in the importance of future welfare (approximately 5%). (By way of comparison, with a 1% discount rate the welfare of current agents is worth twice that of those in 69 years' time and nearly three times that of agents in 100 years.)

However, where future generations are expected to be better off than present agents, there is scope for discounting on grounds other than pure time preference. To look at this in another way, if future agents will consume more than current agents, then the current agents should not have to sacrifice as much even though the welfare of both groups is equally important.

While interesting, how is this relevant to climate change adaptation? As noted above, if it is assumed that consumption will grow over time, then discounting future welfare is appropriate on the grounds that relatively less welfare will be gained in the future than now. For this reason, Garnaut (2011) assumes a per capita income growth rate of 1.3% per annum until 2100 and a discount rate of 1.35%, which is the sum of the pure time preference and the consumption growth rate. (Note that in the sensitivity analysis, he uses a discount rate of 2.65%, i.e., two times the growth rate plus the 0.05% pure time preference rate).

The pure time preference question is involved and complicated. On the one hand, the principle of non-discrimination among generations has intuitive appeal. Yet, on the other, pure time preference does appear to be an identifiable aspect of individual behaviour (and hence a characteristic of the preferences of each generation). So arises the question of whether the "authoritarian" response (Marglin 1963) of overriding those preferences is justifiable in a democratic context. Furthermore, the argument is based on the (possibly questionable) assumption of homogeneous preferences across time. Lastly, one might challenge the assumption that a local government or decision-maker functions as the guardian of future generations of ratepayers in the same way that a national government does with regard to future citizens according to the advocates of low social discount rates. Overall, the choice of an appropriate discount rate for examining adaptation to climate change is a complex issue.

5.7 Cost-Benefit Analysis

Once the potential losses have been determined using an appropriate discount rate, the costs vs expected losses of different adaptation strategies against a 'no-action' strategy, can be evaluated over a time horizon. Since adaptation and mitigation strategies at the local level may only pay off after several years, it is important to take these longer time horizons into account in any analysis.

Generally, with an investment or cost-benefit analysis, the aim is to find the investment or strategy with the highest net present value (*NPV*). In our problem, the benefit of a project comes from reducing the risks associated with catastrophic events given the expected frequency and/or severity of the events. The cost component of the cost-benefit analysis includes: the cost of maintaining the project; and the initial investment or expenditure required to get the project underway. The *NPV* of a project can then be derived from a two-step procedure. The first step involves estimating the total discounted cost (*TDC*) of the initial investment and the expected costs or 'losses' from extreme weather events:

$$TDC = \sum_{t=1}^{T} \frac{\text{Loss}_t + \text{Cost}_t}{(1+\theta)^t} + \text{Investment cost},$$

The present value of the expected costs is calculated in the second step, i.e., the total discounted losses (*TDL*) from the extreme weather events if no adaptation project were to be implemented. In this case, the annual losses (Loss_{t*}) are expected to be higher since no adaptation action has taken place.

$$TDL = \sum_{t=1}^{T} \frac{\text{Loss}_{t*}}{(1+\theta)^t}$$

To derive the *NPV* of the adaptation project, we then simply need to subtract the *TDC* of the project from the *TDL* under a no-action scenario.

$$NPV = TDL - TDC$$

Clearly, the *NPV* of the project will be positive when the present value of the reduction in expected losses is greater than the present value of the discounted costs for the project. Note that different adaptation strategies or projects will have different effects on the frequency and severity distribution parameters, which will lead to differences in the calculated or simulated loss figures for each year.

With unlimited funding, investing in any project with a positive *NPVs* is advised. Otherwise, funding should be allocated among the projects so as to maximise the total *NPV*.

5.8   Risk and Losses Assessment: Bushfires in the Ku-ring-gai Area

This case study is a good illustration of risk and loss assessment for extreme events. The case study deals with bushfire management in the Ku-ring-gai Shire of northern Sydney.

5.8.1   Background Information

Over the last decade, research has suggested there will be an increase in the number of days conducive to bushfires in many areas of Sydney (Lucas et al. 2007).[1] The Ku-ring-gai Shire is one such area. According to McAneney et al. (2009), the annual probability of property loss due to bushfires in Australia during the 20th century was around 50%. In addition, the most recent IPCC WG2 report states that "there is high confidence that increased incidence of fires in southern Australia will increase risk to people, property and infrastructure" (IPCC 2014, p. 25). The final report of the 2009 Victorian Bushfires Royal Commission (2010, p. 1) notes that it would be a mistake to treat the Black Saturday bushfire event that claimed hundreds of lives and destroyed thousands of homes as a "one-off" event and that "with populations at the rural-urban interface growing and the impact of climate change, the risks associated with bushfire are likely to increase". The challenge of climate change adaptation and the need to build resilience against natural disasters within the Australian context has also been pointed out by Ross and Carter (2011). Local-level management of bushfire risk has also been emphasized by McGee (2011), who examined neighbourhood-level wildfire mitigation programs and their impact on reducing wildfire risk and enhancing community resilience.

The Ku-ring-gai Shire is an interesting case to study due to the high risk of bushfire in this area. The region spans around 18,000 ha of bushland with 89 km of

---

[1] This also means that the extended fire seasons may reduce the number of days suitable for controlled burning which is an important adaptation measure currently practised in Australia (Lucas et al. 2007).

urban/bushland interface (Taplin et al. 2010). In addition, around 13,000 homes in the region (approx. 36%) are rated as high-risk for property damage (Chen 2005). The large number of houses at the bushland interface means that Ku-ring-gai is highly vulnerable to bushfires. Figure 5.4 shows the extent of this vulnerability. The first category of bushfire-prone land, Vegetation Category 1, includes areas of forest, woodlands, heaths, forested wetlands, and timber plantations with a 100-m buffer zone of vulnerable land. Vegetation Category 2 includes grasslands, freshwater wetlands, semi-arid woodlands, arid shrublands, and rainforests with a 30-m buffer zone (NSW RFS 2015).

Following the procedure outlined in the Modelling section above, we conducted a bushfire risk assessment on the Ku-ring-gai Shire.

5.8.2   Choice of Parameters

The parameters for the frequency distribution and the severity distribution are based on information provided by a bushfire expert for the Ku-ring-gai area. Usually, expert advice would be sought from multiple experts and synthesised. However, in cases where the focus is on the local level, it may be difficult to engage with more than one suitably qualified person. We consulted with the Ku-ring-gai Council's bushfire management officer. The officer's estimates were based on more than 5 years of experience working with the Council as well as on discussions with other staff from both the Council and the New South Wales Rural Fire Service. We accepted this as sufficient expertise. The estimates were as follows:

Frequency: Under current conditions, a severe bushfire is expected to happen approximately once every ten years. Therefore, the Poisson distribution is estimated as $\lambda = 0.1$.

Severity: The estimates for the 50th percentile of the distribution, i.e., the median, were $q_{0.5} = 30$ houses damaged ($P(X \leq 30)$), and $q_{0.95} = 200$ for the 95th percentile, i.e., a worst-case scenario ($P(X \leq 200) = 0.95$). As illustrated by Keighley et al. (2018), a lognormal distribution can be derived from this information with a location parameter $\mu = 3.40$ and a scale parameter $\sigma = 1.15$. A plot of the corresponding loss distribution is provided in Fig. 5.1.

5.8.3   Estimates of the Number of Houses Damaged

The resulting lognormal distribution provides estimates of the number of houses damaged for a wider range of percentiles, as shown in Table 5.1. As our case focuses on extreme events, the probabilities of losses are low but, having derived an entire distribution of the losses, the expected losses for a worst-case scenario, in other words, the 95, 99, and 99.5 percentile, become apparent. This provides decision-makers with

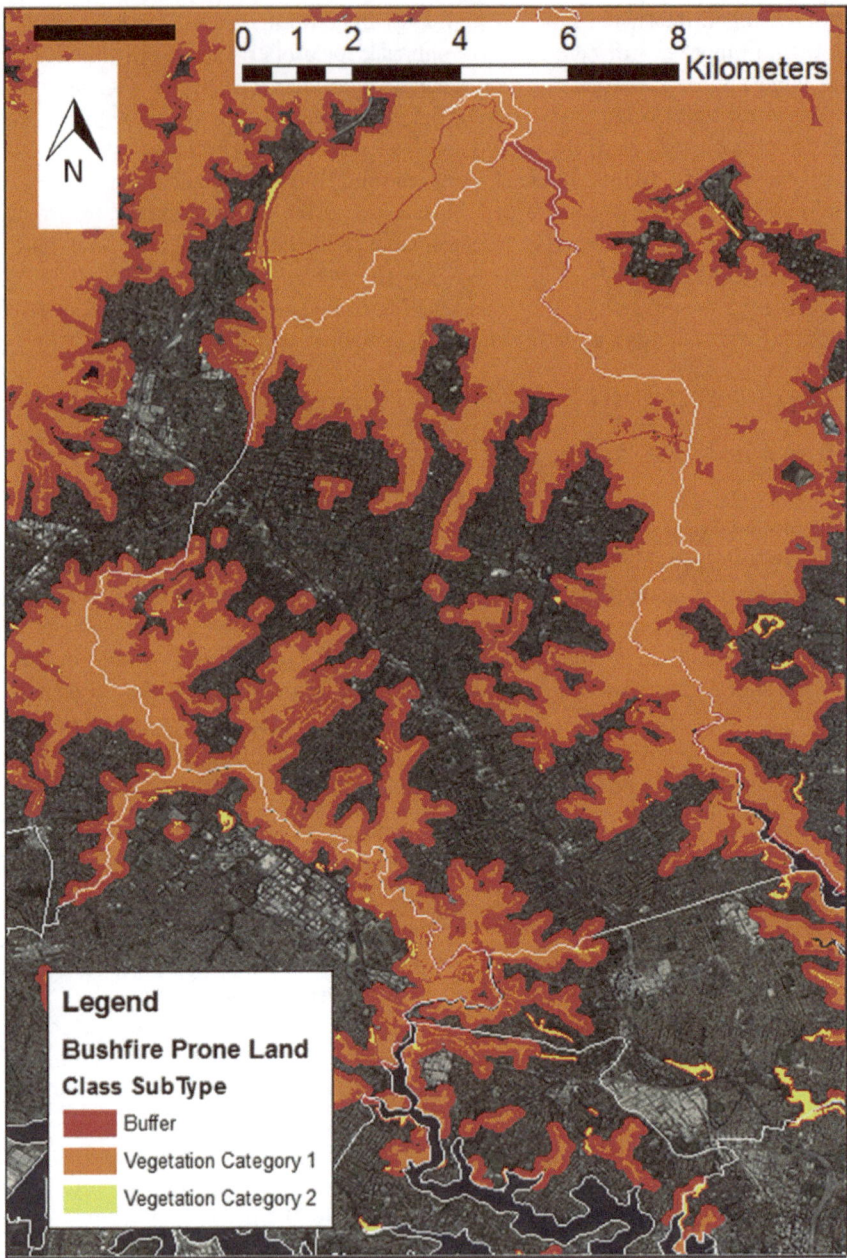

Fig. 5.4 Bushfire-prone land in Ku-ring-gai and surrounds. *Source* Created using GIS data from NSW RFS, 2015

Table 5.1 Descriptive statistics for the number of destroyed houses

Percentiles	No. houses damaged
25	13.80
50	30.00
95	200.00
99	439.38
99.5	587.01
Mean	**58.37**

Based on the derived lognormal distribution with a location parameter of $\mu = 3.40$ and a scale parameter of $\sigma = 1.15$

additional information about the uncertainty involved in a severe bushfire, as well as the potential for extreme losses associated with such an event. The results in Table 5.1 suggest that there is still a 1% chance that more than 439 houses would be destroyed in a bushfire and a 0.5% chance that over 587 houses would be destroyed. Also note that using another type of distribution, such as the Weibull and Burr XII distributions would produce quite different numbers even when using the same expert estimates. We have only presented the results from the lognormal distribution here. Readers interested in the results from the other distributions can refer to Keighley et al. (2018).

5.8.4 Estimates of Total Losses for Ku-ring-gai

The total losses from bushfires are estimated based on the severity distribution. The mean cost of reconstruction per house is $422,000, and the current risk-prone property value is approximated by subtracting the average land value per property from the average property sales price in the area to obtain the property construction cost (see, e.g., Truong and Trück 2016).

Recall that the frequency of bushfires in the Ku-ring-gai area was specified to be $\lambda = 0.1$. However, due to the efforts of fire brigades and other existing resources, the expert has specified that the number of severe bushfires that would actually lead to property damage would be 1 out of 5 events. Further, the maximum number of property losses in any one bushfire would not exceed 1000. As a result, the frequency model (Poisson distribution) needs to be slightly modified by introducing a Bernoulli variable to account for the actual occurrence of houses lost per event. In addition, we have imposed a restriction so that the upper bound on losses is equal to 1000 properties.

Table 5.2 contains the estimates for the total discounted cost of losses from property damage resulting from the adjusted LDA over 40 years based on a lognormal severity distribution. To examine the impact of the discount rate and the severity of climate change, four scenarios were examined as follows:

Table 5.2 Simulated *TDC* losses from bushfires over a 40-year time horizon

Losses ($AUD millions)	Percentiles					Mean
	25	50	75	95	99	
Scenario 1: base case (financial discount rate 4%)						
	0	1.43	9.42	38.83	87.42	8.60
Scenario 2: social discount rate (discount rate 1.35%)						
	0	2.54	15.88	61.79	136.62	13.77
Scenario 3: climate change impact with adaptation (4% discount rate, frequency doubles over 40 years)						
	0	4.46	14.67	48.12	99.37	11.89
Scenario 4: climate change impact without adaptation (4% discount rate, frequency doubles over 40 years, damage occurs in 33% of the bushfires)						
	3.07	10.91	25.78	69.75	130.97	19.78

Scenario 1 The base scenario is at a discount rate of 4%, which is approximately in line with the average cost of borrowing for a local government over the last two decades.

Scenario 2 The second case is based on a significantly lower social discount rate of 1.35%, as used in Garnaut (2011).

Scenario 3 In this scenario, we assume the frequency of bushfires will double over the 40-year timeframe, i.e., the parameter λ increases from $\lambda = 0.1$ to $\lambda^* = 0.2$ but the severity will stay the same.

Scenario 4 This is an exacerbated scenario where the frequency of bushfires doubles and the severity of the fires is also increased. Thus, houses are assumed to be damaged in 33% of bushfire events instead of 20%, as originally specified by the expert.

Note that the 25th percentile estimate for the *TDC* of property damage is zero across all but one of the scenarios. This is because the frequency of severe bushfire events is low ($\lambda = 0.1$) and only 1 in 5 of those events results in a loss of houses. Given these specifications, we would expect a severe bushfire in the Ku-ring-gai area approximately every ten years, with 20% of those events damaging houses. With a focus on a 40-year time horizon, there is a relatively high percentage of simulation runs with no losses.

5.9 Discussion of the Main Results

Scenario 1 (the base case) shows that the median estimate for total losses is $1.43 M over the 40-year period based on a lognormal distribution of severity. The mean estimate or expected loss is $8.60 million, while the 99th percentile estimate is $87.42 million, which is approximately 10 times higher than the expected loss. This is due to the skewness and the heavy tail of the lognormal distribution. These numbers also emphasize the challenge for decision-makers: if decisions are based on the mean estimate only, an expected discounted cost of $8.60 million might not seem very high. On the other hand, if decision-makers are more worried about a worst-case scenario, the significantly higher discounted costs of $87.42 million might justify more investment into adaptation.

If we compare the base case with Scenario 2, the results show that using a social discount rate instead of a financial one leads to significantly higher total losses for all percentiles and the mean. This is because the lower discount rate (of 1.35% instead of 4%) places greater weight on later time periods and increases the simulated *TDC* of damage to houses by approximately 60%. Scenario 2 highlights how significantly the chosen discount rate can affect the results since all the other parameters in the simulation are exactly the same. The difference between the results for *TDCs* between a higher (financial) and lower (social) discount rate becomes even more substantial when longer time horizons are considered, e.g. 100 years. Further, Table 5.2 illustrates that the 95th and 99th percentiles of the loss distribution also increase substantially. Based on the estimated distribution and applied discount rate, there is a 5% chance that the *TDC* will be higher than $61.79 million and a 1% chance that the *TDC* will exceed $136.62 million. The latter figure is approximately 10 times higher than the mean of the *TDC* distribution. Thus, risk-averse decision-makers will be aware of this low-probability/high-risk scenario when making adaptation investment decisions.

The result from Scenario 3 shows how increasing the frequency of events impacts adaptation—specifically, that doubling the frequency of bushfires within the 40-year period increases the total loss estimates by approximately 40%. Scenario 4 shows the impact of increasing severity as well. Here, the losses increase by approximately 65% in comparison to Scenario 3, and by approximately 130% in comparison to the base case.

In summary, *TDC* estimates are quite sensitive to the choice of the discount rate and will typically increase substantially when a lower discount rate is chosen. Therefore, considerations of intergenerational equity will play a major role when it comes to quantifying potential losses from extreme events.

An expected increase in the frequency of catastrophic events will also lead to higher TDC estimates. In our case study, the most substantial effect on the expected loss occurred when both the frequency and the severity of bushfires were assumed to increase. The greatest impact on the 99th percentile of the *TDL* was found when a social discount rate was applied.

5.10 Investment into Adaptation

Now, we turn to sustainable decision-making and the costs and benefit of adaptation investment. Generally, adaptations to an increasing bushfire risk can be made at various levels. For example, governments could revise building codes or adjust funding for investment projects to reduce risks associated with bushfires. Education or awareness programs could be implemented. Owners could make their homes more resilient to bushfires or else pay higher insurance premiums, and so on.

Our analysis focusses on possible adaptation investments by local governments and, more specifically, on several adaptation options identified by the Ku-ring-gai Shire as having the potential to reduce the risk of bushfires. The options involve constructing new fire stations and/or creating new fire trails (Ku-ring-gai Council 2010). Constructing more fire stations reduces the response times to fire, which should, in turn, reduce the amount of damage. Fire trails allow for hazard controls, such as reduction burning, breaks in the spread of fire, and possibly more time for fire brigades to respond.

Consider the fire trail adaptation project as an example for evaluation. Let's assume that the total discounted cost of building the fire trails and maintaining them over the next 40 years is $3 million, but that this investment reduces the risk of losses by 30% because the new trails should allow for more efficient reduction burning and will interrupt the fire's spread. For simplicity, let's now assume that the estimated numbers in Table 5.2 for the distribution of TDCs are reduced by 30% in all four scenarios.

To provide adequate information for decision making, the *NPV* of the project ($NPV = TDL − TDC$) needs to be considered and compared to the *TDC* of the project and the *TDL* of a no-action scenario.

Beginning with Scenario 1, the initial focus should be on the mean or expected loss. If new fire trails are built, the expected mean loss over 40 years will be reduced by 30%, i.e., by $8.60 M * 0.3 = $2.58 M to a *TDC* of $6.02 M (the mean of discounted losses when the projected is implemented). Add the $3.00 M of present-day costs for the project, and the *TDC* = $9.02 M. The mean of the *TDL* distribution without adaptation is $8.60 M. Thus, the *NPV* of the adaptation project for Scenario 1 over 40 years is

$$NPV_{\text{Scenario 1}} = TDL_{\text{Scenario 1}} - TDC_{\text{Scenario 1}}$$
$$= \$8.60\,M - \$9.02 = -\$0.42\,M < 0$$

Thus, for Scenario 1, where the financial discount rate is 4%, an adaptation investment is not favourable since it yields a negative *NPV*. In this scenario, when only the expected value of the loss distribution is considered, the recommendation would be to not invest in building fire trails.

However, the results for the other scenarios are quite different. In Scenario 2, with a social discount rate of 1.35%, the expected loss is reduced from $13.77 M to $13.77 M − $4.13 M = $9.64 M, i.e., a positive *NPV*:

$$NPV_{\text{Scenario 2}} = TDL_{\text{Scenario 2}} - TDC_{\text{Scenario 2}} = \$13.77\,M - (\$9.64\,M + \$3.00\,M)$$
$$= +\$1.13\,M > 0.$$

Scenarios 3 and 4, which represent a more dramatic impact of climate change, give rise to the following results:

$$NPV_{\text{Scenario 3}} = TDL_{\text{Scenario 3}} - TDC_{\text{Scenario 3}} = \$11.89\,\text{M} - \left(\$8.32\,\text{M} + \$3.00\,\text{M}\right)$$
$$= +\$0.57\,\text{M} > 0$$

$$NPV_{\text{Scenario 4}} = TDL_{\text{Scenario 4}} - TDC_{\text{Scenario 4}} = \$19.78\,\text{M} - \left(\$13.85\,\text{M} + \$3.00\,\text{M}\right)$$
$$= +\$2.93\,\text{M} > 0$$

Thus, while the *NPV* of the project in Scenario 1 is negative, the *NPV* of the adaptation project is positive for the scenarios that either apply a social discount rate or assume that climate change will have a more severe impact.

The 'Precautionary principle' offered by the IPCC might encourage decision makers to place significant weight on scenarios that reflect a stronger effect of climate change. The principle is based on the 1998 Wingspread Statement, which states: "When an activity raises threats of harm to human health or the environment, precautionary measures should be taken even if some cause and effect relationships are not fully established scientifically" (IPCC 2014). Principle 15 of the 1992 Rio Declaration (United Nations 1992, p. 3) on Environment and Development reflects the same sentiment: "Where there are threats of serious or irreversible damage, lack of full scientific certainty shall not be used as a reason for postponing cost-effective measures to prevent environmental degradation." In this context, Scenarios 2–4 illustrate that building new fire trails at a total cost of \$3 million today is a beneficial adaptation investment, supported by a cost-benefit analysis that yields a positive *NPV*.

As a last note, it is worth mentioning that applying the precautionary principle might also encourage more risk-averse decision-making that is not based on the mean but rather on a worst-case scenario, e.g., the 95th or 99th percentile of the *TDC* distribution. Under these circumstances, the present value of the adaptation costs could be compared to the expected reduction in losses in the worst-case.

Overall, our example illustrates that sustainable decision making for adaptation investments strongly depends on the assumptions made for quantifying future losses from extreme events. As pointed out, given the long time horizon that needs to be used for evaluation, two key factors in adaptation investment evaluations are the discount rate used in the decision-making process and the assumptions about the severity and impact of climatic change.

5.11   Teaching Notes

5.11.1   Synopsis of the Case

Measuring the potential costs of catastrophic climatic events is a challenging but important exercise, as the occurrence of such events is usually associated with substantial damage and high uncertainty. Risk assessments and measures to evaluate adaptation should focus on an appropriate time horizon that is consistent with the frequency of events since a short-term view may disproportionally deflate the risk involved. This chapter illustrates key concepts that need to be considered when quantitatively evaluating adaptation to extreme climate events. Important issues include: measuring uncertainty using a probability distribution; the time value of money; the choice of discount rate values; the costs and benefits of adaptation; and sustainable decision making.

5.11.2   Target Learning Group

- Level of study—BA and MA students
- Subject areas—management; economics; finance; statistics.

5.11.3   Learning Objectives

5.11.3.1   Key Issues

- Understand how climate change can impact the frequency and severity of extreme events.
- List the possible impacts o f dfferent extreme events.
- Model the impacts of extreme events using the loss distribution approach, including modelling the frequency and severity of events.
- Understand the concept of the time value of money. Choose the appropriate discount rate and use it in the discounting process to find the present value of future losses.
- Understand the use of a cost-benefit analysis for climate adaptation decision making.

5.11.3.2   Specific Objectives

- Examine the case study: Bushfires in the Ku-ring-gai area.

- Identify the key parameters i n he case study, and understand how the values have been chosen for these parameters.
- Draw contrasts between the four cases to fully understand the research aim of the study and to create awareness that the future holds many possible scenarios and such possibilities should be accounted for properly.
- Closely study the discussion of the main results and how conclusions are drawn from the statistics.

5.11.4 Reading Activities

5.11.4.1 Pre-reading

Read through the section headings of this chapter. What do they tell you about the main issues associated with modelling extreme events? Are they linked to each other in some way? Can you see how these concepts fit into the big picture without understanding the specifics?

Examine the plots in Figs. 5.1, 5.2, and 5.3.

- What does Fig. 5.1 suggest about the annual total of insured economic losses from extreme events in Australia for the period 2000–2017?
- What is the difference between the distributions displayed in Fig. 5.2 and the one in Fig. 5.3?
- Figure 5.3 shows a highly skewed distribution. Why would such a distribution be appropriate to model losses from climate events?

Before you read the section on cost-benefit analysis, list the key issues you would consider before making a decision on adaptation to extreme events. Then compare your list to the key issues mentioned in the cost-benefit analysis section.

Examine Table 5.1.

- Why is there such a big difference between the mean and the median in the distribution for the number of destroyed houses?
- What are the 50th, 95th, and 99th percentiles of the distribution? Explain in your own words, how these numbers should be interpreted.

Examine the different scenarios in Table 5.2.

- What impact do the different scenarios have on the losses?
- Which scenario seems to create the highest losses?

5.11.4.2 In-Depth Reading

The loss distribution approach

- Examine the section "Modelling the impacts of extreme events". Note that the section highlights three important concepts related to the loss distribution approach (LDA)

  - the frequency of events
  - the severity of events
  - the cumulative losses over time.

- Describe in your own words how these three concepts are combined to calculate the present value of future losses from extreme events.

Discounting and the time value of money

- What do the terms 'financial discounting' and 'economic discounting' mean? What are the main differences between these two approaches?
- According to economic theory, what is the relationship between welfare, consumption, and utility? What is measured by a utility function?
- How is the discount rate related to intergenerational equity? What is meant by the principle of non-discrimination among generations?
- What is the present value of $100,000 in 40 years with a discount rate of: (i) 0%; (ii) 1%; (iii) 5%; and (iv) 10%?

Cost-benefit analysis

- How does a cost-benefit analysis relate to the net present value?
- What are the costs and benefits in the context of an adaptation investment?
- Explain how different projects and a no-adaptation action scenario can be compared using a cost-benefit analysis.

The case study

Examine the background section of the case study.

- Why has the Ku-ring-gai area been chosen as the basis for the analysis?
- What is the main risk of extreme events identified for this area?
- What are the key challenges for quantifying an appropriate distribution for the frequency and severity of extreme events for this region?
- What is the benefit of comparing different scenarios for losses from bushfires?
- Provide a brief summary of the main results of the case study.
- Explain in your own words how investment into an adaptation project can be analysed in the proposed framework.

5.11.5   Assignment Questions

5.11.5.1   Objective

In this assignment, you will perform computation tasks similar to the Ku-ring-gai case study to review important concepts associated with modelling the costs of extreme climate events. As a first step, familiarise yourself with the steps involved in the case study and see if you can replicate these steps. If you get stuck, you can always go back to the Kur-ring-gai case study.

Building a spreadsheet to calculate the relevant numbers, using functions is very helpful for this question and highly recommended.

5.11.5.2   Assignment

Case

A small coastal town has been the victim of flooding in the past decades. Assume the local government would like to invest in a climate change adaptation strategy to reduce risk to the area. Before the government proceeds with the plan, it must establish the likely cost of future flooding. This task has been assigned to you.

Based on your research, you were able to simulate data on the occurrence and severity of flood events over the next 10 years. This data appears in Table 5.3. The number of floods per year was generated from a probability distribution. The cost per flood was generated from a lognormal distribution, which has been estimated based on a local expert's opinion.

Table 5.3   Simulation data on the occurrence and severity of flood events over the next 10 years

Year	Floods per year (base case)	Cost per flood (base case)	Floods per year (severe case)	Cost per flood (severe case)
1	1	$869,652	1	$873,650
2	0	$2,212,675	1	$1,931,440
3	0	$559,520	1	$994,551
4	2	$279,714	2	$298,301
5	0	$498,164	0	$813,136
6	0	$1,016,906	1	$1,096,495
7	1	$228,712	1	$975,850
8	0	$949,254	1	$1,530,189
9	1	$235,586	1	$951,998
10	1	$1,141,965	1	$682,264

(One difference between this case and Ku-ring-gai is that the numbers here are only based on one simulation. The results in the Ku-ring-gai case study are based on many simulations, and running a high number of simulations, e.g., $k = 10,000$ or $k = 100,000$, allows the total costs in present-day terms to be calculated at various quantiles).

The first two columns are the numbers in the base case. Assume that the expected numbers of floods per year can be modelled using a Poisson distribution with $\lambda = 0.6$. The cost per flood is generated from a lognormal distribution ($\mu = 13$, $\sigma = 1$).

In a more severe case, we are likely to have a higher expected number of events per year, compared to the base case. These values appear in the next column. The numbers have been generated from a Poisson distribution with $\lambda = 1$.

Similarly, the expected mean cost per flood is likely to increase as well. Let's assume that in a more severe case, the cost per flood can be modelled using a lognormal distribution with parameters $\mu = 13.2$ and $\sigma = 1.2$, resulting in a distribution with a higher mean and variance than for the base case.

Questions

(a) Calculate the present value of the costs associated with flooding in the next 10 years in the base case. For this question, assume the appropriate discount rate is 5%, which is the interest rate paid by the government if it wants to borrow money to undertake the project.

(b) Now re-calculate the present value of the costs from flooding assuming a discount rate of 1%. Do you expect the present value to be higher or lower than the base case? Is the result consistent with your expectation?

(c) Repeat (a) and use the number of floods in the severe case instead, combined with the cost per flood in the base case. Do you expect the present value to be higher or lower than the base case? Is the result consistent with your expectation?

(d) Repeat (a) and use the number of floods as well as the costs from the severe scenario. Do you expect the present value to be higher or lower than the base case? Is the result consistent with your expectation?

(e) Compare your results in the four cases above. What conclusions can you draw?

Practice Questions:

Question 1: Use NPV rule to determine whether to invest in a project

Assume that a local government would like to invest in a climate change adaptation strategy to reduce the risks from flooding in a coastal area. Further, assume that, currently, the average damage per year due to flooding is $1,500,000.

The strategy requires an initial investment in $t = 0$ of $10,000,000 and a yearly maintenance cost of $300,000. The strategy is assumed to reduce the average damage per year by 60%.

• Assume that the government has to borrow the money for the investment for a yearly rate of $r = 5\%$ (financial discount rate). What is the net benefit of the project in present-value dollars if the project has a lifetime of: (i) 20 years; and (ii) 30 years. What would be the total net benefit of the project?

- Climate change studies forecast that the average flooding damage per year will increase at the rate of 3% per year. So, if the current average flooding damage per year is $1.5 million, the average flood damage per year in 10 years' time is $2,024,788. What would be the effect with respect to the calculated NPV of the project?

Question 2: What general difficulties arise when evaluating the costs and benefits of climate change adaptation strategies at the local scale?

5.11.6   Discussion Activities

In a group of 3 to 4 students, discuss and list relevant issues regarding the following case study.

There is a remote small town located in a hilly district. It is a peaceful and quiet place to live but, in recent years, more and more frequent mudflows have caused significant damages to the little town, especially during summer when there is heavy rainfall.

The local government is discussing a plan to relocate the population of the small town to nearby villages and other possible plans to reduce the costs of future mudflows. They invite you to express your opinion on this matter as well.

Using the knowledge you have learned from this chapter, work in a group to discuss and identify relevant issues from the following aspects:

- What is the main risk to this small town?
- What are the possible impacts of climate change?
- If we try to project future costs of the extreme events, what numbers are necessary for the calculation process?
- What information needs to be gathered to forecast the number of mudflows?
- If we want to estimate the cost of a mudflow, what number should we acquire?
- What factors will you consider when choosing the appropriate discount rate?
- What adjustments will you make to the base case estimates to create a better understanding of the distributions of the total costs?
- After you get the modelling results, what kind of conclusions can you draw to help the government make a decision?
- Other than relocating the entire town, what other alternatives you can think of to reduce the costs of future extreme events?

5.11.7   Multimedia Supplementary Activities and Readings

- **Adapting to a changing climate**
  https://www.youtube.com/watch?v=lGMx2xP3dcM

A new video documentary by the UNFCCC Adaptation Committee to raise awareness of climate change adaptation. The 20-min documentary "Adapting to a changing climate" introduces viewers to the topic of climate change adaptation, weaving in inspiring stories of adaptation action and interviews with experts.

- **A climate adaptation decision support tool for local governments: CATLoG**
  https://www.nccarf.edu.au/publications/climate-adaptation-decision-support-tool-local-governments
  A decision support tool for investment into climate adaptation developed as part of a research project for the National Climate Change Adaptation Research Facility. The tool uses a combination of quantitative (cost-benefit analysis) and qualitative (multi-criteria analysis) methods. It allows users to conduct sensitivity tests and examine the impact of uncertain parameters ranging from climate impacts to discount rates. The final product is a user-friendly decision tool in the form of an Excel add-on, together with a user manual booklet that demonstrates sample worked out projects. The tool is made flexible so that stakeholders can adopt or refine or upgrade it for their context-specific applications.

- **Climate change adaption: It's time for decisions now**
  https://www.youtube.com/watch?v=FO46sPwm4xk
  Animation film by the International Climate Initiative (ICI) of the Federal Ministry for the Environment, Nature Conservation and Nuclear Safety (BMU), produced by the Deutsche Gesellschaft für Internationale Zusammenarbeit (GIZ) GmbH in cooperation with the Potsdam Institute for Climate Impact Research (PIK).

- **Climate change is happening. Here's how we adapt**
  https://www.youtube.com/watch?v=fw01_q0cxM8
  TED Talks: Imagine the hottest day you've ever experienced. Now imagine it's 6°, 10°, or 12° hotter. According to climate researcher Alice Bows-Larkin, that's the type of future in store for us if we don't significantly cut our greenhouse gas emissions now. She suggests that it's time we do things differently—a whole system change, in fact—and seriously consider trading economic growth for climate stability.

- **The Intergovernmental Panel on Climate Change (IPCC)**
  https://www.ipcc.ch/
  IPCC is the United Nations body for assessing the science related to climate change. It publishes assessment reports on climate change, its causes, potential impacts, and response options. It also oversees the Data Distribution Centre, which provides data sets, scenarios of climate change and other environmental and socio-economic conditions, as well as other materials.

References

Bank for International Settlements (2001) Consultative document: operational risk. Retrieved from https://www.bis.org/publ/bcbsca07.pdf

Chen K (2005) Counting bushfire-prone addresses in the greater Sydney region. In: Morrison RJ, Quin S, Bryant EA (eds) Planning for natural hazards—how can we mitigate the impacts? Proceedings of a symposium, 2–5 Feb 2005, University of Wollongong, GeoQuEST Research Centre, pp 1–10

Fishman GS (1996) Monte Carlo. Springer, New York, NY

Garnaut R (2011) The Garnaut review 2011: Australia in the global response to climate change. Cambridge University Press, New York, NY

Hasson AEA, Mills GA, Timbal B, Walsh K (2009) Assessing the impact of climate change on extreme fire weather events over Southeastern Australia. Clim Res 39(2):159–172

IPCC (2014) Climate change 2014: impacts, adaptation, and vulnerability. Part B: regional aspects. In Barros VR, Field CB, Dokken DJ, Mastrandrea MD, Mach KJ, Bilir TE et al (eds) Contribution of Working Group II to the fifth assessment report of the Intergovernmental Panel on Climate Change. Cambridge University Press, New York, NY

Keighley T, Longden T, Mathew S, Trück S (2018) Quantifying catastrophic and climate impacted hazards based on local expert opinions. J Environ Manage 205:262–273

Klugman SA, Panjer HH, Willmot GE (2012) Loss models: from data to decisions, 4th Edn. Wiley, Hoboken, NJ

Lucas C, Hennessy K, Mills G, Bathols J (2007) Bushfire weather in Southeast Australia: recent trends and projected climate change impacts. Consultancy report prepared for The Climate Institute of Australia. Retrieved from http://royalcommission.vic.gov.au/getdoc/c71b6858-c387-41c0-8a89-b351460eba68/TEN.056.001.0001.pdf

Marglin S (1963) The social rate of discount and the optimal rate of investment. Quart J Econ 77:95–111

Mathew S, Trück S, Henderson-Sellers A (2012) Kochi, India case study of climate adaptation to floods: ranking local government investment options. Glob Environ Change 22(1):308–319

McAneney J, Chen K, Pitman A (2009) 100-years of Australian bushfire property losses: is the risk significant and is it increasing? J Environ Manage 90(8):2819–2822

McGee TK (2011) Public engagement in neighbourhood level wildfire mitigation and preparedness: case studies from Canada, the US and Australia. J Environ Manage 92(10):2524–2532

Murphy BF, Timbal B (2008) A review of recent climate variability and climate change in south-eastern Australia. Int J Climatol J Royal Meteorol Soc 28(7):859–879

NSW Rural Fire Service (2015) Guide for bushfire prone land mapping. Retrieved from http://www.rfs.nsw.gov.au/__data/assets/pdf_file/0011/4412/Guideline-for-Councils-to-Bushfire-Prone-Area-Land-Mapping.pdf

Ramsay FP (1928) A mathematical theory of saving. Econ J 38(152):543–559

Ross H, Carter RW (2011) Natural disasters and community resilience. Australas J Environ Manage 18(1):1–5

Shevchenko PV, Wüthrich MV (2006) The structural modelling of operational risk via Bayesian inference: combining loss data with expert opinions. J Oper Risk 1(3):3–26

Stern N (2006). Stern review: the economics of climate change. United Kingdom. Retrieved from http://mudancasclimaticas.cptec.inpe.br/~rmclima/pdfs/destaques/sternreview_report_complete.pdf

Taplin R, Henderson-Sellers A, Trück S, Mathew S, Weng H, Street M, Bradford W, Scott J, Davies P, Hayward L (2010) Economic evaluation of climate change adaptation strategies for local government. Ku-ring-gai Council case study

Trück S, Bradford W, Henderson-Sellers A, Mathew S, Scott J, Street M, Taplin R (2010) Assessing climate change adaptation options for local governments. In: You Y, Henderson-Sellers A (eds) Climate change monitoring and strategy. Sydney University Press, Sydney, Australia, pp 362–400

Truong C, Trück S (2016) It's not now or never: implications of investment timing and risk aversion on climate adaptation to extreme events. Eur J Oper Res 253(3):856–868

Truong C, Trück S, Mathew S (2018) Managing risks from climate impacted hazards—the value of investment flexibility under uncertainty. Eur J Oper Res 269(1):132–145. https://doi.org/10.1016/j.ejor.2017.07.012

UNISDR (The United Nations Office for Disaster Reduction) (2016) 2015 disasters in numbers. Retrieved from http://www.unisdr.org/files/47804_2015disastertrendsinfographic.pdf

United Nations (1992) The Rio declaration on environment and development. Retrieved from http://www.unesco.org/education/pdf/RIO_E.PDF

Victorian Bushfires Royal Commission (2010) 2009 Victorian Bushfires Royal Commission final report. Summary. Retrieved from http://royalcommission.vic.gov.au/Commission-Reports/Final-Report.html

West JJ, Small MJ, Dowlatabadi H (2001) Storms, investor decisions, and the economic impacts of sea level rise. Clim Change 48(2–3):317–342

Dr. Stefan Trück is a Professor of Business Analytics and Co-Director of the Centre for Financial Risk at Macquarie University. Previously, he has held positions at Queensland University of Technology and Karlsruhe Institute of Technology in Germany where he received a Ph.D. in Business Engineering. Stefan's research interests focus on risk management, financial econometrics and business analytics, including the fields of energy and commodity markets, credit risk, systemic risk, emissions trading, climate change economics and international financial markets. He has published in several high impact journals including the European Journal of Operational Research, Journal of Banking and Finance, Global Environmental Change, Energy Economics, and Journal of International Money and Finance. He also received various research grants, including two Discovery Grants from the Australian Research Council in the area of risk management and major grants from the National Climate Change Adaptation Research Facility (NCCARF).

Dr. Chi Truong is a Senior Lecturer at the Department of Actuarial Studies and Business Analytic, Macquarie University. He has taught various courses in the area of investment and risk management, applied portfolio management, corporate finance and data analytics. His research interests are in the fields of environmental economics, real options analysis, catastrophic risk management under climate change and systemic risk quantification and forecast. Dr. Truong has published in highly ranked international journals including European Journal of Operational Research, Conservation Biology, Environmental and Resource Economics, Canadian Journal of Agricultural Economics, and Agricultural Water Management.

Mr. Tim Keighley is a data scientist and senior learning designer. He has worked in proteomic research, capital markets research and runs the *Excel Skills for Business* specialisation for Macquarie University with Coursera. He is an expert in *R* and *Excel*.

Dr. Feng Liu holds a Ph.D. degree in Actuarial Science and Applied Finance. She has published papers in the leading academic journals in actuarial science and applied finance. Her research projects focus on the application of mathematical and statistical models in empirical studies. She is also a CFA charterholder. Over the last decade, she has been actively involved in teaching activities in Australian top universities including curriculum development and has accumulated substantial teaching experience.

Dr. Supriya Mathew is a multi-disciplinary researcher whose research interests' focus on assessing the impacts of extreme environmental conditions on various communities and devising potential adaptive responses. She is currently a research fellow at the Menzies School of Health Research and based in Alice Springs.

Chapter 6
Institutionalising Sustainable Production Practices: Malaysia's Solar Photovoltaic Industry

Brian Low and Stephanie Kay Ann Cheah

Abstract The case study explores the role of institutions, their effectiveness, and their legitimacy in developing sustainable production practices over time. Set against the backdrop of government reforms in Malaysia's emerging SPV industry, developing these practices requires a combination of particular macro-institutional conditions and policies. Although the new policies provide wide-ranging opportunities for many businesses, they also impose constraints on how businesses conduct sustainable production practices. Institutional theory points to the role of several factors in legitimising these practices, such as reducing uncertainty and information costs, pathways to transfer solar technology and knowledge, and providing better financial support. Institutional theory also calls into question how a wide array of actors at the macro-institutional level are able to conduct sustainable production practices. This question has two implications for those within the network:

1. How does sustainable production emerge over time and, by extension, what are: (a) the roles of the network actors; and (b) the actors' effectiveness in driving business sustainability?
2. How do actors' relational dynamics legitimise or delegitimise sustainable production practices?

The case study explores these and other questions by tracing four key sustainable production practice indicators from the perspective of both institutional and network theory.

Keywords Policies · Institutions · Network · Sustainable production practices · Renewable energy sources

B. Low (✉) · S. K. A. Cheah
Monash University, Subang Jaya, Malaysia
e-mail: brian.low@monash.edu

© Springer Nature Singapore Pte Ltd. 2020
L. Wood et al. (eds.), *Industry and Higher Education*,
https://doi.org/10.1007/978-981-15-0874-5_6

6.1   The Case at a Glance

Key theories	• Institutional theory • Network theory
Key concepts	• Formal and informal institutions • Institutional reform policies • Institutions' effectiveness and legitimacy • Network actors, activities, and resources • Networks of relational ties • Institutionalising sustainable production practices • Sustainable value chain
Level of study	• Undergraduate, and particularly MBA/Ph.D.students
Subject areas	• Sustainability, economic policy, regional development, business networks

Graduate capabilities	**Graduate outcomes**	**%**
	Critical thinking	25
	Problem solving	25
	Teamwork	10
	Communication	5
	Ethical thinking	5
	Sustainability	30
	Total	**100%**

Time required	• Out-of-class preparation: 90 min • In-class discussion: 120 min

6.2   Introduction

As a nation, Malaysia has committed to reducing carbon dioxide emissions by up to 40% of its 2005 levels by 2020. By 2015, the country had already achieved a 33% reduction and, as a result, re-pledged to a 45% reduction by 2030 (Bernama 2016). Malaysia has several natural renewable energy sources to help it achieve its goal. Among these, solar energy has demonstrated great potential as a solution alongside biomass, biogas, mini-hydro, and the less technologically mature wind and geothermal energy. However, solar energy's full potential has yet to be realised, and installations of solar photovoltaic (SPV) systems across the nation have remained low. As of 31 December 2016, the cumulative operating capacity of SPV installations was only 3.3 million megawatts (MW), and around 20% of that energy was generated in 2016 alone (SEDA 2016a).

Paradoxically, Malaysia's SPV manufacturing industry is substantial. Within the space of 20 years, the country has risen to third globally behind China and Germany, with solar cells and modules produced in Malaysia currently accounting for 15% of the world's production (Performance Management and Delivery Unit 2014). Moreover, Malaysia has companies operating across the entire value chain, from silicon production (e.g., Tokuyama) to component and solar cell manufacturing (e.g., Sunpower and Q-Cell) to module assembly (e.g., Flextronics, Solartiff, First Solar Putrajaya).

However, there are pressures to balance Malaysia's long-term commitment to reducing carbon emissions with short-term competitiveness through reform policies that encourage foreign and local investment. These policies are highly localised and focus on export-oriented, low-end, low-technology solar products that involve labour-intensive assembly, processing, and manufacturing. Against the backdrop of these policy changes and pressures, business and regulatory agencies work in partnership to produce and regulate solar energy. In the context of an industry that has only begun to emerge over the past 10 years, sustainable production practices require a particular combination of macro-institutional conditions and policies. In this case study, we combine institutional theory (Scott 1995) and network theory (Håkansson and Snehota 1989) to analyse the sustainable production practices that underpin development in Malaysia's SPV industry.

Malaysia's SPV industry began in 2004 with the launch of the Malaysian Building Integrated Photovoltaic (MBIPV) Project, a joint initiative between the federal government of Malaysia, the United Nations Development Program, and the Global Environment Facility. The aim of the MBIPV Project is to promote a widespread and sustainable SPV market in Malaysia. The nation's first SPV initiative began in 2006 with the introduction of National Suria 1000 programme (2006–2010). This was initiated to provide financial capital incentives to commercial and residential building owners wishing to install SPV systems. The system consists of photovoltaic modules, inverters (to convert sunlight to energy), power-control systems, mounting, cabling, and a tracking and storage device. Ultimately, the goal was a 30% per year-on-year increase in the use of SPV products as a way to trigger cost reductions in solar systems.

Three subsequent policies have been established to pursue some form of sustainable development within the industry: Feed-in-Tariff (FiT) (2011–2016); Net Energy Metering (NEM), 2016–2020; and Large Scale Solar (LSS), 2016–2020. These policies provide wide-ranging opportunities for many businesses, but they also impose constraints on how businesses conduct their sustainable production practices. To accommodate new government priorities, businesses have needed to respond quickly with new resources and new o r changed practices. Not surprisingly, these constraints have led to tension, especially when a business interprets a policy differently or arrives at a different evaluation of the requirements.

Institutional theory points to the roles of several industry stakeholders in legitimising organisational practices. But it also calls into question whether a wide array of stakeholders at a macro-level are capable of maintaining sustainability in the way they do business. For example, how is uncertainty and the cost of information reduced across a complex network of actors? How is knowledge and technology transferred? Can all who need it access adequate financial support? Can import tariffs remain low to increase direct foreign investments without undermining the local industry? And so on. There is also a bigger question: Can a wide array of stakeholders conduct sustainable practices? This has two important implications for the behaviour of players in the network:

- How d o sustainable production practices emerge over time and, by extension, what is (a) the role of the stakeholders and (b) the stakeholders' effectiveness in driving business sustainability?
- How do the dynamics within stakeholders' relationships legitimise or delegitimise sustainable production practices?

Through both institutional theory and network theory, this chapter explores these and other questions by tracking four key indicators of sustainable production and its institutionalisation.

The basic premise of institutional theory is that businesses conform to 'respectable' behaviour by compromising rules and regulations in a way that is deemed acceptable within the system (DiMaggio and Powell 1983). Over the course of a company's interactions with external partners, businesses ensure their survival by undergoing a process of evolution and co-evolution to earn legitimacy. The network approach, however, is concerned with creating resources through relationships, many of which should be stable and durable. When businesses interact with each other, they form bonds by sharing and combining both their resources and their practices. While some business practices can be completely internal, more often than not they involve interactions with other firms. These interactions produce interdependencies, but they also limit the firm's independence. For example, resources become shared in these partnerships, but a firm's ability to control its own resources is tremendously reduced (Håkansson et al. 2009).

6.3   Policies and Sustainable Production Practices

Three policies form the backdrop that has influenced sustainability in Malaysia's SPV industry over the past 10 years. From a series of semi-structured interviews, we explored 19 significant network stakeholders and their myriad of economic, social, technological, and economic entanglements. Coupled with extensive content analysis of secondary material, we found these policies seem to have defined and redefined the mix of heterogeneous resources, transformed practices, and created an evolving network of ties stakeholders over time. The policies are presented in Table 6.1, each of which represents the three main phases of the SPV industry's development to date.

Table 6.1 Malaysia's solar photovoltaic policies

Policy	Period	Description	Quota (MW)	Target audience	Gvnd/implemented by
FiT	2011–2016	Subsidised with the opportunity to generate passive income	~250	Individuals and communities Industry and business	SEDA
NEM	2016–2020	Unsubsidised—participants must be willing to invest in reducing electricity costs	500	Industry and business	The Energy Commission/SEDA
LSS	2016–2020	Provides the opportunity to become a power producer	1250	Large investors	The Energy Commission

***Phase* 1**: In 2011, the FiT policy was introduced to act as a catalyst for boosting the industry nationwide. This policy licensed individuals and business owners to act as micropower plants for 21 years, by producing electricity and selling it to the government through Malaysia's power company. Primarily directed toward homeowners, the policy was designed to increase renewable energy growth through government subsidies (SEDA 2016b). After its implementation, Malaysia's take-up of SPV installations grew exponentially. Essentially, the initiative provided a low-risk, high-return investment with zero marginal costs and access to a renewable energy source with far easier set-up requirements. As a result, costs rapidly declined (SEDA 2017). The quotas allocated to the FiT policy were fully subscribed by 2016, which suggests that, if local institutional conditions are conducive, similar policies might work even when transferred to another place.

***Phase* 2**: The NEM policy was introduced in November 2016 to further support industry growth. This policy does not offer subsidies. Rather, it provides savings through self-consumption. For this reason, the initiative is less financially attractive than FiT and the population's interest in using solar energy rapidly decreased. Unlike FiT, where 100% of the electricity is sold to the grid, under the NEM policy, the converted energy is first used to power the building—i.e., self-consumption—and any excess energy is sold to the grid at a fixed rate.

***Phase* 3**: The LSS scheme was introduced in 2010 to attract large-scale investment in SPV growth. Where the FiT and NEM policies cater to local end-users (private consumption), the LSS scheme is directed toward large investors capable of supplying between 1 and 50 MWs of power at the utility level. In other words, LSS is a scheme run by Malaysia's power producer. The project aims to contribute an additional 1 GW to the nation's utility grid between 2017 and 2020 (Tenaga Nasional Berhad 2016). The government has also introduced tax incentives, known as the Green Technology Financing Scheme, for businesses involved in green projects, such as SPV installations on factory roofs. The scheme is managed by Green Technology Malaysia, an organisation under the purview of the Ministry of Energy, Green Technology and Water.

6.4 Sustainable Production Practices in Malaysia's SPV Industry

At an industrial level, sustainable production can be viewed as "industrial production resulting in products that meet the needs and wishes of the present society without compromising the ability of future generations to meet their needs and wishes, and all phases during the lifetime of a product have to be considered" (Ron 1998, p. 105). The challenge when evaluating sustainability, however, is identifying and selecting an appropriate suite of indicators (Fernandez-Sanchez and Rodriquez-Lopez 2010). Given that Malaysia's emerging SPV industry is witnessing: (a) several reform policies with impacts on institutional roles; and (b) a collective industry landscape that is dynamically changing to shape legitimacy for those within it, we opted for the indicators set out by the Lowell Centre for Sustainable Production (LCSP) (LCSP 2011). These indicators are detailed, comprehensive, and practical guides. They are ideal for demonstrating analytical insights, generalisations, and providing theoretical justifications for sustainable development research.

As the industry develops and as new policies are adopted, any new sustainable production activities indicators must remain flexible. New formal and informal institutions are being established with roles that are often specific but can sometimes be conflicting or overlapping. Identifying and developing these institutions and their roles, not surprisingly, is time-consuming and expensive and requires that each network stakeholder acknowledges and accepts their role. Traditional notions of 'how business works' are continually being defined and redefined as a result of these new policies. Businesses not only need to develop new ways of dealing with government and regulatory institutions, they also need to monitor their role in the supply/value chain while staying mindful of their commitments to stakeholders. In short, the complex interrelationships between numerous federal and state government agencies, economic actors, associations, and academia pose some great challenges as Malaysia's nascent SPV industry develops.

These interrelationships dovetail with LCSP's sustainable production indicators. The four indicators are:

- the extent to which an organisation complies with regulatory requirements and conforms to industry and association standards;

- the extent of its concern over inputs, outputs, and performance measurements from a network perspective;
- the extent to which sustainable production practices impact and change value-chain activities; and
- the extent to which an organisations' production processes and output intertwine with a sustainable society's local consumption and the installation of SPV applications.

Each of these indicators is described in detail in the following sections.

6.5 Organisational Compliance with Regulations and Standards

To understand sustainable production practices through organisational compliance with regulations and standards, we analysed two indicators: macro-institutional sustainability and the project management sustainability of significant network actors.

6.5.1 Macro-institutional Sustainability

This indicator seeks to determine the role of both formal and informal institutions, their effectiveness, and, hence, their continued legitimacy in ensuring sustainable production practices in an emerging SPV industry. Numerous types of institutions play various roles at all stages of an industry's development. Formal institutions, particularly government agencies, ensure that SPV industry stakeholders comply with the federal government's development and manufacturing policies. Among these key agencies, a statutory body called the Sustainable Energy Development Authority (SEDA) administers and manages the FiT initiative. SEDA also certifies that systems integrators have the ability and competence to fulfil their responsibilities. This means providing customised solar solutions and appropriate SPV systems to fit individual, commercial, industrial and community customers, and to install and maintain the systems. As a national government agency, the Malaysian Investment Development Authority (MIDA) seeks direct foreign investment for the SPV industry. In collaboration with SEDA, MIDA has compiled a publicly-available list of registered systems integrators and locally-endorsed manufacturers. The Standards and Industrial Institute of Malaysia is responsible for developing industry standards and quality benchmarks based on feedback from the industry. Local standards are important for ensuring sustainable technology is compatible with world standards. In turn, this helps with the transfer of technology and knowledge, and lays the foundation for Malaysia to move up the SPV value chain. However, to ensure a compatible fit with local usage, complying with Malaysia's local standards is not mandatory. In 2016, the Institute launched a solar module testing facility in Malaysia, which signals that local standards are being developed as SPV gains market acceptance and technologies progressively mature.

The challenge is in balancing organisational legitimacy among formal institutions, principally businesses such as manufacturers and systems integrators. However, systems integrators are concerned about how and when to include government regulatory policies into their production processes and product designs, and within their value chains. To ensure their legitimacy, both manufacturers and systems integrators need to heed the advice of these agencies. This is because the component parts and solutions for developing the SPV systems, such as solar modules, inverters, cabling, and mounting structures, are sourced from local and international manufacturers and are always under regulatory and certification scrutiny.

Informal network institutions, such as industry associations, also come under scrutiny and face public doubt over their legitimacy. These associations serve as a collective voice for the industry, and their role typically includes providing a reliable flow of information to the stakeholders they represent. One such association is the Malaysian Photovoltaic Industry Association, a non-profit organisation dedicated to representing the entire solar energy industry in Malaysia. Its members comprise a broad spectrum of systems integrators and manufacturers from first-tier companies to smaller firms. In their role as an advocate, it maintains strong relationships with both manufacturers and the various regulatory agencies and actively works to ensure the legitimacy of the Association and the members it represents. Part of this legitimacy stems from the number and strength of the relationships it has with first-tier firms. From less than 30 members in 2013, the Association has now grown to more than 100 members.

As concerns grow for more high-value-added activities in the industry, manufacturers have also begun to work collaboratively with universities and research institutes to research and develop new SPV-related technologies. However, academic engineers do not necessarily have all the skills needed to bring a product to market, highlighting the need for stronger ties between research institutes and businesses. This is a mutually beneficial relationship as, in the absence of such ties, the technical know-how needed to transform the value chain is further undermined. There is, however, increasing evidence that researchers are reciprocally engaging with the industry to access, learn, and share hands-on knowledge. These relationships both increase the legitimacy of both parties and contribute to sustainable production practices. First-tier manufacturers, in particular, are under growing pressure to collaborate with academia, particularly on research and development. One senior sales manager from a multinational manufacturing subsidiary remarked:

> We have collaboration with the Solar Energy Research Institute [a research centre of a university in Malaysia] doing research and development. Our research and development sector in the Penang factory is jointly set up with a local university. It is still at a very premature stage.

Moreover, as the SPV industry develops, access to finance becomes crucial. However, concerns remain over risk exposure and the unfamiliarity many manufacturers have with delivering financial returns on heavy capital outlays. Hence, commercial banks have been somewhat reluctant to offer loans. This lack of financial support has seen many projects fail to even launch. Despite being wary of financing solar energy projects, and green technology in general, some quasi-government banks, such as the Malaysian Debt Venture, have been willing to assume a banking role. The Malaysian Debt Venture is Malaysia's leading technology financier, and is a wholly-owned subsidiary of the Ministry of Finance. Due to its quasi-government status, it does not compete with commercial banks. Instead, it commits to upholding Malaysia's pledge to reduce carbon emissions and lead the development of green technologies.

Counter to this claim, SEDA's (2017. p 29) recent report on the role of banks notes:

> It was anticipated that participants in the market would have been able to obtain the bank loans needed to finance their projects on account of the high degree of security for investors [as the field of renewable energy was still new to the local market during the earlier days], the problems faced by renewable energy developers [i.e., manufacturers and systems integrators] was not the lack of funds in the capital market, but the lack of skills within the financial institutions to evaluate the applications and provide the fund expeditiously.

The banks' lack of skill is not helped by a general reluctance to offer such loans. One systems integrator explains:

> Commercial banks are not interested in giving this kind of solar loan. Firstly, they don't understand [the nature of this business]. Secondly, they have never tried and they are very reserved [in giving solar loans]. They are focused on giving out housing, car, and business loans. They do not want to open a new portfolio, and they are not willing to change. This is a limitation. A lot of projects fail to kick-start because they are unable to get solar loans.

In other words, sustainable development within the industry and, by extension, sustainable production practices not only require access to quantifiable resources, such as funding, but also skills and training to evaluate the financial viability of projects.

6.5.2 Project Management Sustainability

Beyond the roles of formal and informal institutions at a macro-institutional level, numerous stakeholders undertake technical, financial, market, and social roles and risks associated with commissioning and successfully completing projects at a meso level. As is typical in any SPV project, the systems integrators take centre stage, from identifying relevant consumers, whether they be retail or wholesale, to liaison and consulting. Once a project is conceived, systems integrators undertake the engineering, procurement, and construction tasks. They also draw on the relational capital networks they have built up through previous successful projects, including manufacturers, suppliers, and investors. Previous projects serve as testimony of the integrators' ability and capacity to complete a new project within a given timeframe, which is useful for a smooth approval process. Accordingly, an integrator's relationship network is critical in addressing, and perhaps circumventing, any factors that may present obstacles. Acting on behalf of the consumers, they then submit an approval application to SEDA and apply for tax incentives from MIDA and the Malaysia Green Technology Corporation. Submitted applications undergo a rigorous evaluation by SEDA to ensure the project is both financially and technically feasible. Once the application is approved, the project is commissioned.

Malaysia's power company also plays a key supportive role, especially in programs that sell solar energy to the grid. Relationships between systems integrators and the power company develop spontaneously, either through repeated, relatively straightforward exchanges, or during installation, thus ensuring systems integrators build an SPV system that complies with the power company's standards and requirements. As SPV systems are installed on roofs, approval by the state government and municipal council is required and must be sought in instances where the owner of the building does not own the land. Therefore, the link between land ownership and the approved installation is often complex and may involve lawyers, who draft documents and have strong ties to the municipal council land office.

An important proxy measure of a sustainable SPV industry is the number of successfully-commissioned local projects, including the size (wattage) of the installed projects. Successfully completed SPV projects capture each network actor's contribution to the sustainable development of the industry and help to forge their present and future pathways to legitimacy. While the process of commissioning and managing solar projects have a linear appearance on the surface, sustainability in the SPV industry is anything but linear. Inter-organisational cooperation, trust, and commitment among these stakeholders is essential to securing capital, gaining approval for projects, and producing economically sustainable outputs.

6.5.3   A Network of Inputs, Outputs, and Sustainability Performance Measures

From an industry-as-a-network perspective, sustainable production practices emerge out of a process of change and interactions between institutions such as SEDA, the Standards and Industrial Institute of Malaysia, the Malaysia Green Technology Corporation, industry associations, research institutes, manufacturers, and systems integrators. These institutions are captured in Table 6.2.

In Malaysia's developing SPV industry, sustainable production choices are driven in part by the perceived set of network relationships and exchanges that capture their legitimacy within the limits of past, current, and future expectations. While there may be policy changes, these networks will continue to both facilitate and inhibit changes to sustainable production practices. This, in turn, will further legitimise or delegitimise the respective roles of these institutions. Stakeholders must therefore be willing to discuss their roles, benefits, and interests. Businesses, in particular, must

Table 6.2 Significant institutions and their roles

Key actors	Role and descriptions
Ministry of Energy, Green Technology and Water	Provides strategic direction by planning and formulating policies, regulatory frameworks, and programs involving green technology
Energy Commission	The statutory body established under the Energy Commission Act 2001 responsible for regulating the energy sector—specifically, the electricity and piped-gas supply industries in Peninsular Malaysia and Sabah
Sustainable Energy Development Authority (SEDA)	The statutory body formed under the Sustainable Energy Development Authority Act 2011 [Act 726]/Renewable Energy Act 2011 [Act 725] to administer and manage the FiT project
Malaysian Investment Development Authority (MIDA)	Promotes the manufacturing and services sectors on behalf of Malaysia. It assists foreign companies with investments and/or establishing factories in Malaysia. It also implements its projects as a joint venture partner
The Malaysia Green Technology Corporation	Acts as a catalyst for green technology deployment under the purview of the ministry, as a strategic engine for socio-economic growth. It oversees the Green Technology Financing Scheme, which provides easier access to financing for any project that meets the green technology criteria and the funder's requirements
Tenaga Nasional Berhad	Generates and distributes electricity to consumers
Malaysian Photovoltaic Industry Association	A non-profit industry association dedicated to solar energy serving as a representative for the entire SPV industry in Malaysia
Systems integrators	Their responsibilities include engineering (designing, structuring, planning), procurement (feasibility, financial funds and returns), construction (installation), and commissioning (testing, operation, and maintenance)
The Standards and Industrial Research Institute of Malaysia	An industrial research and technology organisation in Malaysia, wholly-owned by the Ministry of Finance. Its role is to aid research and technology innovation, especially in the private sector, and most importantly, to develop SPV industry-related products, services, and quality standards

(continued)

Table 6.2 (continued)

Key actors	Role and descriptions
Manufacturers	Endorsed recognised local manufacturers/assemblers of SPV modules, inverters, and other SPV components. These manufacturers are eligible for local bonuses
State governments and municipal councils	Responsible for approving installations and other land matters
Education and research institutions	Research and development of SPV-related technology and developing curriculums to train a highly-skilled SPV-aware labour force
Banks	Financing consumers/investors on SPV installations
Insurance companies	Insuring SPV systems, e.g. performance, risk mitigation

restructure and integrate economic, social, environmental, and political practices to reflect sustainability. The crux is whether a network view of a legitimation strategy offers a fresh and useful perspective to reconcile their inputs, outputs, and sustainability performance measures. Such a view would have to emphasize the role of context, the stakeholders' ways of making sense of that context, and how they ought to be reconciling tensions.

To ensure sustainable production practices, network stakeholders must reconcile these tensions through interactive relationships. However, these relationships vary in strength, as summarised in Fig. 6.1.

For example, systems integrators have strong relationships with the local and multinational manufacturers that produce SPV components and systems. It should also come as no surprise that systems integrators and manufacturers have strong relationships with government agencies in view of their accreditation, regulatory, and oversight roles. However, relationships with research institutes are only starting to develop. Manufacturers are collaborating more with universities and research centres. The government is beginning to offer local and international grants for research and development and marketing collaborations activities. Additionally, government agencies are partnering with manufacturers to finance SPV projects.

Thus, at the meso level, the network of firms in the SPV industry holds a range of heterogeneous resources to undertake practice transformation toward sustainability—changes that may or may not complement every role and firm. Yet business

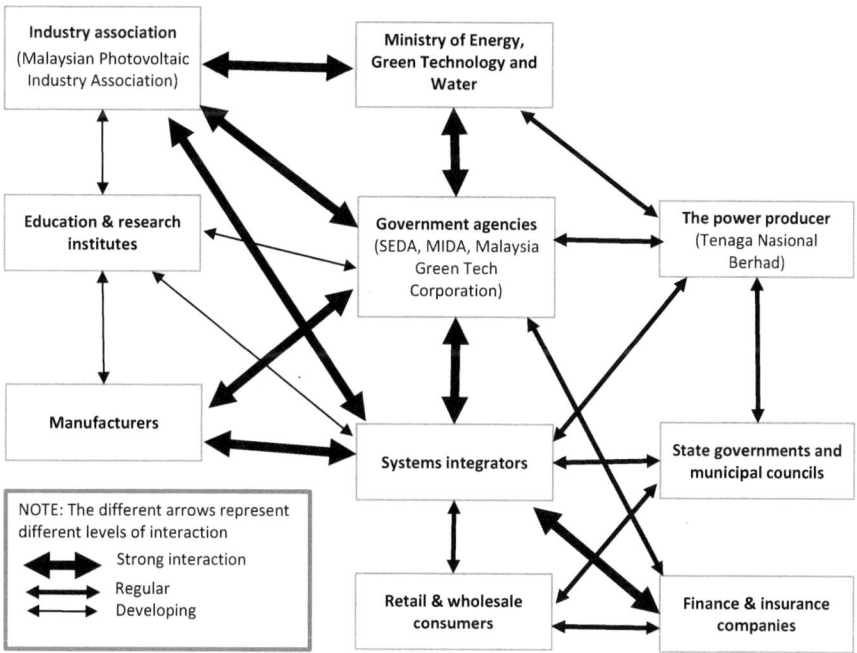

Fig. 6.1 The network of stakeholders in Malaysia's SPV industry

sustainability and sustainable production practices must be continually validated, particularly in view of changing reforms. The issue of legitimacy is, therefore, central to addressing what constitutes sustainable production practices. A business's survival and its licence to operate depends on its legitimacy (Suchman 1995). The need to achieve network legitimacy, therefore, presents a quandary for those involved in the Malaysian SPV industry, whose very existence depends on how well they work with others in the network and how others view their contributions.

It is also apparent that sustainable production activities are constantly being transformed as new resources are defined, and as new production practices are institutionalised. The government plays a major role in institutionalising these practices through its reform policies. In tandem, there is an expectation among manufacturers and service providers that these policies should be made as explicit as possible if formal regulative legitimacy is to be recognised. This view was reflected in the words of several stakeholders:

> The most important thing is policy. Various agencies are driving [the industry] but at one point, there is a limitation [as to what these agencies can or cannot do]. Without the policy, then it is not going to work. (solar panel manufacturer)

> I say we trust the government. Many people asked since FiT is finishing soon, what are you going to do? I say, "It is okay, something will come up." (systems integrator)

> NEM and LSS are some sort of bridging programs. We need many programs until the market becomes independent. (systems integrator)

6.6 The Impact of Sustainable Production Practices on the Value Chain

Throughout its development during the 2000s, the SPV industry faced government pressures to engage in a range of value-adding activities. Even though manufacturers in the industry were relatively young, increasing global and regional competition and international regulations forced these manufacturers to adopt strategic and sustainable production practices. However, domestic regulatory agencies now need to turn their attention to bringing local standards in line with international standards to continue attracting international investments. But while Malaysia's emerging SPV industry is in need of foreign direct investments (FDI), and is ranked highly in the world in terms of output, its reliance on FDIs also means that, so far, it has employed relatively unskilled workers and typically engages in little technological development. The focus decidedly remains on low-end manufacturing and assembly processes and low-value-adding activities. There are many gaps to bridge: the divide between domestic savings and foreign investment; importing the latest technology and management know-how from developed countries, and playing a more important role in rapid economic growth in developing countries (Mottaleb and Kalirajan 2010). Yet the FDIs in Malaysia's SPV industry seem to have reduced the performance of local firms to reallocating workers, managers, and capital elsewhere. The

SPV industry will eventually have to deal with the values and tensions associated with FDIs, internationalisation, and export earnings, as they dovetail with the sustainable production practices that add higher value and lay a path for developing a national SPV industry. Multinational subsidiaries face ongoing and changing local economic and social influences while trying to acclimatise to the local institutional culture. The role of these subsidiaries will require special relationships based on commitment and in-depth understanding of the duality of their practices (Deligonul et al. 2013).

The particular constraints and opportunities surrounding FDIs also appear to have enhanced the activities of local manufacturers and assemblers that sit alongside clusters of multinational subsidiaries. These activities are typically limited to a set of value-chain activities in one sector—the manufacturing of solar panels. What we are witnessing now is a 'module assembly' business model among solar manufacturers. But with national policies, such as Electrical and Electronics 1.0 and 2.0, emphasizing the need for regions to specialise in particular components (e.g., semiconductors, solar panel design, etc.), it is no longer feasible to focus on one sector without considering the impact that development has on other sectors. After all, they share common technologies and production processes. Opportunities for cross-fertilisation could translate into opportunities for specialisation, such as capacity building, high-value-adding activities, or improving productivity. As MIDA (2015, p. 24) puts it:

> A more structured approach [is needed] to develop local industry players in targeted market niches of the solar PV components and supporting industries by giving them a level playing field, developing their capability, decrease their cost, increase quality of products in order to build a stable and cost-effective solar PV value chain and solar cluster in the mid-to-long term.

Finally, while FDIs decidedly focus on exports, low-end manufacturing, and low-value assembly, tensions have also surfaced from Malaysia's drive to become a developed economy and move up the global value chain. Technological "lock-in", including technical interrelatedness, economies of scale, and the quasi-irreversibility of investments exacerbates these tensions (David 1985). Notwithstanding the high technological expertise of local manufacturers and their familiarity with the local value chain, any planned changes would need to be sensitive to their current contributions. The SPV industry, however, is unique in a number of key respects that might impact on these changes. These include: assuring returns on technological investment, high switching costs, and a lack of human capital. Without safety nets to ameliorate these factors, companies have been reluctant to undertake their own research and development. Rather, they have tended to focus on absorbing external technology and know-how and engaging in low-value manufacturing to ensure their sustainability. Implementing and adopting innovations from developed countries is cheaper, faster, and less risky.

MIDA takes a different view, referring to the singular concern of over-reliance on imported raw materials in a largely incomplete SPV supply chain. To create a sustainable and competitive industry, MIDA (2015, p 23) explains:

It is vital to increase the rate of self-supply within the local ecosystem. Dependency on external resources, besides impacting the cost factor, will also expose the industry to various uncertainties and render it more vulnerable to risks. In fact, both manufacturers (module supply chain and supporting industry) and systems integrators expressed concern for the need to increase local material supply and to strengthen the local supply chain.

In practice, this an important factor for the nation's SPV industry to consider when planning an overhaul of existing sustainable production practices. Adding to these tensions is the need to strike a balance between a domestic market-driven expansion and export-led growth, and between low-value and high-value manufacturing—and all this amid the backdrop of changing reform policies. In this context, an industry with domestic market-driven expansion that engages in low-value manufacturing, as is the case now with the SPV industry, is more likely to absorb external technologies than industries with export-led growth and a high-value manufacturing agenda. However, a growing, regional, and global market in renewable energy now offers Malaysia tremendous opportunities to move up the value chain and further differentiate its contribution to this global concern. The shift toward value-added activities in renewable energy is now increasingly evident through various tax incentives, targeted R&D development projects, and incentives to accelerate local solar installations. MIDA's attempt to promote the Domestic Investment Strategic Fund is one of several such initiatives.

According to MIDA (2015, p. 72):

[The] Domestic Investment Strategic Fund is inducing the shift to high value-added, high-technology, knowledge and innovation based industries by enabling Malaysian companies to strengthen their absorptive capacity. Through building capacity to participative in the global supply chain, strengthening training and research and development, promoting the acquisition and acquiring international certification, Malaysian companies (including solar manufacturers) are steadfastly making their way up the value chain. The fund provides matching grants for expenditure on research and development, training, upgrading facilities, licensing of new technology and obtaining international standards.

6.7 Production Processes, Output, and Sustainability Through Local Consumption

Malaysia is increasingly using solar power as an alternative energy source but, nationally, SPV installations and consumption remain low. This has not always been the case. Under the FiT policy, local adoption grew exponentially because people could produce and on-sell the electricity to the government. However, the introduction of the NEM policy disrupted this growth. While not as successful as FiT, the little growth there was mostly involved industrial customers.

Interestingly, the FiT policy was adopted due to its success in Germany, which now leads the world with the most dynamic SPV local electricity market on the globe. Other countries, such as Australia, Brazil, China, Taiwan, most European countries, and some regions in the United States, have also seen some success (Tenaga Nasional Berhad 2012). The market in China (world number 2) is noteworthy in that it has made a conscious effort to accelerate home SPV installations by addressing the financial and regulatory barriers that hampered deployment.

In March 2009, a national SPV subsidy program to promote the use of MBIPV building materials was introduced. SEDA (2017, p. 28), in "An Account of Developing Malaysia's Renewable Energy Resources", reports that among the lessons learned were:

> Besides taking three years to get FiT off the ground, one of the main problem[s] in its introduction was the readiness of policy makers to work with the local ecosystem. A good policy is one that benefits the citizens, the government, and the industry. The main goal is to acquire buy-ins from network operators/Distribution Licensees.

It is apparent that the government, the private sector, and users face multidimensional economic, social, and policy barriers to the sustainable development of renewable energy. A review of recent studies on the adoption of solar energy consumption shows the following:

- The major barriers are limited information about renewable energy technologies, a lack of awareness, and limited private sector engagement. Suggestions for improvement include: increasing policy support from the government to make information more accessible to mass users; providing economic incentives to investors and users; and promoting small community-based renewable energy projects (Alam et al. 2016).
- In a 2018 survey of 603 businesses, 77% do not use solar energy, 16% plan to use it, and only 7% do. Of the 589 CEOs who responded, 73% do not use solar energy at home, 15% do, and 12% are likely to use it in the future (Vistage 2018).

While conscious efforts are being made to accelerate SPV installations by addressing the regulatory and financial barriers that might have hampered deployment, its success has been limited by changes in industry reforms that create ambiguities in deployment policies. Tax and financial incentives and government efforts to attract FDI to promote sustainable production practices have significantly stimulated the development of a sustainable industry, but issues relating to growth in local installations and consumption seem to have been ignored. What is at stake is the dynamic interplay of several elements as they bear on sustainable production practices. The effects of the nation's core cost advantage in SPV cell manufacturing seem to be decoupled from attempts to promote greater use of renewable energy. Local installation programs that could emulate existing technology and contribute to sustainable production practices among domestic and MNCs subsidiaries have also been ignored. In view of the identified facilitators and inhibitors of local consumption growth, what then, is the impact of these programs in fuelling investments that could lead to higher economic production output of the SPV industry, investments in technology, and the pursuit of high-value-adding activities in the SPV value chain?

6.8 Epilogue

Industry sustainability and sustainable production practices are structured according to the interdependence of actors and based on stakeholders' expectations. The challenge for an emerging SPV industry is to understand the impact of the sustainability practices by various actors. The ability to cope with these practices requires a balance between the demands placed on businesses through institutional reform policies and the specific targets or constituents to which the organisation must appear legitimate. Malaysia's strong global ranking in the solar market perhaps vindicates any shortcomings the nation may have in successfully developing and sustaining sustainable production practices, reform policies notwithstanding. However, the presence of ongoing tensions relating to a sustainable reduction in manufacturing cost, investments in new technology, access to financial support, and increasing competition among regional economies for direct foreign investment, pose major challenges.

List of acronyms:

Acronyms	Descriptions
FDI	Foreign direct investment
FiT	Feed-in-Tariff
LCSP	Lowell Centre for Sustainable Production
LSS	Large-scale solar
MBIPV	Malaysian Building Integrated Photovoltaic
MIDA	Malaysian Investment Development Authority
MW	Megawatts
NEM	Net Energy Metering
SEDA	Sustainable Energy Development Authority
SPV	Solar photovoltaic

6.9   Teaching Notes

6.9.1   Synopsis of the Case

The case study explores the role of institutions, their effectiveness, and their legitimacy in developing sustainable production practices over time. Set against the backdrop of government reforms in Malaysia's emerging SPV industry, developing these practices requires a combination of particular macro-institutional conditions and policies. Although the new policies provide wide-ranging opportunities for many businesses, they also impose constraints on how businesses conduct sustainable production practices. Institutional theory points to the role of several factors in legitimising these practices, such as reducing uncertainty and information costs, pathways to transfer solar technology and knowledge, and providing better financial support. Institutional theory also calls into question how a wide array of actors at the macro-institutional level are able to conduct sustainable production practices. This question has two implications for those within the network:

1. How does sustainable production emerge over time and, by extension, what are: (a) the roles of the network actors; and (b) the actors' effectiveness in driving business sustainability?
2. How do actors' relational dynamics legitimise or delegitimise sustainable production practices?

The case study explores these and other questions by tracing four key sustainable production practice indicators from the perspective of both institutional and network theory.

6.9.2   Target Learning Group

- Level of study—BA and particularly MBA/Ph.D. students.
- Subject areas—sustainability; economic policy; regional development; business networks.

6.9.3   Learning Objectives

- Understand the roles of institutions, critique their effectiveness, and, by extension, their legitimacy in institutionalising sustainable production practices over time.
- Analyse sustainability production practices using a combination of institutional and network theory.
- Distinguish contextually relevant sustainable production indicators and how they dovetail with macro-institutional conditions and policies.

- Construct a network map and identify its key actors, resource ownership, and the activities each actor undertakes with respect to their individual and collective roles in institutionalising sustainable production practices.

6.9.3.1 Key Issues

- Key institutional roles in transforming sustainable production practices and resources over time, i.e., Who does what, with whom, why, and when?
- Reform policies and their impact on the sustained currency of these activities and on various institutions' legitimacy over time.
- Sustainable FDIs, technology, low-end manufacturing, and assembly activities, including reliance on imported raw materials in local SPV value chains.
- The paradox of the nation's global challenge of the world SPV market but low domestic SPV installations and consumption.

6.9.3.2 Theoretical Concepts

- Formal and informal institutions; institutional reform policies; institutions' effectiveness and legitimacy; network actors, activities, and resources; networks of relational ties; institutionalising sustainable production practices; and sustainable value chain.

6.9.4 Reading Activities

6.9.4.1 Pre-reading

Read the case study in detail. Under each subheading, identify the keywords and themes and establish their connections.

- From Fig. 6.1:
  - Identify the different types of formal and informal institutions.
  - Understand these institutions' roles and their responsibilities in institutionalising sustainable production practices.

- The case study reports four indicators of sustainable production practices. Relate these practices to the roles of these institutions.
- Examine and understand Fig. 6.2 in the "Additional material" section below, which shows how an SPV system typically functions.

6.9.4.2 In-Class

Skim through the case and summarise no more than five key points. These should include:

- the production and consumption of renewable energy, particularly solar power in reducing global carbon emission;
- the major global SPV producing countries, Malaysia's competitiveness, and its value-adding contributions in the local and global value chain;
- the indicators of contextually-significant sustainable production practices and institutional macro conditions;
- the roles of institutions, particularly government agencies, in institutionalising sustainable production practices, especially at the early stages of industry development; and
- how a combined institutional and network theory offers a fresh perspective in understanding sustainable production practices.

Pay attention to Table 6.1, and distinguish the differences between the FiT, NEM, and LSS policies, and especially:

- the role of contextual factors or triggers in shaping these policies;
- their specific objectives, including their compatibility; and
- their implications in the development of a sustainable SPV industry.

At the end of the lesson, three key takeaways (or conclusions) should be presented to the students:

- Understanding the roles of government, business, and non-business actors is key to developing sustainable production practices.
- Formal and informal institutions and significant network actors must be willing to monitor and revise their policies, business models, and the underlying business processes to ensure the sustainability of the SPV industry.
- Apply a combined institutional and network theory to analyse and identify sustainable production practices.

6.9.5 Discussion Activities

The following questions could be discussed either in the form of a group presentation prior to a group written submission, or as a general classroom discussion prior to an individual written submission.

- What are some of the key formal institutions that oversee the development and deployment of key reform policies? How effective have they been? Support your position.
  (*Discussion points:* formal institutions, roles, policies, effectiveness, i.e., legitimacy)

- What are the roles of associations, banks, universities, and consumers in institutionalising sustainable production and consumption practices? How effective have they been? Support your position.
  (*Discussion points:* informal institutions, roles, legitimacy)
- What are some of the key challenges facing the nation's emerging SPV industry? Focus on: (a) the local and global value chain; (b) the role of FDIs; (c) reliance on foreign technology and raw materials; and (d) low domestic consumption of solar energy.
  (*Discussion points:* value chains, low-end manufacturing and assembly, FDIs, technology)
- "A combined institutional and network theory offers unique insights in understanding how sustainable production practices could be institutionalised." Do you agree or disagree with this statement? Support your position.
  (*Discussion points:* market-as-stimulus-response exchanges (i.e., 4P's), institutional theory, markets-as-networks, institutionalising practices)
- "Institutional policies without the support of key network actors would result in failure, rendering such policies illegitimate in charting the sustainable development of the solar industry." Do you agree or disagree with this statement? State your position and explain why.
  (*Discussion points:* heterogeneous networks of actors, owning resources others value, resource transformation activities).

Additional material
See Fig. 6.2.

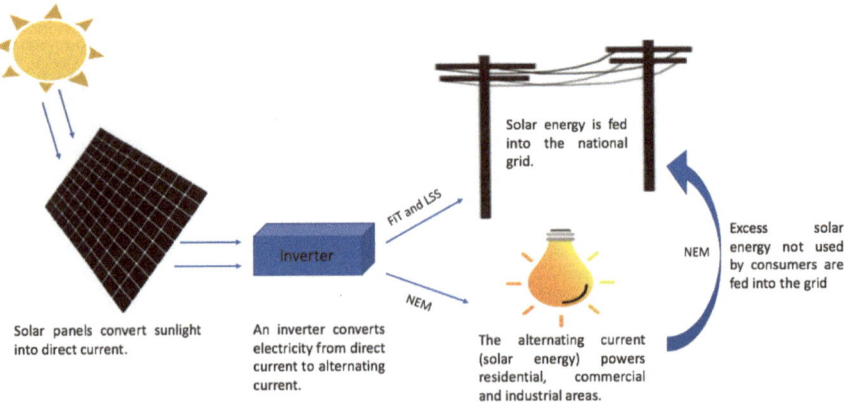

Fig. 6.2 The typical functioning of an SPV system

References

Alam SS, Nor NFM, Ahmad M, Hashim NHN (2016) A survey on renewable energy development in Malaysia: current status, problems and prospects. Environ Clim Technol 17(1):5–15

Bernama (2016, April 22) Malaysia re-pledges to achieve 45 percent CO_2 emission by 2030. New Straits Times. Retrieved from https://www.nst.com.my/news/2016/04/140725/malaysia-re-pledges-achieve-45-cent-co2-emission-2030

David PA (1985) Clio and the economics of QWERTY. Am Econ Rev 75(2):332–337

Deligonul S, Elg U, Cavusgil E, Ghauri PN (2013) Developing strategic supplier networks: an institutional perspective. J Bus Res 66(4):506–515

DiMaggio PJ, Powell W (1983) The iron cage revisited: institutional isomorphism and collective rationality in organisational fields. Am Sociol Rev 48(2):147–160

Fernandez-Sanchez G, Rodriquez-Lopez F (2010) A methodology to identify sustainability indicators in construction project management—application to infrastructure projects in Spain. Ecol Ind 10(6):1193–1201

Håkansson H, Snehota I (1989) No business is an island: the network concept of business strategy. Scand J Manag 5(3):187–200

Håkansson H, Ford D, Gadde LE, Snehota I, Waluszewski A (2009) Business in networks. Wiley, United Kingdom

Lowell Centre for Sustainable Production (LCSP) (2011) What is sustainable development? Retrieved from https://www.uml.edu/research/lowell-center/

Malaysia Investment Development Authority (MIDA) (2015) Malaysia investment performance report: driving sustainable growth. Retrieved from http://www.mida.gov.my/home/administrator/system_files/modules/photo/uploads/20160301100315_MIPR2015-2.pdf

Mottaleb KA, Kalirajan K (2010) Determinants of foreign direct investments in developing countries. A comparative analysis. J Appl Econ Res 4(4):369–404

Performance Management and Delivery Unit (2014) Economic transformation programme annual report 2014. Retrieved from https://govdocs.sinarproject.org/documents/prime-ministers-department/performance-management-delivery-unit

Ron AJ (1998) Sustainable production: the ultimate result of a continuous improvement. Int J Prod Econ 56–57:99–110

Scott WR (1995) Institutions and organisations. Sage, Thousands Oaks

SEDA, Sustainable Energy Development Authority (2016a) SEDA annual report 2016

SEDA, Sustainable Energy Development Authority (2016b) National survey report of PV power applications in Malaysia 2016

SEDA, Sustainable Energy Development Authority (2017) Transitioning the nation towards sustainable energy Malaysia—an account of developing Malaysia's RE resources, vol 1, no 3, pp 1–60

Suchman MC (1995) Managing legitimacy: strategic and institutional approaches. Acad Manage Rev 20(3):571–610

Tenaga Nasional Berhad (2012) Moving on track towards customer demands. Tenaga Link 1:1–20

Tenaga Nasional Berhad (2016) Towards a brighter future driving sustainable and efficient energy. Tenaga Link 1:1–44

Vistage-Mier (2018) 2Q 2018 Vistage-Mier CEO confidence index 2018. Retrieved from http://vistage.com.my/ceo-confidence-index/

Dr. Brian Low is currently an Associate Professor in Marketing and Head of the Marketing Discipline with Monash University, Malaysia. He was previously on the faculty at Western Sydney University, Australia. Brian's research interests are in the areas of Business-to-Business Marketing, and more specifically in industrial networks and economic geography. His background includes marketing management experience that involved market research services, marketing planning, channel management, and product management. Brian holds a Bachelor and a Master degree in Commerce (Hons.) from the University of Auckland, New Zealand, and a DBA from the University of Western Sydney, Australia.

Dr. Stephanie Kay Ann Cheah is a Marketing Lecturer in the School of Business at Monash University, Malaysia. She teaches Principles of Marketing, Retail Marketing, Business Marketing and Marketing Strategy. Her current research interests include business networks, industrial marketing and macro-marketing, particularly on policy evolutions.

Chapter 7
Sustainable Tourism Development and Stakeholder Analysis: The Freycinet Lodge Case in Tasmania

Peter Dixon and Leigh N. Wood

Abstract Tasmania is a small island state of Australia with approximately half a million people. The Tasmanian government would like to encourage tourism to improve employment opportunities for its people, and one popular national park in Tasmania's eastern region has been earmarked as a destination with the potential. However, to increase visitor numbers, both accommodation and the park's facilities will need to be improved. How do we do this? How do we balance the needs of the government, the developer, and the environmental value of the national park? This case study presents the views of three stakeholders. The teaching materials require participants to develop their own stakeholder plan and to investigate stakeholder tools.

Keywords Tourism · Development · Environment · Sustainability · Finance · Stakeholder analysis

Peter Dixon is a non-executive Director of the RACT. The views expressed in this chapter are his own and not necessarily those of the RACT.

P. Dixon
University of Tasmania, Launceston, Australia

L. N. Wood (✉)
Macquarie University, Sydney, Australia
e-mail: leigh.wood@mq.edu.au

© Springer Nature Singapore Pte Ltd. 2020
L. Wood et al. (eds.), *Industry and Higher Education*,
https://doi.org/10.1007/978-981-15-0874-5_7

7.1   The Case at a Glance

Key concepts	• Stakeholder theory and analysis • Multiple perspectives business cases • Environment vs development • The role of government
Level of study	• Undergraduate, capstone, and postgraduate
Subject areas	• Tourism, human resources, finance, public sector management, marketing, and media

Graduate capabilities

Graduate outcomes	%
Critical thinking	20
Problem solving	20
Teamwork	20
Communication	20
Ethical thinking	
Sustainability	20
Total	**100%**

Time required	• Out-of-class preparation: 120 min • In-class discussion: 60 min • Out-of-class assignments: 120 min • Longer assessments are also offered
Activity type	• Team-based with individual components • Work-integrated learning
Additional materials	• **Royal Automobile Club of Tasmania** https://www.ract.com.au • **Freycinet Lodge** http://www.freycinetlodge.com.au

7.2 Introduction and Background

This case study on the Freycinet Lodge concerns a proposal for a tourist development in a national park from the perspectives of three key stakeholders.

Australia is a country in southern hemisphere close to Asia. Tourism is its third most important industry and is an area with strong potential for growth. One of its states, Tasmania, is a small island located at the bottom of the country (Fig. 7.1). Tasmania has beautiful scenery, clean water, healthy food and wine, and is a safe place to visit.

In 2017, the Tasmanian state government announced $4 million in funding to create and support tourism infrastructure across the region through two initiatives: the Tourism Demand-Driver Infrastructure Fund and the Regional Tourism Infrastructure and Innovation Fund. Both funds were dedicated to boosting tourism expenditure in the State and open to grants for infrastructure projects that would bring more visitors to Tasmania and/or improve visitor experiences. The government's target is to attract 1.5 million visitors to Tasmania every year by 2020.

Tasmania is a small state with a population of 520,000. In the past, it has relied on large projects to support economic growth. The most notable of these was a government-supported 'hydro-industrialisation' project, which involved constructing hydro-electric infrastructure to supply industry with power at attractive rates. That avenue was largely closed in the 1980s due to environmental concerns and, as a result, no further hydro-electric development has been undertaken. Another large project was the Tamar Valley pulp mill to exploit the State's timber reserves. At the

Fig. 7.1 Map of Australia with Tasmania located in the bottom right

time of construction, the endeavour was subject to intense environmental opposition, which ultimately led to the demise of the proposal.

Tourism has since emerged as a key industry for the state with visitor numbers and visitor expenditure showing consistent growth year-on-year. However, in some respects, the ability to develop tourist attractions is limited by preservation mandates. For example, much of Tasmania's coast is protected through the National Parks system, so development is regulated by the state government. As of 2016, 51% of Tasmania's land had some form of preservation classification. About 42% of this area is managed by the Tasmanian Parks and Wildlife Service. Marine protected areas cover about 7.9% of the state's waters.

In 2014, the Royal Automobile Club of Tasmania Ltd ('RACT') diversified its operations into tourism with the acquisition of tourism properties and associated activities at Strahan (on the west coast), Cradle Mountain (in the Central Highlands), and at Coles Bay on the east coast (Fig. 7.2). Coles Bay is situated wholly within the boundaries of the Freycinet National Park and includes the acclaimed Wineglass Bay.

To contribute to the cost of adding more accommodation to the 'Freycinet Lodge' facility at Coles Bay (Fig. 7.3), the RACT has been successful in securing a grant from the government's Tourism Fund. Part of this proposal includes expanding the footprint of RACT's lease in the national park to allow for the development.

Fig. 7.2 Coles Bay, East Coast, Tasmania. *Photo* Allan Sharp (https://www.flickr.com/photos/97920783@N05)

Fig. 7.3 Freycinet Lodge, Coles Bay, Tasmania. *Source* Freycinet Lodge (http://www.freycinetlodge.com.au)

To allow for this expansion, the government proposed that the Freycinet National Park Management Plan be amended to remove the restriction on building new accommodation outside of existing leases. The amendment would also give the Minister unlimited power to issue new licences and leases for similar projects. In other words, subject to approval by the Minister, the Coles Bay Zone would be open to further built developments by anyone, not just the RACT.

The RACT proposal raises the following questions:

- Should developing tourist accommodation within the Freycinet National Park beyond that already permitted be allowed? And, if so, on what terms?
- What are the legitimate interests of various stakeholders in assessing whether or not commercial development should be allowed within National Parks?

7.3 Perspective of the RACT

RACT is a member-based organisation with about 190,000 members that offers services to a large proportion of Tasmania's population. These services include roadside assistance, driver training, insurance, travel, automotive repairs, and, more recently, tourism.

Currently, the potential for further development of Freycinet Lodge is limited. The RACT only leases 11 ha, which are ostensibly fully built, and the land is completely surrounded by the Freycinet National Park.

RACT argues that extending the Lodge will not adversely affect the environment because:

- The area of expansion is relatively insignificant, and its use will be no different from what the lease already permits.
- The architectural design will be sensitive, have no visual impact, and adhere to the requirements set out in the Management Plan.

The RACT is aware of opposition by the conservation lobby to its proposal. Therefore, the options open to the Club are:

- Maintain its position and continue with the development;
- Restrict further development to the currently leased area only; or
- Abandon the proposal.

7.4   Perspective of the Tasmanian State Government

The Tasmanian government announced that an expression of interest submitted by the RACT had been approved and that $AUD 1 million in funding would be available to assist with the development of the Freycinet Lodge. Part of the expression of interest included an expansion of the lease boundaries to allow for the development of 12 cabins and 12 serviced sites for motor homes.

Accordingly, the Freycinet National Park Management Plan would need to be amended to remove the current restrictions on building new accommodation outside of existing leases. Hence, the government proposed that the Minister should have the power to issue licences or leases for newly built accommodation without limits on that power. As such, the government's proposal does not merely help the RACT achieve its goals; it opens up the Coles Bay Zone to further development by anyone subject to ministerial approval. The proposal was advertised for public comment, and many representations were received protesting the change.

The government's growth strategy is a key priority. Through growth, businesses can innovate and expand, create jobs, help to build the state's economy, and secure a sustainable future. The kick-start to the plan came from money formerly allocated to another development project (the Cadbury factory in Hobart), which was partly subsidised by the Commonwealth Government. When that project fell through, the funds were diverted into the growth strategy and a new incentive scheme called the Jobs and Investment Fund. The strategy is inextricably linked to the stellar performance of the tourism sector, which has demonstrated clear year-on-year growth against almost all indicators. For the year ended December 2017, total visitors, total nights, visitor expenditure, interstate visitors, and international visitors all showed sustained increases. Importantly, visits to the east coast region of Tasmania increased by 10% (Tourism Tasmania 2017).

7.5 Perspective of the Environmentalists

Opposition to the government's proposal to amend the boundaries of the Freycinet National Park was initially led by a local group, the Freycinet Action Network, which largely comprises local residents. Mainstream conservation groups soon became involved—notably the Tasmanian Conservation Trust, BirdLife Tasmania, the Wilderness Society, and the Tasmanian Greens.

The major arguments of the conservation lobby include:

- The project exploits public land for commercial gain.
- The proposed amendments to the Freycinet National Park Management Plan would give the Minister unlimited licence to approve further development of the entire Coles Bay Zone.
- The government's consultation document only justified the changes in terms of the proposed Freycinet Lodge development but does not address the full implications of the changes, thus setting a misleading and dangerous precedent.
- There is widespread opposition to the proposal as evidenced by the 463 separate representations submitted against it.
- Limiting the amendment to one proponent could create an unfair advantage and might lead to further requests being made, thus possibly threatening the status of the Freycinet area as a National Park.
- Further developments to land within the park's boundaries should be subject to both competitive tender, public consultation, and zoning controls.
- The development would be visible to more than 200,000 people who walk the Wineglass Bay track annually.

They are seeking the following outcomes:

- The RACT withdraws its application and reconsiders planned extensions to Freycinet Lodge.
- The government withdraws its proposed changes to the Freycinet National Park Management Plan.

7.6 Stakeholder Theory and Analysis

Whatever you do (or don't do) has an effect. In this chapter, we discuss a case where: the government has an agenda to increase opportunities for people in the state; a member organisation would like to provide more services for its members; and there is an environmental concern.

How do we balance competing needs? How do we find a solution that is in the interests of all and accords with the United Nations definition of sustainable development?

Recall the UN's definition of sustainable development: "meeting the needs of the present without compromising the ability of future generations to meet their own needs" (Report of the World Commission on Environment and Development 2008).

The inclusion and explicit engagement of stakeholders, beyond shareholders, is a comparatively new area of study with the topic's first publication in 1983. Since then, it has become a key area of business teaching, research, and practice and has been especially useful in forming the corporate social responsibility agenda. During periods of major change or when a sensitive project is being developed, companies often turn to tools to help with stakeholder management, one of which is hiring business consultants with strengths in stakeholder management.

This Freycinet Lodge case study provides an opportunity to engage in stakeholder analysis. According to Goodpaster (1991), this involves gathering facts about the available options and the implications of those choices for the affected parties. The various goals, objectives, and values of each stakeholder need to be synthesised so as to develop a recommendation for the ultimate decision-maker.

Stakeholder analysis is particularly useful for environmental groups and marketing or advocacy campaigns. It is also foundational to developing business cases. In the Freycinet Lodge case study, we use a multi-perspective approach as a lens for the awareness, management, and engagement of stakeholders. However, this is only one possible starting point for developing a business case. There are other many tools and guides available. Leaders need to review these tools and select the ones that are appropriate for their situation. Additionally, cultural and local contexts may mean the tools available need to be adapted or revised as most have been developed for Western countries.

7.7   Teaching Notes

7.7.1   Synopsis of the Case

Tasmania is a small island state of Australia with approximately half a million people. The Tasmanian government would like to encourage tourism to improve employment opportunities for its people, and one popular national park in Tasmania's eastern region has been earmarked as a destination with the potential. However, to increase visitor numbers, accommodation and the park's facilities will need to be improved.

7.7.2   Target Learning Group

This is a broad case study that can be used at all levels of learning. It is particularly useful for courses involving decision making, finance, stakeholder analysis, business ethics, and corporate social responsibility. It could be used as a brief introduction to stakeholder theory and its application in a one-hour tutorial, or as an in-depth study over half a semester. You can emphasize the case study's tourism aspects, financial aspects, or stakeholder aspects depending on your teaching aims.

7.7.3   Learning Objectives

The learning objectives depend on the outcomes and subject matter of your course. Here is a sample:

7.7.3.1   Theory

- List the key definitions in stakeholder theory.
- Compare and contrast the approaches of two theorists in stakeholder theory.
- Evaluate the current state of development of stakeholder theory.
- Critique stakeholder theory.
- Describe any ethical dilemmas posed by stakeholder theory.

7.7.3.2   Application

- List the advantages and disadvantages of the available tools for stakeholder analysis.

- Argue for a recommendation to a board (or CEO) to purchase a program to use for stakeholder analysis.
- Create an application to use in stakeholder analysis.
- Investigate a project and analyse it using stakeholder analysis.
- Write a grant application for a tourism infrastructure project.

7.7.4   Teaching Strategy—The Jigsaw Method

The jigsaw method is a good way to introduce the ideas of stakeholders. The method is described in more detail in Wood and Dixon (2011) but, in summary, this method introduces participants to the idea of stakeholders and involves both stakeholder analysis and stakeholder synthesis. It is suitable for online or face-to-face teaching.

The Freycinet Lodge case study presents the views of three groups: the Tasmanian State Government, the RACT, and the conservation lobby. In the jigsaw method, the class is divided into three groups. Each group assumes one of the three roles, and they have 20 min to workshop their position. All three groups receive the Introduction and Background sections, but each group only receives the Perspective sheet for its own role. The class then redivides into groups of three comprising one 'stakeholder' from each group. These teams must make a joint recommendation.

To illustrate the power of the jigsaw method, we quote one student from a similar case:

> I thought it was good to get different views on things. That was probably the most significant [activity]. This has changed my understanding of sustainability … straight away my thoughts were, look at it from this person's view then this one, then this one et cetera. It's almost like a natural way of thinking now.

After the activity, the facilitator helps the participants articulate the importance of stakeholder perspectives.

7.7.5   Discussion Questions

These questions are designed to be discussed after reading and role-playing the Freycinet Lodge case study:

- How do we identify stakeholders?
- Were there other stakeholders who were not represented in this case study?
- Can we consider the environmentalists as one stakeholder? Who has the power in this group?
- How does an organisation like the RACT create value for its members? How do they manage differing member perspectives?

7.7.6   In-Depth Learning

The Freycinet Lodge case study poses deeper questions about stakeholders, differing viewpoints, power, and progress. As such, it is a micro case that can be extended to examine tourism and progress in general or to examine hegemony and power relationships among stakeholders.

Therefore, there are a wide variety of extension activities and different teaching methods that could be pursued:

Research	Individual	Conduct a critical literature review of stakeholder theory
Debate	Teamwork	Facilitate a class debate between the three groups
Work-integrated learning	Teamwork industry/community participation	Participants work in teams with a practitioner who is writing a grant application, developing, or implementing a project. Business, local government, and NGOs often welcome participants to assist with drafting plans
Capstone project	Online Face-to-face Individual or team	A local project manager can present their project and discuss the design and implementation of their project with the group as a potential client. The participants then return a proposal to the client, including a stakeholder analysis and an engagement plan
Intercultural competence	Individual or team	Many tools and theories have been developed in Western contexts. Participants can review current models and tools for cultural bias and make recommendations for adaptations/different methodologies in a specific context

7.7.7 Suggested Assignments

7.7.7.1 Introductory Assignments

- What is an infrastructure project? List three reasons for targeting infrastructure for tourism.
- List the key definitions in stakeholder theory.
- Compare and contrast the approaches of two theorists in stakeholder theory.
- List the advantages and disadvantages of the available tools for stakeholder analysis.
- Choose a tourism or development project in your area. Find available information and identify the stakeholders. How are the stakeholders engaged and who is coordinating their management?

7.7.7.2 Higher-Level Assignments

- Describe ethical dilemmas posed by stakeholder theory.
- Evaluate the current state of development of stakeholder theory.
- Critique stakeholder theory.
- Create a tool to use in stakeholder analysis.
- Argue for a recommendation to a board (or CEO) to purchase a program to use for stakeholder analysis.
- Choose a tourism (or other) project in your area. Identify the stakeholders and develop a plan to engage and manage the stakeholders to achieve an outcome.
- In this case study, what should have happened? Did the right outcome occur? Why/why not?
- Write a grant application for a tourism infrastructure project. You can adapt a real grant application process.
- Design a grant application process and procedure that is appropriate for your country or local area. This should be detailed with grant amounts, guidelines, and application forms.

7.7.7.3 Work-Integrated Learning Project

- Identify a partner who wishes to implement a tourism project.

7.7.8 Additional Resources

There are many resources available on the web. The reader needs to filter what is available depending on their context. Most resources are developed and applied in Western nations; therefore, they may need adapting for context and purpose.

- A useful resource is the New Zealand government *Guide to Developing the Detailed Business Case*: https://treasury.govt.nz/sites/default/files/2015-04/bbc-detbus-gd.pdf
- There are many examples and tools for stakeholder analysis. Here is one example of how to do stakeholder analysis: https://www.groupmap.com/map-templates/stakeholder-analysis/
- Here is a guide which compares different methods of public consultation: http://www.citizenshandbook.org/compareparticipation.pdf
- The engagement spectrum from International Association for Public Participation (IAP2) may be useful: https://i2s.anu.edu.au/resources/stakeholder-participation-iap2-public-participation-spectrum/
- A government community participation planning procedure and report: https://www.planningportal.nsw.gov.au/major-projects/community/community-participation-plan.

References

Goodpaster KE (1991) Business ethics and stakeholder analysis. Bus Ethics Q 1(1):53–73
Report of the World Commission on Environment and Development (2008, Jan 10) Retrieved from https://sustainabledevelopment.un.org/milestones/wced
Tourism Tasmania (2017) Tourism research. Retrieved from https://www.tourismtasmania.com.au/__data/assets/pdf_file/0010/62992/2017-Q4-Tasmanian-Tourism-Snapshot-YE-December-2017.pdf
United Nations Sustainable Development Goals. Retrieved from https://sustainabledevelopment.un.org/
Wood LN, Dixon P (2011) Stakeholder analysis: using the jigsaw method for ethical dilemmas in business. J Asian Soc Sci 7(4):77–83. Retrieved from http://ccsenet.org/journal/index.php/ass/article/view/9378

Mr. Peter Dixon is a Lecturer in the Tasmanian School of Business and Economics which is a College of the University of Tasmania. After many years of commercial legal practice, Peter joined academe in 2001 and has taught and researched in the areas of management, business ethics, and commercial law. He is currently coordinating the offshore teaching program of the School in China and Hong Kong. Peter was Associate Dean, Learning and Teaching for the former Faculty of Business for 7 years and has been involved in a range of teaching and learning projects including Graduate Skills.

Professor Leigh Wood is a pioneering leader in student success. Her research spans the transition to university and the transition to professional work as well as curriculum design to facilitate these transitions. Her research contribution includes five books, 150 articles and multimedia learning resources. She has had over $A2 million in learning and teaching grants. She is proud of her student experience teams, her students and her Ph.D. graduates and their contributions to our communities.

Chapter 8
Supply Chain Management and Social Enterprise Towards Zero Hunger: The Akshaya Patra Foundation in India

Meena Chavan and Yvonne A. Breyer

Abstract The Akshaya Patra Foundation is a not-for-profit social enterprise that provides a lunch program to schools across India. With funding and logistical support from local and state governments, Akshaya Patra seeks to eradicate malnutrition in 1.2 million underprivileged children (Garg et al. in Cases on supply chain and distribution management: issues and principles. IGI Global, Pennsylvania 2012). As a model social enterprise that relies on software applications and automated mechanisms, Akshaya Patra's kitchen facilities mirror pioneering technologies, such as blockchain, artificial intelligence, and Microsoft Dynamics. Two-fold distribution policies sit at the heart of its supply chains to counteract inefficiencies in mass meal production and delivery (Somashekar and Balasubramanian in Accenture Labs and Akshaya Patra use disruptive technologies to enhance efficiency in mid-day meal program for school children. Retrieved from https://www. akshayapatra.org/accenture-labs-and-akshaya-patra-use-disruptive-technologies-to-enhance-efficiency-in-midday-meal-program-for-school-children 2017). This corporate social responsibility (CSR) ethos creates a nexus between collective grassroots action, the traditional values of the International Society for Krishna Consciousness (ISKCON), and a more progressive India. The Foundation's mission is to feed 5 million children by 2020 (Garg et al. in Cases on supply chain and distribution management: issues and principles. IGI Global, Pennsylvania 2012).

Keywords Business sustainability · Government, business and education · Supply chain and logistics challenges · CSR · Innovation and entrepreneurship

M. Chavan (✉) · Y. A. Breyer
Macquarie University, Sydney, Australia
e-mail: meena.chavan@mq.edu.au

© Springer Nature Singapore Pte Ltd. 2020
L. Wood et al. (eds.), *Industry and Higher Education*,
https://doi.org/10.1007/978-981-15-0874-5_8

169

8.1   The Case at a Glance

Key concepts	• Sustainability in business
	• Supply chain management
	• Not-for-profit venture
	• Corporate social enterprise
	• Education

Level of study	• Undergraduate, postgraduate

Subject areas	• Management, operations, supply chain management

Graduate capabilities

Graduate outcomes	%
Critical thinking	20
Problem solving	30
Teamwork	10
Communication	
Ethical thinking	
Sustainability	40
Total	**100%**

Time required	• Out-of-class preparation:	60 mins
	• In-class discussion:	60mins
	• Out-of-class assignments:	120 mins

Activity type	• Individual case analysis
	• Group case analysis presentation

Additional Materials

- https://www.akshayapatra.org/
  The Akshaya Patra Foundation is a not-for-profit organisation headquartered in Bengaluru, India. It strives to eliminate classroom hunger through its Mid-Day Meal Scheme in government and government-subsidised schools and actively supports the right to education for disadvantaged children. Akshaya Patra has been providing fresh and nutritious meals to children every single day of school since 2000. Its state-of-the-art kitchens, designed to extend the reach of the program, have attracted visitors from around the world, and its innovative use of a range of technologies have become a subject of study.

In partnership with the Government of India and various state governments, Akshaya Patra's along with persistent support from corporations, individual donors, and well-wishers, has grown from serving just 1500 children in five schools in 2000 to 1.6 million children in 14,314 schools across 12 states in 2018. Currently, it is the world's largest not-for-profit school lunch program.

8.2 Introduction

This case study documents the complex interplay between business sustainability, education, and profitability. We use theoretical tools, such as social capital theory, to highlight the Akshaya Patra Foundation's response to supply chain challenges in their national school lunch program—the Mid-Day Scheme (Shastri and Banerjee 2010). These challenges centre on the growing complexity of meal distribution; as new schools join the program daily and, as the Scheme grows, so does the complexity of its distribution logistics. Vehicle capacity needs to be increased, ad hoc route extensions need to be created, the increased cost of delivery needs to be budgeted, and so on. These issues have led to delays in meal delivery as the Foundation's distribution model tries but fails to accommodate unexpected changes in traffic and road conditions (Mahadevan et al. 2013). Akshaya Patra's logistical challenges can best be solved with a recommendation model that maximises the capacity of deployed delivery vans but still maintains the "quality-critical metric: cooking-to-consumption time". This time window is six hours (Mitra et al. 2013). Akshaya Patra has an additional self-imposed challenge—to deliver mid-day meals to 5 million children by 2020. However, the government funding that Akshaya Patra has relied on is now being splintered across other social programs, for example, the Right to Food initiative. This is bringing issues of economic sustainability to the fore.

Using first-hand data collected from a study tour of the Foundation along with secondary research that traces Akshaya Patra's kitchen facilities, this case study focuses on sustainability and delineates the role distinct processes play in the value chain, and how those processes contribute to business innovation.

With individual kitchen units accommodating average cooking capacities of 50,000–185,000 meals per day, the Akshaya Patra Foundation has executed a double-edged strategy to confront two of the most urgent and intertwined dilemmas in India: hunger and education (Mahadevan et al. 2013). Through its Mid-Day Meal Scheme, the Foundation delivers free, nutritious lunches to every student in participating public schools. The ultimate goal is to lift national education standards. Therefore, the program is designed to: improve poor student attention spans due to hunger; promote inter-caste relations; increase school attendance rates; and, notably, empower women through employment prospects (Upton et al. 2007). Akshaya Patra commits itself to the philosophy that "no child in India… be deprived of education because of hunger" (Upton et al. 2007). Thus, the core question of this study is: How will the Akshaya

Patra Foundation accomplish this goal while overcoming the operational challenges associated with a burgeoning middle-class population as the demand grows?

8.3 Background

India is rich in diversity and is becoming increasingly relevant as a global power. The country has a variety of religions, languages, ethnicities, geography, fashion, food, and films (Paris and Alim 2014). It is the largest democracy in the world, consisting of over 1.21 billion people (Khandelwal and Bakshi 2014), which creates great potential for growth and influence over the global economy. In 2014, India's GDP exceeded US $2 trillion and, with an annualised growth rate of 7.3%, it is now one of the world's fastest-growing economies (World Bank 2014). However, India is still a developing country. As such, its ability to compete against more developed nations is limited. Nevertheless, it is attempting to compete regardless. For example, there is a trend within start-up enterprises to operate as socially responsible business entities rather than as purely profit-seeking ventures. Such a goal is difficult in a developing market (Agrawal and Sahasranamam 2016); however, it does highlight that India's outlook is positive and optimistic as it searches for solutions to balance economic prosperity with the social ideals of a democracy and a free market. While there is great socio-economic diversity across India's 28 states and 7 union territories, all work under a common national framework. This makes for an ideal setting to investigate the impact of numerous social developments in an evolving economy (Monsen et al. 2012). It also presents an excellent opportunity for other nations and multinational corporations to learn from India's social initiatives and to make investments that capitalise on the knowledge and growth that is taking place in India.

8.4 Literature Review

A range of literature offers analyses of the strengths and limitations of method-ologies for operational models of growth akin to the Akshaya Patra Foundation's business strategy. In a perceptive article, Mahadevan et al. (2013) argue for inte-grating technological innovation with traditional supply chain logistics and using software analytics as a tool to redesign mid-day meal distribution. In fact, many of the changes Akshaya Patra has made to its logistics operations can be credited to a Microsoft-based design solution. The solution proposed in this article has brought the Akshaya Patra Foundation to the forefront of digitisation. However, new approaches must also be viewed within the framework of India's legal policies and minimal federal funding. It is important to look beyond the simple issue of service coverage. A new approach means re-appraising the philanthropic and religious discourse that underpins Akshaya Patra's philosophy. Although the Hindu religious paradigm of *prasadam* (a holy offering of food), exemplified by the ISKCON movement, is not an influential factor, it does critique the organisation's scalability and growth. But in a country like India, where religion is a part of daily life, these pious values may be points of profitability and viability. For example, employment, funding, and investment opportunities are not inconsistent with the religious sentiments of Hare Krishna that inform Akshaya Patra.

8.5 Two-Fold Distribution Strategy

Akshaya Patra's operating model is based on a series of central cooking hubs that service all schools in the surrounding area. Delivery vans transport the meals by road and, therefore, both kitchen capacity and the size of the delivery fleet relative are integral to meeting regional demand (Upton et al. 2007). When a facility is established, the Foundation plans a routing schedule to dispatch cooked meals from the kitchen to each individual school according to a standard data-driven agenda.

Originally, Akshaya Patra provided meals from one central kitchen in Bangalore and concentrated its efforts on thriving urban precincts. A "hub-and-spoke model" was implemented to "cook mass quantities of food", which was then distributed in smaller quantities to individual schools in neighbouring villages (Upton et al. 2007). However, as the Foundation expanded its service into rural areas, this centralised model proved ineffective. Geographical spread and poor road networks were an obstacle to both distribution and communication. As a result, Akshaya Patra transitioned to a decentralised model with smaller regional kitchens (Upton et al. 2007).

Business innovation is imperative to securing funding and support from local governments and charity groups. In Akshaya Patra's case, innovation meant reconfiguring an entire distribution process and specifically tailoring its value chain to fulfil the need in rural areas. It is worth noting that 80% of India's population live in rural regions. Hence, on a wider scale, this decision also involved developing mechanisms to feed a much greater number of children (Upton et al. 2007). It is argued that sustaining this standard of efficiency in rural/semi-urban regions is highly unfeasible in terms of monetary gain, and will "work only when it's in a more densely populated place, and there are economies of scale". This view i s asceptical construction of the strategic duality prevalent in Akshaya Patra's distribution framework. However, it provides a point of departure for more robust models to devise services that satisfy the pressing needs of urban versus rural demographics.

8.6 Supply Chain Processes

The logistics of Akshaya Patra's supply chain are a direct response to trends in the Indian economy. Here, we deconstruct the unique elements in the Foundation's business model and analyse how they have been designed to complement financial and political realities.

In India, procuring rice is a linear operation: Akshaya Patra obtains rice from the Gujarat State Civil Supplies Corporation, which receives supplies from the Food Corporation of India (Mitra et al. 2013). Likewise, the Government of Gujarat estimates the state's requirements for food-grain (e.g., rice) over successive months and informs Akshaya Patra of its forecast, ensuring a seamless, first-stage operation (Mitra et al. 2013). These *atta* (wheat flour) and grain yield calculations are assessed according to monthly school attendance (Mitra et al. 2013), but the funding equations used pose a striking concern. In an attempt to increase the stream of federal government resources at a steady rate, statements show that their 3-year debt has accumulated to a collective bill of approximately INR ₹ 1.5 million (Mitra et al. 2013). According to Sridhar Venkat, CEO of Akshaya Patra, "making our income more predictable while scaling up" is equally important (Keim 2015). The economic volatility of India's food industry further amplifies this challenge, as food is highly sensitive to price escalations. In the context of India's financial position, the past decade has witnessed unremitting price spikes and long-standing inflation that has far surpassed the nation's economic growth (Timmer 2008). To cope with this period of economic turmoil, Akshaya Patra now only procures produce from commodity brokers with whom it has established, stable relationships and long-term contractual agreements (Nair and Eapen 2012). Additionally, the wholesale procurement of turmeric, chilli, coriander, cumin seeds, and high-value raw materials has been centralised to guard against price spikes (Mitra et al. 2013). However, these measures do not guarantee price stability as many other ingredients and components of the supply chain cannot be acquired at fixed prices over the long term.

Akshaya Patra's urban-area kitchens purchase vegetables from local markets through third-party vendors. Vegetables, oil, pulses, and spices are locally procured from mandis (wholesale markets) in Ahmedabad at reduced market rates through vendor trust and negotiation (Mitra et al. 2013). Storage facilities are also a critical element of Akshaya Patra's supply chain. Without storage, the Foundation could not conserve perishables, leverage economies of scale by buying in bulk, or maintain low inventory prices. Inventory donated as a government grant are rated at the lower end of the market spectrum at a standardised price (for accounting purposes). A purchase request is sent by the storage department when a restock is required (Mitra et al. 2013). However, sometimes goods take longer to arrive than expected and, in these cases, emergency purchases may be required (Mitra et al. 2013). Additionally, a team of quality controllers request quotes and sample produce from a number of suppliers and choose vendors that meet specific criteria: market versus bid price; the quality of the product at raw material level; and their history of on-time deliveries (Mitra et al. 2013).

Like any corporate supply chain, Akshaya Patra also faces legal, political, and operational setbacks (Fernie and Sparks 2014). In the past, it procured rice through a grant from the central government, which was subsequently wholesaled by farmers through a middleman (Upton et al. 2007). However, because costs are subject to weight, the intermediaries often hid heavy objects in the rice, such as stones, metal, nails, etc. When Akshaya Patra publicised the practice as a "very open secret" to exploit profits, they attracted negative media attention (Upton et al. 2007). Hence, to manage this corruption, they purchased destoning machines to separate the rice from any 'alien' substances and found that one-fifth of each bag of rice was disinfected. To complicate matters further, new regulations have been imposed that prevent Akshaya Patra from trading their government-subsidised rice for the better quality rice sold by retail chains. As a result, it has become even more pressing for the Foundation to find ways to overcome the poor yields that drive up prices (Upton et al. 2007). More importantly, these challenges have paved the way for some fundamental questions about Akshaya Patra's business model: Is a compromise between public and private sector interests truly a viable strategy for providing the basic right of food and education to schoolchildren? As cautioned by Biraj Patnaik, an advocate from the Right to Food Campaign's steering committee, there is a possibility that the private sector's concerns may overwhelm public sector interests when governments depend on public-private agreements (Keim 2015).

8.7 Incorporating Increased Automation

Digital India, a 2015 government initiative, has significantly improved the nation's online infrastructure, and most citizens can now readily access government resources electronically. This migration toward economic digitisation has prompted positive responses from traditional commercial institutions, such as "venture capitalists and public and private investors" (KPMG in India and NASSCOM 10,000 Start-ups, 2016). To this end, Akshaya Patra re-modelled its business strategies in an alliance with Accenture—a leader in global professional IT services. Disruptive tools, such as artificial intelligence, the Internet of Things, and blockchain, are now an integral part of scaling up its mass meal production and delivery (Somashekar and Balasubramanian 2017). Called the "Million Meals" project, these technological assets have positively impacted Akshaya Patra's supply chain and operations. The results are improved meal quality, greater service reach, and sustainable value for stakeholders (Somashekar and Balasubramanian 2017). The nexus between traditional religious sentiments, such as *prasadam* (offerings to God) and the shift toward automation that has become core to Akshaya Patra's operations is a testament to global interconnectivity and its impact on India's digital ecosystem.

Strategic evaluation and design were at the essence of developing a blueprint for the upgrades to kitchen operations as part of the Million Meals project. Advanced technologies were harnessed toward four key findings from an analysis of Akshaya Patra's business model: gathering student feedback, monitoring delivery vehicles, gauging the required amount of food supplies, and supervising meal production (Fig. 8.1).

Akshaya Patra's evolution from a blue-collar collection of feedback to adopting more technological solutions exemplifies how fintech is influencing India's food processing industry. For example, the Foundation has leveraged blockchain technology—a decentralised method of exchanging value over the internet without an

School name										Route number
										Phone number
Date	Total Vessels			Vessels Left at Schools			Delivery Time	College Time	Student		Head Masters Sign	Remarks
	big	small	mini	big	small	mini			enrol	present		

Fig. 8.1 Food delivery index/schedule. *Source* Garg et al. (2012)

intermediary—to restructure complex processes to provide both visibility and digital security (Olleros and Zhegu 2016). These initiatives prove that India is morphing into a knowledge-centric economy and a digital society. Likewise, IT sensor systems gauge the end-to-end cooking procedures in kitchen facilities to improve energy consumption and ensure standardised food quality. The use of blockchain, artificial intelligence, and sensor-enabled devices mean Akshaya Patra's technical department has had to shift part of its focus toward digital maintenance, conserving valuable resources, and predicting the needs and meal specifications for upcoming days (Mehra and Lokam 2018).

As outlined earlier, Akshaya Patra also faces critical logistics issues. It requires solutions that decrease the number of delivery vehicles required for its fleet while continuing to meet delivery timeframes. Hence, the Foundation is experimenting with path-optimising software that relies on real-time data analysis to generate the most efficient paths between each kitchen and the schools they service (Mahadevan et al. 2013). These process modifications have improved Akshaya Patra's "audit proficiencies, attendance recording, invoice processing and payment" (Mahadevan et al. 2013). They have also led to opportunities for expanded production and prototype models for all other kitchens to follow (Mahadevan et al. 2013).

A hallmark that distinguishes Akshaya Patra's Mid-Day Meal Scheme is its automated kitchen facilities. Human contact with food is minimised, vegetables are cut at high speed using machines, and conveyor belts transport goods around the facility. The vegetable processing system is a good reflection of Akshaya Patra's automation and end-to-end processes. After being cleaned and sorted, vegetables are transported from stainless steel holding vessels to automatic cutting machines. These machines have motorised engines like those in a BMW car and can mechanically slice 40 kgs of potatoes in one minute. The size and even shape can be programmed (Upton et al. 2007).

A recently-established kitchen in Hubli integrates complex mechanisms with gravity flow for cost savings and to reduce the manual labour involved in food production. All systems conform to health and safety standards, and automation helps to match what is produced to the diverse needs across the nation. Some examples follow.

Fig. 8.2 An automated *roti* (bread)-making machine. *Source* Mitra et al. (2013)

- In northern Indian regions, where the local cuisine is grain-rich, bread-making machines can produce 60,000 pieces of flatbread in one hour (Keim 2015).
- Rice is a staple in southern India, so large cookers heat 250 lb of rice in 20 min (Keim 2015) (Fig. 8.2).

8.8 Operational Models for Growth

Reconfiguring the logistics of Akshaya Patra's Mid-Day Meal Scheme has resulted in process efficiencies across all its regional kitchens in India, while expanding its service coverage at the same time. However, further improvements may be constrained by the fixed number of vehicles in its fleet and the delivery windows required to ensure the quality of food on delivery. To provide context, Akshaya Patra's head office annually allocated a certain number of delivery vehicles to each district, but operating costs are managed regionally (Mahadevan et al. 2013). Therefore, one of the recommendations resulting from this case study is for regional managers to capitalise on available resources to reduce the number of fleet vehicles that need to be deployed and maximise their service coverage. This would include a review of theoretical models designed to solve vehicle routing problems. For instance, Dell'amico et al. (2007) and Bräysy et al. (2007) deconstructed the vehicle routing issues of a "fleet-size-mix" against static time schedules (Mahadevan et al. 2013). In this problem variant, the elements of a prime fleet-size-mix and viable routing solutions are ascertained with a flexible number of delivery vehicles (Mahadevan et al. 2013). However, translating this theory into practice in Akshaya Patra's case only works to a limited extent because its operational model is strictly bounded by the fixed fleet sizes available to each region. Likewise, a study by Tarantilis et al. (2003) and Li et al. (2007) suggests solutions to fixed fleet vehicle issues that closely parallel Akshaya Patra's core logistics concerns. However, the additional restriction on time windows is not included as a metric in their analyses (Mahadevan et al. 2013). So, although there is ample literature on the topic, the complexity of Akshaya Patra's logistical operations must be tackled through phased incremental solutions (Mahadevan et al. 2013).

8.9 Software Design Solutions

Another recommendation to counter the logistics issues associated with distributing perishable meals at reduced prices is a software-based planning solution. Akshaya Patra's is already using Microsoft Dynamics to help streamline its supply chain, centralise data, and ensure each kitchen operates more like a "single unit" than an amalgamation of single entities. Therefore, capitalising on technological resources that are already available makes sense. Microsoft's tools and software design platforms include a range of untapped potential for further innovations. For example, a range of solutions could be tailored to meet the specific needs of different kitchens based on fleet capacity, rather than a standard solution that tries to address the diverse needs of all regions. The rationale for this approach is two-fold and based on the findings and models already devised by Mahadevan et al. (2013).

First, Microsoft platforms, such as Visual Basic and Excel, are used to input and simulate trial values for demand and fleet size according to geographical divisions backed by real-time data and GPS coordinates (Mahadevan et al. 2013). Second, the results are generated as solution-level reports of graphs and/or tables that provide a detailed outline of the solutions for different fleet volumes, travel distances, and total operating costs (Mahadevan et al. 2013). With this approach, managers at the regional level are able to use a master summary report to make dynamic decisions about the best routing alternatives for the day. Further, trip sheets take variables such as "cooking completion times, local school holidays, traffic conditions, staff absenteeism and vehicle availability" into account (Mahadevan et al. 2013). As affirmed in Mahadevan et al. (2013), these reports were useful for refining Akshaya Patra's policy constraints during the preliminary research on appropriate algorithms and were of specific benefit to the supply chain. This solution has also assisted the Foundation's management to make intelligent compromises between cost-efficiency, service coverage, and time.

The school year in India starts in June. This overlaps with Akshaya Patra's annual planning cycle and aligns with requests for a school to be added to the distribution network (Mahadevan et al. 2013). Operations management during this critical

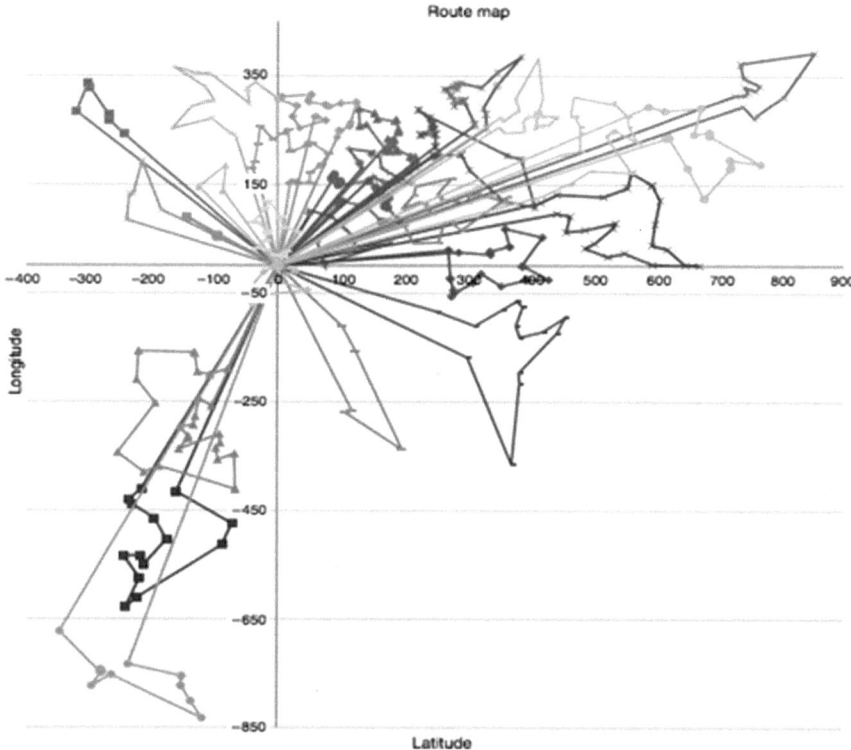

Fig. 8.3 The overlaps in designated routes prior to a software-based solution. *Source* Mahadevan et al. (2013)

period were made more seamless using Microsoft software, especially by considering variables such as information on fleet availability relative to total school demand.

Figure 8.3 illustrates the inefficiencies in Akshaya Patra's operational model. Route path overlaps are obvious prior to implementing a software-based solution in the Vasanthapura kitchen. According to Arun Kumar, Operations Manager of the Foundation, this centrally-managed solution system is assisting Akshaya Patra to meet delivery scales and "long term strategic planning".

8.10 Results

Following the pilot of similar software design models, Mahadevan et al. (2013) note that Akshaya Patra's management successfully decreased their fleet from 35 to 27 delivery vehicles at an annual cost saving of US $75,000 for the Gujarat region alone along with a further reduction of 18.61% to its monthly operating overheads (Mahadevan et al. 2013). Thus, Akshaya Patra is poised to become a key enabler of scalability with an estimated increase in capacity to serve a further 2400 school children regionally, and 62,000 nationally (Mahadevan et al. 2013). Environmental sustainability is also well addressed by the Foundation's push for solutions to reduce its fleet size, as evidenced in the decrease in total trip length by 75 kms, which saves 443 l of diesel fuel per month (Mahadevan et al. 2013). Akshaya Patra's ongoing search for efficiencies in its food processing and delivery models is likely to provide further cost savings and, as a result, expand its operation to include more schools. Additional cost savings may also be found through sales tax exemptions and further discounts on procured goods.

8.11   Conclusion

School lunch programs, especially Akshaya Patra's, are a revolution in understanding and appreciating the socio-economic objectives seminal to India's economic, political, legal, and cultural development. Issues such as enhancing enrolment, student and stakeholder participation, educational retention, and revamping the nutritional state of students are prescient in India (Shalini et al. 2014). Effective mid-day meal schedules can be pivotal in generating stakeholder value and improving the standard of living nationwide. Although Akshaya Patra's decentralised and centralised models to serve the needs of both rural and urban regions have generally received positive responses, it is clear that expanding the program's reach into in rural areas is linked to improvements in food storage, preparation, and delivery. Our findings support Mahadevan et al.'s (2013) argument for a Microsoft-based software solution to Akshaya Patra's distribution issues. Such solutions would result in savings to time, money, and food resources. Akshaya Patra's underlying philosophy—that no child be stripped of the ability to learn due to hunger—is a key factor in the social welfare and societal evolution behind India's emergence as a global business leader. Microsoft's algorithms would help Akshaya Patra tackle these social concerns without compromising the Foundation's traditional religious values.

8.12 Teaching Notes

8.12.1 Synopsis of the Case

The Akshaya Patra Foundation is a not-for-profit social enterprise that provides a lunch program to schools across India. With funding and logistical support from local and state governments, Akshaya Patra seeks to eradicate malnutrition in 1.2 million underprivileged children (Garg et al. 2012). As a model social enterprise that relies on software applications and automated mechanisms, Akshaya Patra's kitchen facilities mirror pioneering technologies, such as blockchain, artificial intelligence, and Microsoft Dynamics. Two-fold distribution policies sit at the heart of its supply chains to counteract inefficiencies in mass meal production and delivery (Somashekar and Balasubramanian 2017). This corporate social responsibility (CSR) ethos creates a nexus between collective grassroots action, the traditional values of the International Society for Krishna Consciousness (ISKCON), and a more progressive India. The Foundation's mission is to feed 5 million children by 2020 (Garg et al. 2012).

The enormous scale of the business landscape in India presents endless opportunities for the development and future progress of numerous firms around the world. The Indian approach to solving business issues centres on holistically addressing all aspects of the problem. By example, India demonstrates that foreign countries and businesses can invest in and observe sustainable practices to further their own advancement. This case study looked at a way India does business differently and how the rest of the world can learn from its example by implementing similar strategies to foster sustainability. CSR, innovation, and entrepreneurship theory can be used to analyse the ways in which foreign businesses and countries can model a sustainable approach from India. It is a good example of how innovation and entrepreneurial ideas have been successfully implemented to solve the issue of education and hunger. The large sample size of India makes it an ideal landscape to trial and implement innovation and entrepreneurial business ideas. As a result, the entrepreneurial business environment is thriving.

This knowledge can be drawn on by both Indian and foreign businesses to optimise their own potential for future global growth. Moreover, the businesses and non-government organisations showcased in the case study could be potential investments and/or examples for further research to better understand the business and CSR landscape in India. The role of CSR is explored as an example of the practices adopted by Indian firms and organisations to be more socially responsible by their own volition and not out of obligation.

The underlying principle of the Foundation is that if children are offered a meal at school, not only will their parents encourage them to attend they will also be sufficiently nourished to retain as much information as possible. This is summarised in their vision that "no child in India shall be deprived of education because of hunger" (Akshaya Patra 2017). This simple vision demonstrates an awareness of the broader issue of world hunger that plagues the world today. The Foundation's solution is in keeping with Indian business philosophy that identified problems should be solved holistically and not through a short-term fix or an approach that only works for a small number of people. From the humble beginnings of serving mid-day meals to 1500 children in five government schools to serving more than 1.6 million children across the Indian subcontinent in the short space of 17 years (Akshaya Patra 2017), Akshaya Patra has demonstrated that simple yet effective policies and collaborations with governments and other partners can create steady and sustainable growth.

8.12.2 Target Learning Group

- Level of study—BA and MA students
- Subject areas—CSR; management; innovation and entrepreneurship; government, society and education.

8.12.3 Learning Objectives

- Innovation and entrepreneurship in emerging economies like India
- CSR in India
- Social enterprise partnership between government, society, and business
- Educating the disadvantaged
- Operations management.

8.12.4 Teaching Strategy

This case study examines how social innovators, such as the Akshaya Patra Foundation, are leveraging technology to scale social value and how these technologies integrate CSR initiatives with traditional belief systems, such as Krishna Consciousness.

The video "Accenture Lab's Tech4Good—Million Meals Pilot" with Akshaya Patra summarises how technology is being used to improve the Foundation's operational processes, enabling it to deliver more meals to Indian school children.

The suggested assignments promote research and discussion on the relationships between food and education, public-private partnerships (PPP), technology and social enterprise, and sustainable supply chains.

8.12.5 Reading Questions

- What is the two-fold outcome of Akshaya Patra's Mid-Day Meal Scheme? Why are these so important? What are the program's broader or more holistic benefits?
- How has India's economic volatility impacted on Akshaya Patra's procurement processes?
- What are some of the challenges listed for Akshaya Patra's PPPs?
- What data sources were used to review Akshaya Patra's business model?
- What benefits have been achieved in Gujarat by decreasing the Akshaya Patra delivery fleet from 35 to 27 vehicles?
- What non-technology solution does the author suggest as a cost-saving measure?

8.12.6 Discussion Questions

- What is the Mid-Day Meal Scheme? Is Akshaya Patra the only provider?
- What is *prasadum?* What connection does the author make to the Akshaya Patra Foundation's mid-day meal program?
- In the context of an economically progressive India, how does the case study create touchpoints between CSR, collective grassroots action, and the more traditional values of the International Society for Krishna Consciousness (ISKCON)?

8.12.7 Suggested Assignments

8.12.7.1 Public-Private Partnerships (PPP)

The author notes that supply chain "challenges pave the way for fundamental questions to be raised, pertinent to Akshaya Patra's business model: Is the compromise between public and private sector interests truly a viable strategy to provide the basic rights of food and education to schoolchildren?"

- Work in groups to research Akshaya Patra's PPP model. Present your findings to the class:

  - What is a PPP model?
  - How is PPP implemented at Akshaya Patra?
  - What are the successes of this model?
  - What are the challenges?
  - What improvements or alternatives do you recommend?

8.12.7.2 Blockchain

Blockchain technology through Accenture's Tech4Good initiative is being used as part of Akshaya Patra Foundation's

- Work in groups to research the benefits of blockchain for Akshay Patra. Present your findings to the class:
- What is blockchain?
- How does blockchain influence the Akshaya Patra supply chain?
- How might blockchain be Akshaya Patra's technology equivalent of India's traditional *dabbawalas* (men who deliver lunches in India)?

8.12.8 Multimedia Activities

- **Accenture Labs Tech4Good—Million Meals Pilot with Akshaya Patra**
  https://www.youtube.com/watch?v=Fsn51Z8ujQI

   This video summarises how social transformation can be accelerated using technology. It showcases how Accenture Labs is partnering with Akshaya Patra to drive the Million Meals pilot. The video is suitable as a listening activity prior to reading the case study.

- What are some of the statistics provided at the start of the video? Why are they important?
- According to the CEO of Akshaya Patra, what is the vision for the Foundation?
- On a daily basis, how many children does Akshaya Patra serve meals to? In how many schools?
- How many meals has Akshaya Patra served to children since 2000?
- Natraj Kuntagod, Senior Principal of Accenture Labs, says that the purpose of leveraging human-centred design is to cut through the complexity and incorporate diverse technologies. Which technologies are used? Why?
- What example does Kuntagod give?
- Vinay N Kumar is the Head of Operations at Akshaya Patra. How does he summarise the role of technology at the Foundation? Why is this important?
- What elements is Accenture looking to improve at Akshaya Patra to benefit the Foundation?
- Akshaya Patra's process streamlining consists of which three key areas?
- According to the Sanjay Podder, MD Accenture Bangalore, every *pesa* saved is how many more meals? What is the significance of this statement to Accenture's Million Meals initiative?

8.12.9 Supplementary Materials

- **Mid-Day Meal Scheme**—https://en.wikipedia.org/wiki/Midday_Meal_Scheme
  A Wikipedia article summarising the Mid-Day Meal Scheme, including its history and program evaluation.
- **Bangla-Pesa: Slum Currency and Implications for the Poor in Developing Countries**
  https://www.brookings.edu/blog/up-front/2013/07/17/bangla-pesa-slum-currency-and-implications-for-the-poor-in-developing-countries/
  This article summarises the "pesa", a currency being used by the poor in developing countries
- **In India, 100-Year-Old Lunch Delivery Service Goes Modern**
  https://www.npr.org/sections/thesalt/2012/08/28/159982983/in-india-100-year-old-lunch-delivery-service-goes-modern
- **This Indian meal service is so efficient it's the envy of FedEx**
  https://www.pri.org/stories/2014-07-15/indian-meal-service-so-efficient-it-s-envy-fedex
  These articles and videos establish connections between India's traditional lunch delivery service—*dabbawalas*—and innovation
- **The PPP model best suited to implementing a school lunch program**
  https://blog.akshayapatra.org/ppp-model-best-suited-for-implementing-mid-day-meals/
  This article from the Akshaya Patra blog outlines the role of Public-Private Partnerships to the Foundation's Mid-Day Meal Scheme and report on how it is implemented in the Foundation.
- **What are Public-Private Partnerships?**
  https://ppp.worldbank.org/public-private-partnership/overview/what-are-public-private-partnerships
  This World Bank resource provides a selection of resources related to PPPs.

Further Reading

- **Keim, B. (2015, 9 November 2015).** Akshaya Patra. Impact India. Accessible at: https://ssir.org/articles/entry/case_study_akshaya_patra

Technical ingenuity and private funding enable Akshaya Patra to serve hot, healthy lunches to 1.4 million Indian children every day. This online and downloadable Stanford Social Innovation Review article summarises the Akshaya Patra Foundation innovation to bring lunches to children in India.

References

Agrawal A, Sahasranamam S (2016) Corporate social entrepreneurship in India. South Asian J Glob Bus Res 5(2):214–233

Akshay Patra (2017). Retrieved from https://odisha.akshayapatra.org/history

Bräysy O, Gendreau M, Hasle G, Løkketangen A (2007) A survey of heuristics for the vehicle routing problem, part II: demand side extensions. Working paper, Sintef Ict, Norway

Dell'amico M, Monaci M, Pagani C, Vigo D (2007) Heuristic approaches for the FSMVRP with time windows. Trans Sci 41(4):516–526

Fernie J, Sparks L (2014) Logistics and retail management: emerging issues and new challenges in the retail supply chain. Kogan Page Publishers, London

Garg M, Gupta S, Pal S, Ranjan Praveer S (2012) Cases on supply chain and distribution management: issues and principles. IGI Global, Pennsylvania

Keim B (2015) Akshaya Patra. Retrieved From https://Ssir.Org/Articles/Entry/Case_Study_Akshaya_Patra

Khandelwal MR, Bakshi MS (2014) The new CSR regulation in India: the way forward. Procedia Econ Financ 11(14):60–67

Li F, Golden B, Wasil E (2007) A record-to-record travel algorithm for solving the heterogeneous fleet vehicle routing problem. Comput Oper Res 34(9):2734–2742

Mahadevan B, Sivakumar S, Kumar DD, Ganeshram K (2013) Redesigning midday meal logistics for the Akshaya Patra foundation: or at work in feeding hungry school children. Interfaces 43:530–546

Mehra A, Lokam S (2018) Vishrambh: trusted philanthropy with end-to-end transparency. Retrieved from https://www.hciforblockchain.org/wpcontent/uploads/sites/25/2018/04/mehra.pdf

Mitra S, Raghuram G, Ghosh A (2013) Akshaya Patra, Gandhinagar: supply chain challenges. Vikalpa 38:105–126

Monsen E, Mahagaonkar P, Dienes C (2012) Entrepreneurship in India: the question of occupational transition. Small Bus Econ 39(2):359–382

Nair SR, Eapen LM (2012) Food price inflation in India (2008 to 2010): a commodity-wise analysis of the causal factors. Econ Polit Weekly 47:46–54

Olleros FX, Zhegu M (2016) Research handbook on digital transformations. Edward Elgar Publishing, Massachusetts

Paris D, Alim HS (2014) What are we seeking to sustain through culturally sustaining pedagogy? A loving critique forward. Harv Educ Rev 84(1):85–100

Shalini C, Murthy N, Shalini S, Dinesh R, Shivaraj N, Suryanarayana S (2014) Comparison of nutritional status of rural and urban school students receiving mid-day meals in schools of Bengaluru, India: a cross sectional study. J Postgrad Med 60(2):118–122

Shastri V, Banerjee PM (2010) From corporate social responsibility to global social entrepreneurship. In: Shastri V, Banerjee PM (eds) Social responsibility and environmental sustainability in business: how organizations handle profits and social duties. Sage, New Delhi, India, pp 1–14

Somashekar N, Balasubramanian K (2017) Accenture Labs and Akshaya Patra use disruptive technologies to enhance efficiency in mid-day meal program for school children. Retrieved from https://www.akshayapatra.org/accenture-labs-and-akshaya-patra-use-disruptive-technologies-to-enhance-efficiency-in-midday-meal-program-for-school-children

Tarantilis CD, Kiranoudis CT, Markatos NC (2003) BoneRoute: an effective memory-based method for effective fleet management. In: Conference: 6th Italian conference on chemical and process engineering, Pisa, Italy, June 2003

Timmer CP (2008) Causes of high food prices. ADB Economics Working Paper Series. Asian Development Bank

Upton D, Ellis C, Lucas S, Yamner A (2007) Akshaya Patra: feeding India's schoolchildren. Harvard Business School Case 608038. Harvard Business Review, Boston, MA

World Bank (2014) Retrieved from https://www.worldbank.org/en/news/press-release/2014/06/20/india-strong-position-to-tap-global-growth-says-new-world-bank-report

Dr. Meena Chavan is a leader in teaching and research in the areas of International Business, Management, Cross Cultural Management, Entrepreneurship, and Small Business Management. She possesses an effective blend of 30 years' experience in industry and academia. She is an advocate of experiential learning and adopts an experiential teaching style. Her innovative approach to teaching has earned her a Vice Chancellor's citation for sustained leadership in experiential and work integrated learning approaches in order to transform students into employable graduates with strong social and community values.

Associate Professor Yvonne A. Breyer is an award-winning academic with expertise in student success, online learning and digital transformation in the higher education sector. Yvonne has led several highly successful strategic initiatives with national and international reach. Most recently, she led the 'Excel Skills for Business' specialisation, which received the Coursera Outstanding Educator Award for Student Transformation on the back of exceptional learner feedback, global reach and impact. She holds a Ph.D. (Macquarie University), a Master of Arts (University of Essen, Germany) and a Postgraduate Certificate in Higher Education, Leadership and Management (Macquarie University).

Chapter 9
Industry-Academia Partnerships for Sustainability: Project Genesis in India

Meena Chavan and Yvonne A. Breyer

Abstract As a pioneer in IT services, business consulting, and business process outsourcing, Infosys drives economic growth and prosperity through global solutions to service delivery. Powered with an AI platform that automates 'people processes' to free up employees for solving higher-level problems, Infosys "prioritises the execution of change" and demonstrates India's rise as a global destination for software services expertise (Infosys in Infosys—AI-powered core | Navigate your next. Retrieved from https://www.infosys.com/navigate-your-next/ai-powered-core/ 2018b). Infosys stands at the forefront of the digital and social revolution with a host of disruptive technologies to fuel innovation. This case study examines the organisation's flagship endeavour, Project Genesis, which is a testament to the firm's corporate social responsibility (CSR) policies and filters throughout its entire business. Project Genesis creates a nuanced connection between grassroots social activism, industry, and academia to improve India's employability index. However, as a growing number of outsourcing companies in India compete to hire employees, the lack of skilled graduates and the attrition rates intrinsic to IT are becoming problematic. In response, Project Genesis seeks to align curriculums with industry needs in an integrated campus-to-corporate transition. The result is a sustainable economic benefit for all (Infosys in Infosys Corporate Social Responsibility | Project Genesis | Infosys BPO Training. Retrieved from https://www.infosys.com/newsroom/press-releases/ Pages/project-genesis.aspx 2012).

Keywords Social activism · Industry-academia partnerships · Business sustainability · Education and industrial skill-enhancement

M. Chavan (✉) · Y. A. Breyer
Department of Management, Macquarie University, Sydney, Australia
e-mail: meena.chavan@mq.edu.au

© Springer Nature Singapore Pte Ltd. 2020
L. Wood et al. (eds.), *Industry and Higher Education*,
https://doi.org/10.1007/978-981-15-0874-5_9

189

9.1   The Case at a Glance

Key concepts	• Sustainability in business
	• Corporate social enterprise
	• Employability
	• Corporate social responsibility models

| Level of study | • Undergraduate and postgraduate |

| Subject areas | • Business management, MBA |

Graduate capabilities

Graduate outcomes	%
Critical thinking	20
Problem solving	30
Teamwork	10
Communication	
Ethical thinking	
Sustainability	40
Total	**100%**

Time required	• Out-of-class preparation:	60 mins
	• In-class discussion:	60 mins
	• Out-of-class assignments:	120 mins

| Activity type | • Individual case analysis |
| | • Group case analysis presentation |

Additional Materials

- https://www.infosysbpm.com/newsroom/press-releases/Pages/project-genesis.aspx

   Project Genesis is an initiative that aligns teaching and curriculums in Graduate Schools with industry requirements to give students an employment advantage. Students who complete the program are equipped with skills they need to be considered 'industry-ready'. The curriculum, called "Global Skills Enhancement" was developed from the results of a skills-level assessment conducted at colleges in Tier II and III towns in various parts of India. To date, the program has been deployed in seven states: Andhra Pradesh, Karnataka, Maharashtra, Orissa, Punjab, Rajasthan, and Tamil Nadu. In June 2012, Infosys also used Project Genesis to train a pilot batch of lecturers from the Royal University of Bhutan.

9.2   Introduction

This case shines a critical light on the complex interplay between business sustainability, education, and industry skills. Using theoretical tools, such as social capital theory and CSR models, we examine one company's response to social welfare issues in India—Infosys. Project Genesis is a CSR initiative developed by Infosys with the aim of instilling strong eco-sustainability management values at the graduate level of India's education system. The program leverages software to create long-term value for state-level and global stakeholders and empowers business graduates with an inspiring and constructive culture of skills enhancement. The net result is an investment in positive reforms to partnerships between industry and academia that promotes social stewardship and contributes to India's social and economic growth (Fig. 9.1).

Fig. 9.1 The four-pronged leadership strategy at Infosys. *Source* Infosys (2018a, p. 44)

9.3   Challenges in the Available Talent Market

Investing in solutions to develop human capital is integral to the Infosys business model and its commitment to strengthening its corporate assets. However, while the employee value proposition at Infosys is designed to ensure continued revenue growth, it is also a response to a tenuous equilibrium between labour demand and lack of skills. Demand for labour in India's IT services industry is saturated, but companies struggle to find employees with suitable skills and knowledge to fulfil their available roles. Industry trend reports indicate that only 35% of India's graduates are equipped for a career in business process outsourcing companies (BPOs) (Thite and Russell 2009). This highlights the failure of academic curricula to meet realistic labour demands in a significant contributor to the nation's GDP. Further, a growing number of BPOs are competing for talent, which only exacerbates the gap between labour supply and demand.

Many scholarly articles report that corporations with CSR frameworks are able to move their strategy between business and social domains (Geva 2008). Moreover, creating a governance model that addresses both strategy and execution is essential for innovation. Internal business forces include employee engagement, growing human capital, and product/service viability (Tiwari et al. 2014). These mechanisms for innovation underpin Project Genesis and Infosys's efforts to unite its external environment with meaningful outcomes at a systemic level (Fig. 9.2).

Infosys recognises that the hiring process is one of the cornerstones to enriching its business value. Accordingly, Project Genesis is a proactive solution to parallel industry demand with access to talent. These solutions revolve around three main principles: upskilling the budding talent market; expanding the existing talent pipeline; and fostering credibility with academia and local communities (Thite

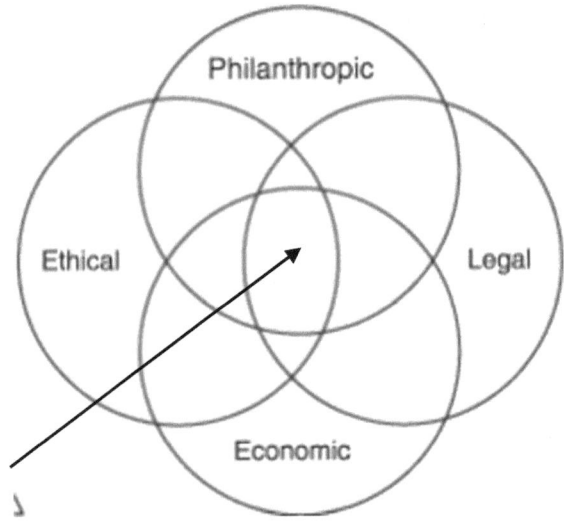

Fig. 9.2 Sustainability lies at the core of the intersecting circles CSR model. *Source* Geva (2008). Project Genesis: Its agenda in a nutshell

and Russell 2009). Project Genesis focuses on youth in economically-marginalised regions of India with qualitative reforms to graduate student education. These regions are known as Tier II and Tier III towns. The ultimate goal is to equip students with the skills they need to meet proficiency standards for employment in the IT services sector (Infosys 2018c). Hence, this initiative partners industry with academia to extend the value chain, improve revenues in a sustainable way, and define a wider interpretation of 'commerce' in a global economic context. This initiative also paves the way for other corporations to re-evaluate their business models. With these two goals in mind, Project Genesis establishes a constant source of skilled employees for its own operations while striving to be a paragon to the rest of the BPO industry.

At first glance, the primary objective of Project Genesis is to reduce the turnover rates characteristic of BPOs and, in turn, stabilise salary overheads (Thite and Russell 2009). Achieving these goals has far-reaching value for an organisation because creating a strong talent pipeline means there is less pressure to headhunt skilled staff from other employers at higher salaries (Thite and Russell 2009). In addition, Project Genesis exclusively invests its resources into solving one of India's most pressing socio-economic issues—employment. The corporate governance strategy behind the project enriches civic amenities and improves employability across the wider community.

9.4 The Project Genesis Model: A Four-Pronged Approach

As one of the current frontrunners in emerging markets, India leverages economic liberalisation as a primary mechanism for increasing its productivity (Tiwari et al. 2014). Over the last two decades, large IT organisations, like Infosys, have boosted India's gross domestic product (GDP) through "export consulting services and urban employment" (Tiwari et al. 2014). Project Genesis embraces this agenda with an effective building-block approach to teaching students material that is tailored to their constrained industry exposure.

9.4.1 The Final Verdict: How Effective Is Project Genesis?

India's BPOs march forward at unrivalled speed. However, with this advancement, the word 'attrition' has become a household term. For India, attrition means the failure of the BPO industry to cope with a labour shortage that is now reaching crisis levels. For graduates, BPOs are seen as a stop-gap while they find a better job. This sentiment is confirmed in meta-analytic reports, which cite "job satisfaction, organisational commitment and the perceived ease of (securing alternative employment" among the causes of turnover at BPOs (Ranganathan and Kuruvilla 2008). Hence, this case analysis examines the impact of Project Genesis on employee retention.

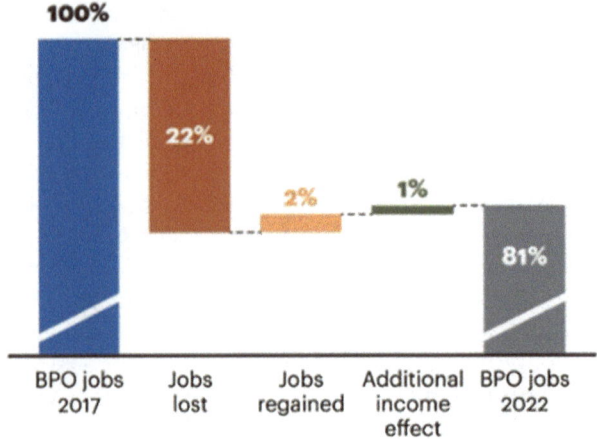

Fig. 9.3 Job losses in India's BPO sector. *Source* Kearney (2017)

In an industry that faces economic unrest and struggles to source enough staff to meet its plans for expansion, Project Genesis serves as a blueprint for how to combat the leading issues associated with employee retention in BPOs (Fig. 9.3).

As such, Infosys has prioritised transformation and, in turn, sparked an evolution in human resources context from employee management to employee engagement (Thite and Russell 2009). In this vein, its corporate governance agenda is underpinned by a business model that sets out the 'essential' skills an employee needs to fulfil their role, and the ways those skills can be cultivated (Thite and Russell 2009). The main objectives of this model are to: hone both an in-house and an external talent market; create an internal portfolio for the talent supply chain; and become a sustainable business faster by reducing attrition rates (Thite and Russell 2009).

Project Genesis is a platform for communal learning. It forges tactical linkages between primary public sectors that support two-way flows of information and, in doing so, creates synchronicity, equips students with industry skills, and sheds light on a range of academic perspectives that make them employable. As a result, this initiative has received a positive response from employees, education institutions, society, the government, and, of course, Infosys itself.

9.4.2   Phase 1: Skills-Level Assessment and the Design of a New Curriculum

The first step in developing Project Genesis was to conduct a preliminary investigation into the basic proficiencies of graduate students. A skills-level assessment was piloted in select colleges in Tier II and III towns to benchmark various skills and identify any knowledge gaps (Thite and Russell 2009). Additionally, the initiative was also promoted to students, academia, and families to increase broad local awareness.

Next, Infosys developed a curriculum, called "Global Skills Enhancement" (GSE), according to deficiencies found from the skills assessment. Tailored to BPOs, the skill gaps fell into two broad streams: language enhancement and numerical analytical skills. The course also contains modules on corporate etiquette, resource and conflict management, and professional growth and training to benefit both mentors and students (Infosys 2018c).

Perhaps more importantly, this process established the groundwork for developing a sound set of organisational values. From an internal perspective, the skills collated through the assessment could be mapped to various client service hubs, and the human resources team could use those maps as a blueprint for recruiting appropriate staff (Thite and Russell 2009). Hence, from the outset, Project Genesis bred a vaster degree of employee engagement by steering potential talent toward aptly selected positions (Thite and Russell 2009).

9.4.3 Phase 2: 'Train the Trainer' and 'Principal's Conclave' Programs

In charting strategies to develop the untapped markets in Tier II and III regions, Infosys created a 'learner-centred experiential' training methodology for universities to drive knowledge pathways through the curriculum (Infosys 2018c). Within this methodology, professors are mentored by in-house trainers at Infosys who pass on a nuanced understanding of BPOs. Professors use this knowledge to augment courses for business graduates (Thite and Russell 2009). The courses are strictly developed by the faculty, but successfully completing a course provides a GSE certification and, therefore, students must demonstrate proficiency in the prescribed skills. This approach serves a dual purpose. It provides students with a comprehensive understanding of integrated end-to-end outsourcing and, from a broader perspective, improves general education standards (Thite and Russell 2009).

The symbiosis between industry-academic partnerships requires commensurate effort on both sides of the equation. Infosys sponsors the course (Thite and Russell 2009), and the host colleges invest their knowledge, infrastructure, and resources. A critical component of the training is an emphasis on contributing to India's growth and creating a long-term career in the BPO industry. That way, all sides benefit. Data on these issues are provided to graduates in regular workshop sessions throughout the course. Astonishingly, subsequent research has confirmed a nil attrition rate in GSE-certified hires (Thite and Russell 2009) (Fig. 9.4).

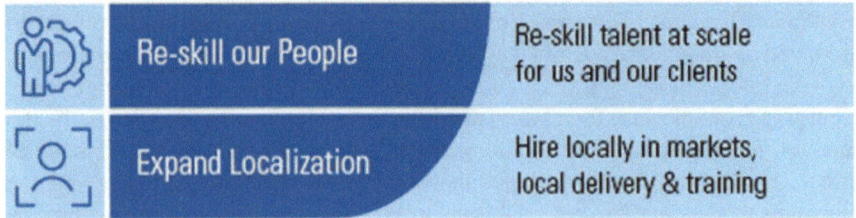

Fig. 9.4 The twin levers of Infosys's strategy to accelerate value creation. *Source* Infosys (2018a, p. 40)

9.4.4 Phase 3: Review and Assessment

Phase 3 involved establishing an institutional network to serve as a centralised online forum for GSE-licensed academics to exchange periodic reviews, evaluations, and constructive critiques on training methodologies, subject content, etc. (Thite and Russell 2009). Beyond expediting synchronicity and real-time professional correspondence, the platform complies with Infosys's governance framework of proactively considering community responses. Academics can also access periodic refresher training seminars, which is an integral facet of Project Genesis. The seminars keep professors up-to-date with recent advances in the BPO landscape and serve as an opportunity to provide feedback and recommendations on the curriculum—for example, removing or revising obsolete portions of the program (Thite and Russell 2009). They also provide financial benefits for both parties. Prior to the seminars, Infosys had fixed curricula covering both long courses and short courses, largely to ensure homogenous training standards. The short programs were for those who already have most of the skills required, and the long programs were for those starting from scratch (Thite and Russell 2009). However, these programs failed to account for the discrepancies in skills across institutes or regions, or fluctuations in aptitude test scores from year to year (Thite and Russell 2009). By allowing changes to suit the needs of the specific students in a course, both partners save time and money. That being said, the cost of the long courses were typically triple the amount of their short-course counterparts (Thite and Russell 2009).

While employee capability and instructor training remain ongoing challenges for Infosys, Project Genesis has resulted in a cohesive program that produces a standardised and skilled talent pool across a broad spectrum of socio-economic backgrounds to match the client services Infosys and other similar BPOs offer. At its crux, the methodology has initiated a critical shift in organisational thinking. The cost of human resources has been offset or decreased. And graduates are able to transition into the corporate sphere as employees in a more seamless manner.

9.4.5 Phase 4: Regional Job Fairs

The last phase of the framework culminates in Infosys expanding its business footprint by aligning human capital with industry needs, and translating these efforts into quantifiable business performance. Job fairs are an important component of this objective. These career expositions invite BPOs to scout recruits from a freshly certified talent pool, offering a gainful solution to the snowballing staffing requirements associated with export consulting services (Thite and Russell 2009). Owing to the well-designed partnership between industry and academia, Project Genesis students can showcase the skills associated with their GSE certification and, hence, their value proposition to potential employers.

The unseen, and, arguably, most important benefit of Project Genesis and these job fairs, is the effect it has had on reducing salary costs (Thite and Russell 2009). Research shows that the largest cost to BPOs is employee salaries (Thite and Russell 2009). Further, there is a causative link between low staff retention in India's dwindling talent pipeline and the swelling salary packages advertised by BPOs (Ranganathan and Kuruvilla 2008). The competition for skilled employees has created a price war that is both driving up salary expectations and negatively impacting business performance—either through a lack of proficient staff, higher staff costs, or both.

Project Genesis and the job fairs provide a stable stream of new and skilled talent for all BPOs. As a result, the employability index in states with a GSE programme has surged by up to 28% (Ranganathan and Kuruvilla 2008). Further, the initiative has increased the likelihood of retaining an employee once hired. Part of this stems from skilling up a larger labour force; the other part rests on a tacit industry policy of 'no poaching', which instils a sense of social stewardship in businesses. Both combined reduce competition and, therefore, the need for high salaries to attract a skilled workforce (Ranganathan and Kuruvilla 2008) (Fig. 9.5).

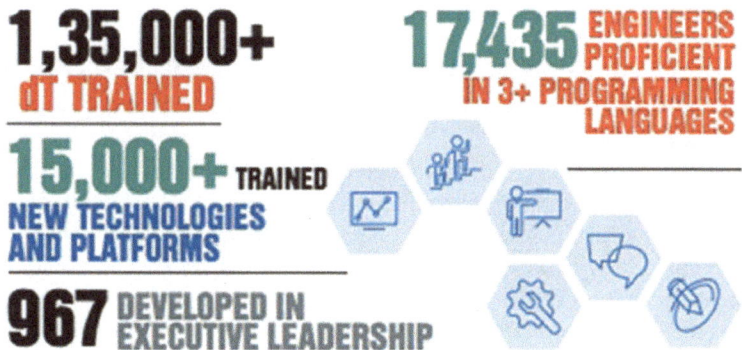

Fig. 9.5 Infosys's integrated education efforts. *Source* Infosys (2017)

9.5 Key Issues: Encouraging Collaboration Between Industry and Faculties in Business Studies

Deconstructing the potential that industry-education alliances hold as an engine for better CSR practices raises the question: What value can be gained if academic institutes and businesses collaborate? Given the stereotypes that abound over classrooms and corporate executives, the issues exposed in these collaborations are appropriate for study.

India's BPO industry faces an increasing scarcity of manpower each year because the national curriculum strongly focuses on theory and not on practical skills (Infosys 2012). To adapt, both the commercial and educational sectors must nurture the knowledge economy if India is to be sustainable in a global market.

Infosys's approach to philanthropy and solving some of the social problems prevalent in India extends beyond monetary support. It develops employment systems, encourages environmental awareness, and establishes research partnerships to synchronise and solidify business-community affairs (Mahajan and Ives 2003). The firm's enthusiastic interest in society and the environment reflects an equally manifest concern for its stakeholders. In pursuing these interests, Infosys has elicited responses from a myriad of civil society groups. Some highly praise Infosys's commitment to social rehabilitation and rural upliftment. Others are far less positive. For example, the Kalpataru Research Foundation supports an all-inclusive business-community ecosystem (Mahajan and Ives 2003) and believes that engaging stakeholders through dialogue and shared learning, such as through programs like Project Genesis, strengthen the fibres of corporate citizenship in BPOs. However, opponents of CSR argue that these programs result in an unbiased representation of labour and resources in the context of the so-called triple bottom line. They claim that resources are limited and inherently fluctuate in line with socio-economic volatility, which seriously compromises the long-term viability of such ventures across the value chain.

Although partnerships pose an ideal means to consolidate corporate interaction with society, balancing conflicting stakeholder interests raises an inescapable question that sits at the forefront of all governance structures: Which stakeholder gets priority if all parties have an equal right to be served by the organisation? This dilemma is one of the core tenets of business ethics and is neatly captured in a statement by (Charkham and Ploix 2005): "There is a real danger with CSR of competing, contradictory, and incompatible objectives." This critique reflects the complexity and power of stakeholder relationships that may subtly drive corporate alliances.

To overcome some of these reservations, Infosys integrates the concept of "shared value creation" in its governance agenda—a progressive move for a BPO. Moreover, it extends this idea to long-term value and within its mainstream business operations (Porter and Kramer 2011). To mitigate the potential powerplays inherent in industry partnerships, the four-phase structure of Project Genesis offers a practical solution for BPOs, where social accountability is commensurate with the entity's scope of influence. Proponents of the industry-academia collaboration model—the position

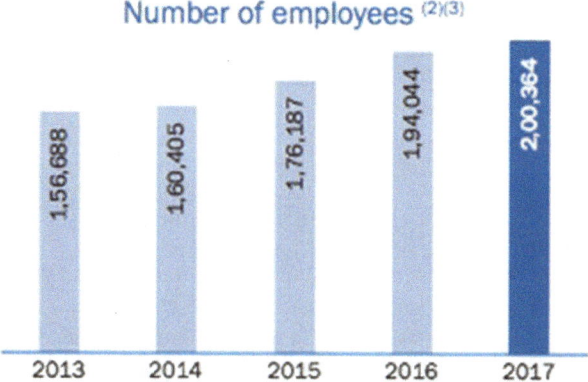

Fig. 9.6 The steady rise in BPO employees. *Source* Infosys (2017)

taken in this case study—support an open-source backbone for co-creating a research infrastructure (Fig. 9.6).

One potential issue in industry-academic collaborations is that research or curricula will be commercialised by corporate forces. The second stage of Project Genesis mitigates this issue through seminars and rigorous training that engage academia in two clear purposes—growth for India and better learning outcomes and job prospects for students. As Han Wensink, Chairman of NEVASCO, asserts: "The industry would be able to create together with academia long-term sustainable consortia… and develop new products and services" (Dasgupta 2017). Therefore, Infosys orients its management functions toward scalable innovations, such as academic partnerships, that help to generate a sustainable employment pipeline in parallel with its corporate governance strategy.

9.6 Epilogue: Teachings for Undergraduate Business Students

A closer inspection of Project Genesis at the undergraduate level suggests that the further study of this initiative would suit budding entrepreneurs and venture capitalists. This case study offers noteworthy principles on leveraging business ethics while still meeting a corporation's appetite for risk. Business students should be able to see the significance of enriching civil society as one of the ways to achieve a corporation's governance strategy. However, forming an interactive collaboration model requires comprehensive cross-sectoral discourse to deepen the authenticity of the strategy and alleviate external bias (Mahajan and Ives 2003). Further, studying partnerships is an important part of instilling a sense of social stewardship in students (and society as a whole) as they bridge the gap between an organisation's style and pace of development and the views of its stakeholders. Students may like to consider possible directions for future research in the vein—for instance, using Project Genesis as a benchmark to draw strategic comparisons with cross-cultural collaborations and their social, legal, political, or economic impacts.

9.7 Conclusion

As India's economic development gains momentum, its corporate landscape is strewn with idiosyncrasies and "burgeoning secondary markets" that push progression (Raj 2017). Project Genesis is a foray into increasing India's chances of becoming a global superpower by tapping into the, as yet, untapped Tier II and III labour markets. By its nature, this initiative leverages value creation through complex synergies between industry and academia and is seminal to improving the nation's present staff retention rates. By commercialising public research and development products, Project Genesis represents a different business model—a model that establishes cross-sectoral collaborations and nurtures those relationships as a sustainable investment in marginalised socio-economic regions. As the pool of skilled talent grows, so does per capita income. In essence, the philosophy that underpins corporate citizenship at Infosys is a compelling argument for business sustainability.

9.8 Teaching Notes

9.8.1 Synopsis of the Case

As a pioneer in IT services, business consulting, and business process outsourcing, Infosys drives economic growth and prosperity through global solutions to service delivery. Powered with an AI platform that automates 'people processes' to free up employees for solving higher-level problems, Infosys "prioritises the execution of change" and demonstrates India's rise as a global destination for software services expertise (Infosys 2018b). Infosys stands at the forefront of the digital and social revolution with a host of disruptive technologies to fuel innovation. This case study examines the organisation's flagship endeavour, Project Genesis, which is a testament to the firm's corporate social responsibility (CSR) policies and filters throughout its entire business. Project Genesis creates a nuanced connection between grassroots social activism, industry, and academia to improve India's employability index. However, as a growing number of outsourcing companies in India compete to hire employees, the lack of skilled graduates and the attrition rates intrinsic to IT are becoming problematic. In response, Project Genesis seeks to align curriculums with industry needs in an integrated campus-to-corporate transition. The result is a sustainable economic benefit for all (Infosys 2012).

9.8.2 Target Learning Group

- Level of study—BA and MA students
- Subject areas—CSR; management; innovation and entrepreneurship; government, society and education.

9.8.3 Learning Objectives

- Sustainability in business
- Corporate social enterprise
- Employability
- Corporate social responsibility models.

9.8.4 Teaching Strategy

This case study examines how the Project Genesis program developed by Infosys equips students in smaller cities and regional areas across India with the skills required by BPOs. For Infosys, the CSR philosophy that underpins this initiative serves to future-proof its talent pipeline in a competitive talent market by providing education opportunities specifically tailored to a career in the sector.

The case highlights the benefits of industry-academic partnerships to help ensure sustainable employment in the BPO industry. The suggested activities that follow are designed to promote awareness and discussion on how geographic distribution impacts staffing prospects, and how industry and education collaborate to find solutions that benefit both individuals and organisations.

9.8.5 Reading Activities

9.8.5.1 Pre-reading

Prior to class:

- Divide the class into groups and assign one of the supplementary reading activities to each group for pre-reading.
- Each group member should read and briefly summarises the key points of their assigned reading.

9.8.5.2   In-Class

- Groups should share and discuss their summaries.
- Then form new groups with at least one representative member of each pre-reading activity.
- These groups should share the key points of their respective articles.

9.8.5.3   Skim Reading

Examine the figures in the case study.

- What is their relationship to Project Genesis?

9.8.5.4   In-Depth Reading

- What is Project Genesis?
- What are its four components or streams?
- How does Project Genesis create links between students, academia, and BPOs?
- How has Project Genesis influenced change in Infosys's HR strategies?
- What are some of the arguments the authors levy against CSR initiatives?
- How does Project Genesis counter these arguments?

9.8.6   Discussion Questions

- Why does Infosys Project Genesis focus on youth in Tier II and Tier III cities?
- How does Project Genesis co-create its educational curriculum with academia? And how does this help Infosys deliver its philosophy of shared value creation?

9.8.7   Suggested Assignment

To what degree is Project Genesis extensible globally or to other industries and emergent markets with talent supply-demand gaps?

For this assignment, participants should work individually or in small groups, then select and research an industry with a supply-demand gap. Students should examine the extent to which Project Genesis and/or the four prongs of its approach are replicable. The four elements are:

- gap analysis and curriculum development;
- knowledge and awareness cascade through 'train the trainer' initiatives;
- project success evaluation; and
- initiative dissemination through fairs and roadshows.

Emerging economies or economically challenged countries/regions are preferred as subjects of analysis. The results can be shared in class as presentations or brief reports. Participants should consider:

- How suitable is Project Genesis as a generic model for industry upskilling?
- How applicable is Project Genesis to countries outside India?/to industries other than BPOs?
- To what extent do the concerns of CSR critics about undue markets and political/economic/social dominance apply to other industries?
- What changes or further innovations might be required to tailor the Project Genesis model to your selected industry?
- How well does Infosys's corporate citizen strategy and industry-academic-community collaboration work for other industries?

9.8.8 Additional Resources

9.8.8.1 Suggested Assignment Resources

- **Loiselle, B. 2016**. How Entrepreneurs Can Fill The Demand Supply Gap In The Education Industry. Retrieved from https://www.entrepreneur.com/article/280535.
  Loiselle makes the case for how entrepreneurs can fill the talent supply gap, presenting a similar approach to that of Infosys.
- **Vaiman, V., Sparrow, P., Schuler, R. & Collings, D. G. 2018**. Macro Talent Management in Emerging and Emergent Markets: A Global Perspective, Routledge.
  This was the first book to specifically focus on country-level activities aimed at attracting and retaining high-level talent in emerging markets for economic success. The book is a guide that orients readers toward activities that increase their country's global competitiveness, attractiveness, and economic development through strategic talent management.
- **London, T. & Hart, S. L. 2004**. Reinventing strategies for emerging markets: beyond the transnational model. *Journal of International Business Studies*, 35, 350–370.
  With established labour markets becoming saturated, multinational corporations have increasingly turned to emerging markets in the developing world. Such strategies almost exclusively target the wealthy elite. However, a number of multinationals have recently launched new initiatives to explore the untapped potential at the

base of the economic pyramid. This labour market is the largest and fastest-growing segment of the world's population. However, reaching these four billion people poses both tremendous opportunities and unique challenges. Conventional wisdom about the global capabilities of multinationals and the strategy of establishing subsidiaries in emerging markets may no longer be appropriate.

- **The Economist. 2015**. *Mind the gap: A lack of skilled workers and managers drags the country down*. The Economist. https://www.economist.com/britain/2015/04/11/mind-the-gap
  Sir James Dyson explains his challenges with finding 3000 engineers when Britain only produces about 25,000 engineering graduates a year, and how he faced a huge shortfall in recruitment.

9.8.8.2 Supplementary Materials

- **Kolanu, P. 2013**. What are Tier II and Tier III Cities?. Silicon India. Retrieved from https://blogs.siliconindia.com/facilitymanagementservices/What_are_Tier_II_and_Tier_III_Cities-bid-52pLs73x43343767.html
  Brief definition and analysis of the benefits of investing in India's Tier II and III cities.
- **The Economic Times. 2018**. Tier II and Tier III Cities. India Times. Retrieved from https://economictimes.indiatimes.com/topic/tier-II-and-tier-III-cities
  Economic Times search results related to Indian Tier II and Tier III cities.
- **Boddupalli, R. 2018**. India's Tier 2 and Tier 3 Cities: Are They Right for Your Business?. Dezan Shira and Associates. Retrieved from https://www.india-briefing.com/news/india-tier-2-tier-3-cities-right-business-15932.html/
  A listing of India's Tier 2 and Tier 3 cities, including managing investment in these cities.

References

Charkham J, Ploix H (2005) Keeping better company: corporate governance ten years on. Oxford University Press, Oxford, UK

Dasgupta A (2017) Finding the right fight in academia and industry collaboration. Geospatial World. Retrieved from https://www.geospatialworld.net/article/expectations-in-academia-and-industry-collaboration

Geva A (2008) Three models of corporate social responsibility: interrelationships between theory, research, and practice. Bus Soc Rev 113:1–41

Infosys (2012) Infosys Corporate Social Responsibility I Project Genesis I Infosys BPO Training. Retrieved from https://www.infosys.com/newsroom/press-releases/Pages/project-genesis.aspx

Infosys (2017) Annual report 2016–2017. Retrieved from https://www.infosys.com/investors/reports-filings/annual-report/annual/Documents/infosys-AR-17.pdf

Infosys (2018a) Annual report 2017–2018. Retrieved from https://www.infosys.com/investors/reports-filings/annual-report/annual/Documents/AR-2018/financials/pdf/Infosys_AR18_Boards_report.pdf

Infosys (2018b) Infosys—AI-powered core | Navigate your next. Retrieved from https://www.infosys.com/navigate-your-next/ai-powered-core/

Infosys (2018c) Project Genesis. Retrieved from https://www.infosysbpm.com/newsroom/press-releases/Pages/project-genesis.aspx

Kearney AT (2017) Kearney Global Services Location Index—the widening impact of automation. Retrieved from https://www.atkearney.com/digital-transformation/gsli/full-report

Mahajan A, Ives K (2003) Enhancing business-community relations—Infosys technologies case study, India. New Academy of Business, UN Volunteers, The Energy and Resources Institute, India

Porter ME, Kramer MR (2011) The big idea: creating shared value. How to reinvent capitalism-and unleash a wave of innovation and growth. Harv Bus Rev 89

Raj E (2017) Doing business in India: the rise of Tier-II and Tier-III cities. Arsha consulting. Retrieved from https://www.arshaconsulting.com/en/blog/posts/2017/october/doing-business-in-india-the-rise-of-tier-ii-and-tier-iii-cities/

Ranganathan A, Kuruvilla S (2008) Employee turnover in the business process outsourcing industry in India. In: Dariusz J, Jerzy K (eds) Management practices in high-tech environments. IGI Global, Hershey, PA, pp 110–132

Thite M, Russell B (eds) (2009) The next available operator: managing human resources in Indian business process outsourcing industry. Sage, New Delhi, India

Tiwari R, Kalogerakis K, Herstatt C (2014) Technology and innovation management frugal innovation and analogies: some propositions for product development in emerging. In: R&D management conference 2014, 3–6 June at Stuttgart (Germany) proceedings, pp 15–23

Dr. Meena Chavan is a leader in teaching and research in the areas of International Business, Management, Cross Cultural Management, Entrepreneurship, and Small Business Management. She possesses an effective blend of 30 years' experience in industry and academia. She is an advocate of experiential learning and adopts an experiential teaching style. Her innovative approach to teaching has earned her a Vice Chancellor's citation for sustained leadership in experiential and work integrated learning approaches in order to transform students into employable graduates with strong social and community values.

Associate Professor Yvonne A. Breyer is an award-winning academic with expertise in student success, online learning and digital transformation in the higher education sector. Yvonne has led several highly successful strategic initiatives with national and international reach. Most recently, she led the 'Excel Skills for Business' specialisation, which received the Coursera Outstanding Educator Award for Student Transformation on the back of exceptional learner feedback, global reach and impact. She holds a Ph.D. (Macquarie University), a Master of Arts (University of Essen, Germany) and a Postgraduate Certificate in Higher Education, Leadership and Management (Macquarie University).

Chapter 10
Migrant Workers and Corporate Social Responsibility: Workplace Practices in Mauritius

Sevika Varaden, Manjit Singh Sandhu and Fandy Tjiptono

> *When I see the migrant workers' broken bodies and eyes without hope, I want to embrace and wipe away their fears. It makes me angry and helps me to keep fighting the oppressive system.*
> **Irene Fernandez (Malaysian human rights activist)**

Abstract The growth of international migration has brought a plethora of issues to the workplace, particularly in developing countries. Exploitation, inequality, poor working conditions, and non-unionisation have led to reports of migrant workers being treated as "slave labour". Many have called for greater attention to address the human rights and working issues of employees in line with workplace sustainability development goals. However, the treatment of migrant workers still remains an issue in business practice in many countries. In this case study, we explore the workplace issues faced by migrant workers from Bangladesh, India, and Madagascar in Mauritius, an island nation in the Indian Ocean off the coast of Southern Africa. The case describes why and how three Mauritian textile manufacturing companies changed their workplace practices to encompass corporate social responsibility (CSR). The complexity surrounding these issues is examined through an institutional lens.

Keywords Corporate social responsibility (CSR) · Migrant workers · Workplace issues · Workplace practices · Mauritius · Stakeholder theory

S. Varaden · M. S. Sandhu
Monash University, Bandar Sunway, Malaysia

F. Tjiptono (✉)
Victoria University of Wellington, Wellington, New Zealand
e-mail: fandy.tjiptono@vuw.ac.nz

10.1 The Case a Glance

Key concepts	• Corporate social responsibility • Workplace sustainability • Stakeholders • Institutional theory

Level of study	• Undergraduate, postgraduate, executive students

Subject areas	• Management, corporate social responsibility, business ethics, sustainability

Graduate capabilities

Graduate outcome	%
Critical thinking	20%
Problem Solving	20%
Teamwork	10%
Communication	10%
Ethical thinking	20%
Sustainability	20%
Total	**100%**

Time required	• Out of class preparation : 2 hours • In-class discussion : 1 hour • Out of class assignments : 2 hours

Activity type	• Team-based

Ancillary materials	• Journal articles related to CSR/business ethics/sustainability

10.2 Background

In 2013, there were an estimated 232 million migrants across the globe. This statistic represents a staggering increase of 77 million people since 1990 (UN 2013). Induced by globalisation, international migration has, without doubt, become an underlying characteristic of the world economy. Yet it remains a pervasive fact that the non-economic facet of migration—the human rights and workplace conditions of migrants—is a forgotten component of this epoch (De Guchteneire and Pécoud 2009). Regrettably, the residents of a country seldom empathise or relate to the impoverished living and working conditions of migrant workers. As highlighted by de Varennes (2003, p. 6), there is an "erroneous fear that migrants are connected to situations of increased unemployment, crime and homelessness". The overriding belief espoused by many is that a person's rights are tied to nationality and citizenship. Consequently, migrant workers enjoy little protection (Tiburcio, 2001, as cited in de Guchteneire and Pécoud 2009).

Mauritius is a small island nation off the coast of Southern Africa (see Fig. 10.1). With a population of around 1.2 million, Mauritius is one of the most robust developing economies of the African region. Although small, its economy is witnessing an annual growth rate of more than 5.0% (2014–2017) (World Economics 2018).

Fig. 10.1 The island of Mauritius

In the textiles industry, this growth has translated to momentous competition and, in turn, a heavy reliance on migrant workers (Tandrayen-Ragoobur 2014). The industry, defined as the "production of fibres and items of clothing" (Barcelona Activa 2013, p. 2), benefits from preferential trade agreements with a range of markets, including the US and Europe (Joomun 2006), and textiles account for around 50% of Mauritius' overall exports (Russell 2014). In 2014, it was estimated that the industry employed approximately 17,000 foreign workers from countries such as India, China, Bangladesh, Sri Lanka, and Madagascar. This figure represents more than 60% of the total migrant workers employed in Mauritius (Statistics Mauritius 2015). Moreover, in Mauritius, it is guaranteed that migrant workers should enjoy remuneration and other employment conditions which, according to law, are not less favourable than those prescribed for Mauritian workers (Employment Rights Act 2008). However, it has been revealed that migrant workers in Mauritius do face exploitation. They do not benefit from proper accommodation, and they feel discriminated against compared to local workers (Suntoo and Chittoo 2011). As a result, there have been many confrontations between workers and employers over workers' rights and labour standards (Lincoln 2015). Media coverage of their working conditions, low pay, and long hours has been extensive, going as far as calling migrant workers in Mauritius "slave labour" (Newell and Winnett 2007).

10.3   Social Issues in the Global Textiles Industry

The textiles industry is labour-intensive, highly outsourced, and globalised. The industry has been accused of weak health and safety standards, mandatory overtime, and forced labour (Giesen 2008). In a globally competitive market, the demand for lower prices has seen many textile manufacturers turn to cheap labour markets for workers (Abernathy et al. 2006; Daft et al. 2014). Regrettably, this has often resulted in exploitation or super-exploitation (Shelley 2007) and, in turn, increasing pressure from NGOs and human rights activists for corporations to implement socially responsible workplace practices (Allwood et al. 2006; Hale and Wills 2007).

Unlike other industries, companies in the textiles industry are not considered to be socially responsible unless CSR practices are implemented across the entire supply chain (Maon et al. 2008), likely because of the extremely close stakeholder scrutiny and high levels of internationalisation (Lindgreen et al. 2016; Vrijhoef 2011). In the context of the textile industry, De Abreu (2014) suggests four factors affecting CSR practices: stakeholder pressure, firm size, position in the value chain and institutional dynamics. Although CSR is being determined by the management, external stakeholders such as customers and NGOs also play an important role in shaping CSR practices (Turcotte et al. 2007).

As a matter of fact, CSR watchdogs have been concerned about labour exploitation in the textiles industry for a long time (Crinis 2010). The textiles industry relies heavily on migrant workers (Stalker 1994), and migrant workers are a vulnerable population commonly exposed to both exploitation (Waite et al. 2015) and unsatisfactory living conditions (UN 2005). In practice, recruitment agencies play a significant role in sourcing and mobilising migrant workers across the globe (Rudnick 1996; United Nations Office on Drugs and Crime 2015), which presents another avenue of exploitation. Recruitment agencies often charge migrant workers exorbitant placement fees and expenses that leave the victims impoverished or indebted (UN 2015).

Black et al. (2005, p. 1) argue that "international migration is a powerful symbol of global inequality, whether in terms of wages, labour market opportunities, or lifestyles". Migrant workers are known to take on low-wage, low skilled, labour-intensive jobs that are unattractive to nationals. This places migrant workers in an employment structure that is inherently predisposed to discrimination (Wang et al. 2014). Gender-based discrimination is more complex and exacerbated by preconceptions about pregnancy and maternity. However, the end result is often lower wages still for female migrant workers (Krull and Marino 2011). Moreover, poor working conditions are the baseline for many migrant workers no matter their gender (International Labour Office 2008).

Following the ILO's Abolition of Forced Labour Convention of 1957, no practice of forced labour has been found in textile and clothes-producing countries (ILO 2016; Wendelspiess 2010). While this does represent progress, it also allows room to focus on deeper layers of exploitation—long working hours, piece-rate pay, and so on (ILO 2014; Wendelspiess 2010). According to ILO (2014), piece-rate pay can mean many workers need to work very long hours just to earn a minimum wage, i.e., the equivalent of working unpaid overtime. According to Misra (2007), global demand for cheap labour is one dominant pull factor attracting migrant workers to take on low paid jobs overseas. This has resulted in a large proportion of migrant workforce facing unfavourable working conditions while reaping limited advantages (Misra 2007). As a result, migrant workers are now amongst the most vulnerable groups of society, with an enduring absence of legal and social support (Giovannone and Sargeant 2016).

10.4 Selected Cases of Social Issues in the Mauritian Textiles Industry

To illustrate the workplace conditions and practices in the Mauritian textiles industry, three Mauritian-based textile manufacturing firms were carefully selected as specific cases. The companies were classified based on the categorisation specified by Kushnir et al. (2010), i.e., small companies (10–49 employees), medium companies (50–249 workers), and large companies (more than 250 employees). Pseudonyms have been used to preserve confidentiality. To increase the validity of this research, we collected and triangulated three sets of data (Gorard and Taylor 2004). The primary data was gathered through in-depth interviews with 22 participants from three textile companies in Mauritius. The participants represent different stakeholders, such as directors, managers, recruitment agents, trade unionists, and Indian and Bangladeshi migrant workers. We then used a content analysis method to analyse both the interview transcripts and relevant archival documents. In addition, we also made field observations in the factories, dormitories, and offices, which provided additional insights into the workers' living conditions.

10.4.1   Case 1 (Bella)

Bella is a private Mauritian textiles manufacturing company, specialising in the production of woven shirts. Since its inception in 1994, Bella has decentralised part of its production outside Mauritius and established manufacturing facilities in India, Bangladesh, and Madagascar. This is a vertically integrated holding company with its own weaving mill to supply fabrics and a parent company listed on the Stock Exchange of Mauritius Ltd. The company exports to the US, Europe, Australia, South Africa, and India. Its customer base is solely international customers, such as Levi's, Esprit, Hugo Boss, Marks & Spencer, Sacoor Brothers, and Zara.

Bella employs 8000 people worldwide, of which 2700 are located in Mauritius. Nationwide, it employs 487 migrant factory workers, all from Bangladesh, Madagascar, or India. These workers are predominantly female and all work as machinists. In an attempt to increase the transparency of its production facilities by following ethical auditing standards, Bella has sought certification from the Worldwide Responsible Accreditation Award for some of its manufacturing units. This certification endorses harmless, compliant, civilised, and ethical manufacturing. The company also successfully applied for membership in both the Business Social Compliance Initiative, a supply chain management scheme run by the Foreign Trade Association to drive improvements in social compliance, and the Sedex Members Ethical Trade Audits (SMETA) program, which helps its members prepare ethical audit reports.

Some of Bella's CSR practices are managed by a dedicated department within its parent company. For example, each year Bella contributes to a CSR fund for the purpose of developing community projects. Plus, Bella has established its own CSR practices that specifically relate to migrant workers. These are listed in Table 10.1.

10.4.2   Case 2 (Isla)

Isla specialises in knitted garments, especially t-shirts, joggers, and polos. It also offers in-house embroidery, printing, laser printing, and garment dyeing and washing. Originally founded in 1987, the company was acquired by a conglomerate in 2014 as an on-going concern. Its entire production output is exported to internationally-renowned brands in the UK, France, and South Africa, such as ASOS, Debenhams, Arcadia, John Lewis, and Markhams. Isla employs 130 people; 60 are Bangladeshi migrant workers, all of whom work as machinists and all of whom are male. Like Bella, Isla gained membership in SMETA to institute ethical audit reporting practices.

Table 10.1 An overview of Bella's workplace practices pertaining to migrant workers

Workplace practices	Examples	
Health and safety	Accommodation	• Free furnished residences, each housing 10–30 workers • Free water and utilities • A cook and a cleaner for each residence
	Meal allowances	• An allowance for food
Recognition	Equal pay	• For all migrant workers, irrespective of age, religion, gender, and nationality, given similar experience
	Bonuses	• An attendance bonus • Incentives
Diversity	Diversity	• Workers of different nationalities and both genders
Growth and development	Training	• On- and off-the-job training programs in schools
Involvement	Workers' Council	• To resolve grievances and advocate for the contributions of migrant workers
	Open-door management policy	• To raise grievances and complaints directly with the employer
Work-life balance	Recreation	• TVs, VCRs, indoor and outdoor games provided at the dormitories • A weekly cricket match on Sundays • Bus services to attend religious events • Social outings
Additional benefits	Free flights	• One return flight to cover the cost of migration

It also benefits from the ASOS Ethical Trade programme, which assists manufacturers in providing fair and safe working conditions. The company does not have a dedicated CSR department, but it has established specific workplace practices for its migrant workers. These are summarised in Table 10.2.

10.4.3   Case 3 (Shellana)

Shellana, also based in Mauritius, was founded in 1995 and specialises in manufacturing accessories, particularly caps, hats, bags, ties, lanyards and tags, belts,

Table 10.2 An overview of Isla's workplace practices pertaining to migrant workers

Workplace practices	Examples	
Health and safety	Accommodation	• Two free furnished residences • Free water and utilities • A cook and a cleaner for each residence
	Meal allowances	• An allowance for food
Recognition	Equal pay	• For all migrant workers, irrespective of age, religion, gender, and nationality, given similar experience
	Bonuses	• An attendance bonus • Incentives
Growth and development	Training	• On-the-job training
Involvement	Workers' Council	• A committee, administered by the workers, to voice grievances
Work-life balance	Religious observance	• Bus services to attend religious events
Additional benefits	Free flights	• One return flight to cover the cost of migration

gloves, aprons, leather accessories, and other apparel. Since its inception, Shellana has become more vertically-integrated with its own chain of retail outlets in Mauritius. The company sells 50% of its production in the Mauritian market; the rest is exported to Seychelles, the Maldives, and South Africa. Its main client is Truworths, a South African fashion retailer. Shellana has 25 employees; 8 are Bangladeshi migrant workers. All are male, and all work on the factory floor, mostly as machinists. Table 10.3 lists the workplace practices implemented by Shellana relating to its migrant workers.

Table 10.3 An overview of Shellana's workplace practices pertaining to migrant workers

Workplace practices	Examples	
Health and safety	Accommodation	• A free furnished residence • Free water and utilities
	Meal allowances	• An allowance for food
Employee recognition	Equal pay	• For all migrant workers, irrespective of age, religion, gender, and nationality, given similar experience
	Bonuses	• An attendance bonus
Growth and development	Training	• On-the-job training
Work-life balance	Recreation	• Frequent social gatherings
Additional benefits	Free flights	• One return flight to cover the cost of migration

10.5   Workplace Issues for Migrant Workers

In Mauritius, foreign textile workers are authorised to work for eight years (Ministry of Labour 2016a). Given that employment for non-nationals is temporary, migrant workers are a vulnerable and highly-marginalised subgroup of society (De Guchteneire and Pécoud 2009). Workplace issues include methods of recruitment, performance requirements, lack of personal or professional development, and unfair dismissals (Raazaz 2017). There are six further issues that specifically affect migrant workers in Mauritius: (1) segregation based on nationality; (2) segregation based on gender; (3) economic exploitation; (4) lack of access to a labour union; (5) poor living conditions; and (6) unlawful recruitment practices. Each of these is discussed in detail in the following sections.

10.5.1   Segregation Based on Nationality

Migrant workers in Mauritius come from diverse countries, mostly Bangladesh, India, Sri Lanka, and Madagascar (International Organization for Migration 2014). However, the concept of equal treatment for migrant workers has been tainted by the underlying bias Mauritians have toward one nationality over another. As Plender (2015) reports, although most basic salaries are the same, Sri Lankans typically earn more than Indians, and Indians earn more than Bangladeshis for doing the same job. The study notes that general education levels in India and Nepal are higher than in Bangladesh. Therefore, Bangladeshis do not speak Hindi as well as Indians and Nepalese, and this may account for the higher rates of pay.

The Mauritian Employments Rights Act (2008) prohibits discriminatory practices, but holding employers to account for discrimination can be challenging (Rooney 2009). Additionally, many migrant workers may not even recognise that discrimination is occurring, as workers of different nationalities are housed in separate dormitories. Thus, they have minimal interaction outside of work.

10.5.2   Segregation Based on Gender

Interestingly, two of the three cases in this study (Isla and Shellana) 'segregate' their workers based on both nationality and gender. In an industry that is conventionally dominated by women, Isla and Shellana only employ men. Each claims that a male-only workforce presents less of a security risk in that it prevents problems associated with female workers living alone. However, the cost savings associated with not needing to provide extra dormitories may also be a factor.

10.5.3 Economic Exploitation

Economic exploitation is another issue confronting migrant workers in Mauritius. Under the Factory Employees (Remuneration Order) Regulation (2001), there are two legal remuneration systems, piece-rate pay or a basic wage, and the two systems are mutually exclusive. In the piece-rate system, each employee is allocated a manufacturing quota to be completed within a certain period of time and is paid based on how many items they produce once they meet their quota (Wu et al. 2013). This may mean a worker labours until midnight to meet their quota without receiving any overtime. As a system, this works in favour of the employer. They exercise control without the need to monitor workers as heavily. A basic wage means workers get paid for working a specific number of hours. Most Mauritians receive a basic wage since they are somewhat unmotivated to work and are not productive enough to be incentivised by piece-rate pay. Additionally, Mauritians tend to be quite resistant to change.

10.5.4 No Access to a Labour Union

Another issue that affects the welfare of migrant workers is non-unionisation. The Mauritian Employment Relations Act (2008) stipulates that every employee has the right to join a trade union. However, management generally considers trade unions to be agents of unfamiliar and/or undesirable values and principles (Adams 2006). As such, many migrant workers in Mauritius are persuaded against joining a trade union. This is not an issue singular to migrant workers but rather a commonplace tactic in the general workforce. The inference is that corporations like to remain union-free in the belief that trade unions reduce profits, i.e., through collective bargaining, protests, or strikes (Kaufman and Taras 2000).

10.5.5 Poor Living Conditions

The Ministry of Labour in Mauritius states that "the Employer shall provide, free of charge, decent accommodation, inclusive of water, electricity, gas, necessary furniture and sanitary amenities as well as sleeping facilities" (Ministry of Labour 2016b, p. 1), and this provision is usually included in a worker's employment contract. However, in practice, some problems may occur. For instance, during an interview, a participant revealed that "some companies keep the workers in hostile regions and dangerous environments. They are beaten, and their money or possessions stolen. And, the law does not provide a protection for them from such cases" (Varaden et al. 2017, p. 18).

10.5.6   Unlawful Recruitment Practices

In some cases, the hardship facing migrant workers begins prior to even reaching Mauritius. The norm for migrant workers is a costly and largely unlawful recruitment process managed by sub-agents. Moreover, ILO (2013) reports that the potential exploitation of migrant workers by sub-agents has not yet been effectively managed or regulated by authorities. For instance, in Bangladesh, sub-agents are usually well-known individuals who are trusted by Bangladeshi workers. As revealed by a recruitment agent during one of the interviews:

> If I contact the prospective workers directly, they won't come, given they don't know me personally. So, I contact sub-agents. They usually are well-known individuals, trusted by Bangladeshi workers. In any case, in Bangladesh subagents are not allowed by the law, but for everybody's advantage, we have to take their services, otherwise, we cannot recruit. Unfortunately, sub-agents also look for their benefits, and demand for a fee. I don't know how much they charge, but altogether, it is very tough to control. (Varaden et al. 2017, p. 18)

Such practices sentence workers to exploitative working conditions and have the potential to create an endless poverty cycle (UN 2015). Either way, workers must work longer hours over longer periods of time to recoup or pay back all the costs incurred in the recruitment process.

10.6   Workplace Practices by Mauritian Textile Companies

Workplace issues have prompted a new theme in corporate social responsibility dubbed workplace CSR. Workplace CSR concentrates on addressing "human and labour rights for the workforce" (Moon 2014, p. 31). While the previous section provides detailed workplace issues pertaining to migrant workers in Mauritius, in this section, we scrutinise the specific CSR practices implemented by Bella, Isla, and Shellana. In terms of workplace practices, Bella appears to be the one most concerned and attentive to the situation of its migrant workers. Bella is the largest of the companies examined, and it has been observed in past studies that the larger the size of the company, the greater the involvement in CSR activities (Roberts, 1992, as cited in Idowu and Leal Filho 2009).

Although Bella is the most prominent in terms of benefits granted to migrant workers, the corporate responsibilities of Isla and Shellana to the migrant workers are also far-reaching, affecting various aspects of the workplace and their personal lives. Migrant workers at these three manufacturers also enjoy numerous economic rewards. In the case of Bella and Isla, workers are given bonuses for attendance and productivity incentives. Shellana only offers bonuses for attendance, but all three remunerate their migrant workers equally, irrespective of age, gender, and nationality. All three companies practice employment diversity in terms of nationality. For instance, Bella employs migrant workers from a range of countries, although mainly from India, Bangladesh, and Madagascar. However, Isla and Shellana do not practice gender diversity, citing security reasons for their single-gender employment policy. All three companies offer some form of training. Each provides on-the-job training programs, but Bella also offers off-the-job training in its own training school.

Further details are provided below on health and safety as well as work-life balance and employee engagement issues.

10.6.1 Health and Safety

The focal aspect of the health and safety issues when employing migrant workers is the provision of accommodation (China Development Research Foundation 2012). The Mauritian Occupational Safety and Health Regulation (2015) establishes that migrant workers should be provided with accommodation that meets certain standards. In other words, it is the employer's responsibility to relocate workers into lodging that meets standard criteria for health and safety (Maher 2009). In each of the three cases in this study, migrant workers are provided with free accommodation and utilities, i.e., electricity, water, and gas. The houses are fully furnished, including linen and towels, kitchen utensils, a TV, and so on, and the houses are generally within walking distance to the factory or else transport to and from the factory is provided. Prior to occupation, all accommodation must pass a health and safety inspection to receive a lodging accommodation permit.

Beyond the legally prescribed requirements, Bella and Isla go further and also provide a cook and cleaner to each dormitory, along with a meal allowance. Usually, the cook is the same nationality as the residents, or of similar nationality, to help the workers acclimatise to Mauritius while providing some of the comforts of home. Isla provides similar housing benefits to Bella, priding themselves on providing their workers with "a good place to live". Shellana provides housing, free utilities, a meal allowance, and housing but stops short of including a cook and cleaner.

10.6.2 Work-Life Balance and Employee Engagement

Work-life balance represents an aspect of employment that is progressively being supported by CSR programmes globally (Brejning 2012). To promote this balance, Bella and Isla plan short annual 'getaways'. Bella also organises frequent parties for its workers—nationals and foreigners included—but is more active in promoting entertainment for its migrant workers. For example, indoor games are provided in the dormitories and outdoor games, such as cricket, are held weekly on Sundays. Additionally, picnics are organised three or four times per year during religious events. The harmony and amity resulting from social outings may increase team spirit and work morale as well as create a sense of being appreciated as individuals and group members among employees (Lack 2013).

As another measure to help migrant workers integrate into the workplace, Bella and Isla have established workers' councils. This extends their corporate responsibilities to the practice of providing employee support. Johnstone and Ackers (2015) assert that participation in a workers' council tends to create a sense of involvement and engagement among employees. It gives them a voice and, thus, the ability to change their current situation. In a strong demonstration of their commitment to corporate responsibility, Bella has also implemented an open-door management policy. Through this initiative, workers are welcome to raise any issue with their supervisor, and they have the right to seek advice from the factory manager.

10.7   Institutional Factors and the Treatment of Migrant Workers

10.7.1   Role of Formal Institutions

As previously discussed, a command and control guideline directed at the treatment of migrant workers has been the prevailing government retort in Mauritius in which, as Sinclair (1997) attests, non-conformity results in penalties. To incentivise companies to treat their migrant workers well, the government has established laws to regulate the most important aspects of socially-responsible workplace practices for migrant workers. These standards must be stipulated in a contract of employment and then vetted by the Ministry of Labour prior to employing any foreign labour. Government officials also conduct surprise visits to factories and dormitories to ensure that employers continue to comply with the guidelines. For migrant workers, these guidelines often establish better working conditions than in their home country. For example, Mauritian law stipulates that firms must provide their workers with a proper mattress, whereas, in their own country, they may have to sleep on the floor. Thus, the Mauritian legal system has formed a crucial instrument in how migrant workers are treated. Whether or not some firms go beyond the minimum legal CSR requirements, almost all companies, big and small, adhere to the guidelines to some extent.

10.7.2   Role of Informal Institutions

In some cases, informal institutional factors have progressed CSR practices ahead of legislation (Crane et al. 2008). International organisations and the publicity they generate is an influencing factor. And, in the case of Bella and Isla, the codes of conduct their clients practise have generated informal pressure to meet certain standards of corporate responsibility. In fact, the policies set by retailers for conduct within their supply chains are perhaps the most influential agents, particularly when the clients is a global company with an internationally-visible profile. Wholesale buyers adhere to their own codes of conduct, and these must be respected by textile manufacturers. Like government reviews, buyers conduct inspections to ensure that the textile manufacturers are complying with their codes, either once, prior to entering a buying agreement, or on an ongoing basis.

Certifications and memberships can also serve a significant role in improving CSR practices. Bella and Isla willingly registered with several organisations for guidance in maintaining a responsible and sustainable supply chain. For the most part, these organisations are non-profit with a focus on CSR.

Interestingly, our analysis of Bella's workplace practices reveal signs of internal mimicry. Yiu and Makino (2002, p. 672) argue that "the multinational enterprise itself constitutes a micro-institutional environment in which organizational information and practices are transferred between the parent and the subsidiaries and among the subsidiaries themselves". The workplace culture at Bella is shaped, in part, by its parent company—a company that is conspicuous favours the good treatment of employees and rewards its workers at annual ceremonies. As such, Bella follows suit by treating migrant workers well and rewarding them at their own annual award ceremonies.

10.8 Moving Forward

Crane et al. (2014, p. 254) claim that the advent of outsourced supply chains has rendered workplace CSR to be a "major issue for companies everywhere", and that the "need to deal with concrete issues for workers remains". This claim is particularly pertinent to the cases selected for this study, as our analysis shows that the Mauritian government, its textile manufacturers, retailers, and wholesalers are paying a great deal of attention to the way CSR is practised. Within a supply chain, good CSR practice is predominantly influenced by the codes of conduct followed by its retailers and wholesalers. The textiles industry has a complex supply chain with many interdependent relationships, but buyers have the most bargaining power, which provides a novel perspective on how businesses have responded to these workplace issues. We find that the more CSR-oriented the retailer, the more manufacturers are prompted to treat their migrant workers well. In contrast, a weak focus on CSR in the supply chain fosters adverse conditions for migrant workers. Large and medium-sized companies are more likely to be conscious of socially responsible practices toward migrant workers. This is probably due to influence from globally-renowned clients, mostly from developed countries, who exercise considerable normative pressure. Meanwhile, small companies usually serve clients from developing countries. With less reputational risk, these clients exert less pressure and, therefore, textile manufacturers have more latitude to skirt around the periphery of their social responsibilities. Mauritius represents an exceptional case in the global textiles and clothing industry because of the bilateral agreements it holds with both developed and developing countries. However, the bargaining power of industry giants like Levi's has certainly been a major influence on the Mauritian government's decision to highly regulate the workplace environments of migrant workers. These case studies shine a light on CSR practices in the textile industry in Mauritius and how three manufacturing companies responded to growing pressure for better working conditions through an institutional lens.

10.9 Teaching Notes

10.9.1 Synopsis of the Case

The growth of international migration has led to a steep rise in human and labour rights abuses globally. Despite the increasing realisation that the general living and working conditions of migrant workers worldwide is precarious, this issue has gained little prominence and is largely neglected in the broad academic literature on CSR. This case study is designed to explore workplace issues and practices, along with the institutional factors that affect the treatment of migrant workers in Mauritius. The case study examines three Mauritian textile manufacturing companies that employ migrant workers from countries such as Madagascar, India, and Bangladesh. The six main issues that affect migrant workers in the Mauritian textiles industry include: segregation based on nationality and gender; economic exploitation; lack of access to a labour union; poor living conditions; and unlawful recruitment practices. The workplace practices implemented by the three companies under study to address these issues can be categorised into health and safety practices, work-life balance, employee engagement, additional benefits, employee diversity, and growth and development. This study shows that both formal and informal institutions (i.e., governments, retailers, and clients) play an important role in establishing and maintaining CSR practices in the workplace.

10.9.2 Target Learning Group

Undergraduate, postgraduate, executive students.

10.9.3 Learning Objectives

- Identify workplace CSR issues in the Mauritian textiles industry
- Identify the underlying causes of those issues
- Identify how Mauritian textile companies have responded
- Identify the institutional factors that may have influenced how businesses have responded to CSR issues in the Mauritian textiles industry
- Critically assess variations in the CSR practices of the three textile manufacturers examined in this study.

10.9.4   Key Issues

- Human rights
- Labour rights
- Balancing low production costs with good working conditions
- CSR practices as "greenwashing"
- Integrating CSR into an entire supply chain.

10.9.5   Theoretical Concepts

- Institutional theory
- Corporate social responsibility.

10.9.6   Reading Activities

10.9.6.1   Suggested Pre-reading

Crane, A., McWilliams, A., Matten, D., Moon, J., & Siegel, D. (2008). *The Oxford Handbook of Corporate Social Responsibility*. Oxford: Oxford University Press.
de Guchteneire, P., & Pécoud, A. (2009). Introduction: The UN Convention on Migrant Workers' Rights. In R. Cholewinski, P. de Guchteneire & A. Pécoud, *Migration And Human Rights: The United Nations Convention on Migrant Workers' Rights* (1st ed.). New York: Cambridge University Press.
de Varennes, F. (2003). Strangers in Foreign Lands Diversity, Vulnerability and the Rights of Migrants (pp. 5–7). Paris: UNESCO.
Lincoln, D. (2012). *Migration and Development in Contemporary Mauritius*. Southern African Migration Programme.
Lincoln, D. (2015). Sewing machinists and bricklayers abroad: Migrant Labour and development in Mauritius. *Journal of Mauritian Studies, 1*(1), 4–27.

10.9.7   Teaching Strategy

10.9.7.1   Prior to Discussing the Case

Consider showing the students one of the videos on migrant issues and then work in groups to identify the workplace issues faced by migrants and its causes. Students should summarise their main points and group should do a simple presentation.

10.9.7.2   Case Discussions

The case study can be used in several ways:

- As a group assignment (groups of three to four students). The assignment can be divided into a written component (20%) and an oral group presentation (15%). It is important that the main concepts and theories related to the case are covered during the lecture before the class discussion.
- As a 'case discussion' during a tutorial. The case study and several discussion questions can be provided to students in advance with brief guidelines on how to prepare for the discussion (e.g., the Harvard case study format). During the class discussion, divide the class into several groups each representing different stakeholders, such as migrant workers, national/local workers, owners/managers, government bodies, NGOs, and so on. Each group should present their views on the case.

10.9.7.3   After the Case Discussion

Ask the students to reflect what they have learned. Have them relate the issues covered to 'workplace sustainability'.

10.9.7.4   Suggested Debate Topics

- The workplace issues faced by the migrant workers in the case are caused by weak governance. Do you agree? Why or why not?
- It is difficult to find a balance between economic sustainability and social sustainability (workplace sustainability). Do you agree? Justify your arguments.
- Organisations (clothing retailers) in this case are expected to consider their social responsibility across the entire supply chain. Do you agree?

10.9.8   Discussion Questions

- Why do you think the textile and apparel industry is always in the limelight where workplace issues are concerned?
- What are the key workplace issues in the Mauritian textiles industry?
- Why do you think workplace issues are being neglected in the Mauritian textiles industry?
- What are the challenges faced by textile manufacturers in addressing workplace issues in the Mauritian textiles industry?

- What are the institutional factors influencing how businesses respond to workplace issues in the Mauritian textiles industry?
- To what extent there is variation in the way businesses respond to workplace issues? And why?

10.9.9   Suggested Assignment Questions

Similar questions to the above can be used.

Multimedia

- A famous textile company in Mauritius
  https://www.youtube.com/watch?v=POVw67vwvSg
- Doing Business In Africa—Mauritius Part 4—Textile Industry
  https://www.youtube.com/watch?v=CDVwUONkBd8
- Apparel Sourcing Opportunities in Madagascar and Mauritius
  https://www.youtube.com/watch?v=qJvFWzd3FOs
- Mauritius' poor treatment of foreign workers harks back to a dark time in its history
  https://qz.com/828580/mauritius-poor-treatment-of-workers-from-countries-like-sri-lanka-bangladesh-harks-back-to-a-dark-time-in-its-history/
- Made in Bangladesh
  http://www.cbc.ca/fifth/episodes/2013-2014/made-in-bangladesh
- Fashion: Last Week Tonight with John Oliver (HBO)
  https://www.youtube.com/watch?v=VdLf4fihP78
- Accord on Fire and Building Safety in Bangladesh
  https://wsr-network.org/success-stories/accord-on-fire-and-building-safety-in-bangladesh/
- Inside India's Garment Industry
  https://www.smh.com.au/lifestyle/fashion/damning-report-on-exploitation-in-australian-fashion-industry-20150416-1mm4yz.html

Further Reading

Banerjee, S. (2007). *Corporate Social Responsibility: The Good, the Bad and the Ugly.* Cheltenham, UK: Edward Elgar.

Carroll, A. (1991). The pyramid of corporate social responsibility: Toward the moral management of organizational stakeholders. *Business Horizons, 34*(4), 39–48. http://dx.doi.org/10.1016/0007-6813(91)90005-g

Carroll, A. (1998). The four faces of corporate citizenship. *Business and Society Review, 100–101*(1), 1–7. http://dx.doi.org/10.1111/0045-3609.00008

Carroll, A. (1999). Corporate social responsibility: Evolution of a definitional construct. *Business & Society, 38*(3), 268–295. http://dx.doi.org/10.1177/000765039903800303

Carroll, A. (2008). A history of corporate social responsibility: Concepts and practices. In A. Crane, A. McWilliams, D. Matten, J. Moon & D. Siegel, *The Oxford Handbook of Corporate Social Responsibility* (1st ed., pp. 19–41). New York: Oxford University Press.

Carroll, A. (2015). Corporate social responsibility: The centerpiece of competing and complementary frameworks. *Organizational Dynamics, 44*, 87–96.

Grawitch, M.J., Gottschalk, M., & Munz, D. C. (2006). The path to a healthy workplace: A critical review linking healthy workplace practices, employee well-being, and organizational improvements. *Consulting Psychology Journal: Practice and Research, 58*(3), 129–147. http://dx.doi.org/10.1037/1065-9293.58.3.129

Matten, D. & Moon, J. (2008). "Implicit" and "explicit" CSR: A conceptual framework for a comparative understanding of corporate social responsibility. *Academy of Management Review, 33*(2), 404–424. http://dx.doi.org/10.5465/amr.2008.31193458

McWilliams, A., Siegel, D., & Wright, P. (2005). *Corporate Social Responsibility: Strategic Implications*. New-York: Department of Economics, Rensselaer Polytechnic Institute.

References

Abernathy F, Volpe A, Weil D (2006) The future of the apparel and textile industries: prospects and choices for public and private actors. Environ Plan A 38(12):2207–2232

Adams RJ (2006) Labour left out. Canadian Centre for Policy Alternatives, Ottawa, ON

Allwood J, Laursen S, de Rodríguez C, Bocken N (2006) Well dressed? The present and future sustainability of clothing and textiles in the United Kingdom. University of Cambridge, Institute of Manufacturing, Cambridge

Activa Barcelona (2013) Textile industry: sector report. Barcelona Activa, Barcelona

Black R, Natali C, Skinner J (2005) Migration and inequality: world development report. World Bank, Washington, DC

Brejning J (2012) Corporate social responsibility and the welfare state. Ashgate Pub, Farnham, Surrey

China Development Research Foundation (2012) Constructing a social welfare system for all in China. Routledge, London, UK

Crane A, Matten D, Spence L (2014) CSR in the workplace. In: Crane A, Matten D, Spence L (eds) Corporate social responsibility: readings and cases in a global context. Routledge, Oxon, pp 253–290

Crane A, McWilliams A, Matten D, Moon J, Siegel D (2008) The Oxford handbook of corporate social responsibility. Oxford University Press, Oxford

Crinis V (2010) Sweat or no sweat: foreign workers in the garment industry in Malaysia. Journal of Contemporary Asia 40(4):589–611

Daft R, Murphy J, Willmott H (2014) Organization theory and design: an international perspective. Cengage Learning, Boston

De Abreu M (2014) Perspectives, drivers, and a roadmap for corporate social responsibility in the textile and clothing industry. In: Muthu S (ed) Roadmap to sustainable textiles and clothing: regulatory aspects and sustainability standards of textiles and the clothing supply chain, 1st edn. Springer

De Guchteneire P, Pécoud A (2009) Introduction: the UN convention on migrant workers' rights. In: Cholewinski R, De Guchteneire P, Pécoud A (eds) Migration and human rights. UNESCO Publishing, Paris, pp 1–46

De Varennes F (2003) Strangers in foreign lands. Strategy paper. UNESCO Database

Employment Rights Act (2008)

FTA (2016) Fta-intl.org. Retrieved from http://www.fta-intl.org

Giesen B (2008) Ethical clothing. VDM Verlag Dr Mueller, Saarbrücken, Germany

Giovannone M, Sargeant M (2016) Vulnerable workers. CRC Press

Gorard S, Taylor C (2004) Combining methods in educational and social research. Open University Press, Maidenhead

Hale A, Wills J (2007) Women working worldwide: transnational networks, corporate social responsibility and action research. Glob Netw 7(4):453–476

International Labour Office (2008) Skills for improved productivity, employment growth and development: report V. International Labour Office, Geneva

International Labour Organization (2013) Employment practices and working condition in Thailand's fishing sector: report. International Labour Organization, Bangkok

International Labour Organization (2014) Wages and working hours in the textiles, clothing, leather and footwear industries: issues paper for discussion at the global dialogue forum on wages and working hours in the textiles, clothing, leather and footwear industries. International Labour Organization, Geneva

International Labour Organization (2016) Abolition of forced labour convention, C105, 25 June 1957. Geneva, Retrieved from http://www.ilo.org/dyn/normlex/en/f?p=NORMLEXPUB:12100:0::NO::P12100_ILO_CODE:C105

International Organization for Migration (2014) Migration in Mauritius: a country profile 2013. International Organization for Migration, Geneva

Idowu S, Leal Filho W (2009) Global practices of corporate social responsibility. Springer, New York, NY

Johnstone S, Ackers P (eds) (2015) Finding a voice at work? New perspectives on employment relations. Oxford University Press, Oxford

Joomun G (2006) The textile and clothing industry in Mauritius. In: Jauch H, Traub-Merz R (eds) The future of the textile and clothing industry in Sub-Saharan Africa. Friedrich-Ebert-Stiftung, Division for International Development Cooperation, Africa Dept, Bonn, pp 193–211

Kaufman B, Taras D (2000) Nonunion employee representation. M.E. Sharpe, Armonk, NY

Krull C, Marino S (2011) Cuban studies 41. University of Pittsburgh Press, Pittsburgh

Kushnir K, Mirmulstein M, Ramalho R (2010) Micro, small, and medium enterprises around the world: how many are there, and what affects the count? MSME Country Indicators. The World Bank, Washington, DC

Lack J (2013) Plan to turn your company around in 90 days. Apress, Berkeley, CA

Lincoln D (2015) Sewing machinists and bricklayers abroad: migrant labour and development in Mauritius. J Mauritian Stud 1(1):4–27

Lindgreen A, Kotler P, Vanhamme J, Maon F (eds) (2016) A stakeholder approach to corporate social responsibility: pressures, conflicts, and reconciliation. Routledge, New York, NY

Maher S (2009) False promises: migrant workers in the global garment industry (discussion paper). Clean Clothes Campaign, Amsterdam

Maon F, Lindgreen A, Swaen V (2008) Designing and implementing corporate social responsibility: an integrative framework grounded in theory and practice. J Bus Ethics 87(S1):71–89

Ministry of Labour, Industrial Relations, Employment and Training (2016a) Checklists for applications for work permit. Ministry of Labour, Industrial Relations, Employment and Training, Employment Division, Mauritius

Ministry of Labour, Industrial Relations, Employment and Training (2016b) Contract models. Mauritius. Retrieved from http://labour.govmu.org/English/Pages/Contract-Models.aspx

Misra N (2007) The push & pull of globalization: how the global economy makes migrant workers vulnerable to exploitation. Washington College of Law. Retrieved from https://www.wcl.american.edu/hrbrief/14/3misra.pdf

Moon J (2014) Corporate social responsibility. Oxford University Press, New York, NY

Newell C, Winnett R (2007, August 12). Revealed: topshop clothes made with 'slave labour'. The Sunday Times

Occupational Safety and Health (Employees' Lodging Accommodation) (Amendment) Regulations (2015) Mauritius: Ministry of Labour, Industrial Relations, Employment and Training

Plender R (ed) (2015) Issues in international migration law. Brill-Nijhoff, Boston, MA

Raazaz S (2017) A challenging market becomes more challenging: Jordanian workers, migrant workers and refugees in the Jordanian labour market. Retrieved from https://www.ilo.org/wcmsp5/groups/public/—arabstates/—ro-beirut/documents/publication/wcms_556931.pdf

Rooney T (2009) The equality bill. Stationery Office, London

Rudnick A (1996) Foreign labour in Malaysian manufacturing. INSAN, Kuala Lumpur

Russell M (2014) Mauritius snapshot: textile and apparel industry in brief. Just-style Home (9 June 2014). Retrieved from https://www.just-style.com/analysis/textile-and-apparel-industry-in-brief_id121536.aspx

Sedex. (2016). SEDEX Global. Retrieved 21 October 2016, from http://www.sedexglobal.com/

Shelley T (2007) Exploited. Zed Books, London, UK

Sinclair D (1997) Self-regulation versus command and control? Beyond false dichotomies. Law & Policy 19(4):363–565

Stalker P (1994) The work of strangers: a survey of international labour migration. International Labour Office, Geneva

Statistics Mauritius, Ministry of Finance and Economic Development (2015) Digest of Labour Statistics

Suntoo R, Chittoo H (2011) Working and living conditions of Chinese migrants in Mauritius. Glob J Hum Soc Sci 11(7):1–8

Tandrayen-Ragoobur V (2014) Foreign labour in the manufacturing sector: evidence from Mauritius. Paper presented at the Third International Conference on Global Business, Economics, Finance and Social Sciences, Mumbai

Turcotte MB, de Bellefeuille S, den Hond F (2007) Gildan Inc. J Corp Citizensh 2007(27):23–36. Retrieved from http://dx.doi.org/10.9774/gleaf.4700.2007.au.00005

United Nations Human Rights, Office of the High Commissioner (2005) The international convention on migrant workers and its committee. United Nations, Geneva

United Nations Office on Drugs and Crime (2015) The role of recruitment fees and abusive and fraudulent practices of recruitment agencies in trafficking in persons: report. United Nations, Vienna

United Nations, Department of Economic and Social Affairs, Population Division (2013) International migration report 2013. United Nations, New York, NY

Varaden S, Sandhu MS, Tjiptono F (2017) Business' response to workplace issues: a case of migrant workers in the Mauritian textile industry. Paper presented at the 2017 Annual Meeting of the Academy of Management, Atlanta, Georgia, 4–8 Aug

Vrijhoef R (2011) Supply chain integration in the building industry. Ios Press, Amsterdam

Waite L, Craig G, Lewis H, Skrivankova K (2015) Vulnerability, exploitation and migrants. Palgrave Macmillan UK, London

Wang H, Guo F, Cheng Z (2014) A distributional analysis of wage discrimination against migrant workers in China's urban labour market. Urban Studies 52(13):2383–2403

Wendelspiess R (2010) Firm response to advocacy campaigns. Books on Demand, Norderstedt

World Economics (2018) Gross domestic product. Retrieved from https://www.worldeconomics.com/GrossDomesticProduct/Mauritius.gdp

Worldwide Responsible Accredited Production (WRAP) (2016) Wrapcompliance.org. Retrieved from http://www.wrapcompliance.org/

Wu B, Yao S, Chen J (eds) (2013) China's development and harmonization. Routledge, Oxon

Yiu D, Makino S (2002) The choice between joint venture and wholly owned subsidiary: an institutional perspective. Organ Sci 13(6):667–683

Ms. Sevika Varaden Being of Mauritian Nationality, she has been, since the past couple of years, assisting in the implementation of biodiversity and renewable energy projects within intergovernmental organisations. Sevika is an International Business postgraduate who completed two postgraduate degrees from Monash University Malaysia, one within which she conducted extensive research on migrant workers in Mauritius. Dedicated to ongoing learning and development, she also has a passionate interest for research, and her areas of interest include corporate social responsibility, sustainability and social entrepreneurship.

Dr. Manjit Singh Sandhu is currently a Senior Lecturer in the Department of Management, School of Business, Monash University Malaysia. He also holds the Deputy Director's post for Graduate Research. His principal research interest is mainly in internationalization of firms, knowledge sharing, entrepreneurship and corporate social responsibility. He has published in several top ranked journals such International Business Review, Journal of Knowledge Management, International Journal of Public Sector Management, International Journal of Entrepreneurial Behaviour & Research, and Asia Pacific Business Review. Dr Manjit has done corporate training work for several organizations that include Malaysian Airlines and Vietnam Chamber of Commerce. He is a member of the Academy of Management and Network for Business Sustainability.

Dr. Fandy Tjiptono is a Senior Lecturer at the School of Marketing and International Business, Victoria University of Wellington (VUW). He has more than 20 years of teaching experience in Malaysia, Indonesia, Australia, and New Zealand. His main research interest is consumer behaviour and marketing practices in emerging markets. His research has been published in several reputable journals such as Journal of Business Ethics, Marketing Planning and Intelligence, International Journal of Consumer Studies, Internet Research, and Journal of Travel and Tourism Marketing. His more than 12 years of consulting experience covers a wide range of industries, such as FMCG, publishing, telecommunication, and banking.

Chapter 11
Mainstreaming Neurodiversity for an Inclusive and Sustainable Future Workforce: Autism-Spectrum Employees

Anna Krzeminska and Sally Hawse

Abstract People with autism have the highest rates of unemployment among any group of people with and without 'disabilities'. Yet their skills are essential to meeting current and future workforce needs, particularly in STEM areas. Traditionally defined as a disability, the strengths and limitations of autism are now recognised as valuable differences and increasingly harnessed by employers in the workplace. This case illustrates people with autism at work, as well as the history of autism employment through a movement that was started by a small Danish social innovator in 2004 and is now spreading globally in large for-profit companies. This case further showcases the various HR practices of these organisations, which are moving from affirmative action programs to regular front-door modes of employment and other models in between. The study concludes with a discussion on issues in this area to be addressed in future.

Keywords Workforce sustainability · Workforce diversity · Autism-spectrum employees · Inclusiveness in the workplace · Neurodiversity

A. Krzeminska (✉) · S. Hawse
Macquarie University, Sydney, Australia
e-mail: anna.krzeminska@mq.edu.au

© Springer Nature Singapore Pte Ltd. 2020
L. Wood et al. (eds.), *Industry and Higher Education*,
https://doi.org/10.1007/978-981-15-0874-5_11

11.1   The Case at a Glance

Key concepts	• Autism spectrum employees • Workplace inclusion and diversity • Neurotypical and neurodiverse
Level of study	• BA and MA students
Subject areas	• HRM, management, social policy, economics

Graduate capabilities	Graduate outcomes	%
	Critical thinking	10
	Problem solving	10
	Teamwork	5
	Communication	5
	Ethical thinking	40
	Sustainability	30
	Total	**100%**

Time required	• Out-of-class preparation: 45 min • In-class discussion: 30 min • Out-of-class assignments: 120 min
Activity type	Individual activities: • Pre-reading • Assignment questions based on the Autism at Work initiative and the development of a brief business case for integrating AS employees into the workplace • Supplementary multimedia activities — YouTube videos • Supplementary further reading Team activities: • Group discussion questions

Additional Materials

Online Resources

- **Autism at Work: Releasing Talent and Harnessing Creativity**
  https://www.youtube.com/watch?v=aVXElNak3sU
  In the run-up to World Autism Awareness Day on 2 April, a diverse panel featuring an employer, an academic, an Autism at Work expert, and an autistic employee, gather to ask: How can workplaces adapt to offer greater opportunities to those with autism, and benefit themselves as a result?

- **Neurotypical**
  http://www.pbs.org/pov/neurotypical/
  This video explores autism from the point of view of AS people themselves. It presents AS perspectives on neurotypical behaviours and challenges the concept of 'normalcy'.

Journal Papers

- **Krzeminska et al.** (2018)
  Advantages and Challenges of Neurodiversity Employment in Organizations. Journal of Management and Organization.
  The Journal of Management and Organization provides global perspectives on management and organisations of benefit to scholars, educators, students, practitioners, policymakers, and consultants worldwide. This special issue focuses on neurodiversity.

Autism at Work Programs

- **EY (Ernst & Young), Neurodiversity program**
  https://www.ey.com/Publication/vwLUAssets/ey-ey-neurodiversity-driving-innovation-from-unexpected-places/$FILE/ey-neurodiversity-driving-innovation-from-unexpected-places.pdf
  EY is one of the first professional services organisations with a neurodiversity program. This organisation believes people on the autism spectrum can spur innovation and provide valuable talent and skills.
- **DXC, Dandelion Program**
  http://www.dandelionprogram.com/
  The Dandelion Program (formerly Hewlett Packard Enterprise) is an initiative to build valuable Information Technology, life, and executive functioning skills to help establish careers for people on the autism spectrum.
- **Microsoft, Autism Hiring Program**
  https://www.microsoft.com/en-us/diversity/inside-microsoft/cross-disability/hiring.aspx
  The Autism Hiring Program is part of Microsoft's recruitment, retention, and career development strategy related to diversity and inclusion, and to increase the percentage of employees with disabilities at Microsoft.
- **SAP, Autism at Work**
  https://www.sap.com/corporate/en/company/diversity/differently-abled.html
  https://news.sap.com/australia/2018/05/08/sap-launches-autism-at-work-program-in-new-zealand/
  SAP's Autism at Work program is part of is broader diversity and inclusion/'business beyond bias' ethos. The program leverages the unique abilities and perspectives of people with autism to foster innovation that contributes to SAP's business offerings.

11.2   Introduction

The characteristics of what we now term "autism" were first identified in the 1940s (Asperger 1991; Kanner 1943). Since then, it has become a condition of interest for researchers, the media, and the workplace. Autism spectrum (AS) disorders are determined on the basis of behavioural criteria. There is currently no medical testing available to diagnose these disorders (ABS 2017; Aspect 2018). Research and media focus have encouraged greater awareness and acceptability of AS and have encouraged better workplace inclusion for people with autism. Autistic individuals increasingly represent a largely untapped source of workforce talent, particularly in science, technology, engineering and mathematics (STEM). This chapter focuses on the benefits of including AS people in employment, and how this inclusion contributes to economic growth and workforce sustainability. This case study promotes the business case for neurodiversity within organisational diversity policies, and examines the advantages and challenges of a neurodiverse team. Different pathways to employment are also explored.

11.2.1   Defining Autism

> Over the years, different diagnostic labels have been used, such as autism, autism spectrum disorder (ASD), autism spectrum condition (ASC), classic autism, Kanner autism, pervasive developmental disorder (PDD), high-functioning autism (HFA), Asperger's syndrome and Pathological Demand Avoidance (PDA). This reflects the different diagnostic manuals and tools used, and the different autism profiles presented by individuals. Because of recent and upcoming changes to the main diagnostic manuals, 'autism spectrum disorder' (ASD) is now likely to become the most commonly given diagnostic term. (NAS 2018)

Autism has traditionally been defined as a developmental disability that affects how people communicate, relate to other people, and experience the world around them. It is a lifelong condition with no known 'cure'. AS is "characterised by difficulties in social interaction and communication, restricted and repetitive interests and behaviours, and sensory sensitivities" (AHRC 2018).

Autism is a 'hidden' disability, which means we can't always tell if someone is autistic, and this lack of visibility can create lifelong challenges, although support can improve quality of life (NAS 2018).

The definition of "disability" used in the Commonwealth Disability Discrimination Act 1992 (DDA) is broad. It includes physical, intellectual, psychiatric, sensory, neurological, and learning disabilities. From the DDA, statements relevant to AS are:

- A disorder or malfunction that results in the person learning differently from a person without the disorder or malfunction.
- A disorder, illness or disease that affects a person's thought processes, perception of reality, emotions, or judgment or that results in disturbed behaviour.

Australian legislation defines disability discrimination as "when a person with a disability is treated less favourably than a person without the disability in the same or similar circumstances" (DET 2012). AS is thus protected under the DDA. Implicit in these definitions is a particular worldview as to what constitutes 'normal', and the consequences of being 'disabled'. For example, although many employing organisations empower people to disclose an AS diagnosis at the point of recruitment, there is a debate that diagnosis and/or self-disclosure may, in fact, lead to unintended or hidden workplace inequalities. These may include being delegated semi-skilled work involving repetitive tasks. Disclosure may adversely affect how AS people see themselves, damaging their concept of themselves or their reputation. AS adolescents "reported using 'masquerading'—pretending to know how social situations work—to hide their social difficulties from typical peers" (Cage et al. 2016, p. 13). Thus, disclosure can result in diminished opportunities, reputational risk, and social exclusion. Cockayne (2018, p. 42) argues that while positive discrimination encourages affirmative action leading to greater inclusion, the concepts of 'disability', 'diversity', and 'skill' are socially constructed: "categorisation of difference depends very much on the 'others' who label differences, the norms against [which] these differences are being identified and from which the term 'neurodiverse' has emerged".

AS encompasses a complex group of developmental differences that share many of the same characteristics, e.g., difficulties with social interaction, communication, or unusual or repetitive patterns of behaviours (Hendricks 2010; Iemmi et al. 2017). The term "autism spectrum disorders" identifies symptoms that can occur in different combinations and can range along a spectrum of diagnostic profiles from very mild to quite severe. The causes of autism are still unknown, but research suggests a combination of genetic and environmental factors may result in developmental differences. Autism is not caused by a person's upbringing, their social circumstances, nor is it self-inflicted (Aspect 2018; NAS 2018).

The Diagnostics and Statistics Manual of Mental Disorders (DSM) is one of the main tools for clinically diagnosing AS. It suggests the diagnostic criteria clinicians can use in determining which mental and behavioural disorders people might have and, notably, the diagnostic criteria for AS has changed with each revision of the DSM. These variations may have, in part, contributed to the increase in the number of cases of AS in Australia and globally (ABS 2017).

Spectrum diversity means some AS individuals can attend university and hold down jobs while others may require a lifetime of specialist support. Comprising autism and two related disorders, Asperger's syndrome and pathological demand avoidance (PDA) (Hendricks 2010; NAS 2018), AS individuals with Asperger's are often of average or above-average intelligence but may still have difficulties with social communications and interactions. PDA individuals appear to have better social communication and social interaction skills than others on the autism spectrum but have an anxiety-based need to be in control, which may display in social strategies, such as avoidance and role play behaviours.

11.2.2   Strengths and Limitations of People with Autism

I spot things and see patterns in numbers that my supervisor and no one else can.

Gareth Moreton (Clegg 2018)

While many AS people are viewed as disabled, the concept of 'neurodiversity' promotes a strengths-based perspective, which fosters a view of valid and different pathways within human diversity. That is, from a strengths-aligned philosophy, neurotypical and neurodiverse are merely different approaches to capability. This area of diversity has historically been overlooked in the employment context, despite clinical studies which identify that AS people possess talents and special abilities (Chen et al. 2015; Cockayne 2018; Hedley et al. 2016).

Strengths Jeanette Purkis was diagnosed with Asperger's in 2004. She is an experienced employee and works for the Australian Public Service. Jeanette is an employee advocate for AS. She believes that in addition to their focus, passion, and attention to detail, AS employees bring empathy and "also come equipped with a great deal of respect for diversity a lot of the time" due to their own personal experiences of discrimination (Swinburn Commons 2015). As Purkis herself exemplifies, AS individuals are increasingly contributing their own voices to the workplace experience conversation.

Limitations Difficulties in social interaction; rigidity in thinking; and over- or undersensitisation to surrounding sounds, lights, and textures typically characterise AS. Those on the spectrum "are frequently troubled by loud noises and feelings of being different from their peers, which have created adverse impacts upon job satisfaction, earnings and securing meaningful employment" (Cockayne 2018, p. 39). Table 11.1 summarises some of the strengths and limitations of individuals on the spectrum.

Clearly articulating the strengths and shortcomings of people with AS provides opportunities to make "rapid headway in understanding how to better support employment among these individuals" (Vogus and Taylor 2018, p. 2). There is an emerging consensus that narrow or limiting views of the capabilities of those with disabilities are often socially constructed (Cockayne 2018). One AS person refers to this as "creating difference where there isn't real difference as such" (MacLeod et al. 2018, p. 690). An alternative and potentially more viable approach long term than affirmative action interventions is to flip the focus from normative behaviour to one that focuses on the strengths and benefits AS employees bring to employers (Vogus and Taylor 2018). AS advocates often champion a more sustainable social model of disability. This approach aims to identify systemic barriers, negative attitudes, and either purposeful or inadvertent social exclusion as the main contributing factor in disabling a person's agency. The social model of disability has its origins in a 1976 statement from the Union of the Physically Impaired Against Segregation (UPIAS):

In our view it is society which disables physically impaired people. Disability is something imposed on top our impairments by the way we are unnecessarily isolated and excluded from full participation in society. (cited in Oliver 2013a)

Table 11.1 Strengths and limitations of people with AS

Strengths	Limitations
• Intense focus and concentration • Good writing skills • Good colour perception • Advanced auditory ability • Attention to detail • Creative capacity • Lateral thinkers, inclined toward innovation • Independence of thought • Affinity with technology • Reliable meeting of deadlines • Capacity to gather and store expert knowledge • Enhanced memory • Highly productive	• Difficulties in social interaction • Interacting with colleagues, managers, and clients • Engaging in conversation • Understanding abstract concepts, metaphors, or sarcasm • Interpreting and using non-verbal communication • Working with distractions • Decision making and problem-solving • Difficulties receiving feedback and criticism • Maintaining concentration and motivation on some tasks • Working in unfamiliar environments • Time management and organisation • Changes to work routines, tasks, or workplace arrangements

Source Cockayne (2018), Engelbrecht and Silvertant (2018), NDCO (2013–2017)

The social model underpins disability equity training and serves as a vehicle for shared disability understanding. It distinguishes between *impairment*, which is when a person i s unable to do something, and *disability*, which is when someone is prevented from full participation in society on the basis of an impairment. Oliver (2013b) maintains that a compelling argument for the social model is that "too much is invested in individually based interventions with ever-diminishing returns". He believes that while the social model has identified disabling barriers in the employment market and with employer behaviours, the challenge remains to move beyond individual interventions and toward collective solutions.

11.3   The Social Issue of a High Employment Rate

> Without jobs, they lack the financial freedom to make decisions about their lives and miss out on other aspects of working such as the social networks that people develop through work. (ABS 2014)

> The problem is that…if no one gives me a chance, if I don't get hired, I will lose my house…I have no one to support me, I don't have any family…there is no one to take care of me. So then the state is going to wind up paying for me for decades, for a person who could contribute in a very valuable way but isn't given a chance. Neil (in the workforce for 40 years) (Taylor 2017: 24)

Employment and job satisfaction are important parts of emotional well-being and fulfilment. Research emphasizes that employment is a key enabler to adult life satisfaction. "Being employed means earning one's own living, contributing to society, integrating into a social network, being seen as part of society, and being less reliant on taxpayer-funded programs" (Chen et al. 2015, p. 3016). Participation in employment promotes personal dignity, supports self-esteem, and contributes to the development of transferable skills. Job and life satisfaction contribute to the United Nations (UN) and OECD annual reports on happiness. These reports use a range of social and economic indicators that shape people's well-being, such as income, jobs, education, work-life balance, social connections, subjective well-being, and economic and social capital (OECD 2017). Subjective well-being is a self-reported measure of individual happiness that describes how people experience their lives. However, in his 2015 statement on World Autism Awareness Day, Secretary-General of the UN, Ban Ki-moon, pointed out that despite their enormous collective potential, the majority of AS individuals remain unemployed. He highlights that "recognising the talents of persons on the autism spectrum, rather than focussing on their weaknesses, is essential to creating a society that is truly inclusive" (Ban 2015). He identifies unique AS strengths as enormous untapped potential coupled with remarkable visual, artistic, or academic skills. Despite these strengths, AS individuals are less likely to be employed than non-disabled adults and up to six times more likely to be unemployed than other adults with a more recognised disability (ABS 2017).

The Australian Bureau of Statistics (ABS) frames this dilemma as impacting the economic security of a sizeable part of the population since jobs and work make financial freedoms and social networks possible, which contribute to positive mental health, personal well-being, and a sense of purpose and identity:

> Employment contributes to mental health, personal well-being and a sense of identity. These are issues with which people with autism may already be struggling with; lower labour force participation can further restrict their ability to participate and contribute. (ABS 2014)

The high rate of unemployment for those with AS suggests that awareness programs for business and programs specifically targeting a transition to employment may help shift these statistics. In August 2018, the UK National Health Service (NHS) identified "autism and learning disability" as a priority area in its 10-year plan. While acknowledging the medical needs of autistic individuals, the plan also underscores the societal contributions they can make. Prioritising AS also signals that support for autism is central to the UK's future health and people strategies, and provides an opportunity to shape care around autistic people's often hidden needs (NAS 2018).

Data from the ABS presents a snapshot of autism in Australia (see Fig. 11.1). Based on the 2015 census information, there has been a 42% increase in autism diagnoses in the last decade. Males comprise the majority of Australians on the autism spectrum. Almost 41% of people with autism aged 15–64 participate in the workforce, representing almost 60,000 people, and 83% of Australians with autism are under 25 years old (ABS 2017; AIHW 2017).

The UK and USA present similar figures, with NAS reporting more than 1 in 100 people in the UK are on the autism spectrum. "If you include their families, autism is a part of daily life for 2.8 million people in the UK" (NAS 2018). The US Autism

A profile of Autism[1] in Australia

Australian Bureau of Statistics

Autism[1] may present substantial challenges for those affected, their families and friends. It can also have an impact on a person's education, as well as their social and economic participation.

In recent years an increasing number of Australians with Autism[1] have been identified. There are numerous factors that may contribute to this increase in reporting. The results from the 2015 Survey of Disability, Ageing and Carers can provide insights into this complex and varied condition.

There were **164,000** Australians with Autism[1] in **2015**

2012   2015

The number of Australians with **Autism[1]** increased by **42.1%** since 2012

4 out of 5 people with Autism[1] were **male**

More than **3/4** of those with Autism[1] were **young** (5-24 years)

64.8%

Almost **2/3** of those with Autism[1] had profound or severe **disability**

74%

Almost **3/4** of those with Autism[1] needed help with **cognitive** and **emotional** tasks

49%

Almost **half** of those with Autism[1] needed help with **communication**

83.7%

Around **4 out of 5** children[2] with Autism[1] had difficulties at **school**

40.8%

People with disability

83.2%

People with no reported disability

40.8% of people with **Autism[1]** participated in the workforce[3], compared with **83.2%** people with **no reported disability**

[1] 'Autism' includes people with Autism Spectrum Disorder, Asperger's Syndrome, Rett Syndrome, Childhood Disintegrative Disorder and Pervasive Developmental Disorder, not otherwise specified. For more information, see *Autism in Australia*, 2015 (cat.   4430.0).
[2] Living in households.
[3] Labour force figures are for persons aged between 15 and 64 years living in households.

Further information is available in *Autism in Australia*, available in *Disability, Ageing and Carers, Australia: Summary of Findings, 2015* (cat. no. 4430.0) available from the ABS website (www.abs.gov.au). A pdf version of the information sheet is available from the Downloads tab of this publication.

Fig. 11.1   A profile of autism in Australia. *Source* ABS (2017)

Science Foundation (ASF) reports that 1 in 59 children have been identified with AS. There are global similarities in reports of AS prevalence:

> AS continues to be over 4 times more common among boys (1 in 37) than among girls (1 in 151) and they are reported in all racial, ethnic, and socioeconomic groups. Studies have been conducted in several continents (Asia, Europe, and North America) that report a prevalence rate of approximately 1 percent. A 2011 study reported a 2.6 percent prevalence of autism in South Korea. (ASF 2018)

There are social and economic implications of increased numbers of AS diagnoses. These include the emotional costs of not being able to participate equally in work and life and the economic burden of managing this exclusion. Participation in the workforce is important for social inclusion and economic independence, but people with AS disorders may encounter barriers to entering the labour market.

Employment studies conducted in the USA, UK, Canada, and Australia indicate high rates of unemployment for those on the spectrum compared to other disability groups (Hedley et al. 2016). Recent Australian statistics show the labour rate participation is 40.8% among the 75,200 people of working-age (15–64 years) living with AS. This is compared with 53.4% of working-age people with developmental differences and 83.2% of people without a disability. The unemployment rate for people with autism spectrum disorders was 31.6%, which is more than three times the rate for people with a disability (10.0%) and almost six times the rate for people without a disability (5.3%) (ABS 2017). Similarly, for the 2015–2016 period, the UK and the US report an employment rate of approximately one third (Lorenz et al. 2016).

Reflecting on navigating the steps to employment, one hiring manager (Alsop 2016) comments that:

> Even if they are called in for an interview, people with autism often make a poor showing. They may fail to make eye contact with the interviewer, have trouble reading body language and understanding ambiguous questions, and give short, direct answers without elaborating on their positive attributes. And if asked to talk about their weaknesses, they readily reveal their foibles.

Self-disclosure and low self-esteem can also present barriers to employment. Researchers at Rutgers and Syracuse universities found that when people revealed in their cover letters that they were on the AS spectrum, they were about 25% less likely to be contacted by the employer than those who had not mentioned a disability (Alsop 2016). Low self-esteem can result from repeated employment rejections. Self-efficacy is "the optimistic self-belief in our competence or chances of successfully accomplishing a task and producing a favourable outcome" (Akhtar 2008). Self-belief plays an important role in job roles we believe we are capable of doing. A 2014 survey of young adults with AS found that "45% of respondents were 'overqualified' for their current job, which was correlated with low job satisfaction and poorer working conditions" (Taylor 2017, p. 4). Self-efficacy may have influenced their selection of lower-skilled jobs than they were qualified for.

11.3.1 Looking to Future Workforce Needs

> Once they are hired, most organizational cultures rely so heavily on social and communication skills that it can be hard for a person with autism to break through without support. (Oesch 2017)

ABS statistics highlight that people with AS are less likely than others to complete further education, and that learning and support needs may be a factor. ABS 2015 census data identifies that, at 49%, almost half of those on the AS spectrum require help with communication. People with other forms of disability are more than twice as likely to have a Bachelor's or higher degree than those with AS, while people with no disability are more than four times as likely to have received a further education qualification. "All people with disability and those with no disability were 1.6 times more likely to have an Advanced Diploma, Diploma or Certificate III or IV than people with autism" (ABS 2017). Figure 11.2 shows educational attainment for these groups.

The education gap is most noticeable in higher education. 2015 ABS figures for educational attainment indicate that Australians with no disability have 28.7% participation in higher education, while individuals across the autism spectrum comprise only 6.5% of this participation rate. These figures imply barriers to participation in higher education (MacLeod et al. 2018). They also suggest two things that may assist with closing this gap: learning models that leverage the strengths of AS people and employment models that address learning, support, and professional development needs. In this, employers have a valuable role. As the data in Fig. 11.3 from the US Bureau of Labour Statistics (Fayer et al. 2017) for 2009–2015 shows:

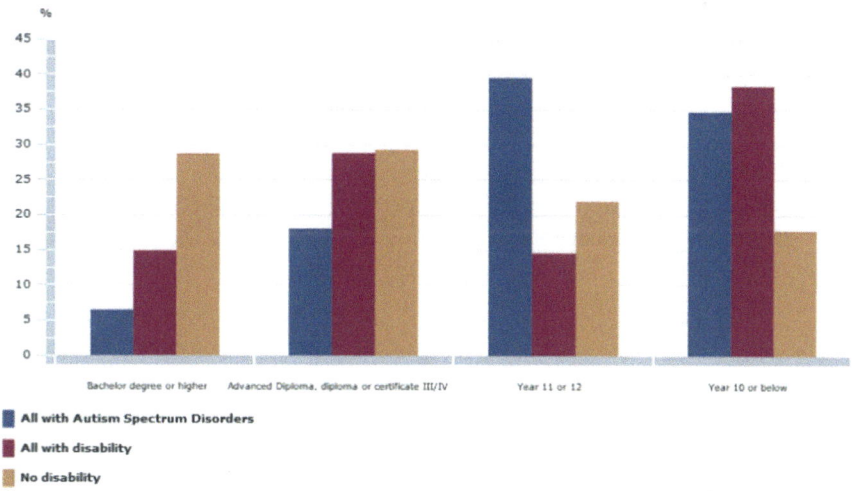

Fig. 11.2 Highest level of education attained by people with autism, a disability, or no disability. *Source* ABS (2017)

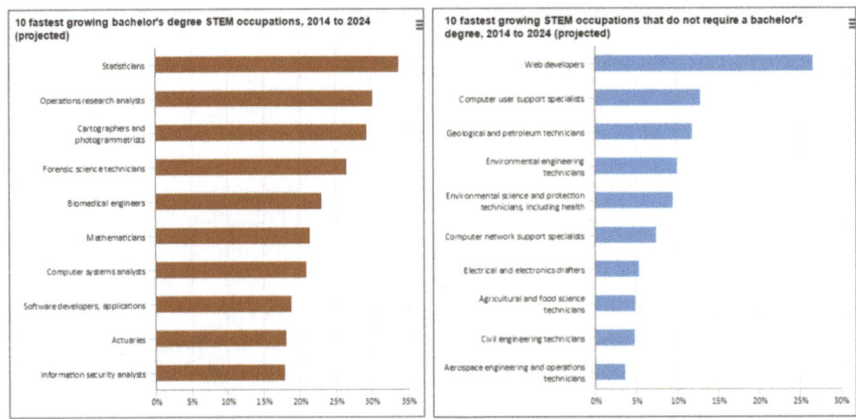

Fig. 11.3 Projected growth in STEM occupations by education level. *Source* Fayer et al. (2017)

- Over 99% of STEM employment is in occupations that typically require some type of higher education for entry, compared with 36% of overall employment.
- Substantial growth in degree and non-degree STEM occupations is projected from 2014 to 2024.
- STEM jobs account for more than half of the employment in five industries—computer systems 66.7%, architecture and engineering 64.5%, software publishers 63%, computer manufacturing 58%, and scientific research 55.7%.
- Over 800,000 net STEM jobs were added to the US economy between May 2009 and May 2015.
- There were nearly 8.6 million STEM jobs in May 2015, representing 6.2% of US employment.
- STEM jobs accounted for two-thirds of employment in the computer systems design industry.
- Nearly 900,000 STEM jobs were in architecture and engineering.
- Employment in computer occupations is projected to increase by 12.5% from 2014 to 2024; engineering is projected to add 65,000 new jobs.
- The STEM group that is projected to grow the fastest from 2014 to 2024 is the mathematical science occupations group at 28.2%, compared with the average projected growth for all occupations of 6.5%. This group includes occupations, such as statisticians and mathematicians.

These figures underscore the need for increasing the capacity of the STEM talent pipeline. They also highlight the natural alignment between AS strengths and STEM industry needs. Focus, attention to detail, and affinity with technology are surface STEM strengths of AS workers. However, as Table 11.1 indicates, a more valuable AS skill set going forward may be their creativity, or lateral thinking that contributes to innovation. A neurodiverse workforce is important for innovative decision making. According to Michael Fieldhouse, Dandelion Program executive at HPE/DXC, neurodiversity "drives diversity of thinking and innovation". In 2017, DXC Technology was formed from the merger of Computer Sciences Corporation (CSC) and the Enterprise Services business of Hewlett Packard Enterprise (formerly Electronic Data Systems). The company now offers internships and jobs to AS individuals in cybersecurity, data analytics, and software testing. Similarly, Amy Conn, marketing director of Integrate observes that people with autism often "have a propensity to think outside the box and can be extremely creative" (Oesch 2017). Integrate helps companies recruit and retain professionals on the autism spectrum.

11.4 The History and Development of the AS Employment Market

11.4.1 Specialisterne: The Social Innovator of Harnessing the Strengths of People with Autism

> The reason autistic people are often unemployed or underemployed is rarely their attitude or aptitude for work. We still live in a world where many employers lack understanding of the potential gains to their business from employing us, where recruitment processes—interviews especially—are exclusionary by their very nature and where workplaces need to be more understanding, supportive, and respective. Jeanette Purkis, AS advocate (2017)

Until recently, AS employment opportunities have largely been limited to disability-related government and civic employment support interventions. Amaze (amaze.org.au) and ASA (autismspectrum.org.au) are examples of autism support bodies that assist with the transition to employment. Specialisterne (which is Danish for 'The Specialists') is a social business concept originally founded in Denmark in 2004 by IT and telecommunications professional, Thorkil Sonne, whose son was diagnosed with AS. Sonne established Specialisterne to provide AS people with the opportunity to use their specialist skills to a business's advantage. Today the company is internationally acknowledged as the first and leading example of how autistic adults can become effectively included in society and provide valuable, high-quality services to their employers. Specialisterne provides both employment opportunities and education to succeed in the workplace. It "works to enable jobs for autistic adults through social entrepreneurship, innovative employment models and a national change in mindset. We believe that it is not the autistic individual who needs to change, but rather the way the labour market is conducted" (Specialisterne 2018). The model has been implemented around the world, with offices in Europe, South America, North America, and Australia. Other companies in the IT sector that specifically employ people with AS include Passwerk in Belgium and Auticon in the UK, Europe, and the US. Auticon extends the Specialisterne model to the provision of IT and compliance consulting (Clegg 2018). Its approach is to "offer sustainable careers [and] activate the extraordinary talents of autistic adults in complex IT and compliance projects ... in an autism-positive work environment" (Auticon 2018).

Fig. 11.4 Specialisterne business partners. *Source* Specialisterne (2015)

The Specialisterne Denmark website showcases some of its business partners (see Fig. 11.4). The number of partnerships with leading international brands is a testament to matching talent with needs and a shift in how AS people are increasingly seen as abled rather than disabled workers.

11.4.2 *AS Employment in Large for-Profit Companies*

> SAP's Autism at Work program was launched in 2013. It leverages the unique abilities and perspectives of people with autism to foster innovation as we help customers become intelligent enterprises. The program taps into an underutilised talent source, reducing barriers of entry so qualified individuals can fully develop their potential. Autism at Work employs over 140 colleagues in 12 countries. SAP (2018)

Research focussed on "identifying effective vocational interventions has received relatively less attention than identifying the barriers to employment" (Chen et al. 2015, p. 3017). Since 2012, the social innovation of harnessing the strengths of people with autism in the workplace has spilled over to large for-profit companies. SAP may be one of the most committed employers of autistic people. The software company expects that by 2020, autistic employees will account for 1% of its total workforce, which currently numbers about 75,600. This 1% represents 756 new employees (Alsop 2016). DXC Technology employs around 60 people with AS through its Dandelion Program, which offers internships and jobs in cybersecurity, data analytics, and software testing largely in government agencies (Oesch 2017).

The annual Autism at Work summit contributes to this awareness and employment ecosystem. The Autism at Work summit was established by SAP and other leading autism employers, such as DXC, Microsoft, and EY (Ernst & Young) in 2013, and brings together companies, individuals, civic groups, universities, and philanthropists to share ideas and collaborate on advancing neurodiversity in the workplace.

More than 70 autistic employees have been hired in the past three years at JPMorgan Chase, a financial services firm and one of the largest banking institutions in the US. While job performance results have been stellar at Chase, a shift in awareness and perspective has been a further benefit. James Mahoney, executive director and head of Autism at Work at JPMorgan Chase observes that (Fig. 11.5 and Table 11.2).

"Our autistic employees achieve, on average, 48% to 140% more work than their typical colleagues, depending on the roles … They are highly focused and less distracted by social interactions."

"Mentoring some of the people we've hired has opened my eyes to challenges we take for granted," Mahoney says. "I used to be impatient with a person's communication style, and I've learned to see the value and merit of the individual standing before me."

Fig. 11.5 Program success at JPMorgan Chase. *Source* Eng (2018)

Table 11.2 GEM case study

Grenoble Ecole de Management
Grenoble Ecole de Management is creating a programme to help school leavers with Asperger's pursue careers in big data, software development, and cybersecurity
The programme will launch in January 2019 with a cohort of 25 students, in partnership with the autism educational body C3R. To participate, students must have an autism diagnosis and have graduated from secondary school
Laurence Sirac, who heads GEM's MBA and masters job placement service and has Asperger's herself, will direct the programme. It mixes online classes in data skills, which are taught by professors at the school, and specialist face-to-face tuition in the social skills that autistic workers sometimes find hard to acquire
Students will be helped to find jobs and have access to job coaches as they adjust to their new roles
For more information visit: https://en.grenoble-em.com/news-asperger-profiles-gem-and-c3r-join-forces-offer-data-training-program-supervised-professional

Source Clegg (2018)

11.5 From Affirmative Action to Front-Door Employment

11.5.1 Affirmative Action

Employment equity is the policy of promoting employment opportunities for groups that have been discriminated against or marginalised. The principles of affirmative action help achieve the goals of equal pay, employment, and development opportunities. Enacting these goals also promotes increased diversity and including neurodiversity. Under the *Australian Disability Discrimination Act*, AS constitutes a disability. But, spearheading a focus on *ability*, the Australian Human Rights Commission notes that individuals must be assessed on their current ability to do the job, and that where an individual cannot perform the core requirements of a job because of a disability, "the employer must consider how the person with a disability could be provided with reasonable adjustments to help them do the job" (AHRC 2018).

To fulfil this obligation, the Commission promotes access to employment through employer education programs and resources. *Willing to Work*, a 2015 *National Inquiry into Employment Discrimination Against Older Australians and Australians with Disability*, engages with employers to understand the opportunities and challenges employing people with a disability. One of the inquiry recommendations was to review recruitment and development opportunities to ensure inclusiveness, as shown in Table 11.3.

InfoXchange, a not-for-profit social enterprise that leverages technology for social justice, provides a *Willing to Work* good practice example. Table 11.4 summarises InfoXchange's partnership approach to inclusive hiring.

Other examples from *Willing to Work* relevant to supporting the transition of AS individuals to employment include self-identification during the recruitment process at Commonwealth Bank of Australia and US Microsoft, and employee awareness at US Microsoft. Candidate self-identification enables the organisation to tailor aspects of the recruitment process to the individual, while 'disability etiquette' training helps to maximise understanding and communication between all team members (AHRC 2016).

'Impact sourcing' is another model that harmonises with autism-specific employment. The Global Impact Sourcing Coalition defines impact sourcing as "a business practice where companies prioritise suppliers that intentionally hire and provide

Table 11.3 Non-discriminatory recruitment practices

Ensuring non-discriminatory recruitment and retention practices
Businesses should ensure that their recruitment and retention policies do not discriminate against older people and people with disability. This could include reviewing recruitment processes to ensure that they are accessible and making promotional and training opportunities equally available to all employees, including older people and people with disability

Source AHRC (2018)

Table 11.4 Willing to work case study

Partnership with Social Firms Australia and Alpha Autism to employ people with Asperger's syndrome
In 2011, InfoXchange Australia, in partnership with Social Firms Australia and Alpha Autism established a software testing social enterprise firm called TestIT, which leverages the unique talents of people with Asperger's syndrome. Its purpose is to create accessible and durable employment for people facing barriers to work as a result of Asperger's syndrome, while at the same time generating the majority of its income through commercial activity Software testing requires long periods of concentration and the ability to recognise flaws in repetitive information. Hiring people with Asperger's syndrome has proven to be a competitive advantage in software testing firms IT companies all over the world are picking up on this previously hidden human resource. In 2015, Microsoft announced a pilot program to hire people with autism spectrum disorder. The company sees diversity as a strength in the organisation and many people with autism bring particular skills in retaining information, detailed thinking, and excellence in maths or code For more information, visit: http://www.testit.infoxchange.net.au/about

Source AHRC (2016, p. 39)

career development opportunities to people who otherwise have limited prospects for formal employment" (GISC 2018).

However, it is worth considering that affirmative action can also be divisive and provoke resistance and controversy. Education and clarity around the target group can moderate this debate. Ng (2016) points out that individuals may be resistant to affirmative action because of a lack of understanding of the philosophy that underpins it and who the policy is targeting. Those resisting affirmative action often invoke principles of employment based on merit. Particularly for recruitment, this emphasizes the need to communicate affirmative action objectives and to counter views that affirmative action is about "giving people who cannot succeed in the normal workplace an advantage" (Ng 2016). The AHRC (2016) suggests that shifting attitudes, changes in communication practices, and positive business impact are visible elements of affirmative action.

11.5.2   Toward Front-Door Employment

The emergence of offerings that target AS recruitment signal the effectiveness of affirmative action in enacting policies. AS advocacy bodies, such as the UK NAS and Australian ASA, promote awareness and education on how to recruit, employ, and manage AS employees. Barriers to employment for AS individuals can include the recruitment process, such as resumes, phone calls, and interviews; adapting to new work routines; workplace communication; and social engagement (Lorenz et al. 2016). Guidance encompasses the language of job advertisements and role specifications; application forms that enable applicants to provide information about any special interview or workplace needs; or interviewing techniques, such as the situation task action result (STAR) method, which focuses on concrete language and specific examples. Work trials or tests are also techniques that allow AS candidates to demonstrate their suitability for a role (Table 11.5).

Highly visible employers, such as Microsoft, DXC, SAP, and EY, are making the business case for neurodiversity in the workplace by emphasizing the benefits of AS employees. In viewing autism as a form of diversity, employers take a strengths-based view and promote the value of different ways of thinking and how innovation often comes from 'edge' thinking (Vogus and Taylor 2018). While social interaction and communication skills can be a challenge for people with autism spectrum disorder, companies looking to hire untapped talent for tech-related jobs are discovering that those with autism are unusually detail-oriented, highly analytical, and able to focus intensely on tasks, making them valuable employees (Eng 2018).

In late 2017, six companies—Ford Motor, DXC Technology, EY, Microsoft, JPMorgan Chase, and SAP—formed the Autism at Work Employer Roundtable to share best hiring and workplace practices and to help other companies see the return on investment in hiring autistic employees (Eng 2018). Several Autism at Work programs and their HR practices are summarised in Table 11.6.

Collaboration between employing organisations and autism advocates may provide a bridge to employment. Vogus and Taylor (2018) suggest that creating a climate receptive to diversity, psychological safety, and leader inclusiveness are key to creating meaningful AS employment. Markers of a diversity climate are broad employee

Table 11.5 Translink case study

Meeting AS employment needs at Translink
Mark has autism, and attended courses run by a specialist support organisation to help him to develop employment skills. He has a very keen interest in vehicles and was offered a supported work placement with Translink in Lisburn. This has been so successful that he is now in part-time paid employment with the company
From the outset, the support partnership developed an individual job description that matched Mark's skills and abilities. His employer recognised that Mark learned and worked in a different way and made reasonable adjustments in both his daily tasks and the training processes used to take this into account. The support partnership helped both Translink and Mark gain knowledge and skills through disability awareness training for staff, assistance for Mark during training sessions, as well as ongoing guidance and advice. Over time the support has been reviewed and adjusted to Mark's and Translink's needs
Mark says, "Getting this job is one of the best things that has happened to me in my life. I'm glad I got the job and someone else didn't get it. I enjoy my job and I like the work I do; it's good to get paid as well"
Mark's employer at Translink, Roy Hamilton, commented, "Mark follows direction well and completes all his jobs to a high standard. At the start, a new job needs to be demonstrated to him but Mark follows a very structured routine, is methodical, and very meticulous. He does things to the letter and is eager to learn new tasks as well. As he got more confident in the job he started to use his initiative and now when it's not busy he will head off and complete his list of duties. Over the time Mark has been with us he has become an asset to our team"

Source NAS (2011, p. 10)

Table 11.6 Example Autism at work programs

	EY — Building a better working world	Hewlett Packard Enterprise / DXC.technology	Microsoft	SAP
Screen	Phone, Skype video Simulation exercise	One day workshop	Phone Technical Skills Assessment	Phone, Skype video, in-person
Assess	One week in-person training: soft skills; team-based skills/problem solving exercises; introduction to the role, to EY organisation, and business	Four-week training and assessment robotics and autism assessment exercises	One week in-person event Collaborative activities, interview preparations, team interviews	One week in-person soft skills training Five-week SAP Autism at Work Enterprise Readiness Program

↓ Job offer

Manager & team training	In-person group job training In-person customised onboarding	Supported three-year training program Candidate: technical skills, professional and life skills	In-person team session Online training	Autism sensitivity training for manager and immediate colleagues
Onboarding	Cohort community Peer mentoring Employee Resource Groups Job coach	Supported onboarding process Three-year support team: Autism Spectrum Consultant, technical specialists	Support Circle: Peer Mentor, Community Mentor, Job Coach Employee Resource Groups	Supported onboarding process Support-Circle: Job-Coach, Mentor and Team Buddy

↓ Workplace contribution

Role types	Account Support Associate: data analytics, quality control, robotics, cybersecurity	Software testing Cyber security Data analytics Infrastructure monitoring and automation	Software Engineer Data Scientist Service Engineer IT Operations	21 roles in 9 countries Across functions ranging from Human Resources to Engineering
Employment types	Full-time	Full-time Part-time Work experience opportunities	Full-time	Full-time Part-time Contract University student

Source Autism at Work Summit 2017, SAP Palo Alto

agreements in which the organisation promotes diversity and inclusion for those from under-represented groups. Psychological safety is the belief that interpersonal risk and self-disclosure will not incur reprisals or punitive results. Leadership inclusiveness is a set of behaviours that promote diversity through policy and organisational strategies, fosters a sense of inclusiveness and belonging, and visibly supports and appreciates contributions from across the talent spectrum (Vogus and Taylor 2018). Similarly, the AHRC (2016) recommends a range of strategies including: leadership commitment; inclusive recruitment and retention practices; providing flexible work options through job design, work location, and flexible hours; facilitating a transition to employment; providing targeted workplace training and development; and building healthy workplaces (Table 11.7).

One important initiative in this regard is the establishment of 'neurodiversity hubs' that focus on improving the employability of neuro-atypical students by helping them obtain work experience and internships. Neurodiversity hubs are collaborations between universities and autism employers, such as DXC, and have been established at, for example, Swinburne University of Technology, the University of Queensland, Macquarie University, and Curtin University. Strategic partnerships between employers and universities also support research, which provides a solid evidence base for an employer's HR practices.

11.5.3 Different Models for AS Employment

AS employment models range from supported employment services that help AS individuals gain employment in work settings to ongoing assistance, such as job coaching and co-worker mentoring, to competitive or front-door employment, where individuals are directly recruited for jobs with the same benefits, employment support, and conditions as co-workers. Research with AS adults has provided insights

Table 11.7 SAP Autism at Work program case study

SAP Autism at Work
Overview
In 2013, SAP launched what was to become a ground-breaking initiative—the Autism at Work program. Its goal was to integrate people on the spectrum into the workplace. SAP's Autism at Work program was designed to hire skilled colleagues "in spite of autism and because of autism". The program taps into the unique strengths of neurodiverse people, such as creativity, attention to detail, and out-of-the-box thinking, and innovation
Since 2013, the Autism at Work program has grown at SAP and has served as an example for other organisations like Microsoft, EY, HPE, and DXC Technology, who are investing in workforce diversity and operating autism inclusion and employment programs. AS employment initiatives have scaled to include global summits and work fairs, such as the 2017 Australian Autism Employment Fair, hosted by Autism CRC and DXC in conjunction with the Asia Pacific Autism Conference. The focus of the Autism at Work summits is to share learnings and good practice from organisations that are effectively hiring and integrating neurodiverse candidates into their workforces
Autism at Work initiatives work closely with specialist partners such as Specialisterne and civic advocates and government departments such as Autism Spectrum Australia, the UK National Autistic Society, Integrationsamt in Germany, all of whom promote diversity and disability inclusion in the labour market to support employment for people with autism across a wide range of roles and industries
Integrating the program
Employing employees on the spectrum also means providing training to support their skills—and training for the organisation to create an inclusive culture

Source ASPECT (2018), Loucks (2018), Oesch (2017)

Table 11.8 AS employment models

Supported employment	Job placement and help with the transition to autism-specific employment. Ongoing support assists with maintaining employment. Job coaches, peer and supervisory guidance, and mentoring are used
Customised employment	An individualised approach that helps tailor capabilities and job fit. The focus is to align an AS employee's skills, strengths, interests, and on-the-job-training with an employer's needs. Elements can include: – *environmental modification*: minimising distractions – *role realignment*: some job tasks of current employees are re-assigned to strengthen productive gaps or workplace needs, and a new role is created – *job carving*: an existing job description is adjusted so that it contains selected tasks from the original job description – *job sharing*: two or more people share the tasks and responsibilities of a job based on individual strengths
Competitive employment	Full-time or part-time work that pays market rate, with standard benefits and conditions
Self-employment	Guided business start-up support An entrepreneur success story is Nathan Young of Autism Candles.com (2006). Based on an interest in smells. Nathan started Autism Candles to employ himself and others. The Chamber of Commerce and the autism community provided start-up capital and business development support

Source Adapted from Autism Speaks (2013), Hendricks (2010)

regarding their vocational needs. This research suggests that the most constructive interventions are: (1) job placement; (2) supportive supervisors and co-workers; (3) customised job tasks; (4) environmental modification; and (5) ongoing support (Hendricks 2010). Table 11.8 summarises the main employment models.

Lorenz et al. (2016, p. 3) maintain that supported, or

> … autism-specific employment creates a better person-organisation and person-environment fit than a non-autism-specific employment. As a result, this fit may lead to a higher life and job satisfaction. Supported employments have previously been found beneficial for individuals with autism, relating to improvement in cognitive skills even outside the work domain and in quality of life.

11.6   Challenges Ahead

"If they do secure a job, some autistic employees find the work belittling. When Dan Peters worked at a supermarket, people assumed he was intellectually limited and assigned him to bag groceries. "They discriminated because of their stereotypes and gave me low brainpower jobs", he said. (Alsop 2016)

Hedley et al. (2016, p. 930) identify meaningful and purposeful employment is a risk area. They point out that, "even when individuals with AS are employed, the meaningfulness of their employment is questionable as it tends to be in low paying jobs with limited working hours and in jobs that are most often well below the individual's level of education and expertise". While employers are increasingly receptive to neurodiversity and hiring on the spectrum, Cockayne (2018) raises ethical concerns about their intense focus and attention to detail as potential risks to the exploitation of AS employees. She cites a number of examples of highly capable and often senior personnel being delegated menial tasks:

It's just the fact that a lot of it is really strong, it's just the speed, accuracy and quality that comes back is above her pay grade. I think it's a strength—it's really big. He doesn't let himself get distracted. He is one of the people I go to when I have a complex task that I need to know that it will get done.

We had a new box to put the keys in for the filing cabinets. It takes ages to number all the cabinets and the keys and then write on hooks. She took her time over it enjoyed doing it. I knew I couldn't give it to another person-it's those jobs that don't belong to anybody.

A major barrier to long-term sustainable employment for companies is the co-morbidity of people with autism. Autism at work has a high incidence of co-morbidity that affects how people cope in the workforce that is unrelated to their primary autism support needs (Hedley et al. 2016). Estimates indicate 65–80% of individuals with AS present with additional psychiatric symptoms (De Bruin et al. 2007; Ghaziuddin et al. 1998; Leyfer et al. 2006; Mukaddes and Fateh 2010). Organisations are in urgent need of an effective identification and management framework to avoid overwhelming autistic employees team leaders or managers with the responsibility of managing co-occurring mental health needs.

Finally, employing people with autism on a large scale requires fundamental changes to organisational culture and values, which will remain a challenge for large organisations embracing neurodiversity in particular and diversity in general. As Anka Wittenberg, SAP's head of diversity observes, diversity is an essential component of innovation. Organisations need to look beyond their usual goals of recruiting people with excellent teamwork and communication skills. They need to be open to the reality that AS candidates are not strong in these areas and make them a part of broader diversity strategies (Alsop 2016).

11.7 Teaching Notes

11.7.1 Synopsis of the Case

People with autism have the highest rates of unemployment among any group of people with and without 'disabilities'. Yet their skills are essential to meeting current and future workforce needs, particularly in STEM areas. Traditionally defined as a disability, the strengths and limitations of autism are now recognised as valuable differences and increasingly harnessed by employers in the workplace. This case illustrates people with autism at work, as well as the history of autism employment through a movement that was started by a small Danish social innovator in 2004 and is now spreading globally in large for-profit companies. This case further showcases the various HR practices of these organisations, which are moving from affirmative action programs to regular front-door modes of employment and other models in between. The study concludes with a discussion on issues in this area to be addressed in future.

11.7.2 Target Learning Group

- Level of study—BA and MA students
- Subject areas—HRM; management; social policy; economics.

11.7.3 Learning Objectives

11.7.3.1 Key Issues

- Foster awareness of the need to extend workplace diversity conversations to include neurodiversity.
- Create awareness of initiatives focussed on sustaining and scaling autism employment.
- Create an understanding that diversity and inclusion underpin workforce sustainability, which has broad economic benefits.
- Introduce current thinking around mainstream awareness of neurodiversity and promote receptivity to neurodiversity in the workplace.

11.7.3.2 Specific Objectives

- Examine the social construction of 'disability' and how education underpins affirmative action policy.
- Explore AS through the lens of the Australian Disability Discrimination Act, and how affirmative action initiatives underpin the transition to work practices that are creating new HR paradigms in front-door recruitment.

11.7.4 Reading Activities

11.7.4.1 Pre-reading

Skim the chapter for each of the textboxes.

- What do they tell you about the key themes and ideas in the chapter?

Examine the statistics infographics and charts.

- What are the unemployment rates for AS people?
- Assuming stable future prevalence, what percentage of the Australian workforce is likely to be on the AS spectrum? What might this mean for future Australian workplaces?
- What are possible social, economic, and HRM implications of the high AS rate reported for South Korea?

Examine the US BLS STEM data for 2009–2015:

- What are the two largest STEM growth industries?
- What are the top 5 STEM industries for employment:
- STEM jobs represent what percentage of US employment?
- Which STEM group is projected to have the fastest growth rate from 2014 to 2024? Why do you think this is?
- Which industry requiring a university degree is predicted to have the most growth?
- Which industry that doesn't require a university degree (vocational/workplace training) is predicted to have the most growth?

11.7.4.2 In-Depth Reading

Defining autism

- What is autism? And what are its defining characteristics?
- How does the hidden nature of autism impact AS people? What is the social implication?

- What do the terms, "neurodiversity" and "neurotypical" mean? What are the main differences that characterise these two groups?

Strengths and limitations of people with autism

- What are some of the strengths and limitations of AS people? How might these positively or negatively impact on employment?
- Why are these limitations so problematic for gaining employment: Difficulties in social interaction; Interacting with colleagues, managers and clients; Engaging in conversation.
- Can you summarise the concept "social model of disability"? How can HR use this model to benefit AS recruitment and employee well-being?

The social issue of a high employment rate

The ABS (2017) reports that: AS people are less likely to be employed than non-disabled adults and up to six times more likely to be unemployed than other adults with a more recognised disability.

- What are the personal implications for AS people?
- What are the social implications?
- How might this affect the economy and impact government health and social welfare budgets?
- How has the UK responded? What are some of the reasons given?

Looking to future workforce needs

- What reasons are suggested for the low completion rate of further education for AS people?
- There is a global focus on STEM industry talent gaps—how do AS strengths align with these gaps?

Different models for AS employment

- What four models for AS employment are discussed?
- What are the possible strengths and limitations of each of these employment models?
- What are some of the initiatives listed to help scale the recruitment and workforce integration of AS employees?

Challenges ahead

- What are the ethical issues involved in the examples provided?
- What are the possible legislative implications?
- How can HRM shift these behaviours to make workplaces more neurodiversity aware?

11.7.5 Suggested Assignment

Making the business case for AS employees

Prominent employers, such as Microsoft, Hewlett Packard, SAP, EY, and DXC, are making the business case for neurodiversity in the workplace by emphasizing the benefits and strengths of AS employees. This aligns with the good practice recommendations in *Willing to Work* and demonstrates leadership commitment.

- What is the goal of SAP's Autism at Work initiative?
- When was it launched? How has the program evolved?
- What are some elements of the AS employment ecosystem?
- What is the focus of the Autism at Work summits? How do these contribute to scaling AS employment?
- Look at Table 11.1 in the Autism at Work case study. What are some of the similarities and differences in these programs?

Task A business case is a form of gap analysis. It describes the business problem, the current and desired future state, and outlines implementation strategies for the organisation to achieve its goals. SHRM (Mayberry 2008) summarises the ten components of an HR business case.

Select one of the listed organisations and research its Autism at Work program to develop a 5–10 page neurodiversity business case for including AS employees as part of the workforce. Alternatively, develop a business case for an Autism at Work program for your own workplace.
The following structure may be useful.

Problem statement: Briefly state the specific business problem.
Background: Outline the business context. Include information relating to skills, costs, and performance that contribute to the business problem. In general terms, indicate what is required to address the problem.
Project objectives: In a few bullet points, list what the proposed solution is trying to accomplish, e.g., help the organisation lift its STEM capability.
Current process: Identify current business processes that will be impacted by the proposed solution, e.g., recruitment, training, other departments, relationships with clients, external partners, and the competition.
Requirements: List the resources required for the project, e.g., staff, technology, training materials, time, budget.
Alternatives: Outline other options for implementing the proposed solution, e.g., the 'do nothing', 'do the minimum', 'implement the proposed solution'. Include the basic requirements for each option and estimate the project risks.
Compare alternatives: Compare and contrast each of the alternatives with the proposed solution and the other alternatives. State similarities and differences, benefits and detriments, and costs associated with each option.

Additional considerations: List what is essential to the success of the project, e.g., organisational changes to management, changes to existing partnership arrangements, training.

Action plan: Propose specific action steps. State your short-term (first three months) and long-term (three months to conclusion) action plans, including major milestones. This section should also include proposed metrics to measure success.

Executive summary: Write a concise summary of the proposed solution. Tailor it to your audience and offer a high-level overview of research that leads you to the proposal.

11.7.6 Discussion Activities

11.7.6.1 Good Practice Recommendations for Inclusive Workplaces

- In pairs or small groups, participants discuss what constitutes good practice under the AHRC recommendations for: leadership; recruitment and retention practices; workplace flexibility; supporting the transition to work; workplace training and education; and healthy workplaces.
- Alternatively, following Vogus and Taylor (2018), discuss what good practice might look like for employers and for AS employees under each of these headings.

  - leadership commitment
  - ensuring non-discriminatory recruitment and retention practices
  - building workplace flexibility
  - facilitating transitions
  - provide targeted education and training in the workplace
  - build healthy workplaces.

11.7.6.2 Group Activity to Complete the Impact Sourcing Visualisation

https://gisc.bsr.org/files/BSR_GISC_What_is_Impact_Sourcing.pdf (GISC 2018).

- Remove some of the text from selected boxes to provide an incomplete visualisation to small groups, or divide parts of the visualisation among the group. Participants complete and then compare their version to the original. Discuss differences and the possible outcomes of impact sourcing to HRM recruitment practices and AS workers.
- Alternatively, participants can develop a similar impact sourcing model tailored to workplace neurodiversity, using the key points in the chapter.

11.7.6.3 Distributed Reading Impact Sourcing Model

- What is impact sourcing?

11.8 Discussion Questions

- What are the differences and similarities between impact sourcing and established AS employment models? (Fig. 11.6).
- Can the principles of impact sourcing be leveraged in AS recruitment? If yes, how?
- How might impact sourcing influence how AS individuals report their subjective well-being?
- What is the connection to Ban Ki-moon's 2015 UN statement on World Autism Day, and the ABS statement on the importance of work to a person's well-being?

11.9 Multimedia Activities

- **Swinburn Autism MOOC**
  https://www.youtube.com/playlist?list=PLdVESrjTNUXtzX0e0EmupCxG-cJDBExq4
  Swinburne University of Technology's Autism MOOC is designed for parents and carers of people with autism and those who work with people with autism. It seeks to equip them with the skills and knowledge to solve practical issues in the lives of individuals who have autism. The course uses real scenarios, draws on experiences, and aims to foster a supportive network of parents and carers.
- **Autism and employment**
  https://commons.swinburne.edu.au/items/7217b8ce-6acc-4829-8da9-880ebd77f7f6/1/
  In this video, Jeanette Purkis talks about the challenges and possibilities of employment for people with AS. This presentation presents learnings from Jeanette's extensive employment experience as a person with an autism spectrum condition.

  - According to the speaker, what is the average percentage of employment participation for the general public?
  - What is the participation rate for people on the autism spectrum?
  - What are the implications?
  - What are some of the challenges the speaker outlines for AS people?
  - What are some of the strengths the speaker lists for AS people?
  - What does the author suggest to support AS people gain meaningful employment?

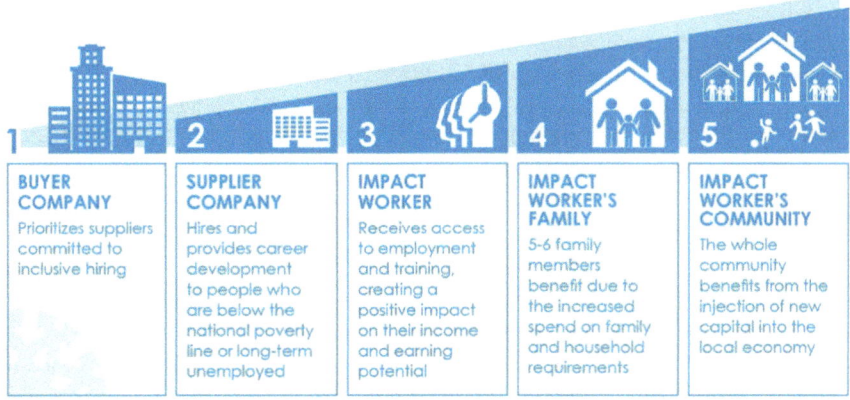

Value to buyers

Value to suppliers

Incomplete impact sourcing model

Fig. 11.6 Sourcing models

- **Autism Awareness Centre**
  https://autismawarenesscentre.com/
  The Autism Awareness Centre focuses on education to assist those with AS. It focuses on providing current information about intervention methods. This video provides an overview of the autism spectrum.
- **Hiring Autistic Workers**
  https://www.cbsnews.com/video/hiring-autistic-workers/

A CBS video case study of Microsoft's hiring process for autistic workers, and the business opportunities of hiring neurodiverse staff.
- **Controversial anti-neurodiversity Twitter thread**
  To promote debate around anti-diversity sentiment, and the need for affirmative action policy. Select a current controversial hashtag. For example: https://twitter.com/hashtag/EndAutismNow?src=hash

  Example questions:

  – What is the focus of this Twitter thread?
  – How do you think it relates to the concept of 'social construction of illness'?
  – How do you think it relates to affirmative action practices?
  – Why might there be such a reaction to affirmative action and the emergence of neurodiversity?

  One person calls this a "disability hate tag" (https://twitter.com/alyzande/status/1027406601731366912).

  – How do contributors to this thread balance the *for* and *against* sides of the neurodiversity argument?

  For example, the thread https://twitter.com/OverlordMarie/status/1027245234365898753 asks readers to consider a world without the contributions of AS individuals.

  Marie Porter 🇨🇦 @OverlordMarie · Aug 9   ⌄
  If people like @JennyMcCarthy want to **#EndAutismNow**, I humbly suggest they try to live a week without ANYTHING that autistics have contributed to the creation of.

  I predict that they would not manage a day.

- **The Aspie quiz**
  https://embraceasd.com/the-aspie-quiz/
  A research-based questionnaire developed by diagnosed AS academics that provides results in chart format.

Further Reading

- **Cockayne, A. (2018).** The 'A' word in employment: Considerations of Asperger's Syndrome for HR specialists. In V. Caven & S. Nachmias (Eds.), *Hidden Inequalities in the Workplace* (pp. 39–65). Cham: Springer International Publishing.
  This chapter reports the findings from an investigation exploring the hidden inequalities that employees with Asperger Syndrome experience in the workplace, providing new knowledge for those concerned with diversity and inclusion, including HR specialists and line managers. Rich descriptions of AS characteristics raise

awareness of how skills can be best used and accommodated and how, at the same time, these characteristics can also create hidden inequalities. These discussions also seek to build some confidence in AS individuals that their unique blend of skills is valuable in contemporary organisations and in roles which neither they nor HR specialists may have considered.

References

ABS (2014) 4428.0 - Autism in Australia, 2012. Australian Bureau of Statistics. Retrieved from http://www.abs.gov.au/ausstats/abs@.nsf/Latestproducts/4428.0Main%20Features62012

ABS (2017) 4430.0 - Disability, ageing and carers. Australia: summary of findings, 2015. Commonwealth of Australia, Canberra, ACT. Retrieved from http://www.abs.gov.au/ausstats/abs@.nsf/Latestproducts/4430.0Main%20Features12015?opendocument&tabname = Summary&prodno = 4430.0&issue = 2015

AHRC (2016) Willing to work: good practice examples for employers. Australian Human Rights Commission, Sydney, NSW

AHRC (2018) Autism. Australian Human Rights Commission, Sydney, NSW. Retrieved from https://www.humanrights.gov.au/quick-guide/11937

AIHW (2017) Autism in Australia. Commonwealth of Australia, Canberra, ACT. Retrieved from https://www.aihw.gov.au/reports/disability/autism-in-australia/related-material

Akhtar M (2008) What is self-efficacy? Bandura's 4 sources of efficacy beliefs. Retrieved from http://positivepsychology.org.uk/self-efficacy-definition-bandura-meaning/

Alsop R (2016) Are autistic employees the best workers around? BBC Capital, London, UK. Retrieved from http://www.bbc.com/capital/story/20160106-model-employee-are-autistic-individuals-the-best-workers-around

ASF (2018) How common is autism? Autism Science Foundation, New York, NY. Retrieved from https://autismsciencefoundation.org/what-is-autism/how-common-is-autism/

ASPECT (2018) Autism spectrum Australia. Retrieved from https://www.autismspectrum.org.au/

Asperger H (1991) 'Autistic psychopathy' in childhood. Cambridge University Press, New York, NY, US

AUTICON (2018) Retrieved from https://auticon.co.uk/

Autism speaks (2013) Employment models

Ban K-M (2015) Secretary-General's remarks on World Autism Awareness Day [as delivered]. United Nations, Geneva, Switzerland

Cage E, Bird G, Pellicano L (2016) 'I am who I am': reputation concerns in adolescents on the autism spectrum. Res Autism Spectr Disord 25:12–23

Chen JL, Sung C, Pi S (2015) Vocational rehabilitation service patterns and outcomes for individuals with autism of different ages. J Autism Dev Disord 45:3015–3029

Clegg A (2018) Hire people who think differently to reap rewards. Financial Times, London, UK. Retrieved from https://amp-ft-com.cdn.ampproject.org/c/s/amp.ft.com/content/583ad27a-38fd-11e8-b161-65936015ebc3

Cockayne A (2018) The 'A' word in employment: considerations of Asperger's syndrome for HR specialists. In: Caven V, Nachmias S (eds) Hidden inequalities in the workplace. Palgrave Macmillan, Cham, pp 39–65

De Bruin EI, Ferdinand RF, Meester S, De Nijs PFA, Verheij F (2007) High rates of psychiatric co-morbidity in PDD-NOS. J Autism Dev Disord 37:877–886

DET (2012) Department of education and training, fact sheet: Disability Discrimination Act 1992. Commonwealth of Australia, Canberra, ACT

Eng D (2018) Where autistic workers thrive. Fortune Magazine. Retrieved from http://fortune.com/2018/06/24/where-autistic-workers-thrive/

Engelbrecht N, Silvertant M (2018) ASD superpowers. Retrieved from https://embraceasd.com

Fayer S, Lacey A, Watson A (2017) STEM occupations: past, present, and future. In: U.S. Bureau of Labour Statistics (ed) Spotlight on statistics. U.S. Bureau of Labor Statistics, Washington, DC. Retrieved from https://www.bls.gov/spotlight/2017/science-technology-engineering-and-mathematics-stem-occupations-past-present-and-future/home.htm

Ghaziuddin M, Weidmer-Mikhail E, Ghaziuddin N (1998) Comorbidity of Asperger syndrome: a preliminary report. J Intellect Disabil Res 42:279–283

GISC (2018) Global impact sourcing coalition. GISC. Retrieved from https://gisc.bsr.org/

Hedley D, Uljarević M, Cameron L, Halder S, Richdale A, Dissanayake C (2016) Employment programmes and interventions targeting adults with autism spectrum disorder: a systematic review of the literature. Autism 21:929–941

Hendricks D (2010) Employment and adults with autism spectrum disorders: challenges and strategies for success. J Vocat Rehabil 32:125–134

Iemmi V, Knapp M, Ragan I (2017) The autism dividend: reaping the rewards of better investment. National Autism Project (NAP), London, UK

Kanner L (1943) Autistic disturbances of affective contact. Nerv Child 2:217–250

Krzeminska A, Austin RD, Bruyère SM, Hedley D (2019) The advantages and challenges of neurodiversity employment in organizations. J Manage Organ 25(4):453–463

Leyfer OT, Folstein SE, Bacalman S, Davis NO, Dinh E, Morgan J, Tager-Flusberg H, Lainhart JE (2006) Comorbid psychiatric disorders in children with autism: interview development and rates of disorders. J Autism Dev Disord 36:849–861

Lorenz T, Frischling C, Cuadros R, Heinitz K (2016) Autism and overcoming job barriers: comparing job-related barriers and possible solutions in and outside of autism-specific employment. PLoS ONE 11:e0147040

Loucks S (2018) Our autism at work program: five years later. Retrieved from https://www.ere.net/our-autism-at-work-program-five-years-later/

Macleod A, Allan J, Lewis A, Robertson C (2018) 'Here I come again': the cost of success for higher education students diagnosed with autism. Int J Inclusive Educ 22:683–697

Mayberry E (2008) How to build an HR business case. SHRM. Retrieved from https://www.shrm.org/resourcesandtools/hr-topics/behavioral-competencies/leadership-and-navigation/pages/businesscase.aspx

Mukaddes NM, Fateh R (2010) High rates of psychiatric co-morbidity in individuals with Asperger's disorder. World J Biol Psychiatry 11:486–492

NAS (2011) Employing people with autism: a brief guide for employers. The National Autistic Society, London, UK

NAS (2018) The National Autistic Society. The National Autistic Society, London, UK. Retrieved from https://www.autism.org.uk/

NDCO (2013–2017) Autism spectrum disorders: key facts. Education to Employment, South Western and Western Sydney National Disability Coordination Officer Program. Western Sydney University, Sydney, NSW

Ng E (2016) Why do individuals oppose affirmative action? Making sense of resistance to affirmative action. Retrieved from https://www.psychologytoday.com/au/blog/diverse-and-competitive/201606/why-do-individuals-oppose-affirmative-action

OECD (2017) How's life? 2017: measuring well-being. FR, OECD Publishing, Paris

Oesch T (2017) Autism at work: hiring and training employees on the spectrum. Retrieved from https://trainingindustry.com/articles/workforce-development/autism-at-work-hiring-and-training-employees-on-the-spectrum/

Oliver M (2013a) The disability movement and the professions. Center for Disability Studies. University of Leeds, Leeds, UK

Oliver M (2013b) The social model of disability: thirty years on. Disability & Society 28:1024–1026

Purkis J (2017) Keynote presentation, autism and employment. Autism CRC Autism@Work Forum. Sydney, Australia

SAP (2018) Differently abled people. Retrieved from https://www.sap.com/corporate/en/company/diversity/differently-abled.html

Specialisterne (2015) Retrieved from http://dk.specialisterne.com

Specialisterne (2018) Retrieved from http://au.specialisterne.com/

Swinburn Commons (2015) Autism and employment. In: SWINBURN UNIVERSITY (ed) Autism MOOC

Taylor C (2017) Employment experiences of people with autism spectrum disorder and workplace supervisors. The University of Utah, MSc

Vogus TJ, Taylor JL (2018) Flipping the script: bringing an organizational perspective to the study of autism at work. Autism 22:514–516

Young N (2006) Autism candles. Retrieved from https://autismadvocacynetwork.com/autismcandles/

Dr. Anna Krzeminska is an Associate Professor in Macquarie University, Senior Research Fellow at the Australian Institute for Business and Economics (AIBE), Research Fellow at the Leuphana University Research Center for Entrepreneurship Evidence in Germany, and the co-founding Director of the Queensland and Macquarie Uni Neurodiversity Hubs. Anna's award-winning research and teaching expertise centers around exploring strategic management issues of social impact organization such as the design of socially and commercially successful business models, growth and scaling strategies, competitive advantage and strategy, as well as leadership and governance practices within those organizations. Anna manages an international research and industry engagement portfolio in strategic management of social impact. She is the Lead Investigator of the Neurodiversity project, an Australian-first project focused sustaining and scaling autism employment.

Dr. Sally Hawse is an organisational knowledge and learning specialist with expertise in knowledge management strategy and project delivery. Dr. Hawse is currently a Learning and Development Consultant, where she is involved in the design, implementation, and evaluation of people development and capability initiatives to support knowledge transfer and workplace learning as part of a NSW Australia local government workforce sustainability and transformation agenda.

Part II
Towards Sustainable Futures
in Higher Education

Chapter 12
F.I.R.S.T: Principles of Discipline for 21st Century Skills

Hana Krskova, Leigh N. Wood, Yvonne A. Breyer and Chris Baumann

Abstract In our digital 21st century, work demands a different set of skills than that of our industrial past. Educational institutions need to do more to help students both complete tertiary education and be ready for a future that will require continual learning. This chapter presents a case for improving non-cognitive skills, and particularly discipline, to achieve these and other goals. Discipline associated with learning often has negative connotations. However, discipline can also be thought of as a powerful tool for enhancing learning and higher achievement as well as overall personal development. Informed by the work of the 2000 winner of the Nobel Prize in Economics, James Heckman, this chapter presents F.I.R.S.T.: five principles of discipline, namely focus, intention, responsibility, structure, and time. A set of corresponding strategies for helping students take control of their own learning, work readiness, and achievement is also presented.

Keywords Academic performance · Achievement · F.I.R.S.T. discipline · Higher education · Work readiness · Completion rates · Graduate employability · Human capital

An earlier version of this chapter formed part of a Ph.D. thesis presented to Macquarie University.

H. Krskova (✉) · Y. A. Breyer
Macquarie Business School, Macquarie University, Sydney, Australia
e-mail: hana.krskova@mq.edu.au

L. N. Wood
Macquarie University, Sydney, Australia

C. Baumann
Macquarie Business School, Macquarie University, Sydney, Australia

Seoul National University (SNU), Seoul, South Korea

12.1 The Case at a Glance

Key concepts	• Discipline • Academic achievement • Work readiness • Human capital
Level of study	• BA and MA students
Subject areas	• HRM, management, business

Graduate capabilities	Graduate outcomes	%
	Critical thinking	30
	Problem solving	30
	Teamwork	10
	Communication	20
	Ethical thinking	5
	Sustainability	5
	Total	**100%**

Time required	• Out-of-class preperation:	45	min
	• In-class discussion:	30	min
	• Out-of-class assignments:	120	min

Activity type	**Individual** • Pre-reading, skim reading, in-depth reading • Assignment questions based on F.I.R.S.T. • Supplementary online resources • Supplementary further reading **Team-based** • Group discussion questions

Additional Materials

Calls for Greater Work Readiness

- ***Workforce of the future: The competing forces shaping 2030*** (**PwC** 2018)
  https://www.pwc.com/gx/en/services/people-organisation/workforce-of-the-future/workforce-of-the-future-the-competing-forces-shaping-2030-pwc.pdf
  A report discussing the competing forces shaping the workplace as we head toward the year 2030—employees need to join the workforce equipped with a framework for adapting to change and learning new skills throughout their lifetime.

- **Global Human Capital Trends 2018: The rise of the social enterprise – Country Report: United Kingdom (Deloitte** 2018b)
  https://www2.deloitte.com/content/dam/Deloitte/uk/Documents/human-capital/deloitte-uk-human-capital-trends-2018.pdf
  A trend analysis that highlights the need for business leaders to empower personal and professional skills development in their employees for success in the 21st-century marketplace.

Non-cognitive (Soft Skills) Emerging as Important

- **The Hard Facts Behind Soft Skills**
  https://www.youtube.com/watch?v=hSmG87MOyV0
  Professor James Heckman, Nobel Prize winner in Economics and expert in the economics of human development, discusses the importance of 'soft'. i.e., non-cognitive, skills for all walks of life.

Call for Increased Completion Rates

- **Joining the Dots**: Completing university in Australia: A cohort analysis exploring equity group outcomes (Edwards and McMillan 2015).
  https://www.acer.org/files/Completion-of-Equity-Groups-JTD-RB-V3-N3-May-2015.pdf
  Using the Commonwealth Higher Education Student Support Number (CHESSN) as a tracking identifier, this briefing paper provides an analysis of individuals in one student cohort as they progress through their studies over nine years.

Journal Papers

- **Krskova, H. & Baumann, C. 2017**. School discipline, investment, competitiveness and mediating educational performance. *International Journal of Educational Management, 31*(3), 293–319.
  In an era of downward budgetary pressure on educational providers, this article highlights that discipline is a more important and more cost-effective solution to academic performance than investing in more staff or funding new infrastructure. Discipline also has an indirect impact on national competitiveness.

- **Baumann, C. & Krskova, H. 2016**. School discipline, school uniforms and academic performance. *International Journal of Educational Management, 30*(6), 1003–1029. *(Highly Commended, 2017 Emerald Literati Network Awards for Excellence).*
  An analysis of student assessment data on school discipline from an international OECD programme showing that levels of discipline vary across different geographic regions and students with higher levels of discipline achieve higher academic scores.

The International Journal of Educational Management

This journal provides a broad overview of developments and best practices in education management. As a forum for sharing ideas, there is a particular focus on how new information and expertise can be applied worldwide. Regular topics of coverage include innovation, delivery, and international perspectives on common problems.

12.2   Introduction

For decades, research has emphasized the importance of cognitive skills in creating human capital (e.g., Becker 1993; Hanushek and Kimko 2000). More recently, however, non-cognitive skills have emerged as also being important for success (e.g., Heckman et al. 2006). Discipline is one such skill, and its contribution to higher academic and workplace performance is receiving increasing attention. In the traditional view, discipline tends to have negative connotations (e.g. Steinberg 2010), particularly in the context of schools (e.g., Lewis et al. 2005; Oplatka and Atias 2007). However, new research[1] offers an alternative perspective: perhaps discipline is only viewed dimly when it is enforced externally. When discipline comes from within, it is commended, even desired. At school, discipline is external. At university, discipline is internal. This chapter discusses F.I.R.S.T.: the five principles of internally-driven discipline, and how these discipline elements can be marshalled to cultivate 21st century skills.

Guided by human capital theory and built on the work of prominent economists, such as James Heckman, F.I.R.S.T. comprises five facets of discipline based on theoretical principles: focus (self-determination), intention (goal-setting), responsibility (self-efficacy), structure (self-regulation), and time (time management). F.I.R.S.T. and its corresponding strategies are useful for improving learning and work readiness in graduates. They can also be used by employers to inspire people to do better and strive for more, or by those wishing to take control of their own learning and achievement.

12.3   Calls for Improved Student Outcomes

Workforce productivity in Western countries is diminishing (e.g., Barro 2016; Bureau 2018). In the search for explanations and possible solutions, human capital theory reveals that enhancing skills and knowledge results in "more productive, flexible, and innovative" people (World Bank 2019, p. 2) so that organisations can "remain competitive in a new global economy" (Zula and Chermack 2007, p. 245). Therefore, human capital theory may both explain and solve three closely-related issues:

---

[1] A project titled "Discipline as a driver for performance in tertiary education: Measurement and associations" (Macquarie University Ethics Approval 5201700175).

- concerns about graduate employability and the growing need to ensure graduates are 'work-ready';
- expectations for educational institutions to improve completion rates; and
- the need to address changing demands for skills given job automation in the 21st century.

Positive graduate employment outcomes have implications at many levels. At the level of individuals, they impact future prosperity and career success. They also impact society in general through enhanced 'organisational effectiveness, national productivity and global competitiveness' (Jackson 2014b, p. 135). As such, the work readiness of graduates has received considerable attention in recent decades. The long-term employability prospects of tomorrow's workforce are concerning, but so is the apparent mismatch between what employers need and what universities seem to be providing (e.g. Jackson 2013). Research suggests that, despite all the recent efforts to equip graduates with the most up-to-date and in-demand skills, industry's expectations are not yet being fully met (Jackson 2014a). Therefore, looking for alternative ways to enhance the work readiness of graduates has become a priority for universities worldwide.

Low completion rates are another concern (Smith et al. 2015). As a result, educational institutions are constantly searching for better retention strategies, especially for at-risk students. In Australia, for example, only 73.6% of the 2007 cohort of domestic Bachelor's students had completed their studies when checked nine years later (DOE 2017). The data also revealed "a notable difference in completion rates between commencers" from high versus low socio-economic backgrounds (Edwards and McMillan 2015, p. 6). The search for innovative ways to help students reach graduation therefore continues.

For organisations to "remain competitive in a new global economy" (Zula and Chermack 2007, p. 245), workforce productivity must, at the very least, be maintained if not increased. Business consulting houses around the world are calling for an increase in human capital through building human capabilities (e.g. Deloitte 2018a; PwC 2018). For industry, skills and abilities that "cannot be fully mimicked by machines" and qualities like "grit" are at a premium (World Bank 2019, p. 50). For better or worse, the world we have built demands relentless increases in efficiency and improvements to service. To achieve these goals, we need to find appropriate skills (Deloitte 2018a). In other words, we need to search for skills that make us agile learners. After all:

> Skills enable people. They are capacities to function. Greater levels of skill foster social inclusion and promote economic and social mobility. They generate economic productivity and create social well-being. Skills give agency to people to shape their lives, to create new skills and to flourish. (Kautz et al. 2014, p. 4)

12.4 Human Capital, Cognitive and Non-cognitive Skills

12.4.1 An Overview of the Human Capital Perspective

Human capital theory highlights the contribution skills and knowledge make to individual-level productivity (Becker 1993) and, in turn, to economic growth (Schultz 1963) at both the macro and microeconomic level. The concept of human capital can be traced back to 1776 when Adam Smith published *The Wealth of Nations* (Smith 1817). It was a controversial concept at first, associated with depicting humans as production units. However, in the mid-20th century, seminal economists, such as Theodore Schultz, Gary Becker, and Jacob Mincer, resurrected the idea with pioneering works that underpin much of our current thinking today. Mincer (1962) highlighted the role of on-the-job training in creating human capital. Schultz (1964) offered investment in human capital as an explanation for increases in agricultural productivity. And Becker (1975) advanced the links between human capital and education by framing college education as a societal investment with a rate of return.

For decades since, researchers have been broadening our understanding of the connections between human capital and economic prosperity (e.g. Barro 1991; Hanushek and Kimko 2000). Within this body of literature, many studies have used human capital theory as a framework for investigating how cognitive skills impact economic growth (e.g., Barro and Lee 1996; Becker and Murphy 2007). Krskova and Baumann (2017), in particular, shed light on the relationship between formal skills and knowledge and competitiveness, while Baumann and Harvey (2018) explored the role of motivation and personality in enhancing competitiveness and productivity.

Recently, some of the controversy surrounding human capital has returned, although from a different perspective. This time the criticism is in response to a preconception that a higher education leads to better opportunities, better job prospects, higher earnings, and overall improvements to economic conditions. These rose-coloured notions have not proven true for all (Hanushek and Woessmann 2008). For example, university education in China is viewed as a way to improve social standing. Yet, in 2013, only one-third of nearly seven million fresh graduates secured a job shortly upon graduation (Mok et al. 2016).

12.4.2 Non-cognitive Skills Are More Important Than Cognitive Skills

Schultz (1961) referred to human capital as skills and knowledge, meaning that human capital encompasses all the skills embedded in the workforce. Over time, 'skills' became synonymous with cognitive skills provided by formal education, with a wealth of literature available about the contribution of education to economic gains (e.g. Barro 2013; Schultz 1960). More recently, however, a growing body of literature finds that all skills—both cognitive and non-cognitive—lead to gains in productivity and economic growth.

Cognitive skills are thinking skills, widely understood as "verbal, reading, and writing abilities as well as those in mathematics, science, music, and art" (Farkas 2003, p. 543). In contrast, non-cognitive skills "go by many names in the literature, including soft skills, personality traits, non-cognitive abilities, character skills, and socio-emotional skills" (Kautz et al. 2014, p. 8). They include, for example, "perseverance (grit), conscientiousness, self-control … self-efficacy, resilience to adversity … and the ability to engage productively in society" (p. 2), all of which are valued by society and the labour market.

Studies into how human capital contributes to economic growth are increasingly shifting toward these non-cognitive skills. Heckman et al. (2006) were among the pioneers of this stream. In a study on the influence of cognitive and non-cognitive abilities on work-life choices and outcomes, these authors challenged the status quo that cognitive skills dictate personal achievements, arguing that: "non-cognitive ability is as important, if not more important, than cognitive ability" (p. 477).

12.4.3 A Case for Increasing Levels of Soft Skills

Evidence for the positive impact of non-cognitive skills is growing. One example is an analysis that shows non-cognitive skills have an influence on wages, schooling, work experience, occupational choices, and risky behaviour. One of the key conclusions drawn by Heckman et al. (2006, p. 478) is that non-cognitive skills "promote success in social and economic life" because, for example, they can boost academic achievement and reduce dropout rates. That particular study also shows that non-cognitive skills play an important role in becoming a productive member of society and, as such, "raise wages through their direct effect on productivity" (p. 413).

While non-cognitive skills have only become a topic of inquiry in the field of economics relatively recently, they have quickly been deemed to be essential to success in learning, work, and life, and "especially critical for entry level and hourly workers" (Kautz et al. 2014, p. 29). In other words, both cognitive and non-cognitive skills contribute to creating human capital.

Like perseverance and self-control (Kautz et al. 2014), discipline is a non-cognitive skill that can be learned. It is key to success in both education and work. Through this analysis, we illustrate the past role of discipline in education, how our view of discipline is changing, and how the theoretical principles of discipline can be used in practice to succeed from within.

12.5 Discipline in Education

Teachers, parents, and the popular press, as well as educational leaders, have been discussing 'discipline'—or the lack thereof—among school students for decades (e.g., Dettman 1972; Pasternak 2013; Slee 1988). It is an important part of parenting (e.g., Baumrind 1966; Pellerin 2005) and of society in general (Charles and Barr 1992). In education, discipline is seen as critical because it is essential to learning (Knight 1988). Further, a lack of discipline has been linked to lower academic achievement (Cohen et al. 2009).

12.5.1 Meanings of Discipline

Discipline, however, has many meanings—for example:

- a synonym for control. This meaning is well known to teachers who use discipline to maintain order. Therefore, it is often linked to rules and regulations (e.g., Smith 1984);
- a deliberate action of "a person who is trained to consider his actions" (Dewey 1916, p. 135);
- a field of study at an educational institution, such as accounting, economics or medicine; or
- what is commonly known as 'self-discipline' (Duckworth and Seligman 2005); the capacity to change one's behaviour to achieve a higher goal, such as controlling anger or not rushing to answer questions in a test before reading instructions.

The focal point of all these interpretations is the theme of control. It is a theme that is especially pertinent to schools, where discipline is 'enforced' as a way to manage students. As Steinberg (2010, p. xi), states, it is "the natural follow-through of getting in trouble" and is used as a "tool of power" to keep order. The underlying "assumption is that students must be controlled, implying that without this control, the class would not be a success". In contrast, discipline at university is imposed internally by students. In this chapter we discuss internal discipline, a mechanism helping individuals achieve more, which is in line with the notion that discipline is "a very effective and useful tool to enhance learning, personal development and overall human betterment" (Baumann and Krskova 2016, p. 1021).

12.5.2 Discipline as a Driver of Academic Achievement

The positive links between increased discipline and academic achievement at school have been firmly established through a plethora of studies, many of which are quantitative and focus on examining data from the three-yearly Programme for International Student Assessment (PISA) administered by the Organisation for Economic Co-operation and Development (OECD) (e.g., Baumann and Krskova 2016; Chiu and Chow 2011; Cohen et al. 2009). Notably, Krskova and Baumann (2017) find that school discipline and academic performance are also linked to national competitiveness based on the OECD data that compares the academic performance of 15-year old students in reading, mathematics, and science across 60 countries.

However, while research into discipline is firmly established at the school level, only more recently has focus begun to shift to discipline at tertiary levels of education. Of the few investigations undertaken so far, Le et al. (2005) is, arguably, the most seminal. These authors designed a 10-item questionnaire for college students in the United States. Since then, other researchers have adopted this instrument, and more investigations into the roles of discipline in the university context have followed including:

- Robbins et al. (2006) who confirm that 'academic discipline' can predict academic performance in terms of grade point average (GPA).
- Komarraju et al. (2013) who examined predictors of academic performance and find that discipline is a significant predictor of college GPAs.
- Mattern et al. (2017) who find in a study of almost 10,000 students across post-secondary institutions, in the context of predicting first-year grade point average during the college admission process, that female students have higher levels of discipline.
- Ndum et al. (2018) who also finds female students have higher levels of discipline and that discipline is strongly associated with success in both composition and algebra.

12.5.3 Perceptions of Discipline in University Students

As opposed to using quantitative questionnaires, qualitative interviews can be used as a way to explore and better understand the concept of discipline. F.I.R.S.T. was born out of such an investigation (see Krskova et al. 2019). Students from Macquarie University in Sydney, Australia were interviewed to examine their perceptions of what discipline in the university context is. How could they become more disciplined and would that make them more work-ready? The students spanned a wide range of cultural backgrounds, different stages of study, and a range of faculties.

The data collected shows that these students already had a self-conception of discipline and recognised its importance in their quest for greater achievement. They described discipline as, for example:

The force to push, push us to study harder. To work harder. (P18[2])

A guideline that individuals put on themselves to ensure that they get particular task done in an education field, or [...] something that they can use to achieve certain goals. (P16)

Other comments indicated that:

People who aren't disciplined don't do well. People who are, usually do well. (P2)

Disciplined students are mostly the most successful students. (P17)

It is unsurprising that discipline at a university would be somewhat different from the concept of discipline in schools. What was unexpected was that the participants described it as an enabler—a way to enhance their focus and purpose, and an empowering force in aspirations for higher performance. Of course, there were a wide variety of responses, but a clear pattern did emerge:

- Students who felt less disciplined were unclear about what discipline means at university.

---

[2]The interview participants are referred to only as, for example, participant "P18".

- Students who felt disciplined had a detailed conception of discipline. And, across the sample, they tended to identify the same five characteristics as being important to discipline: focus, intention, responsibility, structure, and time.

Interestingly, when asked about whether they wished to be more disciplined, the 'more disciplined' students who recognised its benefits said yes, discipline is a continuous goal. They seemed in control of their progress through university and were able to discuss these five elements of discipline in detail. In contrast, the less disciplined students were also less clear about whether or how to improve. They missed the structured discipline they had received at secondary school and focussed on what university could do for them to stay on track.

Moreover, some stages of discipline emerged in the range of responses. Some viewed discipline as an imposed control, like at school. Others recognised the benefits of discipline and enjoyed the feeling of 'being disciplined' from time to time. Still, others claimed that high levels of discipline are required to succeed at work. A few participants also alluded to the highest stage of discipline—creative discipline (Krskova et al. 2019)—citing ideas that accord with Napier and Nilsson (2008, p. 206). The notion is that when "creative organizations have discipline at the heart of what they do", individuals begin "seeking knowledge, and sort of striving for excellence, and not just being mediocre average" (P14).

Discussions of the various stages of discipline generally indicated that discipline is a threshold concept that "takes a very long time to build up" (P16). Figure 12.1 depicts "Discipline as a Threshold Concept". In learning, threshold concepts are sometimes discussed as transformative, troublesome, liminal—and they are often

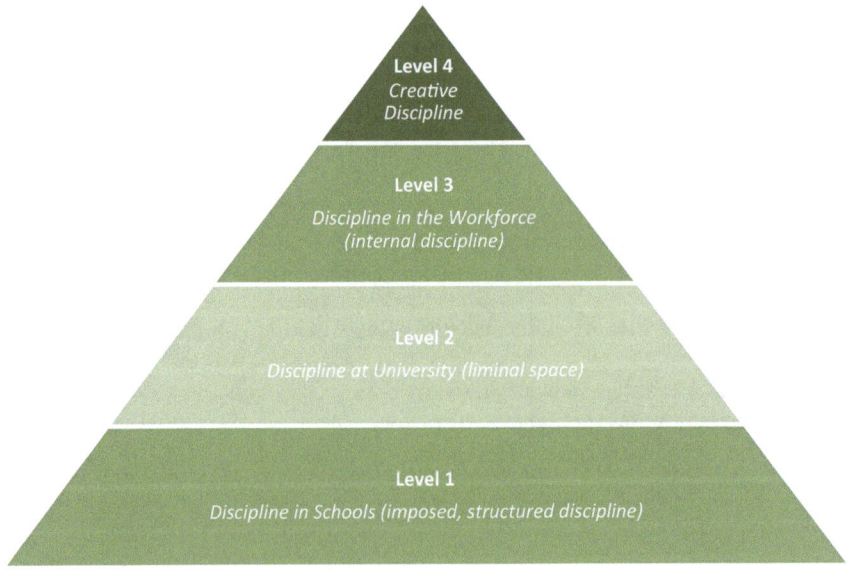

Fig. 12.1 Discipline as a threshold concept. *Source* Adapted from Krskova et al. (2019)

thought of being "akin to a portal, opening up a new and previously inaccessible way of thinking about something" (Meyer and Land 2006, p. 3). Similarly, the discipline threshold is a transformative means by which individuals can interact with the world around them, be it university or the workplace. The foundation of these stages is Level 1, where people seek and need discipline to be imposed. At Level 2, people wander in the liminal space between externally imposed discipline and internally-driven discipline. They recognise that they should be able to discipline themselves but have not yet reached the threshold of discipline required for the workplace. By Level 3, people have clearly moved through the portal and become disciplined. At Level 4, people see themselves as disciplined without external intervention.

Depending on their progress through the layers (discipline at school, at university, in the workforce and creative discipline), some individuals might benefit from structured assistance with only goal-setting, for example. Whereas, others might benefit from learning more about structuring their study or work or time management. The data also suggests that those who need the most support with becoming more disciplined may also need help with understanding what discipline is. Here, F.I.R.S.T. can provide step-by-step guidance with the five building blocks of discipline to progress through the threshold concept of discipline.

12.6 F.I.R.S.T. Discipline

Each of the five discipline elements—focus, intention, responsibility, structure, and time—as illustrated in Fig. 12.2, are discussed in more detail in Tables 12.1, 12.2, 12.3, 12.4 and 12.5. Each theme corresponds to a theoretical perspective discovered in the literature: self-determination (Deci and Ryan 1985), goal-setting (Locke and

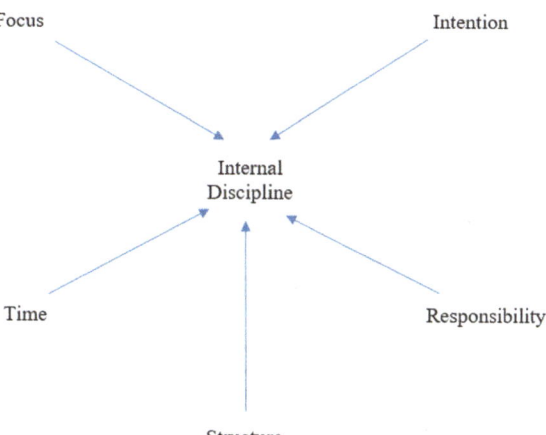

Fig. 12.2 Conceptual model of F.I.R.S.T. discipline. *Source* Adapted from Krskova et al. (2019)

Table 12.1 Focus (self-determination)

In a study of college students, multitasking, e.g., using Facebook and texting while studying, was reported to negatively impact overall college GPA (Junco and Cotten 2012, p. 505). Similarly, a study of middle school, high school, and university students showed that students who "accessed Facebook one or more times during the short study period" had lower GPAs (Rosen et al. 2013, p. 955), Calderwood et al. (2014, p. 19) finds that college students have an "average of 35 distractions of 6 s or longer over the course of 3 h, with aggregated mean duration of 25 min".

The ability to ignore distractions while studying, such as watching YouTube or TV or perusing Facebook, is influenced by self-determination theory (Deci and Ryan 1985), which deals with choices people make during feelings of empowerment and "a higher level of interest in a task" in the absence of external influences (Latham 2012, p. 155).

The not-discipline students may just be easily distracted from many things. (P10)
When they're competing interests, ability to choose the best and most appropriate one. Even [if] it's less enjoyable. (P5)

Table 12.2 Intention (goal-setting)

Goal-setting theory shows that setting goals is a powerful way to enhance performance (Locke and Latham 1990). One of the main propositions of this theory is that "specific high goals lead to higher performance than no goals or even an abstract goal such as 'do your best'" (Latham 2012, p. 56). This theory is equally relevant to undertakings in work and education. Goals such as 'do your best in class' might not be sufficiently specific to galvanise the necessary effort to achieve high academic outcomes, because "maximum effort is not aroused under a do best goal" (Latham and Locke 1991, p. 215). Further, with general, less specific goals, it is possible for poor performance to go unnoticed or to be justified by the vagueness of the general goals.

If you're more disciplined […] you know what you need to achieve. You've got goals. (P6)
I can't see achieving my goal without discipline. (P4)

Table 12.3 Responsibility (self-efficacy)

Self-efficacy theory (Bandura 1986), or the concept of academic self-efficacy (Honicke and Broadbent 2016), concerns the way people choose to behave; for example, how long they dedicate to a task or how persistent they are in pursuit of a certain activity. On the one hand, self-doubt might cause individuals to ease off their efforts and "abort their attempts prematurely and quickly settle for mediocre solutions" (Bandura 1989, p. 1176). On the other hand, students with higher levels of self-efficacy and willingness to take responsibility for their academic performance will display higher levels of perseverance.

[Being disciplined] … I love this feeling, you know, to control my own life and […] fulfilling my plans. (P9)
It's having self-responsibility for all of your studies. (P8)

Latham 1990), self-efficacy (Bandura 1977), and self-regulation (e.g., Zimmerman 1986). The last, time, is known to us all in life and in the literature as time management (e.g. Britton and Tesser 1991; Macan 1994).

Table 12.4 Structure (self-regulation)

The ability to structure tasks well is particularly relevant—both in academia and in the workforce. When individuals attempt to learn new skills and knowledge, they "structure, and create environments that optimize learning" (Zimmerman 1986, p. 308). This might include breaking large tasks or projects into smaller ones or establishing a structure for progression comprising regular interim deadlines before the final due date. Using strategies, such as routines (e.g. Brown et al. 1981), to deal with tasks regularly aligns with theoretical work in self-regulation (e.g., Zimmerman and Schunk 1989). In education, self-regulation means approaching difficult tasks with diligence and confidence (Zimmerman 1990).

I like to have a routine. It's very satisfying when you know you're on top of everything. And you can't achieve that without being disciplined. (P7)
Planning ahead of time. Being structured. You have to know when things are happening and when you need to get something done. (P1)

Table 12.5 Time (time management)

The notion that time management is important in academia was confirmed decades ago. Time management models, such as a model by Macan (1994), are widely acknowledged.
For example, Schuler (1979, p. 854) established that "time management means less stress for individuals, which means more efficient, satisfied, healthy employees, which in turn means more effective organizations". Fisher et al. (1981, p. 2) report that "other things being equal, the more time allocated to a content area, the high[er] the academic achievement".
And yet, despite the availability of a wealth of literature on time management, many people find they lack the discipline to manage their time as they would like.

It seems like when I manage my time better I feel more disciplined and I perform better in my assessments. (P8)
Spend enough time on studying [...] prioritise our time. (P10)
I need to ensure that I have adequate amount of time on a certain subject to do well, essentially. (P16)

12.7 A Way Forward: Applying the F.I.R.S.T. Discipline Principles

The F.I.R.S.T. principles of discipline represent five concrete steps for improving productivity. Each principle has the potential to enhance personal effectiveness. Collectively, these principles allow individuals to deliver their very best work.

In keeping with the notion of human capital theory that enhancing skills and knowledge leads to people becoming "more productive, flexible, and innovative" (World Bank 2019, p. 2), F.I.R.S.T. answers calls from industry for work-ready graduates with a low-cost tool that can narrow focus, eliminate distractions, and put goals and structures in place to help manage time. When paired with the ability to take responsibility for one's own achievement, these five principles can act as either a methodology or an avenue toward success or, ideally, both.

Following the philosophy of Charles and Barr (1992), these principles are not about what not to do; they are about what *to* do. In this context, F.I.R.S.T. is a training program that leads to the "*level of consistent effort*" (P14) required to achieve chosen endeavours.

12.7.1 Assistance for Students

> The more disciplined you are with going to classes or doing your assignments on time or doing the readings before class, the more likely you are to retain the knowledge better and to understand the content better and therefore you should be rewarded with a better mark at the end of the day. (P13)

With discipline linked to both retention and higher academic achievement (Robbins et al. 2006), the F.I.R.S.T. principles can provide a valuable tool for students at risk of academic failure or for those wishing to further enhance their learning and academic achievement. For those at risk, these principles can help with "managing stress" (P16), act as a checklist, help balance the demands of multiple subjects, and so on. In other words:

> If you are disciplined then you are focused on studying [...] if you study hard, then I think at least, if you cannot get HD, at least you can get a C or D. So, discipline can have positive, quite positive impact on achieving [...] a good academic result. (P10)

Further, educational institutions are under significant pressure to ensure their students are more work-ready, which translates to different and higher academic outcomes. In line with Kautz et al. (2014, p. 1), who highlights that high-quality programs can "improve character skills in a lasting and cost-effective way", F.I.R.S.T. is a low-cost alternative to employing more staff or funding new infrastructure that helps graduates contribute from the moment they join the workforce.

Many educational institutions already deliver programs underpinned by self-determination, goal-setting, self-efficacy, self-regulation, and time management. But for those without such initiatives, F.I.R.S.T. could be a guide for establishing frameworks that help students take more responsibility for their own learning and achievement. Programs might be needed for improvement in one specific principle or for assistance with all five. As Baumann et al. (2016) argues, discipline strengthens the work ethic, which is valued by employers (Porter 2005). Therefore, increasing the levels of discipline in students could lead to better-performing students and graduates that are more work-ready.

12.7.2 Structured Internship Programs

During the interviews, the students themselves recognised that there would be a shift in expectations when they transition from university to the workplace (García-Aracil et al. 2018; Wood and Breyer 2017). A toolkit comprising the F.I.R.S.T. principles could enable students and graduates to start "taking initiative or going beyond the direct instructions of what to do" (Porter 2005, p. 340) shortly after beginning a new job.

Together with employers, educational providers could establish structured internship programs based on the five principles as scaffolding for each week of the internship. Each task and each project could be assessed against each principle to ensure that, even with minimum supervision, interns would be fulfilling all the necessary technical requirements of a junior position in an organisation. Mastering how to: keep distractions to minimum, gaining confidence in meeting specific goals and sub-goals (as opposed to "trying their best"), taking responsibility for delivering good work products, structuring all tasks into a well-defined timetable as well as allocating a pre-agreed amount of time to each task—these will enable interns to contribute to organisational success even with limited prior work experience.

12.7.3 Training and Development Programs

I think people that are more disciplined, and have everything planned out, and do things earlier, do definitely well, do better. (P20)

When you go to workforce, you suddenly have expectations from other people. They need a job done, at certain time. You need to stay on top of due dates and that sometimes you need to manage a few projects at the same time. So, if you are not disciplined, you might not get things done on time and you might get in lot of trouble for that. (P1)

When individuals are expected to "take responsibility for lifelong learning" (PwC 2018, p. 29)… when the responsibility for professional and personal development is shifting from employers to employees … when learning is being increasingly viewed "as a lifelong process that involves repeated self-directed efforts to improve one's academic, professional, and personal functioning" (Zimmerman and Schunk 2008, p. 23), mastering the principles of F.I.R.S.T. can help individuals take control of their own learning and development.

Each individual, at any stage of life, can unpack the five principles to assess which components would benefit from enhancement. In turn, this can boost achievement across many a domain. In addition, as "employability is about being capable of getting and keeping fulfilling work" (Hillage and Pollard 1998, p. 2), increasing the levels of discipline has the potential to increase the employability of individuals, regardless of age, industry or geographical location. Each individual could, therefore, seek out a relevant training course aimed at increasing levels of their discipline.

A deficiency in any of the discipline elements can derail a person's efforts to achieve a goal, leaving untapped potential both for them and for their employers. Employers could implement tailored training for staff and embed the discipline elements into continuous professional development (CPD) programs. By offering employees these principles as part of a suite of "learning tools and experiences they will need for continuous development" (Deloitte 2018b, p. 9), employers could empower employees to achieve more.

12.8 Conclusion

If you learn discipline in school or in college, it definitely helps the rest of your life. (P1)

Underpinned by the basic notion in human capital that better skills lead to better productivity (Kell et al. 2018), this chapter outlined the benefits to be had by increasing levels of discipline in our everyday lives. In addition, by viewing discipline as a skill that can be learnt, this chapter offers guidance on how the five principles of discipline in F.I.R.S.T.—focus, intention, responsibility, structure, and time—applied individually or synergistically, can lead to greater achievement across many areas of life.

12.9 Teaching Notes

12.9.1 Synopsis of the Case

In our digital 21st century, work demands a different set of skills than that of our industrial past. Educational institutions need to do more to help students both complete tertiary education and be ready for a future that will require continual learning. This chapter presents a case for improving non-cognitive skills, and particularly discipline, to achieve these and other goals. Discipline associated with learning often has negative connotations. However, discipline can also be thought of as a powerful tool for enhancing learning and higher achievement as well as overall personal development. Informed by the work of the 2000 winner of the Nobel Prize in Economics, James Heckman, this chapter presents F.I.R.S.T.: five principles of discipline, namely focus, intention, responsibility, structure, and time. A set of corresponding strategies for helping students take control of their own learning, work readiness, and achievement is also presented.

12.9.2 Target Learning Group

- Level of study—BA and MA students
- Subject areas—HRM; management; business.

12.9.3   Learning Objectives

12.9.3.1   Key Issues

- Promote awareness of the role of non-cognitive or soft skills in the level of work readiness of graduates.
- Enhance awareness of the positive connotation associated with discipline in higher education, as opposed to the historically negative connotation associated with rigid schools.
- Introduce the theoretical underpinnings of discipline as a concept and identify its relevance to university students for learning outcomes and future employability.

12.9.3.2   Specific Objectives

- Illuminate the five specific elements of discipline in F.I.R.S.T: focus, intention, responsibility, structure, and time.
- Explore the benefits to be had by both students and workers from increasing discipline levels through structured training.

12.9.4   Reading Activities

12.9.4.1   Pre-reading

Skim the chapter headings and each of the textboxes.

- What do they tell you about the key themes and ideas in the chapter?

Examine the text to locate information about why discipline levels in students and workers should be increased.

- What is a priority for universities worldwide?
- What are the completion rates in Australia?
- Business consulting houses such as PwC and Deloitte report on the quest for better work-ready graduates. What skills are attracting a premium in the 21st century?

Examine the text to locate information about the positive impact of discipline, as supported by research.

12.9.4.2   In-Depth Reading

Calls for improved student outcomes

- What are the specific concerns raised in Western countries in relation to workforce productivity?
- What are the three main concerns driving the quest for innovative solutions for student outcomes?

Human capital and the positive impact of skills on achievement and productivity

- What are the main ideas underpinning the human capital perspective?
- What are the differences between cognitive and non-cognitive skills?
- Historically, which set of skills (cognitive or non-cognitive) has been viewed as more important in relation to achievement?
- What are the recent developments in the field of human capital research?
- What are some benefits that can be gained from increasing the levels of non-cognitive skills?

Discipline in education

- What are some of the various meanings of discipline?
- What are examples of the benefits of discipline presented by studies from the school and the higher education sectors?
- What are the five main themes or dimensions that university students have identified as being important in relation to discipline?

The interplay between theory and practice

- What are the five theoretical perspectives discussed in this chapter?

A way forward

- What is presented in this chapter as the way forward?
- What are the three ways discipline levels could be increased (among students and workforce participants alike)?

12.9.5   Discussion Activities

12.9.5.1   Case for Increasing Levels of Discipline in the Workplace

Students should divide into small groups and discuss the following questions:

- What constitutes high levels of discipline?
- How discipline might affect levels of productivity in the individuals, workgroups, and departments of an organisation?

Students should divide into groups based on work experience and discuss what influence the five elements of discipline would have on structuring learning in the following scenarios:

very little or no work experience	a semester-long university unit with high academic outcomes after 12 weeks of lectures and tutorials.
some work experience	week 1 of an internship program for a student in Accounting/Business/Marketing degree.
significant work experience	a major work project, such as creating a new budget template, designing a fundraising program, or setting up a database for reporting to the board on a major business initiative.

The participants should address the following points:

1. Focus

   - design a suitable task;
   - ascertain the importance of the assigned task;
   - assess their ability to become "passionate" about the task, at least for the duration of the project;
   - strategies for reducing distractions;
   - strategies for minimising interruptions;
   - strategies to assist with keeping the goal in sight and focussing on the goal;
   - strategies for resisting social pressures such as taking multiple breaks, answering personal phone calls, or responding to requests on social media.

2. Intention

   - What exactly are you trying to achieve? What will the final work product look like?
   - What do you personally expect to achieve by performing well?
   - How would you rate your expectations of the possibility of the goal being achieved (high, medium, low)?
   - Are you prepared to undertake the task? What do you need in order to succeed?

3. Responsibility

   - If you do not succeed—will you claim responsibility?
   - Do you believe that you are in control of the situation?

4. Structure

   - What is your routine going to be for the duration of the project?
   - How can you split the workload?
   - What steps can you break the task into?
   - What will the project timetable look like (aimed to capture all deliverables and due dates) to ensure successful completion of the project?

5. Time

  – How much time will you allocate to each step?
  – How will you avoid procrastination and distractions?
  – What will galvanise you into action each day?

12.9.6 Assignments

12.9.6.1 Can Increasing the Level of Discipline Make a Difference to You?

- On a scale of 1–10, 10 being the highest, participants should assess their current level in the five dimensions of discipline: focus, intention, responsibility, structure, time.
- Referring to Tables 12.1, 12.2, 12.3, 12.4 and 12.5, participants should discuss how the five theoretical perspectives relate to university students: self-determination, goal-setting, self-efficacy, self-regulation, time management.
- Discuss what changes, relating to the five F.I.R.S.T. discipline principles, you could implement today/this week.
- How could you potentially benefit from such changes this semester? And why?

Further Reading

- **2018 Deloitte Global Human Capital Trends report (Deloitte** 2018a)
  https://www2.deloitte.com/content/dam/insights/us/articles/HCTrends2018/
  2018-HCtrends_Rise-of-the-social-enterprise.pdf
  With organisations no longer being assessed on financial performance alone but also on its impacts on communities and society, the *2018 Deloitte Global Human Capital Trends* **report** outlines the role human capital trends play in successfully achieving organisational outcomes based on a global survey of more than 11,000 human resources and business leaders.

- **World Bank's 2010 Skills Toward Employability and Productivity (STEP) report**
  http://documents.worldbank.org/curated/en/516741468178736065/122290272_
  201511338025153/additional/897290NWP0P132085290B00PUBLIC001421.
  pdf
  These infographics summarise the efforts behind creating a global initiative to create internationally comparative measurements of skills in adults. The overarching goal is to develop the most appropriate skills for increasing productivity and growth.

- **Confucianism, Discipline, and Competitiveness (Baumann et al.** 2019)
  https://www.taylorfrancis.com/books/e/9781351062220
  The CDC book offers a comprehensive look at three interrelated concepts: Confucianism, Discipline, and Competitiveness. By combining three seemingly unrelated dimensions from three different areas of studies - Confucianism from cultural studies, Discipline from the field of education and pedagogy, and Competitiveness from the sphere of business and economics - the CDC book offers a new understanding of pedagogy, contrasting East Asia to other parts of the world. The manuscript highlights the prominent role that a Confucian approach to pedagogy, with its focus on instilling values of hard work, Discipline and education, has played in the rapid economic growth of East Asian societies.

References

Bandura A (1977) Self-efficacy: towards a unifying theory and the organization. Psychol Rev 84(2):191–215

Bandura A (1986) Social foundations of thought and action: a social cognitive theory. Prentice-Hall Inc., Englewood Cliffs, NJ

Bandura A (1989) Human agency in social cognitive theory. Am Psychol 44(9):1175–1184

Baumann C, Winzar H, Viengkham D (2019) Confucianism, discipline, and competitiveness. Routledge, New York

Barro RJ (1991) Economic growth in a cross section of countries. Q J Econ 106(2):407–443

Barro RJ (2013) Education and economic growth. Ann Econ Finan 14(2):277–304

Barro RJ (2016) The job-filled non-recovery. Remarks at the Brookings Institute. Brookings Institute, Washington, pp 1–9

Barro RJ, Lee JW (1996) International measures of schooling years and schooling quality. Am Econ Rev 86(2):218–223

Baumann C, Harvey M (2018) Competitiveness vis-à-vis motivation and personality as drivers of academic performance – introducing the MCP model. Int J Educ Manage 32(1):185–202

Baumann C, Krskova H (2016) School discipline, school uniforms and academic performance. Int J Educ Manage 30(6):1003–1029

Baumann C, Hamin H, Yang SJ (2016) Work ethic formed by pedagogical approach: evolution of institutional approach to education and competitiveness. Asia Pac Bus Rev 22(3):374–396

Baumrind D (1966) Effects of authoritative parental control on child behavior. Child Dev 37(4):887–907

Becker GS (1975) Human capital: a theoretical and empirical analysis, with special reference to education. National Bureau of Economic Research, New York, NY

Becker GS (1993) Human capital: a theoretical and empirical analysis, with special reference to education, 3rd edn. University of Chicago Press, Chicago, IL

Becker GS, Murphy KM (2007) Education and consumption: the effects of education in the household compared to the marketplace. J Hum Capital 1(1):9–35

Britton BK, Tesser A (1991) Effects of time-management practices on college grades. J Educ Psychol 83(3):405–410

Brown AL, Campione JC, Day JD (1981) Learning to learn: on training students to learn from texts. Educ Res 10(2):14–21

Bureau OLS (2018) Productivity and costs. Third Quarter 2018, Preliminary. U.S. Department of Labor, Bureau of Labor Statistics, Washington

Calderwood C, Ackerman PL, Conklin EM (2014) What else do college students "do" while studying? An investigation of multitasking. Comput Educ 75:19–29

Charles CM, Barr KB (1992) Building classroom discipline. Longman, New York, NY

Chiu MM, Chow BWY (2011) Classroom discipline across forty-one countries: school, economic, and cultural differences. J Cross Cult Psychol 42(3):516–533

Cohen EH, Kramarski B, Mevarech ZR (2009) Classroom practices and students' literacy in a high and a low achieving country: a comparative analysis of PISA data from Finland and Israel. Educ Pract Theor 31(1):19–37

Deci EL, Ryan R (1985) Intrinsic motivation and self-determination in human behaviour. Plenum, New York, NY

Deloitte (2018a) The rise of the social enterprise: 2018 Deloitte Global Human Capital Trends. Deloitte, London, UK

Deloitte (2018b) Global Human Capital Trends 2018: the rise of the social enterprise (Country Report: United Kingdom). Deloitte, London, UK

Dettman HW (1972) Discipline in secondary schools in Western Australia. Report of the committee into discipline in Secondary Schools in Western Australia. Education Department of Western Australia, Perth

Dewey J (1916) Democracy and education. The Free Press, New York, NY

DOE (2017) Completions rates of higher education students - cohort analysis, 2005-2015. Commonwealth Department of Education, Canberra, ACT

Duckworth AL, Seligman MEP (2005) Self-discipline outdoes IQ in predicting academic performance of adolescents. Psychol Sci 16(12):939–944

Edwards D, McMillan J (2015) Completing university in Australia: a cohort analysis exploring equity group outcomes. Joining Dots Res Brief 3(3):1–12

Farkas G (2003) Cognitive skills and noncognitive traits and behaviors in stratification processes. Ann Rev Sociol 29(1):541–562

Fisher CW, Berliner DC, Filby NN, Marliave R, Cahen LS, Dishaw MM (1981) Teaching behaviors, academic learning time, and student achievement: an overview. J Classroom Inter 17(1):2–15

García-Aracil A, Monteiro S, Almeida LS (2018) Students' perceptions of their preparedness for transition to work after graduation. Act Learn High Educ 19(1):1–14

Hanushek EA, Kimko DD (2000) Schooling, labor-force quality, and the growth of nations. Am Econ Rev 90(5):1184–1208

Hanushek EA, Woessmann L (2008) The role of cognitive skills in economic development. J Econ Lit 46(3):607–668

Heckman JJ, Stixrud J, Urzua S (2006) The effects of cognitive and noncognitive abilities on labor market outcomes and social behavior. J Labor Econ 24(3):411–482

Hillage J, Pollard E (1998) Employability: developing a framework for policy analysis. Department of Education and Employment, London, UK

Honicke T, Broadbent J (2016) The influence of academic self-efficacy on academic performance: a systematic review. Educ Res Rev 17(1):63–84

Jackson D (2013) Business graduate employability - where are we going wrong? High Educ Res Dev 32(5):776–790

Jackson D (2014a) Testing a model of undergraduate competence in employability skills and its implications for stakeholders. J Educ Work 27(2):220–242

Jackson D (2014b) Factors influencing job attainment in recent Bachelor graduates: evidence from Australia. High Educ 68(1):135–153

Junco R, Cotten SR (2012) No A 4 U: the relationship between multitasking and academic performance. Comput Educ 59(2):505–514

Kautz T, Heckman JJ, Diris R, Ter Weel B, Borghans L (2014) Fostering and measuring skills: improving cognitive and non-cognitive skills to promote lifetime success. National Bureau of Economic Research, Cambridge, MA

Kell HJ, Robbins SB, Su R, Brenneman M (2018) A psychological approach to human capital. ETS research report series. Educational Testing Service, Princeton, NJ

Knight T (1988) Student discipline as a curriculum concern. In: Slee R (ed) Discipline and schools: a curriculum perspective. The Macmillan Company, South Melbourne, VIC, pp 240–312

Komarraju M, Ramsey A, Rinella V (2013) Cognitive and non-cognitive predictors of college readiness and performance: role of academic discipline. Learn Individ Differ 24(1):103–109

Krskova H, Baumann C (2017) School discipline, investment, competitiveness and mediating educational performance. Int J Educ Manage 31(3):293–319

Krskova H, Breyer Y, Baumann C, Wood LN (2019) An exploration of university student perceptions of discipline. High Educ Skills Work-Based Learn. https://doi.org/10.1108/HESWBL-02-2019-0026

Latham GP (2012) Work motivation: history, theory, research, and practice. Sage, Los Angeles, CA

Latham GP, Locke EA (1991) Self-regulation through goal setting. Organ Behav Hum Decis Process 50(2):212–247

Le H, Casillas A, Robbins SB, Langley R (2005) Motivational and skills, social, and self-management predictors of college outcomes: constructing the Student Readiness Inventory. Educ Psychol Meas 65(3):482–508

Lewis R, Romi S, Qui X, Katz YJ (2005) Teachers' classroom discipline and student misbehavior in Australia, China and Israel. Teach Teacher Educ 21(6):729–741

Locke EA, Latham GP (1990) A theory of goal setting and task performance. Prentice-Hall Inc, Englewood Cliffs, NJ

Macan TH (1994) Time management: test of a process model. J Appl Psychol 79(3):381–391

Mattern K, Sanchez E, Ndum E (2017) Why do achievement measures underpredict female academic performance? Educ Meas Issues Pract 36(1):47–57

Meyer J, Land R (2006) Threshold concepts and troublesome knowledge: an introduction. In: Meyer J, Land R (eds) Overcoming barriers to student understanding: threshold concepts and troublesome knowledge. Routledge, Florence, pp 3–18

Mincer J (1962) On-the-job training: costs, returns, and some implications. Eur J Polit Econ 70(5, Part 2):50–79

Mok KH, Wen Z, Dale R (2016) Employability and mobility in the valorisation of higher education qualifications: the experiences and reflections of Chinese students and graduates. J High Educ Policy Manage 38(3):264–281

Napier NK, Nilsson M (2008) The creative discipline: mastering the art and science of innovation Westport. Greenwood Publishing Group, CT

Ndum E, Allen J, Way J, Casillas A (2018) Explaining gender gaps in english composition and college algebra in college: the mediating role of psychosocial factors. J Adv Acad 29(1):56–88

Oplatka I, Atias M (2007) Gendered views of managing discipline in school and classroom. Gend Educ 19(1):41–59

Pasternak R (2013) Discipline, learning skills and academic achievement. J Arts Educ 1(1):1–11

Pellerin LA (2005) Applying Baumrind's parenting typology to high schools: toward a middle-range theory of authoritative socialization. Soc Sci Res 34(2):283–303

Porter G (2005) A "career" work ethic versus just a job. J Eur Ind Train 29(4):336–352

PwC (2018) Workforce of the future: the competing forces shaping 2030. PricewaterhouseCoopers, London, UK

Robbins SB, Allen J, Casillas A, Peterson CH, Le H (2006) Unravelling the differential effects of motivational and skills, social, and self-management measures from traditional predictors of college outcomes. J Educ Psychol 98(3):598–616

Rosen LD, Carrier LM, Cheever NA (2013) Facebook and texting made me do it: media-induced task-switching while studying. Comput Hum Behav 29(3):948–958

Schuler RS (1979) Managing stress means managing time. Pers J 58(12):851–854

Schultz TW (1960) Capital formation by education. J Polit Econ 68(6):571–583

Schultz TW (1961) Investment in human capital. Am Econ Rev 51(1):1–17

Schultz TW (1963) The economic value of education. Columbia University Press, New York, NY

Schultz TW (1964) Transforming traditional agriculture. Yale University Press, New Haven, CT

Slee R (ed) (1988) Discipline and schools: a curriculum perspective. The Macmillan Company of Australia, South Melbourne, VIC

Smith A (1817) An inquiry into the nature and causes of the wealth of nations. Adam and Charles Black, Edinburgh

Smith DD (1984) Effective discipline. Pro-Ed, Austin, TX

Smith J, Trinidad S, Larkin S (2015) Participation in higher education in Australia among under-represented groups: what can we learn from the Higher Education Participation Program to better support Indigenous learners? Learn Communities Intern J Learn Soc Contexts 17:12–29

Steinberg SR (2010) Being in trouble: autoethnography of a not-really bad, white, middle-class Jewish girl. In: Millei Z, Griffiths TG, Parkes RJ (eds) Re-theorizing discipline in education. Peter Lang, New York, NY, pp ix–xii

Wood LN, Breyer YA (2017) Success in higher education. In: Wood LN, Breyer YA (eds) Success in higher education: transitions to, within and from University. Springer, Singapore, pp 1–19

World Bank (2019) World Development Report 2019: the changing nature of work. World Bank, Washington

Zimmerman BJ (1986) Becoming a self-regulated learner: which are the key subprocesses? Contemp Educ Psychol 16(3):307–313

Zimmerman BJ (1990) Self-regulated learning and academic achievement: an overview. Educ Psychol 25(1):3–17

Zimmerman BJ, Schunk DH (eds) (1989) Self-regulated learning and academic achievement: theory, research, and practice. Springer, New York, NY

Zimmerman BJ, Schunk DH (2008) Motivation: an essential dimension of self-regulated learning. In: Schunk DH, Zimmerman BJ (eds) Motivation and self-regulated learning: theory, research, and applications. Routledge, New York, NY, pp 1–30

Zula KJ, Chermack TJ (2007) Integrative literature review: human capital planning: a review of literature and implications for human resource development. Hum Resour Dev Rev 6(3):245–262

Dr. Hana Krskova is a Certified Practicing Accountant and holds a Graduate Diploma in Applied Corporate Governance, an MBA and a Master of Research. During her professional tenure at Macquarie University, Sydney, Australia, she was highly commended in the Vice-Chancellor's Excellence Awards for Professional Staff in the category "Collaboration and Connection" between academic and professional staff. She was also elected onto the Macquarie University Council. Her research interest in student discipline was sparked by years of supervising recent graduates and encountering their somewhat limited level of work readiness.

Professor Leigh N. Wood is a pioneering leader in student success. Her research spans the transition to university and the transition to professional work as well as curriculum design to facilitate these transitions. Her research contribution includes five books, 150 articles and multimedia learning resources. She has had over $A2 million in learning and teaching grants. She is proud of her student experience teams, her students and her Ph.D. graduates and their contributions to our communities.

Associate Professor Yvonne A. Breyer is an award-winning academic with expertise in student success, online learning and digital transformation in the higher education sector. Yvonne has led several highly successful strategic initiatives with national and international reach. Most recently, she led the 'Excel Skills for Business' specialisation, which received the Coursera Outstanding Educator Award for Student Transformation on the back of exceptional learner feedback, global reach and impact. She holds a Ph.D. (Macquarie University), a Master of Arts (University of Essen, Germany) and a Postgraduate Certificate in Higher Education, Leadership and Management (Macquarie University).

Dr. Chris Baumann is Associate Professor at Macquarie University; Visiting Professor at Seoul National University (SNU) and Visiting Associate Professor at Osaka University. Chris' research focus is on the 3Cs: Competitiveness, Cross-culture/Confucianism and Customer loyalty, introducing concepts such as Competitive Productivity (CP), Brand Competitiveness and COSS (country of origin of service staff) effect. Published in leading international journals, Baumann's work with Winzar and Fang introduces the ReVaMB model and "inter-ocular testing", emphasising relativity and "looking at data" to better analyse marketing/cross-cultural statistics. Chris received his doctorate from Macquarie University after postgraduate and undergraduate studies in Canada (MBA Simon Fraser University) and Switzerland.

Chapter 13
Developing Sustainability Discourse Skills for Business

Susan Hoadley and Chris Baumann

Abstract Marketing has a vital role to play in enabling the success and economic viability of sustainable products, services, and experiences. As a result, "sustainability marketing" has emerged as an interdisciplinary area of knowledge, constructed by social and discursive practices. In this chapter, we apply genre pedagogy, which combines developing knowledge of the disciplinary field with developing language skills to successfully produce written and oral texts, to sustainability marketing as a way to understand these social and discursive practices. After a brief introduction to sustainability marketing and genre pedagogy, we use key aspects of genre to explore the context of sustainability marketing and features of sustainability marketing discourse, followed by a discussion of teaching and learning activities. The teaching notes provides activities for reading a sustainability marketing research article on the adoption of environment-friendly cars. These activities make visible the construction of sustainability marketing knowledge, the authors' position and the structure of the article. Our aim is to provide specific approaches that can be used to develop skills to read and understand, as well as produce sustainability marketing texts. These skills are essential for university graduates, not only to demonstrate their sustainability knowledge, skills, and attitudes to future employers, but also so they can make innovative contributions to sustainable businesses, organisations, and communities in their careers.

Keywords Discipline-specific discourse · Genre pedagogy · Scaffolding · Sustainability marketing

S. Hoadley (✉) · C. Baumann
Macquarie University, Sydney, Australia
e-mail: susan.hoadley@mq.edu.au

C. Baumann
Seoul National University (SNU), Seoul, South Korea

© Springer Nature Singapore Pte Ltd. 2020   291
L. Wood et al. (eds.), *Industry and Higher Education*,
https://doi.org/10.1007/978-981-15-0874-5_13

13.1   The Case at a Glance

Key concepts	• Sustainability marketing discourse • Construction of knowledge in sustainability marketing • Representations of stakeholders in sustainability marketing • Intersectionality of sustainability marketing and marketing strategy • Text structure and language choices
Level of study	• Postgraduate
Subject areas	• Marketing, business, management, corporate social responsibility

Graduate capabilities	Graduate outcomes	%
	Critical thinking	30
	Problem solving	
	Teamwork	
	Communication	40
	Ethical thinking	
	Sustainability	30
	Total	**100%**

Time required	• Preliminary reading activities: 90 min • During reading activities: 240 min • Post-reading assignments: 600 min
Activity type	• Individual, pairs, or team-based and/or class discussion depending on the stage of the activities
Additional materials	• Chu, W., Baumann, C., Hamin, H., & Hoadley, S. (2018). Adoption of Environment-Friendly Cars: Direct vis-à-vis mediated effects of government incentives and consumers' environmental concern across global car markets. *Journal of Global Marketing*, 1–10. https://doi.org/10.1080/08911762.2018.1456597

13.2   Introduction and Background

Sustainability is generally understood to include economic, social, and environmental sustainability (Bridges and Wilhelm 2008). This broad understanding extends the responsibility for sustainability education from science and environmental studies to the liberal arts and business schools (Bridges and Wilhelm 2008; McFarlane and Ogazon 2011). Notably, Frisk and Larson (2011) emphasize the role of marketing theory to understand behavioural change in relation to sustainability practices. Sustainability has been a prominent feature of marketing theories and research since the 1970s, particularly in relation to environmentally sustainable products, services, and experiences (Pine and Gilmore 1998). However, since the 1990s, sustainability has taken on a broader definition and is now widespread in the business and marketing literature (Bridges and Wilhelm 2008; McDonagh and Prothero 2014).

According to Bridges and Wilhelm (2008), business has increasingly been taking sustainability seriously since 1999. Borin and Metcalf (2010) highlight the role of sustainability marketing education in preparing graduates for a future where organisations are increasingly integrating sustainable marketing strategies and corporate social responsibility (CSR) throughout their business. However, despite the obvious value of, and need for, sustainability marketing, these not always sufficiently embedded in marketing and other business school programs (Rundle-Thiele and Wymer 2010; Weber 2013)—for example, by incorporating sustainability elements into existing courses, offering electives in topics like entrepreneurship, tourism, or social marketing that emphasize sustainability, or developing specific sustainability marketing courses (Bridges and Wilhelm 2008). Although Borin and Metcalf (2010) identify learning outcomes, activities, and resources for sustainability marketing education, there is limited mention of developing skills in sustainability discourse. And yet, communication is a critical factor for successfully implementing sustainable practices (Djordjevic and Cotton 2011). Therefore, the aim of this chapter is to provide educators with the necessary resources to develop these skills in students. Previous literature has identified texts that can be used to engage students in sustainability marketing education (Bridges and Wilhelm 2008; Borin and Metcalf 2010). However, we go a step further and provide specific approaches to help support this engagement.

Sustainability marketing is an interdisciplinary area of knowledge that acts as an interface between sustainable products, services, experiences, and marketing practice to make both economically sustainable and successful. As with any area of knowledge, sustainability marketing is constructed through discourse, namely, written, oral, and multimodal texts and the social and discursive practices that surround them (Fairclough 1992). It has increasingly become recognised that the best way to develop students' skills in a discipline-specific discourse is to teach students how to critique, create, and control the texts required for success in the discipline. Explicitly teaching students how to produce the texts required at university and beyond has now become an almost commonsense approach that underpins both literacy and advancement in a discipline in the form of genre pedagogy.

Genre pedagogy is a means of teaching students to produce the texts required in their disciplines and has been successfully applied in a range of educational contexts (Humphrey and MacNaught 2011; Dreyfus et al. 2016). As described by Dreyfus et al. (2016), genre pedagogy involves three key aspects:

1. An iterative cycle referred to as the teaching-learning cycle (TLC) (Rothery 1996; Dreyfus et al. 2016), which combines staged construction of target genres with developing knowledge of the disciplinary field through source genres and understanding the disciplinary context.
2. A two-dimensional, 3 × 3 framework to analyse both source and target genres in terms of their function and structure.

   Function refers to the simultaneous functions of language (Halliday and Matthiessen 2004). These functions are:

   – ideational: construing experience as the systems of knowledge and beliefs that constitute discipline-specific knowledge
   – interpersonal: enacting appropriate relationships to discipline-specific knowledge and the (hypothetical) audience of the text
   – textual: organising/delivering discipline-specific knowledge

   Structure has three levels:

   – whole text
   – paragraph
   – sentence

3. Teaching and learning activities for the stages in the TLC are guided by the analytical framework (as above) to develop a better understanding of the genres.

13.3 Applying the Teaching-Learning Cycle to Sustainability Marketing

Figure 13.1 illustrates the TLC as applied to sustainability marketing. The disciplinary context—sustainability marketing—encompasses two types of activities: building the field and text production. Building the field means reading and listening to develop knowledge and inspire ideas to write about. Text production is a three-stage process comprising deconstruction, joint construction, and independent construction. As shown, the central goal is to teach students how to critique, create, and control the genres of the discipline.

13.3.1 Understanding the Context of Sustainability Marketing

As an interdisciplinary area of knowledge, sustainability marketing sits at the overlap between sustainability and marketing, and, specifically, as the interface between

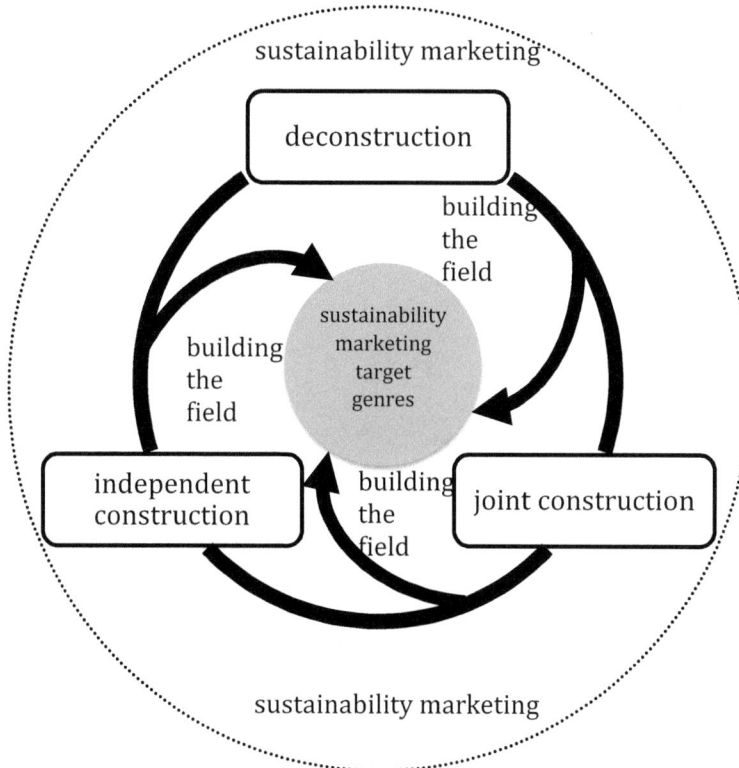

Fig. 13.1 Teaching-learning cycle applied to sustainability marketing. *Source* Adapted from Rothery (1996) and Dreyfus et al. (2016)

marketing practice and environmentally sustainable products, services, and experiences. However, it is also important to take the broader definitions of sustainability and marketing into account, i.e., a definition of sustainability that includes economic and social sustainability, and a definition of marketing that extends to management. As shown in Fig. 13.2, the boundaries between these five areas, and indeed other disciplinary areas, are somewhat porous. Phenomena and concepts overlap and may be understood differently in different areas. For example, sustainability in management may include operational practices, such as turning off the lights to reduce power consumption, or strategies such as developing a corporate mission statement that encapsulates all three aspects of sustainability. In turn, strategies may underpin marketing practices, such as change of markets, marketing communications, or customer education about sustainability (Bridges and Wilhelm 2008). A map of the interdisciplinary context of sustainability marketing allows educators and students to locate source and target texts (with)in the disciplinary field.

Understanding the context of sustainability marketing also involves understanding sustainability marketing discourse in terms of social and discursive practices

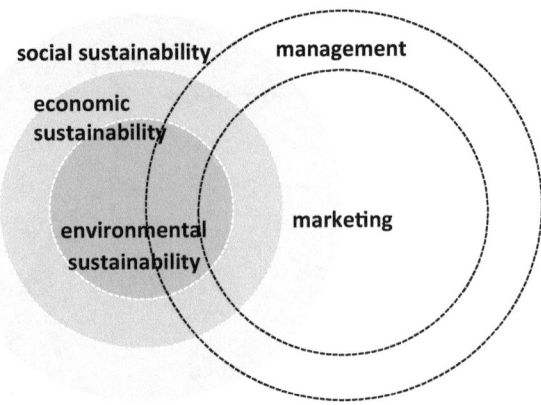

Fig. 13.2 Sustainability marketing context

(Fairclough 1992) in both the source and target genres. Here, the source genres particularly relate to 'building the field' activities, and the target genres relate to 'text production' activities. Bridges and Wilhelm (2008) describe how sustainability marketing is often interpreted in business, higher education, and research. In fact, all three contexts have, to a greater or lesser extent, been examined in both the literature and meta-analyses of the literature. McDonagh and Prothero's (2014) meta-analysis provides a useful starting point for mapping the context of sustainability marketing. Table 13.1 lists five types of sustainability marketing discourse, based on four of the research streams identified by McDonagh and Prothero (2014) to which we have added sustainability marketing education. Each of the selected examples in Table 13.1 can be located within an area in Fig. 13.2. For instance, Porter and Kramer (2006) theorise sustainability marketing by relating CSR (i.e., social, economic, and environmental sustainability) to marketing strategy and competitiveness, which is also a form of economic sustainability. In other words, sustainability should make a positive impact on society *and* contribute to brand competitiveness to be sustainable in itself (Winzar et al. 2018). Hahn and Scheermesser (2006) discuss economic, social, and environmental sustainability in corporate practices, including marketing. In contrast, Rettie et al. (2012) focus on marketing to encourage environmental practices by consumers.

13.3.2   Building the Field in Sustainability Marketing: Source Genres

To build the field in sustainability marketing, students engage with lectures, readings, and other sources to develop their knowledge. Given the relative newness of sustainability marketing, journal articles are a key source of disciplinary knowledge, particularly for postgraduate students. Much of this research is directly applicable to,

Table 13.1 Sustainability marketing discourse

Type	Social practices	Discursive practices	Selected examples
Theorising sustainability marketing	Reformulate sustainability and marketing to reconcile contradictory perspectives	• Produced by marketing academics and practitioners for other academics and practitioners • Published in academic/professional journals	Jones et al. (2008), Kotler (2011), Porter and Kramer (2006)
Sustainability (marketing) frameworks/policy/legislation	Mandate sustainable practices	• Produced by international, national and local organisations and governments for the public and private sector • Published online	Global Reporting Initiative (GRI 2018), Standards International Organization for Standardization ISO 14000
Sustainability (marketing) in organisations	Investigate/inform organisational practices relating to sustainable marketing (and strategy/operations generally)	• Produced by marketing academics and practitioners for other academics and practitioners • Published in academic/professional journals and as books/industry reports	Audebrand (2010), Crittenden et al. (2011), Hahn and Scheermesser (2006)
Consumer concerns, behaviours and practices	Investigate/inform marketing practices relating to sustainable products services, and experiences	• Produced by marketing academics and practitioners for other academics and practitioners • Published in academic/professional journals	Chu et al. (2018), MacDonald and Oates (2006), Rettie et al. (2012)
Sustainability marketing education	Inform pedagogical practices relating to sustainability marketing	• Produced by marketing educators for other marketing educators and students • Published as journal articles, case studies, textbooks, and online	Belz and Peattie (2012), Borin and Metcalf (2010), Bridges and Wilhelm (2008)

and often conducted in collaboration with, industry. Journal articles and other source genres can be analysed using the 3 × 3 framework (Dreyfus et al. 2016), which helps educators to develop learning and teaching activities that scaffold students in building the field of sustainability marketing. The teaching activities provided in the teaching notes are an example of this framework applied to reading a sustainability marketing research article. As adult learners, tertiary-level students are expected to engage in building the field activities independently, but, as many educators will have experienced, scaffolding reading is an essential precursor to scaffolding writing, particularly for diverse student cohorts (e.g., first-in-family, international students, language backgrounds other than English).

13.3.3 Text Production in Sustainability Marketing: Target Genres

Importantly, the source and target genres in sustainability marketing, as with other disciplines, may not be the same. That is, the source genres we expect students to 'consume' are not necessarily the same genres we expect students to produce. There may also be differences between the genres required for university and those required in the workplace, depending on the authenticity of the task at hand (Wiggins 1993). The iterative stages of deconstruction, joint construction, and independent construction in the TLC aim to scaffold the production of texts in the target genres. To identify the target genres in sustainability marketing, we draw on the corpus-based research by Nesi and Gardner (2012). These authors identified 13 genre families of

Table 13.2 Genre families of student writing in higher education

Educational	Family	Examples
Demonstrating knowledge and understanding	Exercise	Calculation, data analysis, statistical analysis
	Explanation	Business, concept, legislation, instrument, methodology, system/process
Developing powers of independent reasoning	Critique	Academic paper review, approach/methodology/result evaluation/interpretation, business/organisation (environment) evaluation, product/service/experience evaluation, project/programme/policy evaluation, legislation evaluation
	Essay	Challenge, commentary, consequential, discussion, exposition, factorial
Developing research skills	Literature survey	Analytical/annotated bibliography, literature review
	Methodology recount	Data analysis report
	Research report	Research article
Preparing for professional practice	Case study	Organisation (issue/start-up) analysis
	Design specification	Product/service/experience design
	Problem question	Organisational scenario
	Proposal	Organisational/marketing plan, project/programme/procedure/policy/legislation proposal, research proposal
Writing for oneself and others	Empathy writing	Expert advice, media article, information leaflet
	Narrative recount	Reflective recount

Source Adapted from Nesi and Gardner (2012)

student writing in higher education and grouped them into five broad educational purposes (see Table 13.2).

A key genre family identified in Nesi and Gardner's (2012) research that is highly relevant to sustainability marketing is the research report. Research reports are, in fact, a macro genre because they consist of other genres such as exercises (e.g., calculations, data analysis, statistical analysis), explanations, critiques (e.g., approach, methodology, method recounts, result evaluation and/or interpretation, and literature surveys. Thus, while research reports are a substantial undertaking for students, they can be broken down into their less complex constituent genres. These constituent genres can then be taught separately and incrementally to scaffold students to produce research reports. Research reports also have the advantage of being a source genre in sustainability marketing in the form of research-based journal articles.

However, although research reports and associated genres aim to develop students knowledge and skills that can be applied beyond university, Nesi and Gardner (2012) argue that case studies, design specifications, problem questions, and proposals are more directly oriented to professional practice. This difference in orientation is less distinct for sustainability marketing because, as mentioned, sustainability marketing research is directly applicable to and often conducted in collaboration with industry. However, it is still important to identify the genre families that involve explorations of industry, such as case studies and problem questions, as distinct from design specifications and proposals as these have a different purpose. Finally, in writing for oneself and others, Nesi and Gardner (2012) identify genres such as expert advice, media articles, information leaflets and narrative/reflective recounts, which are all genres that sustainability marketing students are likely to use beyond university.

13.4 Applying the 3 × 3 Framework to Sustainability Marketing

The 3 × 3 framework shown in Table 13.3 is a distillation of the 3 × 3 framework developed by Dreyfus et al. (2016) for analysing and modelling academic genres. The three rows show the three functions of language: ideational, interpersonal, and textual (Halliday and Matthiessen 2004). The columns show the three structural levels of texts: the whole text, paragraph(s), and sentence (Dreyfus et al. 2016). Across each row is a description of how the language function is expressed at each level of text. At the sentence level, the descriptions are necessarily more 'grammatically' expressed because sentences are grammatical units. This framework provides a starting point for analysing and modelling academic genres in sustainability marketing, such as research articles and reports.

The ideational function is the way language is used to construe sustainability marketing as systems of knowledge and beliefs that constitute discipline-specific knowledge. The interpersonal function is how language is used to enact appropriate relationships between the author and sustainability marketing knowledge, as well as

Table 13.3 3 × 3 framework

	Whole text	Paragraph(s)	Sentence
Ideational	Staged construal of discipline-specific knowledge as appropriate to the purpose	Content/information is: • Grouped into (appropriate/logical) phases; • Related and developed across and within phases	• Vocabulary is discipline-specific and formal, with an appropriate choice of processes to define, classify, relate, and report on participants and circumstances • Tenses are used appropriately
Interpersonal	Convincing expression of a position in relation to the topic by moving through stages	• Content is expressed in an authoritative, objective and impersonal way, supported by appropriate evidence and with appropriate evaluation • The relationship to the audience is appropriately enacted, focussing on giving information (i.e., no questions or commands)	• Adverbs, adjectives, and lexical items are used to evaluate objectively • Modal verbs, adverbs, and interpersonal metaphors are used to negotiate positions • Appropriate source material is incorporated and cited
Textual	Structure is made explicit, and text is previewed at the beginning and reviewed at the end	• Topic and concluding sentences are used to predict/summarise • Repetition, substitution, and reference are used to create cohesion • Conjunctions are used to organise text	• Information flows with appropriate delivery of given and new information, including use of the active/passive voice • Abstract nouns and nominalisations are used selectively and appropriately to express processes, qualities, relationships, generalisations, and track ideas • Articles and pronouns are used to track participants • Layout, headings, paragraphing, bullet points assist the information structure

Source Adapted from Dreyfus et al. (2016)

the author and the (hypothetical) audience. The textual function is the way language is used to organise and deliver sustainability marketing knowledge.

13.5 Teaching and Learning Activities to Develop Sustainability Marketing Discourse Skills

Teaching and learning activities to build the field of sustainability marketing involve scaffolding students to critically read journal articles and other key genres in the discipline (refer to Table 13.1). According to Wood and Petocz (2003), critical reading of discipline-specific discourse means not only being able to describe and interpret the text but also being able to explain how the text interacts with its social and disciplinary context. Frameworks to scaffold reading are generally based on three corresponding stages: pre- or preliminary reading, in-depth reading, and post-reading activities (e.g., Gibbons 2009; Wallace 1992; Hoadley and Wood 2013; Wood and Petocz 2003). Example learning activities for each stage are shown in Table 13.4. The suggested activities can be tailored to suit face-to-face or online learning environments, or a combination of both. Similarly, the activities can be completed independently or collaboratively in small groups or as a whole class. Techniques such as think, write, pair, share (where students write down their individual answers before discussing with a peer), and jigsaw groups (where student groups develop expertise on one particular aspect of the text or topic, and then form new groups where each student has a particular 'expertise' and shares it with the others) are effective ways to give

Table 13.4 Teaching and learning activities to scaffold reading

Preliminary reading	In-depth reading	Post-reading
• Predict content from title, keywords, abstract/introduction, first sentences or images • Share personal narratives related to the topic • Develop a concept map of existing knowledge of the topic • Develop a list of questions the text might answer • Develop a structural outline of the text	• Skim read with a limit on time to identify the argument and evidence (focus on the introduction, conclusion, and topic and concluding sentences) • Annotate key points, questions, ideas, and other sources to follow up • Identify the different stakeholders (including the author(s) and the audience) and their perspectives • Summarise each section/paragraph of the text in one sentence or less • Identify the contribution of each section/paragraph to the overall text • Identify evidence of the authors' voice, views, and/or interactions with the audience	• Summarise the text in words, images, and/or multimodal text • Debate the main argument or most controversial points in the text • Rewrite the text for a different audience • Compare and contrast with similar text(s) • Find and skim read a selection of related texts (i.e., cited in the text and/or that cites the text)

Informed by Gibbons (2009), Hoadley and Wood (2013), Wood et al. (2008), Wood and Petocz (2003)

students the time, confidence, impetus, and environment to successfully engage with the reading.

Teaching and learning activities to scaffold students in writing texts follow the three steps of production in the TLC, i.e., deconstruction, joint construction, and independent construction. The deconstruction stage of the TLC involves teaching and learning activities to develop students' understanding of how the genre is typically structured and expressed (i.e., key language features) (Humphrey and Mac-Naught 2011). Such teaching and learning activities use examples of the target genre, descriptions of the examples based on the application of the 3 × 3 framework, and activities for students to consolidate their understandings (Dreyfus et al. 2016). The joint construction stage asks students to jointly write an example of (a section of) the target genre with the educator (Dreyfus et al. 2016). Key to this stage is that the students need to have developed enough discipline-specific knowledge of the given topic and enough understanding of the target genre to be able to contribute to the joint construction (Dreyfus et al. 2016). Humphrey and MacNaught (2011) identify three educator-led phases of joint construction:

- bridging—making links between analysing the example and constructing a similar text by reviewing the deconstruction and planning to write;
- negotiation—eliciting the wording of the text through iterative discussion using re-reading, questioning, repetition, recasting suggestions, and careful evaluations; and
- review—standing back with the students to assess and edit the jointly constructed text.

Finally, the independent construction stage involves students writing their own example of the target genre. In addition to sufficient knowledge of the field and understanding of the target genre, this stage also requires writing support for the students through consultations, peer review, draft submissions, and so on (Dreyfus et al. 2016).

13.6   Conclusion

Organisations have been increasingly taking sustainability seriously since the late 1990s (Bridges and Wilhelm 2008), and their concern is only growing. As such, there is an urgent need to equip university graduates with the sustainability marketing skills needed to become social entrepreneurs. If sustainability marketing skills are understood as the ability to succeed in the social practice of sustainability, which in turn relies on the consumption, production, and distribution of texts (Fairclough 1992), developing discourse skills in sustainability marketing is key. These skills can be explicitly taught using genre pedagogy. In this chapter, we applied the stages of the teaching-learning cycle (TLC) to sustainability marketing and provided a framework for analysing and modelling sustainability marketing texts. We also described learning and teaching activities that will help to scaffold the consumption and production of sustainability marketing texts for students. In doing so, we mapped the interdisciplinary context of sustainability marketing within sustainability and management more broadly, and also identified the social and discursive practices of key streams of sustainability marketing discourse.

In the teaching notes for this chapter, we have provided a set of activities for the 'building the field' stage of the TLC. All the activities are informed by the 3×3 framework and centre around an example sustainability research article, i.e., Chu et al. (2018). These activities go way beyond a simple reading of the topic content; they require students to examine the discursive and social practices of sustainability marketing discourse as both constraints and enablers to sustainability marketing research. Thus, our aim is not merely to equip students with the skills they need to develop sustainability marketing knowledge, but for them to be able to understand and critique its construction. With an understanding of staging, argument, and structure, students should be able to more successfully inform future sustainability and communication practices. The outcomes for students are the ability to examine the social contexts of sustainability marketing and produce sustainability marketing texts required at university and beyond, underpinned by discipline-specific knowledge.

13.7 Teaching Notes

13.7.1 Synopsis of the Case

This set of teaching and learning activities scaffolds student engagement with a sustainability marketing research article on the adoption of environmentally-friendly cars by Chu et al. (2018). In these activities, students analyse the structure and language of the article, and well as its content and context. More specifically, students examine how the authors construe sustainability marketing as systems of knowledge and beliefs, express their position in relation to the topic, and how they organise sustainability marketing knowledge. The activities are arranged into three stages (pre-, during-, and post-reading) with a range of options for each stage. They are intended as a starting point for developing discourse skills in sustainability marketing so that students can engage with sustainability marketing literature more confidently and independently. In addition to developing sustainability marketing knowledge to address sustainability issues, students will also be able to critique the construction of that knowledge to inform future sustainability and communication practices.

13.7.1.1 The Article

Chu, W., Baumann, C., Hamin, H., & Hoadley, S. (2018). Adoption of environment-friendly cars: Direct vis-à-vis mediated effects of government incentives and consumers' environmental concern across global car markets. *Journal of Global Marketing*, 1–10.

   https://doi.org/10.1080/08911762.2018.1456597

13.7.2   Target Learning Group

Postgraduate students studying sustainability, marketing, or management.

13.7.3   Learning Objectives

The primary aim is to develop sustainability discourse skills, especially in relation to sustainability marketing.

13.7.3.1   Key Issues

- The representations of stakeholders and their beliefs, attitudes, values, and behaviour
- The construction of knowledge in sustainability marketing
- The sufficiency of the research (i.e. evidence/outcomes) to inform practice (i.e. marketing, corporate, consumer, government).

13.7.3.2   Specific Objectives

- Explain the use of discipline-specific terminology.
- Explain the overall text structure and the role of figures and tables.
- Explain the authors' position on a topic using supporting evidence.
- Critique representations of key stakeholders and their perspectives.
- Critique the structure and information flow of key or typical sections and paragraphs.
- Explain the role of repetition, substitution, reference, and conjunctions.

   Note: The model answers and commentaries provided are not exhaustive; there may be other appropriate responses and interpretations.

13.7.4 Preliminary Reading

13.7.4.1 Concept Map (30 min)

Students brainstorm what they already know about sustainability and marketing in pairs or small groups and then create a concept map in larger groups/as a whole class. As the concept map develops, the educator asks prompt questions to focus on the relationship between sustainability and marketing discourse. The final concept map is photographed, saved, and distributed digitally for future reference.

13.7.4.2 Title Translation (30 min)

Students are asked to identify the seven terms that refer to concepts or phenomena in the title of the article and answer the following questions:

- What does the term mean to them?
- Is this meaning a common sense, everyday meaning, or a technical meaning?
- Do they find the term interesting or uninteresting and why?

Students answer the questions by completing a table like the one below. (In practice, the Term column would be blank or, perhaps, with one example.) The first attempt should be individual; then can students discuss with peers to complete the table more fully (Table 13.5).

13.7.4.3 Abstract Analysis (30 min)

Students analyse the abstract using a structured abstract framework (see Table 13.6) and discuss how well the abstract aligns with the framework (see the Commentary

Table 13.5 Title translation

Term	Meaning	Common sense or technical	Interesting? (yes/no)	Why?
Adoption				
Environment-friendly cars				
Direct (effects)				
Mediated (effects)				
Government incentives				
Consumer concerns				
Global car markets				

Table 13.6 Abstract analysis

Component[a]	Text	Key section(s) in the article
Purpose	This study explores the impact of consumers' concern for the environment, government incentives, and consumers' environmental image on the adoption of environment-friendly cars (EFCs)	Introduction
Design/methodology/approach	A total of 2400 consumers across five key car markets (China, Germany, Japan, South Korea, USA) were sampled. Structural equation modelling was conducted, followed by ANOVA and UNIANOVA	Literature review and hypotheses/model development Methodology
Findings	In four of the five markets, environmental concern is key in the adoption of EFCs, whereas government incentives appear generally ineffective. China is contrastive in that government incentives, rather than environmental concerns, are a key factor. Environmental image only (significantly) mediates the adoption of EFCs in China. Examination of the interaction between environmental image and the adoption of EFCs indicates that environmental image has different impacts in different markets	Results and discussion
Research limitations/implications		Introduction Conclusion
Practical implications		Introduction Conclusion
Social implications		Introduction Conclusion
Originality/value		Introduction Conclusion

[a]Structured abstract components according to the Emerald Publishing Group (see Emerald's author guidelines); bold indicates a mandatory component

below). The discussion could be extended to predictions about where various components of the abstract might appear in the article. Students initially work in pairs, followed by a class discussion.

COMMENTARY

The publishing house Emerald suggests a structured abstract for all the articles it publishes. The abstract in Chu et al. (2018) includes three of the four mandatory components of the structured abstract suggested by Emerald. However, the *Journal of Global Marketing,* which is published by Routledge (Taylor & Francis Group) and is where the article appears, requires a non-structured abstract with a limit of 100 words making it difficult for the authors to cover all the typical components of an abstract. Importantly, just because a component is not covered in the abstract does not mean it is not in the article. As indicated in the key section column, four of the seven total components are addressed in the Introduction and Conclusion. This indicates the relative (un)importance of these components in comparison to the others, which have larger, dedicated sections, and may explain why they were not included in the abstract. Thus, a key feature of how sustainability marketing is construed as systems of knowledge and beliefs is the extensive and detailed discussion of research in terms of its design, approach, methodology, and findings. However, arguably, the abstract would be improved if the authors had managed to include the originality and value of the research in the abstract.

13.7.5   In-Depth Reading

13.7.5.1   Mapping the Text (2 × 60 min)

This is a jigsaw reading activity to help students develop an understanding of how the content is organised within the overall structure, and the role each section, paragraph, figure, table, etc. plays in constructing sustainability marketing knowledge in this context. The process is as follows:

1.   Students form five groups. Each group reads and discusses one of the five sections of the article (each group should read a different one). The sections only slightly differ in length, but some are more challenging than others. Therefore, to the extent possible, students should be allowed to choose which section they want to work on, bearing in mind that the groups need to be roughly the same size. If necessary, the more difficult sections could have a few more students in the group.
2.   Students are given time to read the section individually, then time to discuss and map the structure and content of each section.
3.   Once each group has discussed their section, the students form new groups with at least one representative of each section per group.

Table 13.7 Article mapping—introduction and literature review/model development

Section	Content
Introduction	
[Paragraph 1]	
[Paragraph 2]	
[Paragraph 3]	
[Paragraph 4]	
Literature review and hypotheses/model development	
[Introduction]	
Product adoption	
Environmental concern	
Government incentives	
Environmental image	
[Conclusion] Figure 1. Adoption model for environment-friendly cars	

4. In this second set of groups, each student, in turn, explains the section they read and discussed. By the end of the activity, each student will have a reasonable understanding of the whole article.

Table 13.7 provides a model answer for the text mapping for the first two sections of the article. In practice, students might represent the structure and express the content in different and perhaps more imaginative and engaging ways. A more concise, higher-level map of the overall article is shown in Fig. 13.3. The students' article mappings should allow them to consider: the stages of the article; how these stages construe knowledge and express a position; and how the staged structure of the text is made explicit.

COMMENTARY

In sustainability marketing, knowledge is construed as new knowledge by reporting primary research. This new knowledge is expressed as the four hypotheses and model in the Literature review and hypotheses/model development section. The new knowledge is related to existing knowledge both in terms of research and theory, in detail in the Literature review and hypotheses/model development section, as well as throughout the article. The existing knowledge is from both (general) marketing and sustainability marketing literature. The Methodology section explains how new knowledge was collected and tested using statistics theory and is stated, discussed, and further interpreted using statistics theory in the Results and discussion section. The Introduction and Conclusion present the knowledge and research more generally, where the rationale and value of the study are outlined, and the implications of the research are emphasized, respectively.

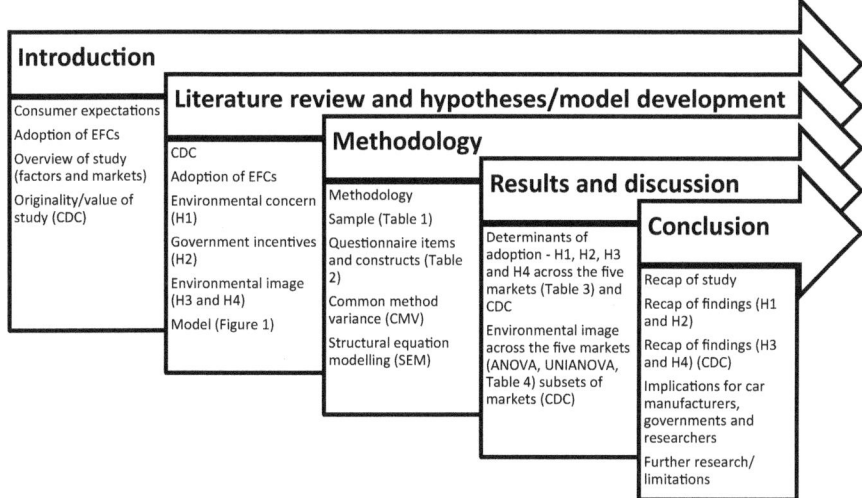

Fig. 13.3 Article mapping—construal of knowledge, position, and structure

The authors introduce their position in the Introduction. They assert that: environmental concern and government incentives are likely to influence the adoption of EFCs; that the effects are likely to be different in different markets; and are likely to be mediated by environmental image. Their assertions are justified with references to selected experts in the field. In the Literature review and hypotheses/model development section, this position is broken down into four different components (being the variables in the subsequent model), and each component is justified with more comprehensive reference to experts in the field and the four hypotheses sequentially stated. The position is amplified/reinforced by the image of the model at the end of the section (Fig. 13.1). The Methodology section explains the methods for testing the hypotheses with references to both statistical experts and sustainability marketing experts (see Table 13.6). The authors' position becomes more nuanced in the Results and discussion section, where the statistical testing of the hypotheses is interpreted. Specifically, the authors' position on differences across different markets is reinforced and amplified by further statistical analysis (i.e. ANOVA and UNIANOVA) theory. The summary of the findings in the Conclusion reinforces their final (nuanced) position.

The structure of the article, made explicit through the section headings, is typical of quantitative research articles. And even though the Introduction does not include a preview of the paper, the aim and overview of the study (paragraph 3) can be used to infer the structure to come. Similarly, the Conclusion does not explicitly review the structure but does provide a brief recap of the study and findings. These two factors indicate that the authors believe their audience is likely to be familiar with the structural conventions of the genre of quantitative research articles.

13.7.5.2 Stakeholder Analysis (60 min)

Students identify the stakeholders mentioned in the article and analyse how they are represented. An examination of the key sections is a good starting point, i.e., the title, abstract, notes, introduction, and conclusion. Alternatively, students could be allocated different sections to analyse. Note that the same type of stakeholder might be referred to in different ways (e.g., automotive industry, car companies, car manufacturers), so the initial list may need to be refined as the activity progresses. Once the stakeholders have been identified, students should then choose a stakeholder to investigate further. Using an electronic version of the article, students should search the article to see how frequently and where their chosen stakeholder is referred to. Remind students to also search for they, their, we, and our. Ask students to identify how the stakeholders are represented and the connections and overlaps between them.

The key stakeholders in the article are consumers, car companies/industry/manufacturers, governments, markets/countries, and researchers. Initially, students should work in pairs and then present their findings to other pairs or the class. Two of the five stakeholder groups—governments and car companies/industry/manufacturers—are less challenging to analyse, so both could be given to one pair of students.

COMMENTARY

Consumers are referred to collectively and variously as consumers, people and, more specifically, in the context of the article, respondents. They are represented as: having concerns, beliefs and needs; acting by adopting behaviours and practices, not least consuming; and receiving government incentives. Consumers' concerns, needs, and behaviours are a key subject of the article given that environmental concern, environmental image, and adoption of EFCs form the basis of the model being tested. Consumers are also classified broadly (e.g., global online consumers) and more narrowly (e.g., Swiss consumers, Canadian, and American consumers).

Car companies/industry/manufacturers are mentioned less frequently than consumers. However, these stakeholders also have 'beliefs' and adopt practices. Car companies are represented as acting in response to consumer beliefs and need as well as acting on governments, i.e., lobbying. Importantly, car companies and companies more broadly are seen as beneficiaries of the research and, in fact, the research was partially funded by an industry body—the Korean Academy of Motor Industry (KAMI).

Governments are represented as actors in that they provide government incentives. The effects of these incentives are a key focus of the research. Consumers evaluate their governments through the questionnaire and, as mentioned, car companies lobby governments. Similar to car companies, governments are represented as beneficiaries of the research. However, for governments, the benefits are extended by the implications of the research for the adoption of other sustainable products for the "greater good".

Markets/countries are mentioned frequently and related to one another. Most often, markets are represented as 'locations' in which the factors in the model have their effects. They are classified in: geographic terms (e.g., global, country) economic terms (e.g., booming); in terms of their market potential or status (e.g., large, target, emerging, saturated); and in cultural terms (e.g., national, Western, Asian). Sometimes the five markets are referred to as a whole group; other times, they are referred to in smaller groups or individually. Interestingly, the markets are also represented as acting in a very abstract sense—i.e., whether they converge, diverge, or crossverge (Ralston et al. 1997) in relation to the factors that influence the adoption of EFCs.

Researchers represented in the article are the authors of the article and other researchers—specifically, collectively, and generally. The authors act through direct reports of research activities (e.g., we test) and through possession of the research (e.g., our study provides). Other researchers are frequently cited throughout the article, particularly in the literature review, both specifically and directly (e.g., Rogers described) or collectively and indirectly (e.g., research indicates), or in other combinations thereof. When referred to generally, researchers are represented as beneficiaries of the research (and, by inference, this includes the authors).

13.7.5.3 Paragraph Analysis

Students analyse the information flow, structure, and evidence of the authors' position for a single paragraph of the article. Students can either: select their own paragraph; select from an identified set; or be allocated a paragraph. Working in pairs, students should then present their findings to other pairs or the class.

Prompt questions for the activity are:
Information flow

- Identify the first part of each sentence (up to the verb) and identify where the thing (noun) being talked about has previously been mentioned in the paragraph. Based on this, and from reading the paragraph, describe the flow of information in the paragraph.

Paragraph structure

- Identify any words that provide key links (conjunctions) between sentences.
- Consider the effectiveness of the first sentence as a topic sentence (i.e., previewing the whole paragraph).
- Consider the effectiveness of the last sentence as a concluding sentence (i.e., providing a conclusion for the whole paragraph).
- Describe the overall structure of the paragraph.

Authors' position

- Identify the words or phrases that express evaluation or a nuanced position and explain the role and effect of these words.

COMMENTARY (Table 13.8)

Table 13.8 Example paragraph analysis

Results and discussion, Determinants of the adoption of EFCs, last paragraph (p. 6)

Overall, **the results** indicate a convergence (Ralston et al. 1997) of the key car markets of Germany, Japan, Korea, and the USA, but a divergence in the case of China, which has a distinct pattern. **The basis of this convergence** appears to be the economic status of the four converging markets as generally saturated and highly developed markets, in contrast to China, which is an emerging market. **The results** indicate little evidence of divergence on the basis of national culture between China, Japan, and Korea as Asian markets, in contrast to Germany and the USA as Western markets. *However*, **the USA** is somewhat ambiguous in that, while it converges with Germany, Japan, and Korea with regards to direct relationships, there is evidence that it diverges from them and converges with China in relation to the mediated relationships. **Ralston et al.** (1997) describe crossvergence as the synthesis of economic ideology and national cultural influences into a different value system. *Thus*, seemingly, **the economic ideologies of the USA's saturated, highly developed car market** are affected by the value of environmental image in the national culture

Notes Bold = first thing (noun), bold italics = linking words, underline = authors' position

Information flow: The first sentence begins with the results and convergence and divergence is introduced as new information. The following two sentences discuss convergence and divergence in the order they appear in the first sentence. The pattern of information flow changes in the second half of the paragraph. The first parts of the next two sentences are the USA and Ralston et al., respectively. Crossvergence is introduced to explain the results for the USA, which is further explained in the final sentence. The first parts of all the sentences in the paragraph can be identified from earlier in the paragraph (with the obvious exception of the first sentence).

Paragraph structure: The first sentence is a topic sentence for the first half of the paragraph. The last sentence summarises the second half of the paragraph. Three conjunctions (in italics) provide an explicit structure for the paragraph. '*Overall*' indicates the finding discussed in the first three sentences is a high-level main finding. '*However*' indicates a switch to an exception in the results. '*Thus*' signals an interpretation of the exception.

Authors' position: Particular words and phrases are used to qualify the absoluteness of the authors' position in relation to their findings (e.g., appears to be, little evidence, somewhat, seemingly). In addition, evaluative words are used to highlight the findings in relation to China and the USA (i.e., distinct, ambiguous).

13.7.6 Post-Reading Suggested Assignments (10 hours per task)

- Summarise the text in words, images, and/or a multimodal text.
- Debate the main argument or more controversial points of the text.
- Rewrite the text for a different audience.
- Compare and contrast with similar text(s).

Further Reading

Morley, J. (2018). Academic Phrasebank. http://www.phrasebank.manchester.ac.uk/.

References

Audebrand LK (2010) Sustainability in strategic management education: the quest for new root definition. Acad Manage Learn Educ 9(3):413–428. Retrieved from http://aom.metapress.com/index/C4672472586P328P.pdf

Belz FM, Peattie K (2012) Sustainability marketing: a global perspective, 2nd edn. Wiley, Chichester

Borin N, Metcalf L (2010) Integrating sustainability into the marketing curriculum: learning activities that facilitate sustainable marketing practices. J Mark Educ 32(2):140–154

Bridges CM, Wilhelm WB (2008) Going beyond green: the "why and how" of integrating sustainability into the marketing curriculum. J Mark Educ 30(1):33–46

Chu W, Baumann C, Hamin H, Hoadley S (2018) Adoption of environment-friendly cars: direct vis-à-vis mediated effects of government incentives and consumers' environmental concern across global car markets'. J Glob Mark 1–10

Crittenden VL, Crittenden WF, Ferrell LK, Ferrell OC, Pinney CC (2011) Market-oriented sustainability: a conceptual framework and propositions. J Acad Mark Sci 39(1):71–85

Djordjevic A, Cotton DRE (2011) Communicating the sustainability message in higher education institutions. Int J Sustain High Educ 12(4):381–394

Dreyfus S, Humphrey S, Mahboob A, Martin JR (2016) Genre pedagogy in higher education: the SLATE Project X. Palgrave Macmillan, New York, NY

Fairclough N (1992) Discourse and social change. Polity Press, Cambridge, MA

Frisk E, Larson KL (2011) Educating for sustainability: competencies and practices for transformative action. J Sustain Educ 2(1):1–20

Gibbons P (2009) English learners, academic literacy, and thinking: learning in the challenge zone. Heinemann, Portsmouth, NH

GRI 2018 (2018) GRI standards. Retrieved from https://www.globalreporting.org/standards

Hahn T, Scheermesser M (2006) Approaches to corporate sustainability among German companies. Corp Soc Responsib Environ Manage 13(3):150–165

Halliday MAK, Matthiessen CMIM (2004) An introduction to functional grammar, 3rd edn. Arnold, London, UK

Hoadley S, Wood LN (2013) How to embed discipline-specific discourse: learning through communication. Macquarie University, Sydney. Retrieved from https://staff.mq.edu.au/public/download.jsp?id=106634

Humphrey S, Macnaught L (2011) Revisiting joint construction in the tertiary context. Aust J Lang Lit 34(1):98–116

International Organization for Standardization (2018) ISO 14000 Environmental management. Retrieved from https://www.iso.org/iso-14001-environmental-management.html

Jones P, Clarke-Hill C, Comfort D, Hillier D (2008) Marketing and sustainability. Mark Intell Plann 27(1):103–126

Kotler P (2011) Reinventing marketing to manage the environmental imperative. J Mark 75(4):132–135

MacDonald S, Oates CJ (2006) Sustainability: consumer perceptions and marketing strategies. Bus Strategy Environ 15(3):157–170

McDonagh P, Prothero A (2014) Sustainability marketing research: past, present and future. J Mark Manage 30(11–12):1186–1219

McFarlane D, Ogazon A (2011) The challenges of sustainability education. J Multidisc Res 3(3):81–107

Morley J (2018) Academic phrasebank. The University of Manchester. Retrieved from http://www.phrasebank.manchester.ac.uk/

Nesi H, Gardner S (2012) Genres across the disciplines: student writing in higher education. Cambridge University Press, Cambridge, MA

Pine BJ II, Gilmore JH (1998) Welcome to the experience economy. Harv Bus Rev 76(4):97–105

Porter ME, Kramer MR (2006) The link between competitive advantage and corporate social responsibility. Harv Bus Rev 84(12):78–92

Ralston DA, Holt DH, Terpstra RH, Kai-Cheng Y (1997) The impact of natural culture and economic ideology on managerial work values: a study of the United States, Russia, Japan, and China. J Int Bus Stud 39(1):8–226. https://doi.org/10.1057/palgrave.jibs.8400330

Rettie R, Burchell K, Riley D (2012) Normalising green behaviours: a new approach to sustainability marketing. J Mark Manage 28(3–4):420–444

Rothery J (1996) Making changes: developing an educational linguistics. In: Hasan R, Williams G (eds) Literacy in society. Longman, London, UK; New York, NY

Rundle-Thiele SR, Wymer W (2010) Stand-alone ethics, social responsibility and sustainability course requirements: a snapshot from Australia and New Zealand. J Mark Educ 32(1):5–12

Wallace C (1992) Reading. Oxford University Press, Oxford

Weber J (2013) Advances in graduate marketing curriculum: paying attention to ethical, social, and sustainability issues. J Mark Educ 35(2):85–94

Wiggins P (1993) Assessing student performance: exploring the purpose and limits of testing. Jossey-Bass Publishers, San Francisco, CA

Winzar H, Baumann C, Chu W (2018) Brand competitiveness: introducing the customer-based brand value (CBBV)-competitiveness chain. Int J Contemp Hospitality Manage 30(1):637–660

Wood LN, Petocz P (2003) Reading statistics. University of Technology Sydney, Sydney, Australia

Wood L, McNeill M, Harvey M (2008) How to lead discussions: learning through engagement. Macquarie University. Available at: http://www/mq/edu/au/ltc/pdfs//FBE_Lead_Discussions.pdf

Dr. Susan Hoadley is a lecturer in Linguistics at Macquarie, specialising in academic, discipline specific and professional communication. She has taught in higher education in Australia for nearly 20 years, focusing on the development of language and communication skills. Prior to joining the higher education sector, Susan worked in industry and had considerable business experience. Her research interests combine her passion for language and education with an ongoing interest in business. She has qualifications in both education and linguistics and is a Senior Fellow of the Advance Higher Education Academy.

Dr. Chris Baumann is Associate Professor at Macquarie University; Visiting Professor at Seoul National University (SNU) and Visiting Associate Professor at Osaka University. Chris' research focus is on the 3Cs: Competitiveness, Cross-culture/Confucianism and Customer loyalty, introducing concepts such as Competitive Productivity, Brand Competitiveness and COSS (country of origin of service staff) effect. Published in leading international journals, Baumann's work with Winzar and Fang introduces the ReVaMB model and "inter-ocular testing", emphasising relativity and "looking at data" to better analyse marketing/cross-cultural statistics. Chris received his doctorate from Macquarie University after postgraduate and undergraduate studies in Canada (MBA Simon Fraser University) and Switzerland.